Heidegger and Modern Philosophy

Heidegger and Modern Philosophy

Critical Essays

Edited by Michael Murray

New Haven and London
Yale University Press

Published with assistance from the
Kingsley Trust Association Publication Fund
established by the Scroll and Key Society of Yale College.

Designed by Thos Whitridge
and set in Janson type.
Printed in the United States of America by
Vail-Ballou Press, Inc., Binghamton, New York.

Library of Congress Cataloging in Publication Data

Main entry under title:

Heidegger and modern philosophy.

  Bibliography: p.
  Includes index.
  1. Heidegger, Martin, 1889–1976—Addresses,
essays, lectures. I. Murray, Michael, 1941–
B3279.H49H343   193   77–21684
ISBN 0–300–02100–3 cloth
    0–300–02236–0 paper

12 11 10 9 8 7 6 5 4 3

Contents

History of Philosophy   201

Politics and Philosophy of History   291

Introduction

MARTIN HEIDEGGER was born in the village of Messkirch on September 26, 1889, and died in nearby Freiberg in Breisgau on May 26, 1976. One of the most original and important thinkers of the twentieth century, Heidegger has exercised more influence on the direction of Continental philosophy during this time than has any other single figure. Almost as important has been his impact on numerous other disciplines—theology, psychiatry, literary criticism, historiography, theory of language, philosophy of science, and the analysis of technological society. Yet while the name of Heidegger is generally familiar in the Anglo-American world, rather little of his thought is really known.

The present collection is aimed chiefly at Anglo-American readers and is written for the most part by authors who write and teach in the setting of British and American thought and culture. It undertakes to answer the question "Can Heidegger Be Understood?" [1] Students and scholars in this tradition will find in this volume a broad and representative coverage of the major topics in Heidegger's philosophy, not of course, every topic, but many in depth. Along the way these essays point out a number of highly interesting relationships between Heidegger's thought and other contemporary developments, such as the substantive and methodological concerns of Frege, Carnap, Dewey, Ryle, Wittgenstein, and Quine.

My general assumption is that Anglo-American readers will be unacquainted with either the content or the variety of Heidegger's thought. For them this Introduction provides a characterization of each paper and its importance, which may be read for an overview or consulted by division and chapter as a guide to the essays. I shall also indicate ways in which Heidegger's concerns are relevant to the concerns of Anglo-American philosophers. Although his answers may differ from theirs, much can be gained by considering Heidegger's alternatives and revisionary proposals. In difficult and radical matters an introduction such as this

---

1. The title of a paper by Richard Schmitt, *Inquiry* 10 (1967) : 53–73.

can at best offer indications; I hope these indications will at least provoke the reader to turn to the papers themselves.

This volume lays claim to being introductory, though it is not elementary. As often as not, the papers lead the reader far into deeply complex and unfamiliar aspects of Heidegger's thought that even advanced scholars of Heidegger wrestle with. The volume does not lead to a coherent view of a system of Heidegger's, for he certainly has no such system, perhaps not even a "philosophy" as that expression is often used. He himself always preferred the more modest designations of pathways and signposts for his thinking.

LOGIC, PHILOSOPHY OF SCIENCE, AND TECHNOLOGY

Questions about logic and its philosophical significance were one of Heidegger's earliest theoretical interests, and were treated in his first publications, "New Research in Logic" (1912) and his "Critical-Positive Contribution to Logic," *The Theory of Judgment in Psychologism* (1914). He was an early admirer of Frege, Russell, and Whitehead; and Husserl's *Logical Investigations*, especially the Sixth, captured Heidegger's attention perhaps even more than his phenomenology.[2]

The thrust of Heidegger's work in this area was to challenge the hegemony of symbolic logic, and it is not insignificant that the first major encounter with his thought by analytic philosophy was made from a commitment to that hegemony. This is Carnap's "The Overcoming of Metaphysics through Logical Analysis of Language" (1932), in which Carnap takes Heidegger's "What Is Metaphysics?" (1929) as a paradigm case of metaphysical nonsense, emblematic of the metaphysical tradition, and devoid of cognitive significance. Heidegger's essay has certainly been so regarded since by many analytical philosophers. But a central mistake in the paper is Carnap's assertion that Heidegger regards the Nothing as a special sort of something. Heidegger warns specifically against this and carefully avoids such phrasing of his thought in that lecture. At the same time he points out how conventional logic is prejudiced to consider Nothingness in precisely this sense. Since Heidegger thinks some important sense can be made of "the Nothing which nihilates," conventional logic must be limited in its power to symbolize.

Heidegger's challenge to the hegemony of symbolic logic is one that he shares with many ordinary-language analysts; yet in some respects his is a more frontal and far-reaching attack. He means to denigrate not the idea of symbolic logic as a calculus of propositions in the narrow, formal sense, but rather the extended use of it as a model for the essence of language,

2. "My Way to Phenomenology," *On Time and Being*, trans. Joan Stambaugh (New York: Harper & Row, 1971), pp. 74–79.

thought, philosophy, science, and even technology. Albert Borgmann, in "Heidegger and Symbolic Logic," provides several examples of how such a logical calculus supplies the model of the linguist's formal rules of sentence formation, the modern urban highway and traffic system, and the architecture of a skyscraper. In each case he attempts to indicate Heidegger's sense of what is absent and precluded by this model.

In the "Critique of Science and Technology," Harold Alderman continues this examination of Heidegger's conception of scientific and technological rationality and their corresponding senses of reality. Modern science is constituted by its unique objectification of nature—established first by a fundamental mathematization of nature with its peculiar interdependence of experimental fact and mathematical projection—and by the institutionalized and specialized character of scientific research. For modern science the stretch of nature that is a mountain consists in what can be established in its calculable objectivity, considered by physics as its measurable microstructure and by geology as its measurable macrostructure. From the viewpoint of modern technology, however, this sense of objectivity gives way to another sense of reality—the mountain as resource or depository—in which nature is reduced to disposable reserves at the command of the subject's will. While technology is a mode of uncovering in its own right, its relentless drive to dominate the whole of Being, man included, poses a momentous danger to Western society. Heidegger calls this the dominating Framework (*Gestell*) of modern technology.

Technology and the logical structure underlying it must be more closely examined. They are not philosophically beyond question. Borgmann explores Heidegger's claims that, though logic may include mathematics and metamathematics, it cannot by itself attain a true philosophy of mathematics, much less a philosophy of science. A widely stated gloss on this position is that Heidegger's work is antiscientific, a view thought to be proved conclusively by his controversial assertion, "The sciences do not think."[3] Heidegger rejects this accusation completely; nor is his assertion meant merely as a polemical exaggeration. What he does mean can be seen more clearly in the programmatic statement that the essence of science and of scientific knowledge cannot be conceived *in* scientific terms, that no proposition about the essence of science is a proposition *in* any science or science generally. Versions of this view had wide acceptance even among those antimetaphysicians who railed against Heidegger. The notion of a metalanguage and the definition of the philosophy *of* science advocated by Carnap and others depends on such a distinction. Yet the Logical Positivists' version contains a double ambiguity, which Heidegger could not accept. This is first of all because they attempt to reduce the meaning of philosophy to the philosophy of science. Such an effort

3. *What Is Called Thinking?*, trans. Fred Wieck and J. Glenn Gray (New York: Harper & Row, 1968), pp. 8, 14.

implicitly recognizes a difference *within philosophy*, since the reduction of the whole to one of its fields can never be justified solely on the grounds of that field. The second ambiguity appears in the claim that the crucial difference is that between science and metascience. For while on the one hand this distinction preserves different orders of signification (object and metalanguage), on the other hand it actually marks a distinction *within science* aiming, as was Carnap, at a comprehensive coordination of the sciences (see the program of "unified science"). That philosophy involves more than this view allows is historically suggested by the failure of the program ever to be carried out. More recently, Quine has argued against all so-called basic differences between science, philosophy, and common sense, and he would presumably criticize Carnap's position as much as Heidegger's. Yet the ambiguities noted in the approach of the Logical Positivists already contain the seeds of Quine's conclusion and so prepare for the collapse of these differences.

A second important facet of Quine's approach is his nominalist and conventionalist interpretation of knowledge, which affects how we take science and ontology alike by denying essences and essential truths entirely. If there were no essences, then for Heidegger, as for the tradition, there could be no proper matter for philosophical thinking. But while Heidegger shares in the historicist turn of post-Hegelian culture, for him it remains shallow and reactionary. He wants instead a new concept of essence and truth that stresses a verbal and historical meaning.[4] Care for the "essencing" of art or for the "essencing" of science is a matter for thinking that no science investigates, and which scientism and nominalism bar from being thought at all. What Heidegger opposes is not science but rather scientism, which attempts to conflate this difference between scientific and philosophical statements. In short, Heidegger is after an adequate philosophy of science, and from *Being and Time* on this was one of his major preoccupations—according to one interpreter, his *only* aim especially in that work.[5]

METAPHYSICS, ONTOLOGY, AND FUNDAMENTAL ONTOLOGY

One of the major themes of twentieth-century philosophy has been its anti-Cartesianism. The attempt to overturn the categories of subject and

4. About essence (*Wesen*) Heidegger writes: "It is from the verb *wesen* that the noun first derives" and "we do not mean [by essence] the inclusiveness of a genus; rather we mean the manner in which [for example] house and state hold sway, administer themselves, develop and decay. It is the manner in which they 'essence,' continue onward. . . ." "The Question Concerning Technology," trans. William Lovitt. *Basic Writings*, ed. David Krell (New York: Harper & Row, 1977), p. 303.
5. Seigfried, Hans, "Heidegger's Longest Day," *Journal of Philosophy* 72 (1975) : 84, who claims that *Being and Time* is "a philosophy of science in a strict . . . sense,

object, mind and body, and consciously to introduce new modes of philosophical description is shared by Ryle, Wittgenstein, Dewey, and Heidegger. Gilbert Ryle recognized this fact about Heidegger in his critical appreciation of *Being and Time*, which he persuaded G. E. Moore to publish in *Mind* in 1929. Ryle interprets that work as a revolutionary and original theory of mind that breaks with the prevailing Cartesian theories of modern thought. This new conception of mind turns out to be surprisingly similar to the one that Ryle himself adopts decades later in *The Concept of Mind*. (The issues between Ryle and Heidegger are summarized in the fourth section of this introduction.)

Karsten Harries's "Fundamental Ontology and the Search for Man's Place" differs from Ryle's in restoring Heidegger's innovative ways of conceiving human existence to the context of basic ontological questions. A fundamental ontology, in contradistinction to an ontology, establishes the necessary conditions under which ontologies of the various realms of Being can have meaning. Descartes sought through the act of reflection to establish a foundation for ontology in the *res extensa et res cogitans*, providing a material basis for mathematical physics in the ontology of extended bodies and an utterly different mental basis in the ontology of the conscious subject. In the *Critique of Pure Reason* Kant similarly claimed to provide an ontological foundation for Newtonian natural science through his "critical" conception of nature. Like these thinkers, Heidegger seeks in *Being and Time* a fundamental ontology, one that elaborates the underlying categories of the possible objects of science and of the experiencing subject. But he revolutionizes the project when he reopens the question of the meaning of Being and argues that subjectivity and objectivity must be rethought. These categories can, in fact, be demonstrated to be abstractions from a more basic sense of man's place and of the things he encounters within the world. This more basic sense is provided through an existential analysis of man as being-in-the-world and things as implements ready for use. These structures, the a priori structures of the social-historical world of everyday life, anonymously shape values and conduct. In making his point of departure the phenomena of the indeterminate "anyone" of everyday existence, Heidegger raises to a philosophical level the social critique of Kierkegaard and John Stuart Mill.

The priority claimed for the everyday world, however, cannot be definitive. This is so because the "authentic" mode of life that Heidegger's analysis is meant ultimately to bring to the fore is one that refuses merely to take over its criteria from the average standards of everyday existence. Furthermore, because the "derivative" Cartesian categories enter into the conduct of science and scientific technology, they importantly determine the everyday world in our time, and this rules out any simple ontological

---

a philosophy of science which resembles in many ways the so-called "new" philosophy of science advanced by Feyerabend, Hanson, Kuhn, Polanyi, and others. . . ."

priority. For these two reasons Heidegger is lead in a quite different direction than, say, the later Wittgenstein or the closely affiliated position of Rorty at the end of his discussion of Heidegger and Dewey, which would dissolve philosophy into everyday existence.

Some noteworthy articles on common themes in Wittgenstein and Heidegger have appeared in recent years. In this section Wittgenstein's sympathetic text on Heidegger's thought on Being and Dread is fully translated for the first time, and my commentary attempts to highlight the chief points of difference and agreement. Wittgenstein recognizes that Heidegger is attempting to say something of real importance here, though it is impossible to *say* it without running up against the limits of language. Possibly Heidegger knew more about Wittgenstein's work than he ever explicitly indicated in his published writings, though the only definite mention is his use of one of Wittgenstein's tales in one of his last seminars.[6] Ross Mandel's paper in the fourth section advances further the critical exchange between Heidegger and Wittgenstein.

Otto Pöggeler's essay brings the discussion of Heidegger's work up through the various stages after the so-called Turn (*Kehre*) from man toward Being. This notable paper examines Heidegger's later thinking on Being, where it is most speculatively bold, difficult, and jarringly new. In the early Greek thinkers Being is thought as *physis*, as the temporal process of emergence, of *kinesis* and *genesis*, from which beings come and go. After Plato, however, Being in the sense of *physis* tends to sink into oblivion, to be replaced by *eidos* and *ousia*, which stress the entities that emerge, in particular the kind that statically endure. This shift is the origin of metaphysical thought, according to Heidegger. In *Being and Time*, where Heidegger first begins to reopen the question of the meaning of Being, he points out how the metaphysical tradition has always conceived reality as something underlying, permanent, invariant; in short, as that which is "continuously present," in contrast to the merely apparent, changing, and intermittent. Theories as different in their ways as that of the Aristotelian substance and that of the Platonic forms share the conviction that reality means continuous presence. Heidegger contends that this meaning of Being as continuous presence implicates a sense of time that has never been investigated by the tradition, and he wants to make a new issue of the hidden relationship between Being and time. He argues further that since presence must be intelligible to us, we must examine how human understanding forms the horizon within which Being as presence manifests itself, and give special attention to the temporal nature of man.

In subsequent writings, Heidegger attempts to approach the meaning

6. Heidegger, with Eugen Fink, *Heraklit* (Frankfurt am Main: Klostermann, 1970), p. 31.

of Being more directly, by finding new ways to speak of Being's presence and primacy. Being is spoken of almost untranslatably as the "event of appropriation" (*Ereignis*), in which man and beings belong together within a historical epoch, and constitute a historical destiny or sending of Being (*Seinsgeschick*). Already in *Being and Time*, Heidegger employs strategies to subvert the traditional metaphysical notions of substance, subject, and object, and to replace them with new existential and phenomenological concepts. Later he deepens the critique of traditional metaphysics, especially of its demand for a securing ground, whether that ground be conceived in the classical form of a highest being or divine *causa sui,* or in the modern form as the subjectivity of the subject. Yet the project of seeking a foundation for ontology—Heidegger's own "fundamental ontology"—still suggests this demand. This insistence on locating the foundation in some privileged being keeps metaphysics and Heidegger himself in *Being and Time* from thinking the crucial *difference* between Being as such and particular beings—in other words, the difference between individual things on the one hand, and the process and truth of Being on the other.

Pöggeler discusses another inadequacy of the tradition that Heidegger criticizes: the radical cleavage it asserts between formal a priori and historical categories. A meditation on language shows this dichotomy to be an illusion. Yet rather than leaving us in a historicist trap, the historicization of language makes possible a "meta-critical" dimension. This point is elaborated more fully by Gadamer and by Hoy in their contributions. Concretely, Heidegger carries this out through his topology of the basic words of Being (*physis, logos, techne, aletheia,* etc.), following out their transformations in Latin and in the modern languages in studies analogous to research done in historical linguistics and conceptual history.

Despite Carnap's confident air in dismissing Heidegger's employment of 'negation' and 'Nothingness,' a satisfactory theory of these notions in contemporary analysis has not proved an easy matter. Stanley Rosen's paper "Thinking about Nothing" takes its point of departure from Heidegger's claim about the philosophical importance of this neglected topic and from his several theses about its meaning. Rosen shows significant connections between these attempts and certain problems in contemporary mathematical logic and ontology, from Frege to Quine and Wiggins. He argues that the problem of Nothingness is indispensable and that it cannot be cleared up by the application of the sense–reference distinction and the methods of quantification theory. While Heidegger's treatment goes deeper and farther than these analytical attempts, it is burdened by its own difficulties. This account of Rosen's invites comparison with the related, though significantly opposed, approaches taken by Wittgenstein and Carnap.

HERMENEUTICS AND LANGUAGE

The development of twentieth-century analytical philosophy has often been described as a "linguistic turn." Continental philosophy has pursued its own version of such a turn in the works of Husserl, Heidegger, Merleau-Ponty, Gadamer, and Ricoeur. We can say that hermeneutics, in its narrow sense the theory of textual interpretation, is an umbrella term for this philosophy of language. Heidegger's contributions to this area are considerable, the fullest collection of them being presented in his *On the Way to Language*. Heidegger's views have some affinity with those of Austin and Wittgenstein, but also sharp differences, though they are most distant from those of Carnap. That Carnap's encounter with Heidegger assumed a certain strategic importance for Heidegger is indicated by his implicit references to Carnapian trends in contemporary thought. In one place in his late writings, Heidegger makes this importance explicit, in a discussion of questions about objectivity, thinking, and speaking. Such questions, he writes, "form the still hidden center of the endeavor toward which the 'philosophy' of our day tends from its most extreme counter-positions (Carnap → Heidegger), the technical-scientistic view of language and the speculative-hermeneutic experience of language." [7] The apparent divergences between the positions are so striking as to obscure any sense of a common center. A sign of that center, however, is that neither position conceives language as merely the regional, provincial subject matter of one of the various "philosophies of." "Rather, both recognize language as the realm within which the thinking of philosophy and every kind of thinking and saying move and rest." [8]

   Paul Ricoeur examines the chief stages in the formulation of hermeneutic theory and Heidegger's seminal contribution to it. He traces the development of hermeneutic theory from a special hermeneutics of textual interpretation to the general hermeneutics of Schleiermacher and Dilthey, and then to the effort of Heidegger and Gadamer to shift hermeneutics from an epistemological model to an ontological one. Heidegger does this by calling into question the assumption of much of linguistics and philos-

7. *Phänomenologie und Theologie* (Frankfurt am Main: Klostermann, 1970), p. 39; *The Piety of Thinking*, trans. James Hart and John Maraldo (Bloomington: Indiana University Press, 1976), p. 24.
8. Ibid. Whether or not Heidegger was a metaphysician as Carnap thought, Heidegger makes it crystal clear in subsequent writings that he aims to *overcome* metaphysics understood as the philosophical framing of things that has dominated Western thought since Plato and Aristotle. Heidegger's published discussion, "The Overcoming of Metaphysics," dating from 1936–41, bears almost the exact same title as Carnap's essay on him.

ophy of language that the primary task is to explain the speaking of the speaker. This approach, whether it adopts the speech–acts model of Austin and Searle or Chomsky's model of grammatical competence, or some combination of them, may be roughly termed a psychological linguistics. For Heidegger's part, what language itself says and reveals—how it discloses the world—is more basic than and prior to the speaking of the subject. Heidegger shares with the French structuralists the decentering of the subject which assigns primacy to the "saying" of language over the "speaking" of the individual speaker.[9] As stress on speaking leads analysis back to the speaking subject, so does a stress on the primacy of saying lead reflection to what is said. But what is said does not merely designate a form, as it does for the structuralists, but the reality revealed as well. Insofar as Heidegger's approach emphasizes the original showing and revealing of language, it may be called an ontological linguistics.

Gadamer's *Truth and Method* is a central work in hermeneutic theory significantly affected by the account of understanding outlined in *Being and Time*. In the major chapter included here, Gadamer takes up the idea that understanding is essentially anticipative; it envisages and conceives in advance the meaning of what is to be interpreted. (A similar problem is stated by Socrates in the form of his mythical answer to the Meno paradox.) Heidegger designates this state of affairs the "hermeneutic circle." Gadamer argues for the importance of the hermeneutic circle by recovering a positive meaning of "prejudice" (*Vorurteil*) that has been suppressed since the Enlightenment. For him, "prejudice" denotes the necessary conditions for every possible understanding of a text: anyone who understands exists a priori in a historically determinate relation to that which is to be understood. Understanding develops out of this encounter, which gives rise to a new prejudgment, and this testifies further to the way that understanding is historically, essentially bound to tradition and language. In this connection Gadamer elucidates how temporal distance plays a positive role in the constitution of understanding.

The last paper in this section is "The Metaphor and Philosophy," by Ronald Bruzina. Heidegger's thought has often been described as metaphorical, and this judgment is apparently confirmed by his attraction to the language of poetry and myth. Bruzina is interested in a much deeper question raised by Heidegger's philosophy of language, which concerns the unexamined metaphysical schema that lies at the base of the distinction between the literal and the metaphorical. The schema is the dualism of the sensible and supersensible, physical and mental, emotive and rational. For a thinking that wants to surpass metaphysics, the literal, "proper," "basic" mode of discourse (philosophical assertion) and the

9. See Jonathan Culler, *Structuralist Poetics* (Ithaca: Cornell University Press), pp. 28–29.

metaphorical, "transferred," "derivative" mode (poetic utterance) must be equally questioned. All traditional accounts or explanations of language are conducted within the metaphysical schema; Heidegger attempts to find a new experience of language that undercuts this schema, and to take steps toward a new sense of Saying.

HISTORY OF PHILOSOPHY

This section includes five papers on relations between Heidegger and other figures or themes in the history of philosophy.

Vick's paper on "Heidegger's Linguistic Rehabilitation of Parmenides' 'Being,' " makes the case that Heidegger is right to claim that Parmenides is *not* the monist he is usually taken to be, and that the philosophical topic of Being in its difference from beings, first dislodged by Parmenides, lies submerged but not at all dispensed with in contemporary as well as other ancient authors. The significance of Heidegger's revisionary studies of the Greek world is only beginning to be appreciated in the work of younger classical scholars.[10]

In their joint paper on Husserl and Heidegger, "Philosophy's Last Stand," Herbert Dreyfus and John Haugeland bring into focus a set of key disputes between the two philosophers, showing the patterns of views and maneuvers that lie behind them. The central issue is the philosophical status of essential and necessary truths, a topic that is once again of active current interest among analytical philosophers. Heidegger's early works seek to satisfy the methodological demand of Husserl's phenomenology, although in the end his responses systematically undercut the demand itself. The authors argue that Husserl was more immediately prescient about this consequence than was Heidegger, and cite in support the unpublished notes of Husserl.

Other papers in this section treat philosophers on whom Heidegger has said little or nothing, namely Dewey, Wittgenstein, and Ryle, though Dewey and Heidegger are known to have orally expressed interest in each other's thought. In his "Overcoming the Tradition," Richard Rorty explains why this should be so by sketching out how Heidegger must appear to Dewey, and how Dewey must appear to Heidegger. He takes up four themes: the classical distinctions between contemplation and action, Cartesian epistemology, skepticism, and the differences between philoso-

10. Philosophers and classicists should look forward to the important papers reinterpreting early Greek thought by Mitchell Miller, Jr., even though the name of Heidegger is nowhere mentioned. See "Parmenides and the Disclosure of Being," *Apeiron*, forthcoming, and "La Logique implicite de la Cosmogonie d'Hesiode," *Revue de Metaphysique et de Morale*, forthcoming; see also Werner Marx, *Heidegger and the Tradition*, part I, chaps. 1–2; part III, chaps. 3–5.

phy, science, and "the aesthetic." Rorty emphasizes the signal importance of Heidegger's account of the history of thought, yet he overlooks or dismisses the historicity of poetic discourse that Heidegger also affirms. The critical juxtaposition of the Heidegger-Dewey surmounting of the Western tradition raises the question of just what *is* philosophy—not only what philosophy once was but also what it might or ought to be. From the standpoints of their different views on the future or futurelessness of philosophy, Heidegger will appear to Dewey "as a final decadent echo of Platonic and Christian otherworldliness," and Dewey to Heidegger "as an exceptionally naïve and provincial nihilist." For himself, Rorty holds that in the end the everyday is our only resort, which represents an end to philosophy still more radical than Heidegger's.

Kant characterized his own critical transcendental philosophy as "a Copernican revolution." During the period of the composition of *Being and Time*, Heidegger was deeply involved in turning the interpretation of Kant away from the epistemologically oriented reading of the neo-Kantians and in reinstating an interest in ontology. This view is most fully worked out in *Kant and the Problem of Metaphysics* (1929). In his paper on "A Second Kantian Revolution," Ross Mandel explores common substantive concerns of Wittgenstein and Heidegger in this light. Central to them is the notion that the procedures of knowing determine our perspectives on the world and that these procedures are grounded in human activities, or forms of life. Yet Heidegger, unlike Wittgenstein, wants to preserve the Being of the things disclosed to us, which is the ontological implication or force of our expressions and behaviors. Second, the analytic of Dasein provides a unified foundation for the forms of life, and the modes of things and the uses of words that belong to these forms. Mandel argues that within this analytic Heidegger provides a dimension to the philosophy of science denied or ignored by Wittgenstein and those under his influence like Toulmin and Kuhn, which he does through his "existential conception of science" and his ontology of the objects of natural science. Along the way, new critical problems arise that call into question the role fundamental ontology is supposed to serve for the special sciences.

The final contribution in this section is my "Heidegger and Ryle: Two Versions of Phenomenology," in which I argue that despite obvious differences in aim, substantial affinities exist between Ryle's *The Concept of Mind* and Heidegger's *Being and Time*. In them one finds the same forms of argument, the same concepts and often the same examples, the same attacks upon Cartesianism with its dualistic theory of "mind," intellectualist model of consciousness, and problem of other minds, as well as such positive distinctions as knowing-that and knowing-how, and disposition, mood, and feeling. Examination of Ryle's early papers on phenomenology, including the review of Heidegger, supports the conclusion that Ryle was significantly influenced by Heidegger and that there is a major convergence of their philosophies. Along with some emendation of an earlier version of this discussion, I have included several comments that Ryle kindly provided in response to the original article.

Though no single paper represents Heidegger's response to Descartes, stated first by him in §§19–21 of *Being and Time*, basic indications are afforded by several other papers in this collection, those by Harries, Rorty, and Murray. Mandel's essay stresses the Kantian themes in comparing the work of Wittgenstein and Heidegger. Had the length of this section permitted, two additional studies would have been included: one on Sartre through whom some of Heidegger's thought has filtered into Anglo-American discussions in ethics and philosophical psychology, and the other on Heidegger's important though controversial Nietzsche interpretations.

These selections, moreover, by no means give a real indication of the rich range of Heidegger's own deconstructive historical interpretations, which, to mention only the major instances, include those of Anaximander, Heraclitus, Parmenides, Plato, Aristotle, Thomas Aquinas, Thomas of Urfurt (alias Duns Scotus), Descartes, Leibniz, Kant, Schelling, Hegel, Nietzsche, and Husserl. And this list omits the entwined sequence of poets from Sophocles to Hölderlin and Rilke that Heidegger thoughtfully interprets. The decision in the face of this to stress the contemporary relations and to situate Heidegger in the field of twentieth-century thought was based on the desire to put him in a discourse with non-Heideggerians. The manner in which philosophy expressly or tacitly conceives its immediate and distant past determines importantly its self-identity. In the end, of course, there can be no adequate placement of contemporary philosophy apart from the tradition, though such placings are always open to being rethought from future vantages and concerns.

Future histories of thought are no less likely to recognize division and conflict among current modes than do present ones. Yet it may well be that the important oppositions they single out will not at all correspond to 'Anglo-American' vs. 'Continental,' or 'Analytical' vs. 'Phenomenological' philosophy, designations now in common use. Rorty anticipates such a conclusion when he writes, "The really fundamental 'split' in contemporary philosophy . . . is between those (like Dewey, Heidegger, Cavell, Kuhn, Feyerabend, and Habermas) who take Hegel and history seriously, and those who see 'recurring philosophical problems' being discussed by everybody from the Greeks to the authors of the latest journal articles." [11] Those analytical philosophers who take their history and

11. Rorty, below, p. 244.

historicity with a grain of salt run into an insoluble impasse when they feel moved to claim that they are making a "revolution in philosophy," since concepts like revolution and overthrow are ineradicably historical concepts. Heidegger takes the historicity of thought with the utmost seriousness, which puts him into opposition to the Enlightenment's history-free paradigm of thinking but also, as Gadamer and Hoy argue, to the relativistic historicism of Romanticism. This brings us to our final section.

POLITICS AND PHILOSOPHY OF HISTORY

Hannah Arendt wrote the first of these essays to review Heidegger's career from the vantage of his eightieth year. In it she accomplishes two things. First, she delineates memorably from personal experiences the character of Heidegger's thinking and how its appearance on the European scene was felt. She indicates how the extraordinary fame of Heidegger, based solely upon his reputation as a teacher and preceding by many years his first major publication, spread "like the rumor of a hidden king." The rumor was that Heidegger was actually attaining "the things themselves" proclaimed by Husserl, that thinking was a thinking of its own matter and not merely "about" something, that it was activity not product, and that in connection with it, the cultural treasures of the past were being made to speak in unheard ways. The residence of the thinker, she says, lies in thinking itself, in a seclusion from the world in which absent things are made present, and present things absent. This makes it the very obverse of our everyday place in the world.

Second, Arendt turns to Heidegger's brief but notorious involvement in political affairs. The episode was Heidegger's ten-month tenure as rector of the University of Freiberg from April, 1933, to his resignation in February, 1934, and his almost simultaneous enrollment in the National Socialist Party. There can be no doubt that this constitutes a major reason why Heidegger's thought has been contemptuously dismissed by many Anglo-American philosophers and scholars. It is common for writers on Heidegger either to ignore this episode entirely or attempt to make it central to an assessment of Heidegger; but neither of these does justice to its importance. In this respect Hannah Arendt and Karsten Harries provide us a much needed corrective, though this can only be the beginning, since a thoughtful and factual study of this matter has not yet occurred in the English-language scholarship. Arendt holds up the case of the thinker who abandons his residence in thinking for political affairs—of which the classical example is Plato's Sicilian expeditions—to a proper measure of understanding, exasperation, and most important, comic derision.

Harries takes a different approach in "Heidegger as a Political Thinker," arguing that the rectoral address of 1933 has its roots in *Being and Time* and points ahead to later writings such as *An Introduction to Metaphysics* and "The Origin of the Work of Art." What links them is the key notion, from the first work, of authentic resolve, which pushes the individual man back into the world in order to discover a communal destiny, and the notion, from the later writings, of a creative work that establishes the place for such a community life. The political work, on this view, is the work of a violent creative leader who attempts to establish a world, one that both lets the earth be itself and that provides man a ground. Two constraints, however, are built into the essence of the creative work thus conceived. The authentic leader must respect the autonomy of the followers, and they in turn must recognize the established place as their own. Moreover, the work that provides the ground is marked by an ineradicable tension; because of life's temporal nature, it can never be finally secured against the precarious and errant. Such a political thought must collide with the designs of every totalitarian ideology because the authentic work remains constantly exposed to question and revocation. It is just such a totalitarian character, however, that Heidegger attributes increasingly to modern technology, whose framework equally grips Europe, Russia, and America, and ever more the Eastern world as well.

As Borgmann and Alderman have made clear, Heidegger denies that science and technology can ever provide the measure of what is. Yet what is a shaping historical destiny cannot be merely rejected; we must rather learn to think it through from its origins in Greek metaphysics, to live through and surpass it, to be free to say yes and no. The question is whether this can be accomplished from the standpoint of the "inner emigration" of Heidegger's later years. Harries criticizes both the exaggerated optimism of his earlier claims about the social mission to his philosophy and the subsequent retreat that seems to deny a social mission in the present.

In his paper "History, Historicity, and Historiography," David Couzens Hoy examines the role of three basic concepts in Heidegger's philosophy of history up through *Being and Time*. Heidegger distinguishes between history as the reality of that which historically happens, historiography as the science of history, and human historicity as the temporal structure (past, present, future) of a life in relation to other lives and the world. Heidegger is concerned to demonstrate that the third notion is the ground of the first two, and besides completing his analysis of human being with this notion, he claims to have established the ontological foundation of historiographical knowledge, and even to provide it with a guiding norm. In this way Heidegger seeks to dissolve the problem of historicism and relativism, interpreted not only as an epistemological problem for theorists but also as the existential nihilism of the modern era.

The best way to combat these is through a foundationalist theory of science and through the incorporation of an essential "critical" role into the structure of history. While defending Heidegger against certain misdirected charges, Hoy makes more pertinent and serious criticisms about the criteria of historiographical validity and truth, which cast doubt on the notion that an ontological philosophy of history can play a normative, as distinguished from a formal, foundational role, in historiographical knowledge.

This doubt is related to those of Ricoeur and Mandel with respect to other fields. Heidegger himself never specifically sought to affect other fields of learning, and these writers argue that his thought, strictly taken, could not achieve "productive" effects. Paradoxically, however, no other European philosopher of this century has had more effect (for good or ill) on other academic fields. Hoy does not consider the very rich treatment of the history of Being that is at the center of what might be called Heidegger's later philosophy of history. Other papers in the collection compensate this omission to some extent, though the best starting point for understanding even the later work remains *Being and Time*.

The five divisions of the present collection should be regarded as loose groupings, and other groupings besides these are possible. Other themes could have received more independent examination; particularly conspicuous is the absence of a paper on Heidegger's theory of art and poetry. It is only a partial answer to say that the extreme importance of this theory for Heidegger is indicated by the way the theory pervades certain of the essays presented, ones supposedly and actually on the nature of philosophy itself and on political thought. And there exist various other useful works that examine this and related areas of Heidegger's thought.[12] The leading edge of contemporary literary theory in America has been deeply affected by French writers like Jacques Derrida and Michel Foucault who have massive debts to Heidegger. While there are the usual justified excuses for the fixed divisions of philosophy, it would be to miss the challenge of Heidegger's work not to see the way he seeks to deconstruct many of our divisions of academic and metaphysical convenience. This is what Derrida means when he speaks of a thinking that deconstructs as it proceeds, which always writes what it writes *sur rature* (under erasure).

There are, of course, the usual ways to read a book like this, from beginning to end, or by turning to individual topics described in the Introduction. For the reader who prefers a select introductory reading sequence, here are three possibilities, roughly arranged in order of their

12. See my *Modern Critical Theory* (The Hague: Martinus Nijhoff, 1975), pp. 10–12; and Harold Alderman, "The Work of Art and Other Things," *Martin Heidegger in Europe and America* (The Hague: Martinus Nijhoff, 1973).

accessibility: (1) Alderman, Harries (ch. 5), Ricoeur, Rorty, Arendt; (2) Borgmann, Ryle, Wittgenstein, Bruzina, Dreyfus–Haugeland, Hoy; (3) Carnap, Pöggeler, Gadamer, Vick, Murray, Mandel, Harries (ch. 18).

By all reports the philosophical waves that Heidegger set in motion are no longer the subject of current discussion in Germany today. One explanation is that he has succeeded in changing the philosophical map of issues, questions, and assumptions, and the practice of many disciplines. Explicitly this heritage is represented by what is commonly called hermeneutic philosophy.[13] The critical achievement is indicated by the way in which Heidegger helped put to rest certain forms of transcendental philosophy, ones associated with Kant and Husserl, but also with his own earlier attempts. A second reason is that the infectious language of his thought has often monopolized and jargonized philosophical German in unfortunate ways. A third reason is that against the current fashion, Heidegger's thought does not promise to change the world, since, he claims, all such proposals for world change rest upon previous thought foundations that his own thinking has found questionable. Seeking to fill this vacuum are the various attractive revisionist Marxisms that appear everywhere in Germany, with as many institutional and political causes as philosophical ones and not without their own jargon. Lastly, but very importantly, displacing Heidegger are certain forms of Anglo-American philosophy, themselves decisively affected by thinkers like Frege, Wittgenstein, Carnap, and Popper. In contrast to Germany, in France Heidegger's influence, which reached its first peak in the existential phenomenology associated with Sartre and Merleau-Ponty, seems to be reaching a second high-water mark in the 1970s with Derridá, structuralism, and the renewed interest in Nietzsche and Heidegger's writings on him.[14]

In any widespread and serious sense, however, the encounter with Heidegger in the United States and England has hardly begun. There is no little irony, and perhaps a special opportunity here as well, in the fact that Heidegger begins to "arrive" or be heard in the English-speaking world about the same time that the German-speaking world is beginning to take up English philosophy. The results that emerge from these newly visible cross-currents should prove to be among the significant developments to come out of this decade.

All of the essays presented below have been specially edited for the purpose of this collection. Five of them were written for it and have not

13. Besides the contributions of Ricoeur and Gadamer in the third section below, see Otto Pöggeler, ed., *Hermeneutische Philosophie* (Munich, 1972), and my *Modern Critical Theory*, ch. 4, "The New Hermeneutic."

14. See, for example, Jacques Derridá, *Of Grammatology*, trans. Gayatri C. Spivak (Baltimore: Johns Hopkins University Press, 1976), and a key periodical, *Diacritics*, and *The New Nietzsche*, ed. David B. Allison (New York: Delta, 1977).

been published previously in any form; some that have appeared elsewhere have undergone major revisions for this occasion; others appear as
they first appeared—with corrections and minor changes made for the
sake of space and clarity—several from journals that are little known and
mostly ignored by a broad philosophical readership. The articles by
Carnap and Ryle appear here in their original forms with those parts not
dealing with Heidegger deleted for reasons of space. The piece by
Wittgenstein appears for the first time in a complete English translation.

At last there exists a fine sequence of English translations of Heidegger's works available and forthcoming, which includes the first anthology,
Basic Writings, edited by David Krell (1977), and a new translation by
Joan Stambaugh of *Being and Time.* At the end of this collection the
reader will find a Bibliographical Guide that lists all the works of
Heidegger in good English translations and a selection of additional
secondary literature.

I wish to thank heartily the many contributors to this volume, and
for their special assistance, Stanley Rosen, Karsten Harries, Jesse Kalin,
B. F. McGuinness, Frank Tillman, Cathy Iino, and finally, Harry Frankfurt, whose simple question one evening about what he might read to see
what was important about Heidegger called to my attention that no
suitable collection of such discussions existed.

Logic, Philosophy of Science, and Technology

1. ALBERT BORGMANN

Heidegger and Symbolic Logic

WE TAKE IT FOR GRANTED that Heidegger's philosophy and symbolic logic are two influential and seemingly incompatible forces within the present philosophical community. An investigation of the relationship between these two types of philosophy may therefore contribute to an understanding of what today's philosophy is both in itself and in its relation to the world.

For reasons of competence and economy, this essay will take Heidegger's writings as the point of departure and reference. Besides, an exploration of symbolic logic limited to Heidegger's writings may contribute in a modest way to the history of philosophy, whereas symbolic logic, if chosen as the primary thematic frame of reference, would be prohibitive in scope and diversity.[1] The first part of this essay is purely doxographical, tracing the term "symbolic logic" as used in Heidegger's works. This survey provides the basis for a systematic confrontation of Heidegger's philosophy and symbolic logic, followed by an attempt at taking a few constructive steps beyond Heidegger and symbolic logic.

Quite obviously, Heidegger scholars and students of symbolic logic have little regard for one another's work.[2] It is therefore worth noting that there is a definite affinity in the ancestry of these two schools. In *Being and Time*, we find Heidegger's acknowledgment: "If the following

This is a substantially revised version of a paper that first appeared in *Heidegger and the Quest for Truth*, ed. Manfred S. Frings (Chicago, 1968). Parts reprinted with permission of Quadrangle Books.

1. The relationship between Heidegger and symbolic logic has received little attention in the literature. Some important remarks and references are to be found in Otto Pöggler's *Der Denkweg Martin Heideggers* (Pfullingen, 1963), pp. 306–07, 313–14. Regarding Heidegger and speculative logic, see Walter Bröcker, "Heidegger und die Logik," *Philosophische Rundschau* 1 (1953–54) : 48–56.

2. A recent illustration comes from J. J. C. Smart, "My Semantic Ascents and

investigation has taken any steps forward in disclosing the 'things themselves', the author has to thank E. Husserl above all. . . ." [3] The preface
of the *Principia Mathematica* says: "In all questions of logical analysis, our
chief debt is to Frege." [4] Both Husserl and Frege were indebted to
Bolzano, and shortly before the turn of the century, both were concerned
with the foundations of arithmetic and each was aware of the other's
contributions.[5] In 1884, Frege published *The Basic Laws of Arithmetic:
A Logical-Mathematical Investigation of the Concept of Number.*[6] When
Husserl's *Philosophy of Arithmetic: Psychological and Logical Investigations* appeared in 1891, it contained a considerable number of frequently
critical references to Frege's work.[7] In the main, Husserl's criticism dis-
puted Frege's rigorous distinction between logic and psychology. In 1894,
Frege published a review of Husserl's book; as was to be expected, Frege
severely criticized Husserl and insisted on the autonomy of logic. He
accused Husserl of what Husserl himself was to call *psychologism.*[8] Although Frege directed his attack against a trend rather than an author, the
sarcastic language of the review is surprising in view of the polite correspondence that had been going on between the two scholars since 1891.[9]
But we may well assume that by 1894 Husserl agreed in principle with

---

Descents," in *The Owl of Minerva: Philosophers on Philosophy*, ed. Charles J. Bon-
tempo and S. Jack Odell (New York, 1975), pp. 57–62. Smart exhibits abysmal disdain for "the purveyors of *angst*," and he insists on "contemporary logic, recursive
function theory, and semantics" as a background of discipline which should be
common to all philosophers proper. The later Heidegger is more conciliatory and
recommends attention to "the as yet hidden center of those endeavors toward which
contemporary 'philosophy' tends from its extreme counterpositions (Carnap→
Heidegger)." The passage, written in 1964, appears in *Phänomenologie und Theologie*
(Frankfurt am Main, 1970), p. 39; translated by James G. Hart and John C. Maraldo
in *The Piety of Thinking* (Bloomington, Indiana, 1976), p. 24.

   3. Heidegger, *Sein und Zeit*, 9th ed. (Tübingen, 1960), p. 38, n. 1 (*Being and Time*,
trans. John Macquarrie and Edward Robinson [New York, 1962], p. 489). The translations of the passages from Heidegger's writings are mine.

   4. Alfred North Whitehead and Bertrand Russell, *Principia Mathematica*, 2nd ed.,
3 vols. (Cambridge, 1963), I : viii.

   5. A more elaborate historical account along with a systematic discussion of the
relationship between Husserl's and Frege's work is now available. See Henry
Pietersma, "Husserl and Frege," *Archiv für Geschichte der Philosophie* 49 (1967) :
298–323.

   6. Gottlob Frege, *Die Grundlagen der Arithmetik. Eine logisch-mathematische
Untersuchungen über den Begriff der Zahl* (Breslau, 1884).

   7. Edmund G. Husserl, *Philosophie der Arithmetik. Psychologische und logische
Untersuchungen* (Halle an der Saale, 1891), p. 12, n. 1; pp. 104, 116, 119, 129–34,
142–43, 148, 156, 164–65; p. 168, n. 1; p. 171, n. 1; p. 174, n. 1; pp. 180, 182–88.

   8. "Rezension von Dr. E. G. Husserl: Philosophie der Arithmetik . . . ," *Zeitschrift
für Philosophie und philosophische Kritik* 103 (1894) : 313–32.

   9. Only fragments of the correspondence are preserved. The earliest letter (May 24,
1891) is by Frege in response to a (lost) letter and some publications sent by
Husserl. My access to the correspondence was arranged by the *Institut für mathe-
matische Logik und Grundlagenforschung* at the University of Münster, where an

Frege's criticism or even that the review brought about Husserl's conversion from psychologism.[10] Volume 1 of the *Logical Investigations* of 1900 was the first forceful presentation of Husserl's new phenomenological approach, and it contains an explicit retraction of his earlier criticisms of Frege.[11] A report on recent work in logic that Husserl published in 1903 mentions Frege's name once more and in a tone of great respect; but Husserl's philosophical concern thereafter led him to ever more fundamental questions and away from his kinship with Frege.[12]

The first record of an encounter by Heidegger with symbolic logic follows directly from the foregoing historical sketch. In 1912 Heidegger published a report on "Recent Research in Logic." [13] He paid tribute to Husserl's refutation of psychologism. Then he continued, "It seems to me that the real significance of G. Frege's logico-mathematical investigations has not yet been appreciated; much less have his writings been exhaustively dealt with." [14] This passage parallels closely Husserl's reference to Frege. More important, it indicates that symbolic logic and speculative thought were still seen as linked in the writings of the early Heidegger, not only in the report of 1912, but also and very similarly in the dissertation of 1914.[15] Both writings shows some acquaintance with the *Principia Mathematica*, and according to the *curriculum vitae* of the dissertation, Heidegger had great interest and some formal training in mathematics and physics and was looking forward to postdoctoral work in these fields.[16] However, although he might have had a more detailed knowledge of the initial works of symbolic logic proper than Husserl did, Heidegger never meant to emulate that school of thought in its method. Both the

edition of the scholarly remains and correspondences of Frege is being prepared. Concerning the history of the term *psychologism*, see Herbert Spiegelberg, *The Phenomenological Movement: A Historical Introduction*, 2nd ed., 2 vols. (The Hague, 1965), I : 56, 93–98.

10. Spiegelberg cautiously and more generally confirms that view; see I : 93.

11. *Logische Untersuchungen*, 2 vols. (Halle an der Saale, 1900–01), I : 169, n. 1. There is one further reference to Frege in II, 53.

12. "Bericht über deutsche Schriften zur Logik in den Jahren 1895–99," *Archiv für systematische Philosophie* 9 (1903) : 395. Husserl returns to the foundational problems of logic and mathematics at a deeper level in *Formale und transzendentale Logik. Versuch einer Kritik der logischen Vernunft* (Halle an der Saale, 1929).

13. "Neuere Forschungen über Logik," *Literarische Rundschau für das katholische Deutschland* 38 (1912): cols. 465–72, 517–24, 567–70.

14. Ibid., cols. 467–68. The parallel to Husserl's report is obvious. But Heidegger may have become aware of Frege through his studies in mathematics. He refers to Frege's "Sinn und Bedeutung" and "Begriff und Gegenstand" while Husserl mentions "Funktion und Begriff."

15. *Die Lehre vom Urteil im Psychologismus. Ein kritisch-positiver Beitrag zur Logik* (Freiburg, 1914), pp. 97–98, n. 3. The treatise is now also available in Heidegger, *Frühe Schriften* (Frankfurt am Main, 1972), pp. 1–129.

16. Ibid., pp. vii, 111. One should not give too much weight to these plans. Heidegger's early writings abound in announcements of projects.

report and the dissertation deny symbolic logic any philosophical authority.

To be sure, Heidegger grants to symbolic logic philosophical *significance*, but as a problem, not as a theory. In the report, he says:

> . . . it seems to me that above all it must be pointed out that symbolic logic
> never gets beyond mathematics and to the core of the logical problems. I see
> the barrier in the application of mathematical symbols and concepts (above
> all the concept of *function*) whereby the meanings and shifts in meaning
> in propositions are obscured. The real significance of the principles remains
> in the dark; the propositional calculus, e.g., is a figuring with propositions;
> the problems of the theory of propositions are unknown to symbolic logic.
> Mathematics and the mathematical treatment of logical problems reach limits
> where their concepts and methods fail; that is precisely where the conditions
> of their possibility are located.

The dissertation puts it more briefly: "It would have to be shown how its
formal nature [that of symbolic logic] prevents it from gaining access to
the living problems of the meaning of propositions, of its structure and
cognitive significance." Heidegger did not take these statements to constitute an exploration and a refutation of symbolic logic. He saw a task ahead
and says so expressly in the report: "The work here outlined is yet to
be done, and it will not be accomplished as quickly as the overcoming of
psychologism." [17]

Heidegger did not formally carry out this project. His *Habilitation*
thesis of 1916 on *The Doctrine of Categories and Meaning of Duns Scotus*
contains no mention of symbolic logic.[18] The absence of such remarks is
initially puzzling, not only because the Scotus book is largely concerned
with logical and semantic questions. The investigation touches on the
very problem of how logic and mathematics are to be distinguished: "Is
logic mathematics or mathematics logic," Heidegger asks, "or does neither
alternative hold true? . . . One thing . . . can be decided on the basis of
what has been said so far, namely, that the two realms in question, though
they both be of an immaterial nature, cannot coincide. The homogeneity
which owes its peculiar nature to the uniformity of the viewpoint varies in
these two worlds. The homogeneity of the mathematical realm has its
foundation in *quantity*. The homogeneity of the realm of logical validity
rests on *intentionality*, the referential ordination." [19]

---

17. "Neuere Forschungen," col. 570; *Die Lehre vom Urteil*, p. 97, n. 3; "Neuere
Forschungen," col. 570.
18. *Die Kategorien- und Bedeutungslehre des Duns Scotus* (Tübingen, 1916).
(Martin Grabmann showed later that Thomas of Erfurt is the author of the *Gram-
matica speculativa*, the primary subject of Heidegger's interpretation.) Heidegger
uses the term modern logic, but with reference to the works of Windelband, E. V.
Hartmann, Bolzano, Husserl, Dilthey, Rickert, and Simmel. See pp. 11, 95; pp. 177–78,
n. 1. This book too has been reprinted in *Frühe Schriften*, pp. 131–354.
19. *Kategorienlehre*, p. 100.

In *Being and Time*, Heidegger has not changed his view of symbolic logic. He has, however, come to speak with more authority. The philosophically derivative nature of symbolic logic is considered evident now, since *Being and Time* explores and discloses precisely those fundamental structures relative to which symbolic logic is derivative: the first part of the published version of *Being and Time* is a "Preparatory Fundamental Analysis of *Dasein*." It discloses *Dasein* as understanding. Understanding issues in interpretation. One of the derivative modes of interpretation, says Heidegger, is the proposition. The discipline that treats of propositions or judgments is logic. But there is yet a further derivation: "In symbolic logic, propositions are dissolved into a system of 'mapping and interconnecting'; they become the object of a 'calculus,' but not of an ontological interpretation." [20]

In the late twenties and early thirties, the philosophical scope and claim of symbolic logic grew considerably. Heidegger himself was chosen the victim of an attempt at making symbolic logic relevant to metaphysics. In 1931, Rudolf Carnap published "The Overcoming of Metaphysics through Logical Analysis of Language," in which he used a passage from Heidegger's *What Is Metaphysics?* to show the meaningless of speculative thought.[21]

Heidegger rejected this broader claim. In his lecture course "Fundamental Questions of Metaphysics," of 1935–36, he says of symbolic logic:

There is an attempt here at calculating the system of propositional connections by means of mathematical methods; hence this kind of logic is also called "mathematical logic." It sets itself a possible and valid task. However, what symbolic logic furnishes is anything but a logic, i.e. a contemplation of the λόγος. Mathematical logic is not even a logic of mathematics in the sense that it determines or could at all determine the nature of mathematical thinking and mathematical truth. Rather, symbolic logic is itself a type of mathematics applied to sentences and sentential forms. Every mathematical and symbolic logic places itself outside whatever realm of logic because for its very own purposes it must posit the λόγος, the proposition, as a mere connection of concepts which is basically inadequate. The presumption of symbolic logic of constituting the scientific logic of all sciences collapses as soon as the conditional and unreflective nature of its basic premise becomes apparent.[22]

In the treatise "Recollection in Metaphysics" of 1941, Heidegger begins to assign symptomatic significance to the growing claim and prestige of symbolic logic. "The signal of the degrading of thinking is the upgrading

20. *Sein und Zeit*, p. 159 (*Being and Time*, p. 202).
21. "Überwindung der Metaphysik durch logische Analyse der Sprache," *Erkenntnis* 2 (1931) : 219–41. Translated by Arthur Pap in *Logical Positivism*, ed. A. J. Ayer (Glencoe, Ill., 1959), pp. 60–81. The section of this article that concerns Heidegger is reprinted in this volume, pp. 23–34.
22. *Die Frage nach dem Ding* (Tübingen, 1962), p. 122 (*What Is a Thing?*, trans. W. B. Barton, Jr., and Vera Deutsch [Chicago, 1967], p. 156). Concerning the con-

of symbolic logic to the rank of true logic. Symbolic logic is the calculative organization of the unconditional ignorance regarding the essence of
thinking provided that thinking, being thought essentially, is that creative
knowledge of fundamental outlines which, in the care of the essence of
truth, rises from being." [23] The rise of symbolic logic is, nevertheless, historically consistent. The "Postscript" of 1943 to *What Is Metaphysics?*
takes symbolic logic as the "consistent degeneration" of logic—logic, in
turn, being the issue of the Greek experience of being where the fundamental concern is with entities, a concern that originates from being
but conceals it. This concern now realizes itself as a consuming attempt
at rendering everything calculable and at reducing thought to endless
and seemingly productive calculation.[24]

The treatise "The Overcoming of Metaphysics" shows in particular
that modern metaphysics in the form of transcendental philosophy is, in
its endeavor to prove and to secure the conditions of objectivity, ultimately preoccupied with objects. And the "mere reverse (the empirical-
positivistic misinterpretation of the theory of knowledge) is signaled by
the advance of symbolic logic." [25] The Parmenides interpretation of 1951
underscores the significance and scope of this reversal of the " 'metaphysics' or 'ontology of cognition.' " "Its presently decisive and most
consequential form is constituting itself under the name of 'symbolic
logic.' " Along with the philosophy of existence and existentialism,
symbolic logic is seen as the most effective offspring of "the unchallenged
power of modern thinking." [26]

The lecture course *What Is Called Thinking?*, of which the Parmenides
interpretation was to be a part, ascribes even greater power and significance to symbolic logic. "Already symbolic logic is widely taken (particularly in the Anglo-Saxon countries) as the only possible form of rigorous
philosophy because its results and procedures immediately yield something
definite toward the construction of the technological world. Hence, in
America and elsewhere, symbolic logic, as the proper philosophy of the
future, begins to assume its reign over the spirit. Through the appropriate
coupling of symbolic logic with modern psychology and psychoanalysis
and with sociology, the concern of future philosophy becomes perfect."
Again Heidegger points out that this development has not sprung from

---

cept of relation in symbolic logic, see also *Unterwegs zur Sprache*, 2nd ed. (Pfullingen, 1960), p. 125 (*On the Way to Language*, trans. Peter D. Hertz [New York,
1971], p. 32).

23. *Nietzsche*, 2 vols. (Pfullingen, 1961), 2 : 487. Translated by Joan Stambaugh in
The End of Philosophy (New York, 1973), p. 80.

24. *Was ist Metaphysik?*, 4th ed. (Frankfurt, 1943), pp. 27–28. Translated by
R. F. C. Hall in *Existence and Being* (Chicago, 1949), p. 356.

25. *Vorträge und Aufsätze*, 2nd ed. (Pfullingen, 1959), pp. 75–76. According to the
textual note on p. 283, the present passage was written sometime between 1936 and
1946.

26. Ibid., p. 234.

willful or mistaken human decisions, but from a higher consistency. "This concerning, however, is by no means the machination of men. Rather, these disciplines are under the destination of a power which comes from afar and for which the Greek words ποίησις [poetry] and τέχνη [technology] remain perhaps the fitting names provided that they name for us, those who think, that which makes one think." The same lecture course once more views the origin and significance of symbolic logic most briefly and comprehensively: "Only because at one time the call to thought became event as λόγος, symbolic logic today is developing into the planetary organizational form of every presentation." [27]

One last remark in *What Is Called Thinking?* indicates more specifically one of the ways in which symbolic logic establishes its reign over reality. "Occidental logic finally becomes symbolic logic, whose irrepressible development is meanwhile bringing about the electronic computer whereby human nature is fitted into that being of objects to which we hardly pay attention, but which appears in the nature of technology." [28] Very similarly, the lecture series *The Principle of Causality* (1955–56) says: "Meanwhile, translation machines have been set to work by modern technology, more precisely by the modern interpretation of thinking and speaking as found in symbolic logic which stands in an elective affinity to modern technology." [29] Here too Heidegger sees in symbolic logic the fruition of a long development, one that is decisively if concealedly influenced by Leibniz.[30] The translation machine is one concrete manifestation of what in *Hebel—The Housefriend* is called the language machine: "The language machine is—and more particularly is still in the process of becoming—a way in which modern technology disposes of the mode and world of language as such." [31]

The appearance of symbolic logic and this final attack on language are aspects of one and the same metaphysical event, as "A Dialogue on Language" of 1953–54 tells us. The lecture series "The Nature of Language" sketches that event:

Recently, the scientific and philosophical investigation of languages aims with ever greater determination at the construction of what is called the "metalanguage." Scientific philosophy which is concerned with the construction of this superlanguage quite consistently interprets itself as metalinguistics. This sounds like metaphysics and not only sounds like it; it *is* like it; for metalinguistics is the metaphysics of the thoroughgoing technifica-

---

27. *Was heisst Denken?*, 2nd ed. (Tübingen, 1961), p. 10; p. 10; p. 102 (*What Is Called Thinking?*, trans. Fred D. Wieck and J. Glenn Gray [New York, 1968], pp. 21–22; p. 22; p. 238).
28. *Ibid.*, p. 145; p. 238 of the translation.
29. *Der Satz vom Grund*, 2nd ed. (Pfullingen, 1958), p. 163.
30. Ibid., pp. 65, 170, 203.
31. *Hebel—Der Hausfreund*, 3rd ed. (Pfullingen, 1965), pp. 27–28. (First published in 1957.)

tion of all languages with a view to establishing a solely functioning inter-
planetary instrument of information. Metalanguage and sputnik, metalinguistics and rocket technology are the same.

However, one should not assume that the scientific and philosophical investigation of languages and of language are being looked at here in a
derogatory manner. This research has its special right and retains its own
weight. There is always much useful information to be learned from it.

The appraisal of metalanguage and metalinguistics is implicitly corrected
in the lecture "The Way to Language," of 1959, where Heidegger points
out that any formalized language must in some way remain dependent on
natural language. But this dependence, Heidegger continues, is viewed as
a tentative and undesirable state of affairs by information theory. Its goal
is still to construct "the formalized language, that type of information by
means of which man is fitted into, i.e., established in, the technical-calcula-
tive realm and where he gradually abandons 'natural language'." [32]

In his final remarks on symbolic logic, Heidegger concedes to symbolic
logic not only symptomatic significance and technological efficacy, but
accepts it as the dominant mode of philosophy, or better perhaps, as the
successor of traditional philosophy. This line of thought first appears in
the essay on "Hegel and the Greeks," of 1958:

> From the title "Hegel and the Greeks" there speaks to us the whole of
> philosophy in its history, and it does so at a time when the decay of philoso-
> phy is becoming obvious; for philosophy migrates off into symbolic logic,
> psychology, and sociology. These independent research areas are securing
> for themselves mounting significance and manifold influence inasmuch as
> they constitute the functional patterns and successful instruments of the
> politico-economic, i.e., of our essentially technological world.[33]

He puts the matter more positively still in the essay on "The End of
Philosophy and the Task of Thought," of 1964. There he says of the unfolding of philosophy into the individual sciences:

> It looks as though this is merely the dissolution of philosophy, and in truth
> it is precisely its completion.
>   It suffices to call attention to the independence of psychology, of sociology,
> of anthropology qua cultural anthropology, and to the role of logic qua sym-
> bolic logic and semantics. Philosophy turns into an empirical science of man,
> of everything that can become for man an accessible object of his tech-
> nology by means of which he establishes himself in the world, working on
> it in manifold ways of making and fashioning.[34]

---

32. *Unterwegs zur Sprache*, p. 166; pp. 160–61; pp. 263–64 (*On the Way to
Language*, p. 25; pp. 58–59; pp. 132–33).
33. *Wegmarken* (Frankfurt am Main, 1967), p. 255.
34. In *Zur Sache des Denkens* (Tübingen, 1969), pp. 63–64. Translated by Joan
Stambaugh in *On Time and Being* (New York, 1972), pp. 57–59.

Similar remarks can be found in the notes of a seminar that Heidegger conducted in 1962 on his lecture "Time and Being" and in an interview he gave in 1966.[35] But at the peak of its significance in Heidegger's thought, symbolic logic must share its position with other disciplines. It now is always mentioned along with such disciplines as psychology, sociology, (cultural) anthropology, semantics, and political science. Moreover, cybernetics now assumes the focal significance that was earlier ascribed to symbolic logic.[36]

The German word that Heidegger almost exclusively uses for symbolic logic is *Logistik*.[37] There is an etymological and semantic equivalent in English, logistic. But this word is now rare as a noun.[38] In the English-speaking world, the term "symbolic logic" stands for roughly the same thing as *Logistik* does in German. But what do these names stand for? Symbolic logic in the narrowest sense is that discipline which deals with the construction and investigation of calculi. A calculus is a formal system that consists of a set of specified symbols and a set of formation rules that indicate how the symbols are to be connected. This kind of calculus is trivial, and so are its properties. We can render the calculus more complex by designating certain groups of correctly connected symbols as axioms and by adding rules that permit the transition from one or more groups of symbols to another group of symbols. We can then inquire into the various properties of the calculus as a whole or into the properties of its parts. We can, for instance, ask whether a given group of symbols can be arrived at by using the formation rules of the calculus or by starting from the axioms and using the rules of transition. We can inquire whether one of the axioms can be arrived at by starting from the others in the calculus, using the rules of transition.

Such a calculus is also called a logistic system, and we say that it is formal or rigorous. We may further say that it is syntactic or uninterpreted. Regarding its philosophical significance we can finally say that it is mute. Such a logistic system does not assert anything; it cannot, there-

35. Ibid., p. 28 (p. 26 in the translation). The interview, under the title "Nur noch ein Gott kann uns retten," appeared in *Der Spiegel*, no. 23 (May, 1976), pp. 193–219. The passage referred to (p. 212) speaks of *logic* rather than *symbolic logic*. But the context is almost literally like that of the passages referred to in this and the preceding notes. I assume there was a slip on the part of Heidegger or in the process of transcription.

36. *Zur Sache des Denkens*, pp. 64–65, 79 (pp. 58, 72 in the translation); "Nur noch ein Gott kann uns retten," p. 212; *Heraklit* (Frankfurt am Main, 1970) pp. 23–27.

37. Concerning the etymology and history of this word, see Günther Jacoby, *Die Ansprüche der Logistiker auf die Logik und ihre Geschichtsschreibung* (Stuttgart, 1962), pp. 119–22.

38. An early book of W. V. O. Quine's has the title *A System of Logistic* (Cambridge, Mass., 1934). *Logistic* is still widely used as an adjective, particularly in the expression *logistic system*. The disappearance of *logistic* as a noun may have brought about in part by the rise of its near-homonym from the military sphere, *logistics*.

fore, be wrong, and one cannot take issue with it. One may challenge the existence of a property that has been attributed to it. But such a controversy can never be fundamental. One can either show that the calculus indeed has the property or that it is impossible for the system to have that property; and if neither can be done at present, the point must remain moot.[39]

Heidegger nowhere in his writings goes very far in dealing explicitly with symbolic logic in this narrow sense. The technically most specific remarks speak of symbolic logic as a propositional calculus. This type of calculus is commonly understood in the following interpreted sense: the variables are said to stand for unanalyzed kinds of propositions of which only the truth or falsehood enters into the construction of the calculus. The constants or connectives are said to express the logical relationships that obtain among propositions. The transitions from one or two strings of variables and connectives to a further string are said to represent logical operations or inferences.

Heidegger does not clearly distinguish between the calculus and its interpretation. Instead, he uses the term "mathematics" in place of "logistic system," and the term "symbolic logic" in place of "propositionally interpreted calculus. In light of this clarification and of Heidegger's initial views on symbolic logic presented earlier, it is clear that at first Heidegger regarded the purely formal domain of the calculus as the proper realm of symbolic logic.[40] But in so limiting symbolic logic, Heidegger had to contend with the claims on the part of symbolic logic that extend beyond its competence in constructing and investigating calculi.

Symbolic logic in its wider sense is delimited by a number of claims. These are manifold, but they are all bound to symbolic logic in the narrow sense to the extent that they regard the logistic system as a decisive model or tool. Symbolic logic in the wider sense is represented by such schools of thought as Logical Positivism, Analytic or Scientific Philosophy, and the like. Rather than listing all claims that have been advanced and then trying to locate the limit proper to symbolic logic, we will, in keeping with our methodological premise, discuss those claims only that Heidegger attributes to symbolic logic; but we will keep in mind that Heidegger, especially in his later writings, uses the term symbolic logic, i.e., *Logistik*, quite loosely. Only the first two claims to be discussed are generally put forth by, let us say, textbooks of symbolic logic.

---

39. A more precise and technical exposition of the logistic systems can be found in Alonzo Church, *Introduction to Mathematical Logic* (Princeton, N.J., 1956), I : 47–58; or in Irving M. Copi, *Symbolic Logic*, 3rd ed. (New York, 1967), pp. 177–247.

40. In *Die Frage nach dem Ding*, p. 122 (*What Is a Thing?*, p. 156), Heidegger seems to grant further the possibility and validity of formally reconstructing the truth-functional connections that obtain between propositions.

According to Heidegger's early views, symbolic logic, in the first place, claims to be capable of laying bare the structure of language and of reasoning.[41] There can be little doubt that natural language embodies formal relations and that a calculus can mirror these explicitly. It is also true that more formal features are being brought into the open as more types of symbolic logic are being developed such as modal, deontic, many-valued, or dialectical logic. But such concessions leave unanswered the crucial question of the significance of revealing formal structures in language: Do these formal structures constitute the core or skeleton of natural language? If yes, then the interpreted calculi of symbolic logic can serve as canons of language, and logical analysis of language would be the most incisive and illuminating approach to natural language. If no, then logical analysis is merely a manner of rendering explicit informally obtained insights, a manner, moreover, which can blind and mislead as much as it can be of heuristic benefit. Heidegger argues the negative case and so essentially if unwittingly takes sides in a controversy that has been carried out at length and in depth under the heading of ideal vs. ordinary language philosophy.[42] Heidegger and the moderate faction of the ordinary language school, as represented by Strawson for instance, have had, it seems to me, the better part of the issue.[43]

In the second place, Heidegger says of symbolic logic that it fails to be, as it claims, a philosophy of mathematics. To clarify this criticism, let us put it in the context of a number of related claims.

1. Symbolic logic includes mathematics.
2. Symbolic logic is a philosophy of mathematics.
3. Symbolic logic includes metamathematics.
4. Metamathematics is a philosophy of mathematics.
5. Mathematics includes symbolic logic.

Heidegger nowhere attributes the first claim to symbolic logic and so has no quarrel with symbolic logic on that score. It is the second claim that is

41. This claim is advanced in varying degrees of explicitness and inclusiveness. Obviously, it is impossible in principle to substantiate it rigorously. And certainly all logicians are aware that there are types of thinking other than (formal, deductive) logical reasoning. But there is often an implication that the latter type of thought is the most reliable and powerful and the highest in dignity; there is, then, the further claim that this type of thought is most fully and adequately dealt with in symbolic logic. See Church, pp. 1–3; Copi, pp. 1–8; Frederick Brenton Fitch, *Symbolic Logic: An Introduction* (New York, 1952), pp. 3–5; Harold Newton Lee, *Symbolic Logic* (London, 1961), pp. 3–16; W. V. O. Quine, *Methods of Logic*, 2nd ed. (New York, 1964), pp. xi–xvii. For further references and refutations of this claim, see Jacoby, pp. 27–64; Brand Blanshard, *Reason and Analysis* (La Salle, Ill., 1962), pp. 127–88.

42. The best collection of documents is Richard Rorty, ed., *The Linguistic Turn* (Chicago, Ill., 1967).

43. See my *The Philosophy of Language* (The Hague, 1974), pp. 91–125.

ascribed to symbolic logic by Heidegger and said to be in error. The ascription and critique might be explicated in the terms of the third and fourth claims, and I assume that Heidegger would agree with the explication. But to say that the explicated claim has not been made good is still ambiguous. It might mean that metamathematics has failed to carry out its entire original program, say that of Hilbert. Or it might mean that regardless of its failures or successes, symbolic logic, in its metamathematical parts, is unilluminating and merely an upward extension of mathematics, not an exploration of its foundations. It is the latter point that Heidegger urges, and in his early writings he put it in the form of the fifth claim. I am inclined to agree with the second claim. Surely symbolic or mathematical logic has thrown important light on the scope and foundations of mathematics. On the other hand, I am quite unsure of the fruitfulness or illuminating force of a primarily speculative philosophy of mathematics, that is, one where formal systems and procedures have little or no part. But this is beyond my competence, and I leave the matter with these attempts at clarification.[44]

Third, Heidegger accuses symbolic logic of not being equal to its pretension that it is a philosophy of science. This claim is an extension of the first and the second; but here the inclusion of the empirical sciences requires not only a rigorous calculus, but an equally rigorous tie between empirical reality and the calculus. One may interpret the verification principle and the theory of logical atomism as attempts at formally bridging the gap between empirical reality and deductive reasoning. The failure of these endeavors supports Heidegger's charge that this third claim is unfounded.[45]

So far we have considered Heidegger's comments on symbolic logic as they appear in his writings from 1912 to 1936. After this period we witness a turn in Heidegger's position. Broadly speaking we can say that the claims of symbolic logic that Heidegger was at pains to deny he now grants to an increasing extent. We may locate the turning point in the passage, written sometime between 1936 and 1946, where Heidegger speaks of symbolic logic as the signal of the final phase of a long effort to obtain mastery over objects through the inquiry into the conditions of their possibility.

Heidegger is still critical of this latest effort, calling it "the empirical-positivistic misinterpretation of the theory of knowledge." [46] Symbolic logic is nonetheless accepted now as the symptom of the final phase of

44. For further remarks on the relationship between mathematics and symbolic logic, see Lee, *Symbolic Logic*, and Quine, *Methods of Logic*.

45. As indicated before, the term *symbolic logic* is used quite loosely in this and the following claims. Examples for statements of these claims can be found in Ayer; refutations of the claims in Jacoby and in Blanshard, pp. 127–307.

46. See n. 25 for reference.

Western thought. From the status of a symptom it is further raised to that of the decisive formative power of the technological era, giving rise and exhibiting closest affinity to electronic computers. Here is a remarkable if narrow point of contact between Heidegger and Quine. In his essay "On the Application of Modern Logic" Quine says, "The utterly pure theory of mathematical proof and the utterly technological theory of machine computation are thus at bottom one, and the insights of each are henceforth insights of the other."[47] But that view is too generous toward symbolic logic in its assessment of symbolic logic's contribution to the construction of computers and it is unfair in burdening symbolic logic with the major responsibility for computer technology. Heidegger credits symbolic logic with having played a major role in promoting the enterprise of machine translation and of a formal language that can be embodied in a machine and that is powerful enough to displace natural language. But machine translation in a serious sense has been one of the spectacular failures of computer technology,[48] and doubt is thus cast on its power to command us. Of course there are many influential philosophers at work today who will not agree with Heidegger when he speaks of the end of philosophy and surrenders metaphysics to symbolic logic.

The result of the foregoing confrontation of symbolic logic and Heidegger's thought is unsatisfactory. It does injustice to symbolic logic in concentrating on the tasks it had set for itself without being equipped for them. And in considering only the immediate environment of the remarks on symbolic logic in Heidegger's writings, it fails to consider Heidegger's thought in larger terms. A more fundamental confrontation is called for. This need is emphasized by the fact that the change in Heidegger's appraisal of symbolic logic coincides chronologically with the turn in Heidegger's thought. What is it precisely that we have to reconsider within a deeper perspective of Heidegger's philosophy? It is the emergence of symbolic logic as a focus of modern technology. How technology comes to be a theme of Heidegger's reflections is a topic in its own right. What we want to do here is lay bare one strand in the development of Heidegger's thought on technology, the strand that is marked by Heidegger's comments on symbolic logic.

Heidegger begins as an undistinguished if solid scholar in philosophy. His work comes into its own with *Being and Time*, a deeply ambivalent book whose distinctive trait is the determination to attain a new level of radical thought. In this determination Heidegger finds himself in competi-

---

47. In *The Ways of Paradox* (New York, 1966), p. 41.
48. A critique of the claims and achievements of workers in computer technology has been given by Hubert L. Dreyfus, *What Computers Can't Do* (New York, 1972). On machine translation see pp. 3–5 in particular.

tion with symbolic logic in the broad sense. There too we find an attempt
to rethink traditional philosophy in a fundamental way. Heidegger is
aware of the challenge and seeks to pursue more radically the tasks that
symbolic logic has set for itself. Consider Heidegger's attempts at exploring the foundations of mathematics and Newtonian physics in the lecture
course "Fundamental Questions of Metaphysics" (1935–36) and the
passage in *Being and Time* that characterizes his enterprise in implicit
opposition to that of symbolic logic:

> Insofar as these regions [i.e. those of the various sciences] are obtained from
> the realm of what is in general, such precursive research which provides the
> basic concepts is nothing but the interpretation of what is with regard to the
> basic constitution of its being. Such research must precede the individual
> sciences; and it *can*. The work of Plato and Aristotle proves it. Laying the
> foundations for the sciences in this way is different in principle from the
> "logic" which limps along after, investigating the status of some science as it
> chances to find it, in order to discover its "method." Laying the foundations,
> as we have described it, is rather a productive logic—in the sense that it leaps
> ahead, as it were, into some area of being, discloses it for the first time in
> the constitution of its being, and, after thus arriving at the structures within
> it, makes these available to the positive sciences as lucid assignments for
> their inquiry.[49]

What tangible effect this laying of foundations had was certainly
limited. Furthermore, the turn in Heidegger's thought signals the abandonment of all such endeavors. It marks Heidegger's realization that
science and technology cannot be understood and overcome by taking
hold of their antecedent and controlling conditions. Such a move is typical
of science and technology and only extends their domain. This insight
of Heidegger's is strikingly illustrated by a passage that almost point by
point modifies the passage just cited. "What philosophy in the course of
its history attempted on occasion, and insufficiently even then, namely to
outline the ontologies of the various regions of what is (nature, history,
law, art), this the sciences now take over as their own task. They are interested in a theory of the various and necessary structuring concepts of
the subject area that is assigned to them." [50]

Science and technology are the forces that are giving shape to our age.
The sequence of Heidegger's comments on symbolic logic reveals how
Heidegger discovers the historical roots and the hegemony of these forces.
The comments also show how the practical and theoretical, technology
and science, are more and more seen as one by Heidegger. To be sure,

49. *Sein und Zeit*, p. 10 (*Being and Time*, pp. 30–31). Heidegger's discussion of
mathematics and Newtonian physics is to be found in *Die Frage nach dem Ding*,
pp. 49–83 (*What Is a Thing?*, pp. 65–108).
50. See *Zur Sache des Denkens*, pp. 64–65 (p. 58 in the translation).

he never identifies science and technology but holds them to be issues of the same phenomenon, the essence of technology, which he calls the framework (*Gestell*).[51]

What is the framework? Roughly speaking, it is the predominant perspective in which everything presents itself, within which we take up with the world, and which finally guides the ways in which we understand ourselves. Specifically, things appear within the framework as challenges (*Herausforderungen*) to which we respond in procuring them (*bestellen*) as a resource (*Bestand*). The questions that arise for us are two: Why is symbolic logic a focus of the framework? And what light can a further consideration of symbolic logic throw on the framework or, more generally, on Heidegger's theory of technology?

Following Heidegger's remarks we have seen that symbolic logic is not, in its explicit claims and arguments, an illuminating theory of our age or of technology and science. Nor is it technologically productive in a central and straightforward way. But it might be revealing as a practice. What are the essential features of technological practice? Let us consider three examples where different experiences and practices help to bring technological practice into relief.

We begin by considering some aspects of the competence that we have in forming and understanding such simple sentences as 'Some man lives in that house' and 'This cat walks on a roof.' In order to make the case more indicative, let us assume that I have no formal grammatical training. I will nevertheless recognize that first string of sounds ('Some man lives in that house') as a meaningful and comparatively independent whole, and I see that the first and second string are alike in just that respect. If asked how many elements each of the whole incorporates, I will, after some deliberation, answer, "Six." The independence of these elements is apparent to me from the possibility of substituting and interchanging them; for instance *this* for *that*, *man* for *cat*, etc. Some results of substitutions sound quite normal to me, others sound strange, and others again quite nonsensical. On the basis of substitutability, I can arrange the twelve elements into different groups, let us say *man, house, cat,* and *roof; lives* and *walks; in* and *on; some, that, this,* and *a*.

Inquiring into the way in which these elements are connected into a sequence, I find that the cohesion in different pairs of sequential elements

51. Heidegger gives his most explicit account of the essence of technology in the two essays published in *Die Technik und die Kehre* (Pfullingen, 1962). The kinship of science and technology is explained on pp. 13–14 and 21–23. Heidegger's views of modern science underwent many changes. In *Die Frage nach dem Ding*, p. 51 (*What Is a Thing*, p. 67) he gives modern science philosophical rank—that is, science inasmuch as it is revolutionary science (to use Thomas Kuhn's term). Further materials on Heidegger's views of science can be found in Karlfried Gründer, "M. Heidegger's Wissenschaftskritik," *Archiv für Philosophie* II (1961) : 316–22.

differs in strength. In the first sentence, *that* and *house* are intimately connected while *in* and *that* do not seem tied together as closely. But if I add *house* to *that*, there is again a close connection between *in* and *that house*, which indicates that the cohesions are determined by relationships that transcend contiguity. In the second sentence, I find similar conditions; and, in general, I know that for any of the observations I have made I could easily produce other examples. Further, I could form sequences that would exhibit traits going beyond my present observations, but that are in some essential way connected with them.

What has been said about the two sentences could be shortened and generalized by using grammatical terms such as noun, verb, subject, predicate, and so on. However, such a systematization would still be lengthy and unclear in the delimitations of the terms. The shortest, most comprehensive and uniquivocal way of presenting all of the above information would be a set of rules of the following kind:

1) Rewrite *Sentence* as *Noun Phrase* plus *Predicate Phrase*.
2) Rewrite *Noun Phrase* as *Determiner* plus *Noun*.
3) Rewrite *Predicate Phrase* as *Verb* plus *Prepositional Phrase*.
4) Rewrite *Prepositional Phrase* as *Preposition* plus *Noun Phrase*.
5) Rewrite *Determiner* as *some* or *that* or *this* or *a*.
6) Rewrite *Noun* as *man* or *house* or *cat* or *roof*.
7) Rewrite *Verb* as *lives* or *walks*.
8) Rewrite *Preposition* as *in* or *on*.[52]

These rules are to be understood in the sense that, after having applied the first rule, I can apply any rule to any element (other than "plus") in the result of a rewriting in the way that the rule being applied prescribes.

I now apply the rules in the following way: I want to generate a certain sentence. So I rewrite *Sentence* as *Noun Phrase* plus *Predicate Phrase* (Rule 1). In the result of that rewriting, I rewrite *Predicate Phrase* as *Verb* plus *Prepositional Phrase* (Rule 3). In the result of that rewriting, I rewrite *Prepositional Phrase* as *Preposition* plus *Noun Phrase* (Rule 4). In that result, I rewrite *Noun Phrase* as *Determiner* plus *Noun* (Rule 2). I have now generated the following string: *Noun Phrase* plus *Verb* plus *Preposition* plus *Determiner* plus *Noun*. Applying further rules, I derive a sequence of elements which is identical to the sentence: 'Some man lives in that house'. If the results of the applications of the rules are arranged one beneath the other with *Sentence* being written in the top line of this

---

52. This is a simplified fragment of a generative grammar. For a full presentation and discussion, see Noam Chomsky, *Aspects of the Theory of Syntax* (Cambridge, Mass., 1965), particularly pp. 106–11; and Jerrold J. Katz and Paul Postal, *An Integrated Theory of Linguistic Descriptions* (Cambridge, Mass., 1964), particularly pp. 6–12.

column, then the entire column can be uniquely transformed into a tree with *Sentence* at the top branching into a left element (*Noun Phrase*) and a right one (*Predicate Phrase*); both branch further, and that process continues till the final elements, read from left to right, yield one of our sentences. For the two sentences, we would have to derive two trees which would turn out to be identical except for the final elements.

By means of the tree I can exhibit clearly and rigorously all the information that was at first presented in an informal way. Since the tree is determined by the column of results of rule applications and since the column is contained in the set of eight rules, we can say that the entire initial information is contained in that set. As a matter of fact, the set of rules contains additional information since it also permits the derivation of the sentences 'The man walks on the roof' and 'That cat lives in some house' and others. The set could, in a simple and consistent way, be extended to cover additional sentences.

We now turn to the second case, which is to contrast an indicative experience of our world with a similar experience of a pretechnological world. Let us start with the latter and consider a simple undertaking such as visiting a friend who lives in the same town as I do. As I leave my house, the sun appears from behind the mountains, and the women go shopping for food. They buy certain vegetables because this is the time of the year when those vegetables are harvested and brought from the villages nearby to the market. I am familiar with most of the houses that I walk past; they seem to have the same physiognomy as the families that have lived in them for generations. As I get further away from the part of the town where I live, the environment speaks less clearly. But I still know quite certainly where I am: the church is to my left and somewhat behind me, the distance to the mountains is greater. There is the fountain that my friend mentioned, and the house to the west, all lit up by the sun, must be his.

Consider now the same enterprise in a big city of today. I get in my car and head for the A-Expressway. Going east on the A-Expressway, I watch for the turnoff to the B-Expressway north. I take that turnoff, and going north on the B-Expressway, watch for the cutoff to the C-Expressway northwest. I take that cutoff, and going northwest on the C-Expressway, I watch for the exit of Thirty-first Street south. I take that exit, and going south on Thirty-first Street, I watch for the second traffic light. At the traffic light, I turn west onto Fairfield Drive. The third house on the north side of the sixth block is my friend's.

Thirdly let us consider the way in which a great building came into being in the Middle Ages and the way it does today. Take a cathedral to illustrate the former. Through a long development, a unique, never exactly repeated outline had come to serve as its ground plan. In its growth from bottom to top, it unfolded itself in a varying, never fully preconceived shape. It grew and changed with the succession and the skill of the master builders and stonemasons. They failed and succeeded with their knowledge of the stone and their experiences in building walls, vaults, arches, and spires. A skyscraper of today is entirely determined by the blueprints and specifications of the architect. These plans are in turn contained in the laws of economics, architecture, and engineering. The building is decisively shaped in an abstract combination of various factors, in a kind of calculus; the concrete execution is trivial.

The same is true of the expressway system as a physical construction. But that case was meant to establish another and more indicative parallel. The expressway system, in its completed state, is itself a kind of embodied calculus. The very language in which the trip was described is very close to the description of how an application of a generative calculus leads to a certain sentence. It is indeed possible to define an expressway system as a calculus and a trip as a proof within that calculus. The decisive point is to realize how far the parallel between the generative linguistic calculus and the expressway system goes. Just as the set of linguistic rules contains a large number of possible sentences, so the expressway contains a large number of possible trips. And just as a complete generative grammar of a certain language would contain all the possible sentences of that language, so a complete expressway system in a certain region would contain all the possible trips within that region.

We must now try to articulate more sharply the technological practice that has been adumbrated in these examples and we must see whether a sharper outline will exhibit an illuminating kinship with symbolic logic. It has been recognized that technological practice draws on the formal sciences such as logic, statistics, queuing theory, and so on, and not just on the substantive ones such as physics and chemistry.[53] But the question we must pose reaches further: does symbolic logic have a paradigmatic and not just an instrumental significance in technology? What is implicit in the examples above is that in technological practice formal features are discovered in the concrete phenomena of our world. Such discoveries lead to the construction of formal models that cover a certain domain of the concrete world. These models form a hierarchy from concrete and limited realizations at the bottom to more abstract and encompassing models in the higher reaches of the hierarchy.[54] What is common to all of them is that ideally they delimit in rigorous form the space of all the possibilities of the domain that they cover. The ideal grammar contains all possible

53. See Mario Bunge, "Toward a Philosophy of Technology," in *Philosophy and Technology*, ed. Carl Mitcham and Robert Mackey (New York, 1972), pp. 62–63.

54. This is a most complex hierarchy. Its global description will always be sketchy though it may be possible to give precise local accounts.

sentences; the ideal expressway system encompasses all possible trips; the ideal manual of architecture contains all possible buildings.

These formalizations can be thought of as a modeling of reality in two senses. First, the modeling sharply captures and represents a certain segment of reality. Second, this modeling amounts to a reshaping of reality. The articulation of a segment of reality in a model severs that part of reality from its historical context. It takes hold of a region of reality by delimiting and exhausting at once all its possibilities and variations. The world in its historical coherence and in its actual and singular presence recedes.

We can think of that kind of modeling as an explication of the way in which technological man, according to Heidegger, meets the challenges of the modern era and of how he procures them as an indefinite resource. We can further think of the eclipse of the singular world by the concern with possibilities as an explication of the peculiar self-concealment of the framework, i.e., of the essence of technology. Technological practice does not overtly deny or suppress any actuality; on the contrary, it seems at pains to expand the scope of actualities ad infinitum. But when all trips, for instance, are equally possible, none will stand out as a commanding actuality.

A striking illustration of this self-concealment is the discussion of the creativity of language in the kind of grammatic analysis sketched above. It is often said that a generative and transformational grammar accounts for the "creative aspect of language use," i.e., for the fact that the competent speaker constantly generates and understands sentences he has not encountered before.[55] This the grammar accomplishes by showing how the (internalized) command of a finite set of rules allows one in principle to produce and comprehend infinitely many different sentences. But in answering the question of creativity by showing how infinitely many different things can be said, one quite conceals the questions of creativity that ask: What in particular needs to be said? What is an eminent and commanding actualization within the infinite possibilities? These questions are usually not posed and are certainly not answerable in generative and transformational grammar.[56]

Symbolic logic may now be seen as the most general modeling of reality. In the first sense of modeling, this is a view of which a variant has been developed by Quine. Logic is the ultimate, that is the most central and least likely to be revised, part of the systematic conceptual structure in which reality is present to us.[57] But for Heidegger symbolic

55. See Chomsky, *Cartesian Linguistics* (New York, 1966), pp. 3–31.
56. See my *Philosophy of Language*, pp. 126–28 and 154–62. Chomsky is aware of the ambiguity of "creativity." See *Cartesian Linguistics*, p. 84, n. 30.
57. *Methods of Logic*, pp. xii–xv.

logic constitutes the ultimate modeling of reality in that other sense as well: it is the most decisive shaping force of our world. As such it is at the center of the framework; it procures it as a resource most incisively and conceals its own significance most resolutely. Finally, symbolic logic as the ultimate modeling of our world, in both senses of modeling, may be taken as the common origin and force of modern science and technology, i.e., of the theoretical and the practical.[58]

I have tried, in this concluding part of the paper, to point out the consistency and fruitfulness of Heidegger's theses as regards the relationship of symbolic logic and technology. Yet it is a view that I cannot share, however much I have learned from it. I dissent for chiefly two reasons. First, it seems to me that a sharp distinction between science and technology is crucial for an understanding and especially for a principled critique of technology. Second, I think we need a more concrete delineation of the essential pattern and direction of technolgy than is provided either by the framework or by symbolic logic.[59] To learn from Heidegger is to think with him and against him.[60]

58. This is a view that Hans Jonas, without reference to symbolic logic, has worked out in detail—whether inspired by Heidegger or not—in "The Scientific and Technological Revolutions," *Philosophy Today* 15 (1971) : 76–101.

59. The arguments in support of these theses are worked out in "The Explanation of Technology," forthcoming in *Philosophy and Technology: An Annual Compilation of Research* 1 (1977).

60. The revision of this paper has benefited from suggestions and critical notes of Michael Murray's.

2. RUDOLF CARNAP

The Overcoming of Metaphysics through Logical Analysis of Language

[EDITOR'S NOTE: In the sections that preface the discussion of Heidegger, Carnap analyzes "cognitive" meaning and states the project of an ideal logically constructed language. Since a language consists of a lexicon and a syntax, we must fix the meaning of each. A word is meaningful if it refers in "observation sentences" to observable sense data, experiences, or things. A sentence is meaningful if it employs meaningful words and if it obeys the rules of a logical syntax, which is one that eliminates all possible nonsensical combinations of words, including those which grammatical syntax permits. In such a language no pseudowords or pseudostatements could occur and thus metaphysics would be eliminated.]

METAPHYSICAL PSEUDOSTATEMENTS

LET US NOW TAKE A LOOK at some examples of metaphysical pseudostatements of a kind where the violation of logical syntax is especially obvious, though they accord with historical-grammatical syntax. We select a few sentences from that metaphysical school which at present exerts the strongest influence in Germany.[1]

From *Logical Positivism,* ed. A. J. Ayer; translated by Arthur Pap from "Überwindung der Metaphysik durch Logische Analyse der Sprache," *Erkenntnis* 2 (1931). Reprinted with permission of the Free Press and the Rudolf Carnap Trust. The first word in the title has been translated as "Overcoming" instead of "Elimination."

1. The following quotations (original italics) are taken from M. Heidegger, *Was ist Metaphysik?* (1929). We could just as well have selected passages from any other of the numerous metaphysicians of the present or of the past; yet the selected passages seem to us to illustrate our thesis especially well.

"What is to be investigated is being only and—*nothing* else; being alone and further—*nothing;* solely being, and beyond being—*nothing. What about this Nothing?* . . . *Does the Nothing exist only because the Not, i.e. the Negation, exists?* Or is it the other way around? *Does Negation and the Not exist only because the Nothing exists?* . . . We assert: *the Nothing is prior to the Not and the Negation.* . . . Where do we seek the Nothing? How do we find the Nothing. . . . We know the Nothing. . . . *Anxiety reveals the Nothing.* . . . That for which and because of which we were anxious, was 'really'—nothing. Indeed: the Nothing itself—as such—was present. . . . *What about this Nothing—The Nothing itself nothings.*"

In order to show that the possibility of forming pseudostatements is based on a logical defect of language, we set up the schema below. The sentences under I are grammatically as well as logically impeccable, hence meaningful. The sentences under II (excepting B3) are in grammatical respects perfectly analogous to those under I. Sentence form IIA (as question and answer) does not, indeed, satisfy the requirements to be imposed on a logically correct language. But it is nevertheless meaningful, because it is translatable into correct language. This is shown by sentence IIIA, which has the same meaning as IIA. Sentence form IIA then proves to be undesirable because we can be led from it, by means of grammatically faultless operations, to the meaningless sentence forms IIB, which are taken from the above quotation. These forms cannot even be constructed in the correct language of Column III. Nonetheless, their nonsensicality is not obvious at first glance, because one is easily deceived by the analogy with the meaningful sentences IB. The fault of our language identified here lies, therefore, in the circumstance that, in contrast to a logically correct language, it admits of the same grammatical form for meaningful and meaningless word sequences. To each sentence in words we have added a corresponding formula in the notation of symbolic logic; these formulae facilitate recognition of the undesirable analogy between IA and IIA and therewith of the origin of the meaningless constructions IIB.

On closer inspection of the pseudo-statements under IIB, we also find some differences. The construction of sentence (1) is simply based on the mistake of employing the word "nothing" as a noun, because it is customary in ordinary language to use it in this form in order to construct a negative existential statement (see IIA). In a correct language, on the other hand, it is not a particular *name*, but a certain *logical form* of the sentence that serves this purpose (see IIIA). Sentence IIB2 adds something new, viz. the fabrication of the meaningless word "to nothing." This sentence, therefore, is senseless for a twofold reason. We pointed out before that the meaningless words of metaphysics usually owe their origin to the fact that a meaningful word is deprived of its meaning through its metaphorical use in metaphysics. But here we confront one of those rare cases where a new word is introduced which never had a meaning to begin with. Likewise sentence IIB3 must be rejected for two reasons. In respect of the error of using the word "nothing" as a noun, it is like the previous sentences. But in addition it involves a contradiction. For even if it were

I. Meaningful Sentences of Ordinary Language	II. Transition from Sense to Nonsense in Ordinary Language	III. Logically Correct Language
A. What is outside? $\qquad$ Ou(?) Rain is outside $\qquad$ Ou(r)	A. What is outside? $\qquad$ Ou(?) Nothing is outside $\qquad$ Ou(no)	A. There is nothing (does not exist any- thing) which is outside. $\qquad$ $\sim(\exists x).Ou(x)$
B. What about this rain? (i.e. what does the rain do? or: what else can be said about this rain? $\qquad$?(r)	B. "What about this Nothing?" ?(no)	B. None of these forms can even be constructed.
1. We know the rain $\qquad$ K(r)	1. "We seek the Nothing" "We find the Nothing" "We know the Nothing" $\qquad$ K(no)	
2. The rain rains $\qquad$ R(r)	2. "The Nothing nothings" $\qquad$ No(no)	
	3. "The Nothing exists only because . . ." $\qquad$ Ex(no)	

admissible to introduce "nothing" as a name or description of an entity, still the existence of this entity would be denied in its very definition, whereas sentence (3) goes on to affirm its existence. This sentence, there-fore, would be contradictory, hence absurd, even if it were not already meaningless.

In view of the gross logical errors which we find in sentences IIB, we might be led to conjecture that perhaps the word "nothing" has in Heidegger's treatise a meaning entirely different from the customary one. And this presumption is further strengthened as we go on to read there that anxiety reveals the Nothing, that the Nothing itself is present as such in anxiety. For here the word "nothing" seems to refer to a certain emotional constitution, possibly of a religious sort, or something or other that underlies such emotions. If such were the case, then the mentioned logical errors in sentences IIB would not be committed. But the first sentence of the quotation at the beginning of this section proves that this interpretation is not possible. The combination of "only" and "nothing else" shows unmistakably that the word "nothing" here has the usual meaning of a logical particle that serves for the formulation of a negative existential statement. This introduction of the word "nothing" is then immediately followed by the leading question of the treatise: "What about this Nothing?".

But our doubts as to a possible misinterpretation get completely dissolved as we note that the author of the treatise is clearly aware of the conflict between his questions and statements, and logic. "*Question and answer* in regard to the Nothing are equally *absurd* in themselves. . . . The fundamental rule of thinking commonly appealed to, the law of prohibited contradiction, general '*logic*,' destroys this question." All the worse for logic! We must abolish its sovereignty: "If thus the power of the *understanding* in the field of questions concerning Nothing and Being is broken, then the fate of the sovereignty of 'logic' within philosophy is thereby decided as well. The very idea of 'logic' dissolves in the whirl of a more basic questioning." But will sober science condone the whirl of counterlogical questioning? To this question too there is a ready answer: "The alleged sobriety and superiority of science becomes ridiculous if it does not take the Nothing seriously." Thus we find here a good confirmation of our thesis; a metaphysician himself here states that his questions and answers are irreconcilable with logic and the scientific way of thinking.

The difference between our thesis and that of the *earlier antimetaphysicians* should now be clear. We do not regard metaphysics as "mere speculation" or "fairy tales." The statements of a fairy tale do not conflict with logic, but only with experience; they are perfectly meaningful, although false. Metaphysics is not "*superstition*"; it is possible to believe true and false propositions, but not to believe meaningless sequences of words. Metaphysical statements are not even acceptable as "*working hypotheses*"; for an hypothesis must be capable of entering into relations of deducibility with (true or false) empirical statements, which is just what pseudo-statements cannot do.

With reference to the so-called *limitation of human knowledge* an attempt is sometimes made to save metaphysics by raising the following objection: metaphysical statements are not, indeed, verifiable by man nor by any other finite being; nevertheless they might be construed as conjectures about the answers which a being with higher or even perfect powers of knowledge would make to our questions, and as such conjectures they would, after all, be meaningful. To counter this objection, let us consider the following. If the meaning of a word cannot be specified, or if the sequence of words does not accord with the rules of syntax, then one has not even asked a question. (Just think of the pseudoquestions: "Is this table teavy?" "Is the number 7 holy?" "Which numbers are darker, the even or the odd ones?"). Where there is no question, not even an omniscient being can give an answer. Now the objector may say: just as one who can see may communicate new knowledge to the blind, so a higher being might perhaps communicate to us metaphysical knowledge, e.g., whether the visible world is the manifestation of a spirit. Here we must reflect on the meaning of "new knowledge." It is, indeed, conceivable that we might encounter animals who tell us about a new sense. If these beings were to prove to us Fermat's theorem or were to invent a new physical instrument or were to establish a hitherto unknown law of nature, then our knowledge would be increased with their help. For this sort of thing we can test, just the way even a blind man can understand and test the whole of physics (and therewith any statement made by those who can see). But if those hypothetical beings tell us something which we cannot verify, then we cannot understand it either; in that case no information has been communicated to us, but mere verbal sounds devoid of meaning though possibly associated with images. It follows that our knowledge can only be quantitatively enlarged by other beings, no matter whether they know more or less or everything, but no knowledge of an essentially different kind can be added. What we do not know for certain, we may come to know with greater certainty through the assistance of other beings; but what is unintelligible, meaningless for us, cannot become meaningful through someone else's assistance, however vast his knowledge might be. Therefore no god and no devil can give us metaphysical knowledge.

MEANINGLESSNESS OF ALL METAPHYSICS

The examples of metaphysical statements which we have analyzed were all taken from just one treatise. But our results apply with equal validity, in part even in verbally identical ways, to other metaphysical systems. That treatise is completely in the right in citing approvingly a statement by Hegel ("pure Being and pure Nothing, therefore, are one and the same"). The metaphysics of Hegel has exactly the same logical character as this modern system of metaphysics. And the same holds for the rest of the metaphysical systems, though the kind of phraseology and therewith the kind of logical errors that occur in them deviate more or less from the kind that occurs in the examples we discussed.

It should not be necessary here to adduce further examples of specific metaphysical sentences in diverse systems and submit them to analysis. We confine ourselves to an indication of the most frequent kinds of errors.

Perhaps the majority of the logical mistakes that are committed when pseudostatements are made are based on the logical faults infecting the use of the word "to be" in our language (and of the corresponding words in other languages, at least in most European languages). The first fault is the ambiguity of the word "to be." It is sometimes used as copula prefixed to a predicate ("I am hungry"), sometimes to designate existence ("I am"). This mistake is aggravated by the fact that metaphysicians often are not clear about this ambiguity. The second fault lies in the form of the verb in its second meaning, the meaning of *existence*. The verbal form feigns a predicate where there is none. To be sure, it has been known for a long time that existence is not a property (see Kant's refutation of the ontological proof of the existence of God). But it was not until the advent of modern logic that full consistency on this point was reached: the syntactical form in which modern logic introduces the sign for existence is such that it cannot, like a predicate, be applied to signs for objects, but only to predicates (see, for example, sentence IIIA in the above table). Most metaphysicians since antiquity have allowed themselves to be seduced into pseudostatements by the verbal, and therewith the predicative form of the word "to be," e.g., "I am," "God is."

We meet an illustration of this error in Descartes's "cogito, ergo sum." Let us disregard here the material objections that have been raised against the premise—viz. whether the sentence "I think" adequately expresses the intended state of affairs or contains perhaps a hypostasis—and consider the two sentences only from the formal-logical point of view. We notice at once two essential logical mistakes. The first lies in the conclusion, "I am." The verb "to be" is undoubtedly meant in the sense of existence here; for a copula cannot be used without predicate; indeed, Descartes' "I am" has always been interpreted in this sense. But in that case this sentence violates the above-mentioned logical rule that existence can be predicated only in conjunction with a predicate, not in conjunction with a name (subject, proper name). An existential statement does not have the form "*a* exists" (as in "I am," i.e., "I exist"), but "there exists something of such and such a kind." The second error lies in the transition from "I think" to "I exist." If from the statement "P(a)" ("a has the property P") an existential statement is to be deduced, then the latter can assert existence only with respect to the predicate P, not with respect to the subject *a* of the premise. What follows from "I am a European" is not "I exist," but "a European exists." What follows from "I think" is not "I am" but "there exists something that thinks."

The circumstance that our languages express existence by a verb ("to be" or "to exist") is not in itself a logical fault; it is only inappropriate, dangerous. The verbal form easily misleads us into the misconception that existence is a predicate. One then arrives at such logically incorrect and hence senseless modes of express as were just examined. Likewise such forms as "Being" or "Not-Being," which from time immemorial have played a great role in metaphysics, have the same origin. In a logically correct language such forms cannot even be constructed. It appears that in the Latin and the German languages the forms "ens" or "das Seiende" were, perhaps under the seductive influence of the Greek example, introduced specifically for use by metaphysicians; in this way the language deteriorated logically whereas the addition was believed to represent an improvement.

Another very frequent violation of logical syntax is the so-called "*type confusion*" of concepts. While the previously mentioned mistake consists in the predicative use of a symbol with nonpredicative meaning, in this case a predicate is, indeed, used as predicate yet as predicate of a different type. We have here a violation of the rules of the so-called theory of types. An artificial example is the sentence we discussed earlier: "Caesar is a prime number." Names of persons and names of numbers belong to different logical types, and so do accordingly predicates of persons (e.g., "general") and predicates of numbers ("prime number"). The error of type confusion is, unlike the previously discussed usage of the verb "to be," not the prerogative of metaphysics but already occurs very often in conversational language also. But here it rarely leads to nonsense. The typical ambiguity of words is here of such a kind that it can be easily removed.

> *Example:* 1. "This table is larger than that." 2. "The height of this table is larger than the height of that table." Here the word "larger" is used in (1) for a relation between objects, in (2) for a relation between numbers, hence for two distinct syntactical categories. The mistake is here unimportant; it could, e.g., be eliminated by writing "larger$_1$" and "larger$_2$"; "larger$_1$" is then defined in terms of "larger$_2$" by declaring statement form (1) to be synonymous with (2) (and others of a similar kind).

Since the confusion of types causes no harm in conversational language, it is usually ignored entirely. This is, indeed, expedient for the ordinary use of language, but has had unfortunate consequences in metaphysics. Here the conditioning by everyday language has led to confusions of types which, unlike those in everyday language, are no longer translatable into logically correct form. Pseudostatements of this kind are encountered in especially large quantity, e.g., in the writings of Hegel and Heidegger. The latter has adopted many peculiarities of the Hegelian idiom along with their logical faults (e.g., predicates which should be applied to objects of a certain sort are instead applied to predicates of these objects or to "being" or to "existence" or to a relation between these objects).

Having found that many metaphysical statements are meaningless, we confront the question whether there is not perhaps a core of meaningful statements in metaphysics which would remain after elimination of all the meaningless ones.

Indeed, the results we have obtained so far might give rise to the view that there are many dangers of falling into nonsense in metaphysics, and that one must accordingly endeavor to avoid these traps with great care if one wants to do metaphysics. But actually the situation is that meaningful metaphysical statements are impossible. This follows from the task which metaphysics sets itself: to discover and formulate a kind of knowledge which is not accessible to empirical science.

We have seen earlier that the meaning of a statement lies in the method of its verification. A statement asserts only so much as is verifiable with respect to it. Therefore a sentence can be used only to assert an empirical proposition, if indeed it is used to assert anything at all. If something wants to lie, in principle, beyond possible experience, it could be neither said nor thought nor asked.

(Meaningful) statements are divided into the following kinds. First there are statements which are true solely by virtue of their form ("tautologies" according to Wittgenstein; they correspond approximately to Kant's "analytic judgments"). They say nothing about reality. The formulae of logic and mathematics are of this kind. They are not themselves factual statements, but serve for the transformation of such statements. Secondly there are the negations of such statements ("*contradictions*"). They are self-contradictory, hence false by virtue of their form. With respect to all other statements the decision about truth or falsehood lies in the protocol sentences. They are therefore (true or false) *empirical statements* and belong to the domain of empirical science. Any statement one desires to construct which does not fall within these categories becomes automatically meaningless. Since metaphysics does not want to assert analytic propositions, nor to fall within the domain of empirical science, it is compelled to employ words for which no criteria of application are specified and which are therefore devoid of sense, or else to combine meaningful words in such a way that neither an analytic (or contradictory) statement nor an empirical statement is produced. In either case pseudostatements are the inevitable product.

Logical analysis, then, pronounces the verdict of meaninglessness on any alleged knowledge that pretends to reach above or behind experience. This verdict hits, in the first place, any speculative metaphysics, any alleged knowledge by *pure thinking* or by *pure intuition* that pretends to be able to do the kind of metaphysics which, starting from experience, wants to acquire knowledge about that which *transcends experience* by means of special *inferences* (e.g., the neovitalist thesis of the directive presence of an "entelechy" in organic processes, which supposedly cannot be understood in terms of physics; the question concerning the "essence of causality," transcending the ascertainment of certain regularities of succession; the talk about the "thing in itself"). Further, the same judgment must be passed on all *philosophy of norms*, or *philosophy of value*, on any ethics or esthetics as a normative discipline. For the objective validity of a value or norm is (even on the view of the philosophers of value) not empirically verifiable nor deducible from empirical statements; hence it cannot be asserted (in a meaningful statement) at all. In other words: Either empirical criteria are indicated for the use of "good" and "beautiful" and the rest of the predicates that are employed in the normative science, or they are not. In the first case, a statement containing such a predicate turns into a factual judgment, but not a value judgment; in the second case, it becomes a pseudostatement. It is altogether impossible to make a statement that expresses a value judgment.

Finally, the verdict of meaninglessness also hits those metaphysical movements which are usually called, improperly, epistemological movements, that is *realism* (insofar as it claims to say more than the empirical fact that the sequence of events exhibits a certain regularity, which makes the application of the inductive method possible) and its opponents: subjective *idealism*, solipsism, phenomenalism, and *positivism* (in the earlier sense).

But what, then, is left over for *philosophy*, if all statements whatever that assert something are of an empirical nature and belong to factual science? What remains is not statements, nor a theory, nor a system, but only a *method:* the method of logical analysis. The foregoing discussion has illustrated the negative application of this method: in that context it serves to eliminate meaningless words, meaningless pseudostatements. In its positive use it serves to clarify meaningful concepts and propositions, to lay logical foundations for factual science and for mathematics. The negative application of the method is necessary and important in the present historical situation. But even in its present practice, the positive application is more fertile. We cannot here discuss it in greater detail. It is the indicated task of logical analysis, inquiry into logical foundations, that is meant by *"scientific philosophy"* in contrast to metaphysics.

The question regarding the logical character of the statements that we obtain as the result of a logical analysis, e.g., the statements occurring in this and other logical papers, can here be answered only tentatively: such statements are partly analytic, partly empirical. For these statements about statements and parts of statements belong in part to pure *metalogic* (e.g., "a sequence consisting of the existence-symbol and a noun is not a sentence"), in part to descriptive metalogic (e.g., "the word sequence at such and such a place in such and such a book is meaningless"). Metalogic will be discussed elsewhere. It will also be shown there that the metalogic which speaks about the sentences of a given language can be formulated in that very language itself.

METAPHYSICS AS EXPRESSION OF
AN ATTITUDE TOWARD LIFE

Our claim that the statements of metaphysics are entirely meaningless, that they do not assert anything, will leave even those who agree intellectually with our results with a painful feeling of strangeness: how could it be explained that so many men in all ages and nations, among them eminent minds, spent so much energy, nay veritable fervor, on metaphysics if the latter consisted of nothing but mere words, nonsensically juxtaposed? And how could one account for the fact that metaphysical books have exerted such a strong influence on readers up to the present day, if they contained not even errors, but nothing at all? These doubts are justified since metaphysics does indeed have a content; only it is not theoretical content. The (pseudo)statements of metaphysics do not serve for the *description of states of affairs*, either existing ones (in that case they would be true statements) or nonexisting ones (in that case they would be at least false statements). They serve for the *expression of the general attitude of a person toward life* ("Lebenseinstellung, Lebensgefühl").

Perhaps we may assume that metaphysics originated from *mythology*. The child is angry at the "wicked table" which hurt him. Primitive man endeavors to conciliate the threatening demon of earthquakes, or he worships the deity of the fertile rains in gratitude. Here we confront personifications of natural phenomena, which are the quasipoetic expression of man's emotional relationship to his environment. The heritage of mythology is bequeathed on the one hand to poetry, which produces and intensifies the effects of mythology on life in a deliberate way; on the other hand, it is handed down to theology, which develops mythology into a system. Which, now, is the historical role of metaphysics? Perhaps we may regard it as a substitute for theology on the level of systematic, conceptual thinking. The (supposedly) transcendent sources of knowledge of theology are here replaced by natural, yet supposedly transempirical sources of knowledge. On closer inspection the same content as that of mythology is here still recognizable behind the repeatedly varied dressing: we find that metaphysics also arises from the need to give expression to a man's attitude in life, his emotional and volitional reaction to the environment, to society, to the tasks to which he devotes himself, unconsciously as a rule, in everything a man does or says. It also impresses itself on his facial features, perhaps even on the character of his gait. Many people, now, feel a desire to create over and above these manifestations a special expression of their attitude, through which it might become visible in a more succinct and penetrating way. If they have artistic talent they are able to express themselves by producing a work of art. Many writers have already clarified the way in which the basic attitude is manifested through the style and manner of a work of art (e.g., Dilthey and his students). (In this connection the term "world view" ["Weltanschauung"] is often used; we prefer to avoid it because of its ambiguity, which blurs the difference between attitude and theory, a difference which is of decisive importance for our analysis.) What is here essential for our considerations is only the fact that art is an adequate, metaphysics an inadequate means for the expression of the basic attitude. Of course, there need be no intrinsic objection to one's using any means of expression one likes. But in the case of metaphysics we find this situation: through the form of its works it pretends to be something that it is not. The form in question is that of a system of statements which are apparently related as premises and conclusions, that is, the form of a theory. In this way the fiction of theoretical content is generated, whereas, as we have seen, there is no such content. It is not only the reader, but the metaphysician himself who suffers from the illusion that the metaphysical statements say something, describe states of affairs. The metaphysician believes that he travels in territory in which truth and falsehood are at stake. In reality, however, he has not asserted anything, but only expressed something, like an artist. That the metaphysician is thus deluding himself cannot be inferred from the fact that he selects language as the medium of expression and declarative sentences as the form of expression; for lyrical poets do the same without succumbing to self-delusion. But the metaphysician supports his statements by arguments, he claims assent to their content, he polemicizes against metaphysicians of divergent persuasion by attempting to refute their assertions in his treatise. Lyrical poets, on the other hand, do not try to refute in their poem the statements in a poem by some other lyrical poet; for they know they are in the domain of art and not in the domain of theory.

Perhaps music is the purest means of expression of the basic attitude because it is entirely free from any reference to objects. The harmonious feeling or attitude, which the metaphysician tries to express in a monistic system, is more clearly expresed in the music of Mozart. And when a metaphysician gives verbal expression to his dualistic-heroic attitude towards life in a dualistic system, is it not perhaps because he lacks the ability of a Beethoven to express this attitude in an adequate medium? Metaphysicians are musicians without musical ability. Instead they have a strong inclination to work within the medium of the theoretical, to connect concepts and thoughts. Now, instead of activating, on the one hand, this inclination in the domain of science, and satisfying, on the other hand, the need for expression in art, the metaphysician confuses the two and produces a structure which achieves nothing for knowledge and something inadequate for the expression of attitude.

Our conjecture that metaphysics is a substitute, albeit an inadequate one, for art, seems to be further confirmed by the fact that the metaphysician who perhaps had artistic talent to the highest degree, viz. Nietzsche, almost entirely avoided the error of that confusion. A large part of his work has predominantly empirical content. We find there, for instance, historical analyses of specific artistic phenomena, or an historical-psychological analysis of morals. In the work, however, in which he expresses most strongly that which others express through metaphysics or ethics, in *Thus Spake Zarathustra*, he does not choose the misleading theoretical form, but openly the form of art, of poetry.

3. Harold Alderman
Heidegger's Critique of Science and Technology

One of the most important motifs in the work of Martin Heidegger is the critique of science and technology he develops as part of his more general critique of Western thought. In this essay I want to clarify the character of Heidegger's critique by examining the interrelation between his conception of science and his interpretation of modern technology.

SCIENCE

UNLIKE MOST CONTEMPORARY ANALYSES of science, Heidegger's critique is undertaken with an eye toward a revolutionary mode of thinking that he believes must supplement scientific thought. This section explicates Heidegger's conception of this supplemental thought, the thought of Being (*der Frage nach dem Sinn vom Sein*), by characterizing his understanding of science. Through this characterization the essential difference of the two styles of thought becomes evident and it is in order to emphasize this difference that Heidegger develops a critique of science. Four preliminary remarks: First, the relation of science to the thought of Being is construed by Heidegger as the relation between a thought which is domineering and beings-oriented, and one which is acquiescent and Being-oriented. Second, for Heidegger a critique of science cannot proceed simply through a logical analysis of scientific language. Such an analysis assumes the foundation of the sciences—logic and mathematics—as its basis, and can, therefore, explain science only to itself. Third, Heidegger avoids this narrow analytic reference by showing that science is the contemporary expression of the

A revised and combined version of "Heidegger's Critique of Science" and "Heidegger: Technology as Phenomenon," which appeared in *The Personalist* 50 (Fall, 1969) and 51 (Fall, 1970). Reprinted with permission of the editor.

metaphysical mode of thought which began when Plato yoked Being under the limits of the Idea of the Good, and when Aristotle set the limits
of reality in terms of the law of contradiction. As Heidegger sees it science is contemporary metaphysics—the logical terminus of metaphysical
thought. Fourth, although there is a negativistic element in Heidegger's
analysis of science, which stems from the fact that science has arrogated
to itself alone the privilege of intelligible and meaningful language, Heidegger is by no means merely opposed to science. The thought of Being,
since it differs in intention from science (a theoretical thinking of beings),
cannot be an opponent of science. The *prima facie* opposition between the
two modes of thought is explained away when it is revealed that they are
after different things. In showing this difference Heidegger hopes to show
that the two modes of thought must be evaluated with respect to different
criteria. To impose the scientific criterion of meaningfulness on the
thought of Being is, in effect, to commit a category error. These statements provide a necessary context for the ensuing discussion.

According to Heidegger, scientific thought turns Being into a picture.[1]
He refers us to Descartes to see how this peculiar development takes place
and what it means. In the metaphysics of Descartes, beings for the first
time get defined as the objectivity of representation: a being is what is
represented to man with certainty.[2] The result of this definition of beings
(and of Being itself) is that the whole of beings (the world) comes to be
regarded as the sum total of these certain representations of being to man.
Since the world comprises both the Being of *res extensa* and *res cogitans*,
a total set of the representations of these two realms of Being would give
an exhaustive account of the realm of Being, and would become identical
with a perfect description of Being itself. Thus Being becomes identified
as the picture which results from the collocation of the representations of
beings to man. It is in this sense that, according to Heidegger, the world
becomes a picture in scientific thought. The development of the conception of Being as a picture becomes a possibility only with the subject-ist
metaphysics of Descartes. Heidegger explains subject-ism as a special case
of subjectivism in which we understand "subject" in its original Greek
sense of *hupokeimenon*, this term designating that being which lies before
us and which gathers to itself all other beings, serving as the foundation
of those beings. In its original sense "subject" bore no special relation to
the term subject meaning man, the ego, the I. Man as subject is only one

1. "Die Zeit des Weltbildes," in *Holzwege* (Frankfurt am Main, 1950), pp. 69–104;
"The Age of the World View," trans. Marjorie Grene and reprinted in *Boundary 2*
(1976), pp. 341–55. Hereafter abbreviated *ZW* and *AW*. In this essay Heidegger uses
the word *Welt* to signify the world of nature investigated by the sciences. For science
and technology, this world is identified with Being itself.
2. *ZW*, p. 80; *AW*, p. 349. Compare *Der Satz vom Grund* (Pfullingen, 1957), p. 148.

possible *hupokeimenon*. In Plato the *hupokeimenon* is the eidos; in Aristotle it is actuality. When man becomes the *hupokeimenon* in the thought of Descartes, the foundation of science and technology has been laid— and that foundation is human subjectivity.

At this point we must further clarify what Heidegger means by "Being becoming a picture," for science, as Heidegger sees it, does not merely construe its set of propositions as a picture of the world. It does something much more emphatic. It decides, in a normative fashion, that the world itself consists in nothing other than the picture drawn by science.[3] The world as a picture, then, does not mean the world understood as a picture. It means instead that the possibilities of Being are exhaustively accounted for in the conception of the world as a picture drawn in the propositions of science. Beings are only what is represented in this picture.

To show the radical nature of this scientific conception of Being, Heidegger contrasts it with the conception of Being which he reads in Parmenides' statement *"To gar auto noein estin te kai einai"*: "the perception of beings belongs to Being, because it is demanded and determined by it." [4] In this conception, beings do not become beings because they are represented to man, but because they are thrust into Being by Being itself. In the pre-Socratic doctrine which understands Being as *physis*, that is, as emergence, as coming-to-be, it is impossible for Being to become conceived as a picture of man's own construction; man stands before Being and lets beings be. This is quite different from the notion of representation which is central to the modern conception of Being, where representation means to "bring what is present before one as something confronting oneself, to relate it to oneself, the person representing it, and to force it back into this relation to oneself as the normative area." [5] Man through this maneuver becomes the representative of Being, and, as its representative, he achieves sole power over it.

Nor, according to Heidegger, is modern science anything like the Aristotelian doctrine of *episteme* or the medieval conception of *scientia*.[6] Central to Aristotle's understanding of *episteme* was his doctrine of *empeiria (experientia)*. *Experientia* for Aristotle meant the observation of things themselves, and an understanding of their properties and relations. Thus, Heidegger argues that in the *episteme* of Aristotle, it is meant to be impossible for man to assume domination over the objects of his study —although, in the end, logic and the law of contradiction make this impossibility impossible.

The medieval conception of knowledge yokes the knowledge of beings

---

3. ZW, p. 82; AW, p. 350. In *Being and Time* (New York, 1962) Heidegger refers to this normative picturing as a "productive logic," p. 30.
4. ZW, p. 83; AW, p. 351.
5. ZW, p. 84; AW, p. 351.
6. ZW, pp. 74–75; AW, pp. 345–46.

under the doctrine of faith, which reserves for itself all final and genuine knowledge. To know about beings in this scheme of things is to know them in relation to a creator and to be able to rank them in a hierarchy of Being. Since the primary reference of the medieval knowledge of beings derived from the revealed works of the church, which had as their central object of concern the knowledge of the supreme being, knowledge of beings became a reflection of the knowledge of the supreme being, and, consequently, a theology. The expression of this theological knowledge was found in documents that were believed to be direct revelations of God. Truth itself was understood as a revelation of God and knowledge of the truth of beings was achieved through an examination of the documents that contained the revealed truths. Such knowledge is an *argumentum ex verbo*—an exposition of doctrines—and therefore cannot be anything like a picture which is constructed on the representations of man. As a corollary of his understanding of the medieval conception of knowledge, Heidegger further argues that science is possible only when God has been displaced from the world so that nature can be studied without reference to God. Because of this, science is regarded by him as godless—not because it is atheistic, but because it necessarily removes god to a distant location. (In this same vein he argues that all contemporary religions are godless.) [7]

What then is unique in contemporary science that sets it apart from these previous attempts at a knowledge of beings? What sets the modern experiment apart from the Aristotelian *experientia* and the *argumentum ex verbo?* The fundamental difference is that the essence of modern science consists in the projection of a conceptual framework onto a sphere of beings.[8] This projection determines the way in which scientific facts must conform to the sphere opened by the initial projection. In making such a projection, one opens a sphere of Being and makes of that sphere a definite realm of Being. All sciences are involved in projection, but it is in physics that the most general features of scientific projection can be seen, and it is around the projection of physics that Heidegger centers his discussion. In fact he assumes, as do many others, that mathematical physics is the paradigm case for the sciences.

Physics projects nature as a nexus of spatio-temporal relations which can be described mathematically.[9] In this conception of nature, there is an a priori condition of mathematical accessibility, and nature is seen as mathematical in its essence. This mathematical condition of physics is but a special case of an a priori approach to Being. Originally, *ta mathemata* meant that which man knows prior to his acquaintance with things: the corporeality of bodies, the animativeness of animals or—as in Euclidean

7. Z*W*, p. 70; *AW*, p. 342.
8. Z*W*, p. 71; *AW*, p. 343; *Being and Time*, p. 445.
9. Z*W*, pp. 72–73; *AW*, p. 344.

geometry—the non-intersection of parallel lines. Numbers then are but one instance of the *ta mathemata*. And because they represent the most obvious *ta mathemata* of things, numbers have taken over for their exclusive privilege the name of mathematics.[10] (By "obvious" Heidegger means only that things are denumerable, and that this is the most evident fact about them.) In general, then, physics is a knowledge of the movement of bodies within the spatio-temporal nexus. This projected nexus assigns no preference to any place or any time. Nor does any class of movements merit special attention; all movements are measured as changes of place. Every motion in this projection is regarded as the product of a force, as a determinate amount of change in a precise location within a measurable time. It is within this nexus that physics determines what a fact in nature is; only occurrences accessible to description within this mathematical framework are facts of nature, are events occurring within nature.

With the projection constructed by physics we see an astonishing thing happen. For it turns out that physics uses its facts to justify the projection,[11] even though a fact is a fact only within the projection. Projection determines fact and the facts determined by the projection support the projection as a warranted conception of nature and Being (for science these are the same). The *ta mathemata* founds fact, and the predictable sequence of facts provides a sufficient and exclusive warrant for the scientific projection. This process of mutual confirmation is carried out in experimentation.

Now we can see the crucial difference between the scientific experiment and the Aristotelian conception of the *experimentum*. In modern science, "to get up an experiment means to assume a situation where it becomes possible to trace a definite nexus of motions in the necessity of its course, that is, to control its calculation in advance." [12] Ideally, (as in physics) all scientific experiments are law-covered, in the sense that they are designed to prove a certain mathematically expressed relationship. The law that the experiment is designed to test is always stated in terms of the initial plan of nature assumed by physics. An experiment, then, is nothing other than a privileged experience which is designed to elicit the facts that either confirm or disconfirm the law it is to test. But what kind of facts will be relevant to confirmation? Obviously, it will be only those that fit consistently into the initial projection of nature as a mathematical nexus. Here again we see the narrowly circular nature of Being determined by modern science. At the same time we can see the essential difference from Aristotle and the medieval doctrine of *scientia*. Whereas for Aristotle an *experimentum* was an *argumentum ex res*, in modern science an experiment is an *argumentum ex ta mathemata*. The difference with

10. ZW, p. 72; AW, p. 343.
11. ZW, p. 74; AW, p. 344.
12. ZW, p. 74; AW, p. 344.

respect to the theological *argumentum ex verbo* is just as great. In each of the cases the direction in which one goes for confirmation differs radically. In modern science one turns in the end to one's self for confirmation of hypotheses, since it is the *ta mathemata* which is brought to experience by man that determines the conception of fact, experiment, and confirmation.

In addition to the mathematical and "experimental" features of the scientific doctrine of Being, science requires of nature that everything in it be readily accessible to investigation.[13] Since science deals with facts that are temporal, science is necessarily a *dynamic* projection which emphasizes the permanence of change. The accessibility of nature is then built into the projection. Since all facts of nature are mathematically measurable, it follows that no level of nature can remain a mystery to scientific knowledge. All that is required to unveil all the secrets of nature is a further sophistication of the projection. One merely makes more, and more *sophisticated* calculations. The difficulty here is merely one of procedure. One must work harder to make nature still more apparent through more and more experiments. To fail in this goal is simply not to have worked hard enough. Given the ultimate possible disclosure of all of nature's mysteries, we see that the doctrine of Being in science allows, at least in principle, for an ultimate perfect knowledge of Being itself.

Another important feature of science is specialization, which is a necessary consequence of the initial projection.[14] Every science must work within the projection in the sense of following the general features of motion, measurability, etc. Specialization takes place as a result of the elaboration of general features of the mathematical ground plan, and is closely related to the demand of precision. The scientific objectification of Being becomes more precise by becoming more specialized. Viewed in this light the specialization and fragmentation of the sciences is not merely a necessary evil that is a result of the accumulation of data. On the contrary, specialization is itself the cause of the accumulation of more and more precise data, which is an essential element in scientific progress. As Heidegger sees it, specialization is logically prior to the accumulation of scientific data and therefore cannot be a consequence of it.

Specialization is itself at the heart of the "businesslike" character of the sciences that results in the institutionalization of procedures and devices.[15] Once scientific procedures become institutionalized, they are explicitly granted the power to manage Being officially, and are given the authority to objectify it as an object of research. Thus the businesslike and institutional character of the sciences marks the final stage of their development:

13. *ZW*, pp. 73–74; *AW*, pp. 343–44.
14. *ZW*, p. 77; *AW*, pp. 346–47.
15. *ZW*, pp. 77–78; *AW*, pp. 347–48.

Being becomes totally objectified only in the institutionalization of the sciences. Once the sciences are institutionalized, the scientific thinker becomes a specialist who approaches Being as a set of problems, the solutions to which can be found by continuous elaboration of the mathematical projection.

With the development of scientific institutions, Being becomes fully objectified as a picture re-presented to man. Thus the scientific doctrine of Being becomes an institutional doctrine of Being. And yet Being can become objectified and institutionalized only because man as *hupokeimenon* determines through his projection of nature the objective character of Being. The more objective Being becomes, the more subjective must be the doctrine of man, since man scientifically encounters only his own projection of Being. In the final analysis we see that the objectivity of Being in science is, in fact, the subjectivity of man.

Because Being becomes objectified and determined by the calculations and measurements of man, the originative, nonsubjectist understanding of Being as *physis* is forgotten. Yet even within the framework of scientific thought a hint of the pre-Socratic notion of *physis* remains. In his calculations scientific man ultimately encounters the incalculable, which Heidegger calls the "gigantic" [16]—that which scientific experience encounters in its researches into the vastness of the universe, and in its study of the infinitesimal atomic particles. Here it seems that something that cannot be definitively calculated remains. Heidegger regards this encounter with the gigantic as an indication of a realm of experience qualitatively different from that of scientific experience. The gigantic then remains to remind contemporary thinkers that not everything is, in fact, calculable, and it is this noncalculable something that the thought of Being seeks to isolate as a datum of thought.

Some tentative confirmation of Heidegger's critique of scientific thought derives from the view of thinkers who are more enthusiastic about the sciences. Carnap, for example, views physics as an interpreted calculus, the structure of the calculus being given independently of its interpretation.[17] This is, I think, in close agreement with Heidegger's conception of a projection. Additional strength is given to Heidegger's understanding in Werner Heisenberg's discussion of "The Idea of Nature in Contemporary Physics." [18] In this paper Heisenberg argues that contemporary thought is endangered by the picture of nature drawn by physics. This danger lies in the fact that the picture is now regarded as an exhaustive

16. *ZW*, p. 87; *AW*, p. 354.

17. "Interpretation of Physics," *Readings in the Philosophy of Science*, ed. Feigl and Broadbeck (New York, 1953).

18. *The Physicists' Conception of Nature* (New York, 1958).

account of nature itself, so that science forgets that in its study of nature it is merely studying its own picture. Heidegger and Heisenberg differ with respect to their understanding of this picturing of nature: Heisenberg sees it as a matter of fact that the picturing takes place, and regards the picture not so much as a picture of nature but as a picture of our relations with nature; Heidegger, however, sees the picturing of nature as a necessary feature of scientific thought. Yet both would agree that so long as science is allowed to speak *ex cathedra*, other modes of thought remain impossible.

It is the concern of Heidegger both to insure a thoughtful alternative to science, and, by guarding against its authoritative airs, to protect science from itself. Given this dual concern it is clear that Heidegger's supplemental thought of Being is not antiscientific and that it cannot therefore constitute a recommendation to abandon the scientific study of beings. The supplementation desired by Heidegger is not Jacobin; within the realm of the thought of Being, the contemporary metaphysics that is science remains intact—although shorn of its pretensions. "To think among the sciences means to pass them by without disdaining them." [19] The thought that supplements metaphysics does not seek to build an empire within the realm of thought.

TECHNOLOGY

The essential attribute of technological thought is its insistent aggressiveness, a feature that stems from the anthropocentric assumption of modern science that man is the *hupokeimenon*, the fundamental subject who determines the nature of Being. This feature is made inevitable given the influential Platonic argument that real Being—the *eidos*—can be only that which is perfectly visible to the light of reason.[20] As Heidegger views it this Platonic argument is decisive on three general counts:

1. It gives Being the characteristic of mathematical rationality and thus assumes that Being can be precisely calculated.
2. Since the measure of Being is its calculability, Being becomes intimately related to human reason (the light of which is mathematics); ultimately it becomes dependent upon reason inasmuch as the properties of mathematical systems are reified as properties of Being.

19. *Holzwege*, p. 195. See also *Identity and Difference*, trans. Joan Stambaugh (New York, 1969).
20. "Plato's Doctrine of Truth," trans. John Barlow, in *Philosophy in the Twentieth Century*, ed. William Barret and Henry Aiken (New York, 1962).

3. What results from this is an aggressive spirit of thought that marks all of Western speculation. Although these developments are not fully realized in Plato, their influence gets more obvious in the subsequent history of Western thought and becomes, for Heidegger at least, most clearly manifest in contemporary scientific technology.[21]

In Descartes the calculative aggressiveness becomes more evident with the development of his epistemological model of clearness and distinctness —a model derived from the knowing subject's acquaintance with itself. According to Heidegger, since the Cartesian subject is essentially defined by its rationality and since its paradigm of knowledge is mathematics, we can views Descartes's thought as just one interpretation of the formal connections that Plato affirms between Being and rationality and between the known object and the knowing subject. In effect Descartes accomplishes a more perfect Platonizing of philosophy by further intruding the human subject into the heart of the philosophic process. We must note, however, that it is the intrusion and not the calculative style of the intrusion that is crucial from the point of view of identifying the special characteristics of Western thought, though of course the style does have much to do with the development of technology.

Nietzsche makes the anthropocentric (and noncalculative) intrusion perfectly overt by arguing that it is the human will which determines the nature of Being. Of course, what Nietzsche's will wills as Being is itself. Thus we have Nietzsche, the arch anti-Platonist, evincing what Heidegger believes to be the essential feature of Plato's thought—the ontological aggressiveness of the human subject. In Heidegger's interpretation, the thought of Plato—the Apollonian—and the thought of Nietzsche—the Dionysian—have the same essential attribute; thus the primary element in Western metaphysics is not its calculative rationality but its insistent aggressiveness. In technological thought we shall see the calculative rationality and the insistent aggressiveness meet in perfect harmony.

Using a characteristic etymological maneuver, Heidegger argues that it is possible to understand technological thought only if we first understand the Greek term "techne." [22] We must, as it were, understand what is left

---

21. For a more complete treatment of this devolutionary history, see my "Heidegger on the Nature of Metaphysics," *Journal of the British Society for Phenomenology* 2, no. 3 (1971).

22. "Die Frage nach der Technik," *Vorträge und Aufsätze* (Pfullingen, 1954), pp. 20–21; "The Question Concerning Technology," trans. William Lovitt, in *Basic Writings*, ed. David Krell (New York, 1977), pp. 294–95. Hereafter abbreviated *FT* and *QT*. By the word *Technik* Heidegger means not merely 'technology' but also the general technological characteristics of modern thought. To indicate this stronger sense of *Technik*, we use the word "technicity" or the phrase "technological thought."

out of technology before we can know what technology is. He interprets the term *"techne"* as signifying any way in which beings can be made manifest, as any mode of lighting up a realm of beings. In this original sense of the word, a technician would be a kind of poet who succeeds in an originative uncovering of beings, that is to say in a disclosure of a particular world. Thus Heidegger emphasizes the connection between the Greek terms *"techne"* and *"poiesis."* He further holds that the term *"techne"* was closely associated with the meaning of *"episteme,"* and that both of these terms connoted a kind of functional cognition in which one could be said to know one's way around within some realm of beings. Thus it was a matter of *techne* to uncover beings in a work of art, or to uncover them for use—as in the crafts. The essential and original meaning of *techne* is then that of "making manifest" and not merely that of "making" in the sense of practical construction. As we shall see, the fundamental difference between the original *techne* of *poiesis* and the modern *techne* of technology is that the first is responsive and contemplative whereas the second is domineering and challenging.

This original sense of *techne* is further explicated by Heidegger in terms of an analysis of the four Aristotelian causes.[23] The Greek term for cause is *aition*, meaning "that which is responsible for something." Heidegger understands this sense of cause as stating a doctrine of responsibility for beings; the four causes form a unity of responsibility and provide an adequate understanding of the way in which beings can be taken care of, i.e., uncovered and made manifest in an appearance. For example, consider the making of a bowl as analyzed in terms of Aristotle's four causes: the formal cause is the design of the bowl, the material cause is the clay from which it is made, the efficient cause is the craftsman, and the final cause is the purpose for which the bowl is made. When we view the bowl as a being brought forth by these four causes, Heidegger says we understand "cause" in its Greek sense of responsibility. The bowl comes to be as a result of the responsibility of the craftsman, and its standing as a being is dependent on his craft. Yet there is a fundamental responsibility that is independent of the *techne* of man and of the Aristotelian causes, and this fundamental responsibility is *physis*.[24] Thus Heidegger argues that the original meaning of cause is closely related to the understanding of Being as *physis*. The ultimate responsibility for beings lies with Being itself: Being is the ultimate "cause" of beings.

We can now, within the scope of the Greek understanding of cause, make clearer Heidegger's analysis of the differences between the original and the modern sense of *techne*. Man can either be responsible for beings in a way which is in harmony with the *aition* of *physis*, or he can take

23. *FT*, pp. 15–18; *QT*, pp. 289–92.
24. *FT*, p. 19; *QT*, p. 293.

responsibility for beings in a way which is opposed to it. The construction of a craftsman—e.g., a potter—has something of both elements. The potter using the earth makes a bowl; he assumes responsibility for the earth as a bowl by bringing it forth through the application of his craft. In this respect the craftsman works in harmony with nature. On the other hand, he also is necessarily violent in the crafting of the pot. His art, therefore, shows elements of both the *poiesis* of *physis* and the *poiesis* which is a mere human making. According to Heidegger, it becomes the fate of contemporary technology to forget the *poiesis* of *physis*—the responsible uncovering that is in harmony with Being itself.

What then is essential in the modern meaning of "cause?" "*Causa*," the Latin translation of the Greek "*aition*," means that which is instrumental, that which produces or fabricates; and it is this sense that determines our present understanding.[25] Because of the adoption of this sense of "*causa*" the idea of the efficient cause overshadows all others and we have come to regard a cause as anything that makes or produces an effect. In consequence of this development man as the maker and producer occupies the center of causality: cause signifies the instrumentality of man. This current doctrine of causality so dominates our tradition that it is often said, with Hume, that there are no causes in nature itself—there are only correlations. Even in Western theological thought—where God is the cause of things—God is conceived as the maker of the world, as the being who through his own instrumentality produces nature. Western thought and contemporary technology fully appropriate the idea of causality as instrumentality: scientific technology as a mode of uncovering does not let beings manifest themselves as what they are, but instead insists on a production (i.e., a domination) of beings by man.

A further significant feature of scientific technology is that technological man denies that technology is anything so mysterious as a mode of making beings manifest. The technician sees technology simply as the means in an ends-means relationship.[26] Ends are chosen in some way (the technician does not ask how), and technology merely shows the most efficient way to produce those ends. Technology is in this view only a set of techniques used by men to achieve some goal or other. But what remains always hidden from the technological understanding of technology is that this ends-means relationship has itself obviously come to determine in a most decisive way a doctrine of Being. In the technological view, there are two possibilities of Being: beings are either ends or means. Furthermore, ends become means to yet further ends—ends that are posited by man. In this way we see that in the technological doctrine of Being, Being becomes subordinated to the goals and purposes of man.

25. *FT*, p. 16; *QT*, p. 289.
26. *FT*, pp. 14, 35; *QT*, pp. 288, 294.

Heidegger shows that it is in fact merely a sophistication of the doctrine of Being as objectivity that is central to scientific thought: beings must first become scientific objects before they can become the mere means and goals of man. Technology is thus much more than simply a practical application of modern science. It is the unique mode of making beings manifest which provokes "nature" into delivering what is required and demanded by man.[27] In this provocation, the Being of the manifest being is simply what man makes of it. However, prior to their manifestation, technological beings first must be moved into an ontological position from which they can be manipulated most efficiently. The fundamental step in this movement is accomplished in the mathematical ground plan projected by the sciences, where beings are objectified as objects of study.[28] A being for science is only what can fit into the mathematical scientific net constructed by man himself. Yet in the scientific objectification of Being there remains at least a pretense—and for Heidegger that is all it is—of the ontological independence of the beings of science. In technology even this pretense vanishes, and man the technologist disposes beings as he wills.

Technological thought can be more deeply characterized by contrasting it with the very scientific thought upon which it depends. To make the contrast as graphic as possible we shall consider two specific examples of analysis. The first case deals with the difference between the scientific and technological approaches to a mountain. For the science of geology, a mountain is viewed as a conjunction of substance and historical processes that can be scientifically described. The mountain lies "over there" in scientific nature and one may study it impersonally and spectatorially as is required in an objective study. If we approach the objectified mountain from the point of a mining engineer who has discovered an ore in the mountain, all traces of this objectivity vanish. The mountain becomes regarded simply as a repository of the ore. It is a being that is a necessary resource in so emphatic a sense that the mountain itself becomes identified with that resource. All of this is made candidly clear in a recent advertisement and self-characterization of Anaconda:

Nature creates ore deposits. Anaconda creates mines.

Further reading reveals that Anaconda "earth scientists" invent techniques "to find and develop potential mines," and that their mining engineers and metallurgists progressively identify the ore and the mountain, everything

27. FT, pp. 22, 30, 38; QT, pp. 296, 301, 308. See also Holzwege (Frankfurt, 1950), pp. 70 and 236; and Gelassenheit (Pfullingen, 1959); Discourse on Thinking, trans. John Anderson and E. Hans Freund (New York, 1966), p. 50.
    28. FT, pp. 26, 29; QT, p. 303.

else being deemed "waste materials." The advertisement further states that ores are not much good until someone uses them; with this use they become natural resources. Thus we have from within contemporary technology a partial recognition of its own nature.

To characterize further the difference between science and technology, we turn to another example: consider the difference between a scientific and a technological construal of a neighborhood. A sociological study of a neighborhood attempts to describe attitudes on employment, home ownership, identification with the neighborhood, and any number of other factors. First, the initial data of the study is gathered; then this data is coded and fed into a computer to yield a statistical description of a sociological object. By contrast, a prospective manufacturer approaches the neighborhood from a technological point of view, intending to determine if it is a desirable site for a new plant. The manufacturer is interested in deciding if the labor pool is adequate, if taxes are prohibitive, if transportation facilities are sufficient, and so on. From this technological perspective, the neighborhood is simply identified with its available economic resources. The difference in the two approaches is clear: (ideally) science moves beings into position as mathematically theorized objects; whereas technology further positions these beings of science in such a way that they become mere resources relative to a predetermined end; thus, their objectivity vanishes.[29] For science, beings are objects, but for technology beings are resources.

In Heidegger's view, technology extends—though not reflectively—Nietzsche's metaphysics of the will and makes the overpowering of Being by man quite explicit. Technology approaches nature as a repository of resources containing energies that are unlocked by technology, accumulated, stored, transformed, and utilized in the production of goods.[30] A being thus technologically uncovered stands in a position to be disposed of in a productive process, and the beings of technology are nothing more than this passive stance of waiting to be used by man. This is true in such a radical sense that technological work becomes identified with Being.[31] But this positioning of beings as resources is an event that takes place only when man himself has moved into a position to be the *hupokeimenon* who determines the nature of Being through his own will.[32] Technology is thus seen to be nothing other than one expression of the will to power, and the machines of technology are the means of expressing this will. Clearly then, the machines of technology are not themselves the decisive factors;

29. *FT*, pp. 24–26; *QT*, p. 300.
30. *FT*, pp. 22; *QT*, pp. 297–98.
31. *FT*, p. 24; *QT*, p. 298. See also *The Question of Being*, bilingual ed., trans. William Kluback and Jean Wilde (New York, 1962), pp. 49, 59.
32. *FT*, pp. 25–26; *QT*, pp. 298–99.

rather they are determined by the mode of uncovering that is technicity.[33] Because technology fully unleashes the human will as the determiner of Being it lies, according to Heidegger, at the logical end of the subjectivist history of metaphysics.

Modern technology is then characterized by man's more complete domination of the scientific object; and it is much more than simply a further sophistication of earlier technologies. The main difference between prescientific and scientific technologies lies in the absence of the illusion of domination and the absence of the necessary attempt at domination in the earlier technologies. In prescientific technologies, man was a being *within* nature, whereas in contemporary scientific technology man sees himself as a being *over* nature. The older technologies do not presuppose the ground plan of the sciences or the power of man as the determiner of Being, and are therefore closer to the sense of *physis* as a mode of letting things be. Concrete examples will help to make this difference clear; we will examine a couple used by Heidegger and add one of our own.

Consider the difference between an old bridge built over the Rhine and a modern power plant that uses the Rhine as a source of energy.[34] The bridge, which is built into the river, lets the Rhine be itself and brings forward its essential character by bridging its separate banks. The hydroelectric plant, however, builds the Rhine into the plant itself so that the river becomes merely part of the machinery needed to generate electricity. The riverly character of the river is denied as it becomes a mere resource used to turn the generators. The mechanical force of the river is transformed into electrical force and the river becomes technologically identified with this electrical power. At the same time, the hydroelectric plant differs fundamentally from a windmill and cannot be viewed simply as a more sophisticated machine.[35] The windmill works in nature as it utilizes the forces of the wind without transforming those forces. Its mechanical power turns the grindstone that grinds the grain harvested in the neighboring regions. The windmill lets the wind be itself, and does not move it into position as a mere resource. In fact the windmill makes the direct power of the wind stand out more clearly. It takes the wind into its responsibility, and at the same time lets it be itself. The manifestation of the wind in the windmill does not presuppose man as *hupokeimenon*, as is the case when man uses water as a resource to generate electricity. The first manifestation is made possible by observing the natural force of the wind; the second is made possible through the elaboration of that part of the scientific projection that is the theory of electricity and magnetism.

33. *FT*, p. 27; *QT*, p. 300.
34. *FT*, p. 23; *QT*, p. 297.
35. *FT*, p. 22; *QT*, p. 297.

The difference that is so crucial here can be made still clearer by contrasting two different styles of boating. In the use of a sailboat one moves on the water through the use of currents and wind directions. In sailboating there is a dependency of the boat upon the wind and the water, and one is always very aware of this dependency. A sailboat is a thing of the water. By contrast, a motor boat is a machine used to overcome the water through the power of its engines. The currents and the winds around a body of water also enter into motorboating, but do so as obstacles to be surmounted. In motorboating one attempts to dominate the river, and can gain the illusion that such domination is possible. No such illusion is possible in sailboating. It is precisely such an illusion of domination that lies at the core of scientific technology.

In summary, the general technicity of contemporary thought is viewed by Heidegger as a metaphysical heritage that determines the way Being manifests itself in the modern epoch.[36] Technicity is itself the manner of thought which provokes man to be the being who makes nature yield its resources to him and which places man in a position to be the provocateur of nature. The heritage of technicity is, however, as with most heritages, an ambiguous one. On the one hand, since it is a way of making beings manifest it is a positive accomplishment. At the same time, since technology is a domineering mode of uncovering, it denies that there are any other beings than those made manifest in science and in scientific technology. Thus, while technicity is a heritage, it is also a danger.[37] It holds sovereignty not only over beings, but at the same time over all modes of uncovering beings.

But it is exactly because we are able to see even technological thought as merely one way of making beings manifest that we are also able to think—in the midst of this danger—about alternative modes of manifestation. And it is thus possible to ask about the meaning of the *techne* that is in harmony with *physis*. Heidegger wants to know if it is possible to modulate the insistent and aggressive *techne* of man and to bring Being itself into some sort of focus for thought. He asks, "But may we simply equate the world of technology with Being?" [38] For Heidegger these questions become imperative when we understand the essential fact of the Western metaphysical heritage—the displacement of a genuine thought of Being by science and technology.

Finally, Heidegger's critique of science and scientific technology does

36. *FT*, p. 32; *QT*, p. 306. See also "Letter on Humanism," trans. Edgar Lohner, in *Philosophy in the Twentieth Century*, p. 287.

37. *FT*, p. 36; *QT*, p. 311.

38. "Principle of Identity," in *Identity and Difference*, trans. Joan Stambaugh (New York, 1969), p. 33.

not constitute a romantic flight from mathematics and machines. If we recall that the technician is a kind of poet—a poet who makes technical
beings—then we can understand what is required of scientific technology:
that it become aware of its own foundations and through this self-
awareness rid itself of the pretense of being the *ur*-voice of Being. The
hope for technological man does not lie in giving up his technology. Since
Heidegger has written so eloquently of man's thrown existence, it would
be inconsistent with the basic spirit of his work to conclude that he urges
modern man to take flight from the basic constituent of his own thrown
fate. We are all finally technicians and if we are to be at home in our own
world we must learn to accept that fate as both a gift and a burden. With
this acceptance will come the chance of moving beyond technology. Thus
the burden of science and technology lies not in their calculative style but
rather in their insistent and aggressive spirit. It is, surely, part of Heidegger's point that the same trait would be pernicious in any style of thought.

Metaphysics, Ontology, and Fundamental Ontology

4. Gilbert Ryle

Heidegger's Sein und Zeit

THIS IS A VERY DIFFICULT and important work, which marks a big advance in the application of the 'Phenomenological Method'—though I may say at once that I suspect that this advance is an advance towards disaster.

Heidegger is probably the most original and powerful of Husserl's pupils; and this book, which is dedicated to Husserl and first appeared in his *Jahrbuch für Philosophie und phänomenologische Forschung*, vol. VIII, presupposes a knowledge of the published works and refers explicitly to more recent teachings and writings, as yet unpublished, of that difficult author. Now if *Sein und Zeit* were nothing more—and it is more—than a reexposition of the ideas of Heidegger's teacher, it would be hard enough for, anyhow, English readers to understand, since, save in chance quotations, not a word of Husserl has yet been translated and no adequate exposition in English of the cardinal positions of Phenomenology or even of the logical, epistemological and psychological doctrines contained in the *Logische Untersuchungen* (1900–01 and reedited with modifications 1913) has yet been given.[1] Moreover, to add to our difficulties, until recently there has been an additional historical obstacle to the understanding of Husserl, namely that no sure estimate could be formed of the nature and extent of the influence upon Husserl of Franz Brentano, though it was known that this was great; as, until Kraus and Kastil devoted themselves to the task, most of the psychological and philosophical teaching of Brentano remained unpublished and inaccessible. And finally the 'logical Realism' of Bernard Bolzano (1781–1848) which, with that of Frege, was so largely formative of Husserl's logical theories, must for the present remain unexplored country for most researchers in this field; since the first and only complete edition of his most important *Wissenschaftslehre* (1837) is

Reprinted from *Mind* 38 (1929) and *Collected Papers*, vol. 1 (London, 1971), pp. 197–98, 202–14, with permission of Basil Blackwell and the executors of Gilbert Ryle.

1. But see Boyce Gibson's article in *Mind*, 1922; references and quotations in Bosanquet's latest writings; and Linke's article in *The Monist*, 1926.

unprocurable, and even Höfler's reedition in 1913 of the first two of the four books is now out of print.

It is, however, now becoming possible to see in some sort of perspective what were the beginnings and what have been the stages in the growth of Phenomenology, and a short sketch of its genesis must preface my attempt to state even the programme and method of Heidegger—many of his conclusions for lack of comprehension I must abandon unexpounded.

[EDITOR'S NOTE: *This sketch has been deleted.*]

It is in the first instance the Phenomenology of those psychic acts that have *logical* Meanings, i.e., of acts of thinking, that Husserl prosecutes; but concurrently he is developing the general theory of Phenomenology and the general theory of its subject matter, the intentionality or meaningfulness of consciousness in general. And this general theory we may now sketch. Phenomenology is for Husserl the science of the 'phenomena of consciousness' (a phrase of Brentano's which Husserl for good reasons came to relinquish) or of 'intentional experiences'. But it is not a 'matter-of-fact' science: it does not deal with actual instances, in the sense that it first records and explores these and then makes inductive generalizations from them. Rather it is a science of Essences; it is the science of the character that any experience must have to be a case of doubting (say) or questioning or fancying or inferring. Its subject matter is the type or type-structure of intentional experiences as discerned *intuitively* in some real or imaginary exemplary instance. In a word its subject matter is Essences and not individuals and its method is by 'exemplary intuition': so that it stands to empirical psychology as geometry stands to geography.[2]

That there *are* Essences and that we can know them has been already established in the more purely logical parts of the *Logische Untersuchungen*.

Now as Phenomenology is the 'eidetic' science of intentional experiences, as such, it covers with its net in a certain sense *everything*. For whatever in any sense *is*, be it an existent or a subsistent, a fancy, a relation, the number 7, a hope, a piece of nonsense, the Equator, etc.; in a word, anything that could conceivably be named or thought about is potentially *for* me; i.e., it is potentially the objective correlate or intentional object of some or other act of my consciousness. I may know it or wonder about it or entertain it or be angry with it and so on, and it is there-

---

2. A good statement in English of what are in fact the subject matter, method, and relations with empirical psychology of Phenomenology is given—of course unwittingly—by Cook Wilson, *Statement and Inference*, vol. 1, p. 328, and the last sentence of § 119 on p. 277. And his analyses, e.g., of Opinion, Conviction, and Belief are admirable applications of the 'Phenomenological Method.'

fore actually or potentially the 'accusative' (I borrow the metaphor from grammar, as we have no separate rendering for '*Gegenstand*' as opposed to '*Objekt*') of an intentional experience. And the sort of intentionality that makes my *Erlebnis* what it is, is in its specific detail as in its generic structure something the analysis of which belongs to Phenomenology. This leads to important and (I think) dangerous consequences; for the science of Phenomenology is given a primacy over all other sciences, and it, itself presuppositionless, is supposed to be sovereign over presuppositions which all other sciences must make.

For already in his *Logische Untersuchungen* Husserl, on the basis of what I regard as a serious error in his theory of Meaning (derived, I suspect, from Brentano's founding of Judgment and Knowledge in *Vorstellung*), had erected a theory of knowledge or self-evident judgment according to which such objects of knowledge as are not experiences 'enjoyed' by the knower of them are tissues of Meanings, which Meanings are the *gift* of consciousness; so that consciousness is *constitutive* of all objects that are (or pretend to be) transcendent. This culminates in a doctrine explicitly formulated in his 'Ideen zu einer reinen Phänomenologie', which reminds us strongly of Kant or Green, that 'pure consciousness' is the only self-subsistent reality and the absolute *prius*. And he speaks accordingly of all objects of psychic acts, *including all objects of knowledge,* as 'correlates of consciousness'—things the being of which is to be 'accusative' to actual or possible intentional experiences.

There is thus a progressive trend visible in the philosophy of Husserl and his followers towards a rarefied Subjective Idealism or even Solipsism, a trend which, in my view, is not necessitated by the idea of Phenomenology, which I regard as good, but only by a particular elaboration of a part of a special theory of Meaning which is, if I am not mistaken, an evil legacy from the Locke-Brentano hypothesis of the existence of 'ideas'—certain mental entities out of which knowledge is somehow composed, though they are neither the objects known nor yet our acts of getting-to-know, but representatives between the former and the latter.

This very sketchy account of a few of the threads in the philosophy of Husserl—I can give here no exposition of the many other elements in it which I believe to be of really notable importance—must serve as a preface to Heidegger.

Heidegger's only previous published book was a little work on Duns Scotus whose doctrine of the Categories, Intentionality, and Meaning he expounds clearly, comparing them en route with kindred views of Husserl.

In *Sein und Zeit*, however, he breaks new ground and in some 440 large pages he builds up what he himself only claims to be the threshold to the solution of a problem vastly more profound and radical than any that Husserl has yet formulated. Moreover, in the course of the book Heidegger sets himself to the construction of a new philosophical terminology, especially designed to denote unambiguously the basic categories of Meaning which he is trying to explicate.

Phenomenology must be presuppositionless; that is to say, phenomenological interpretations or analyses must take for granted no theories or observations made in a state of (phenomenological) naïveté. This is common ground. But in fact—so Heidegger thinks—previous phenomenologists had failed to disembarrass themselves of a weighty inheritance of presuppositions, the presence of which either cramps or vitiates their results. For instance, the historical genesis of Phenomenology from psychology, the survival in that psychology of the simple Mind-Matter dualism of Descartes, as well as the 'chemical' theory of atomic ideas, states, and dispositions, the universal domination of Platonic and Aristotelian categories over all contemporary philosophical and psychological thinking, have stood in the way of the strict application of the phenomenological method; with the issue that even the most radical of its exponents have been tackling, with tools that were not their own, objects that they could only see with a squint.

It is no longer, or rather it is not yet, the time for Phenomenology to analyze the types of psychic acts and their interconnections, to examine the relation of 'act' to 'content' and of these to 'real physical things' and 'the world'; for the original isolation of such things as types, psychic acts, act-contents, physical things, and the world was one inherited from naïve predecessors and not *found* by Phenomenology.

The most fundamental presuppositions are ontological presuppositions; and it is to this field that Phenomenology must go, deliberately postponing the study of the twigs until it has completed its examination of the root. And the root is Being (*Sein*). The root problem of Phenomenology is the Meaning of Being—not in the sense that a *definition* is sought for it, for that would be a nonsensical demand, but that an insight of a new—phenomenological—sort is wanted, in possessing which we shall know 'with a difference' something which, of course, we must understand or know 'in a way' already. And by 'Being' is meant not this or that entity of which we can say that it is or that it is something, but the universal which these exemplify.

Now Husserl, though he reached the point of saying that *Sein* is nothing else than the Correlate of *Bewusstsein*, i.e., Being is just what Consciousness has as its 'accusative', had never quite emancipated himself from the Cartesian point of view that Consciousness and Being are *vis-à-vis* to one another in such a way that in studying Consciousness we are studying something on the outside of which and transcending which lies a region of absolute Reality.

And in this frame of mind he could *separate* the spheres of Phenomenology and Ontology by saying that the former is the science of Consciousness, the latter the science of—something else.

But Heidegger is critical of this naïve assumption; and Phenomenology must, he urges, so far from accepting the alleged cleavage between Consciousness and Being, select as its first task of all the analysis and description of that most primitive level of Experience in which is generated *for us* that seeming polar opposition. Our attitude of regarding Being as the opposite of Consciousness is itself one of the intentional experiences, and perhaps the most important of the intentional experiences that Phenomenology must examine.

In this way Heidegger turns the tables on the objection that a more orthodox phenomenologist would be certain to raise, namely, that Phenomenology, being by definition the science of consciousness, can only take Being into its province on the illegitimate assumption that Being is an *Erlebnis* or a component of an *Erlebnis*.

Next, as well the Husserlian as the Kantian or Cartesian accounts of Thought or Consciousness are stated in terms of the ontological categories of Plato and Aristotle. But as these categories were distilled out of a natural and naïve (i.e., prephenomenological) attitude towards the world and ourselves, they must be not indeed rejected but put, so to speak, in inverted commas; they must be accounted for with the naïve attitude from which they sprang. They cannot supply the terms in which we are to unpack the Meanings for which we are looking, for they are at least under suspicion of being metaphorical. Phenomenology is Hermeneutic and the categories which are the untested framework of our everyday world are among its primary *interpretanda*.

As a practical consequence of this view Heidegger imposes on himself the hard task of coining, and on us the alarming task of understanding, a complete new vocabulary of terms—mostly many-barreled compounds of everyday 'nursery' words and phrases—made to denote roots and stems of Meaning more primitive than those in which Plato, Aristotle, and subsequent scientists and philosophers have so taught us to talk and think, that we, by the strong force of habit, have come to regard as ultimate and pivotal ideas which are in fact composite and derivative. Heidegger's ontological Phenomenology is to turn our eyes back again to contemplate with a new method and a new clarity the springs of Meaning from which flow our most familiar and most 'homely' conceptions and classifications. The principle on which he seems to be designing his new terminology is, I should judge, the hypothesis that certain 'nursery' words and phrases have a primitiveness and freedom from sophistication which makes them more nearly adequate expressions of really primitive Meanings than the technical terms which science and philosophy in the course of a long development have established.

The hypothesis seems to me a perilous one, for it is at least arguable that it is here, and not in the language of the village and the nursery, that mankind has made a partial escape from metaphor.

In *Sein und Zeit* Heidegger does not make the assault upon his final objective; he opens the campaign with a preliminary occupation of a terrain that is nearer home. Indeed it is of the essence of his starting-point that it is as near home as possible, for, before trying to interpret what is the Being which any entity as such has, he tries to examine what sort of Being *we* have who are making the examination.

Like Brentano and Husserl he goes back to Descartes's 'Cogito ergo sum' and enquires more deeply than Descartes could do not merely what is a 'cogitatio' or what can be done by or what can happen to a 'res cogitans', but what the 'I' is and must be for such actions and passions to be possible. The threshold to the Hermeneutic of 'Esse' is the Hermeneutic of 'Sum'; and if he can find out what it ultimately is to be an experiencer having experiences, a door, perhaps the only door, will be open for the next search after the innermost Meaning of Being.

The title that Heidegger appropriates for an 'I' who thinks and in particular is asking the questions, using the methods, and appreciating the answers that I am now doing, is *'Dasein'* (one of numerous loans from established *philosophical* terminology which, however necessary, are certainly confusing). The business, then, of the present work is the 'Hermeneutic' or 'Analytic' of *'Dasein';* and as my being is not a timeless subsistence but a being-myself through a continuum of 'nows', the special problem of the work as indicated in the title is to analyse the intrinsic *temporality* of my being.

Perhaps also Heidegger's interest in the way in which time enters into conscious experience was stimulated by some lectures that Husserl was giving, in 1905 and later, on the inward experience of time. These have just been edited and published by Heidegger.

Now the most fundamental and 'primitive' moment of a *'Dasein's'* being is 'being-in-the-world'—being in it not as a chair is in a room or a cow in a field but as having it or being through and through occupied with it and by it. The world that I am in in this sense is all that it means to me; it is what makes me an experiencer of experiences. 'Being-in-the-world' for a *'Dasein'* is just the tissue of its attitudes, interests, and utilizations. In a word, the world that I am 'in' is simply the sum of what I am *about*. The distinction between theory and practice, or thought and will, between thinking-about and doing-about is derivative from the primitive mode of a *'Dasein's'* being—namely 'being-about . . .' (*besorgen*). Nor is it a mere chance attribute of a *'Dasein'* that it has this character of 'being-about . . .' Rather it is the essence of its being what it is, to 'be about . . .' And so, as the world, namely what I am about, belongs intrinsically to what I am, the pretended Subject-Object dualism is a pure fiction imported from the naturalistic attempt to see the relation between me and my world as akin to a relation between one fragment and another fragment of my world.

One of the derivative ways of 'being-about . . .' is 'thinking-about . . .': and of this one of the derivative modes is knowing; and that this is derivative and not primitive is shown by the fact that before knowing I must 'wonder about . . .' and before 'wondering about . . .' I must be 'interested in . . .' or 'concerned about . . .' which in the end turns out to be close to the most primitive mode of 'being-about . . .' and also of 'being-an-I' that there is.

Now while everything that I am-in-the-world-with has the character of being something that I am-about, this is not yet enough to characterize what we ordinarily term 'Things'. The Meaning of 'Thing' is not primitive but derived, and before the world that I 'have' is stocked with 'Things' it is stocked with *instruments* or *tools*, i.e., what I can 'work-*with*' in the performance of some task for some end. Later comes the conception of a 'Thing', namely what can't or needn't be worked with: the conception of 'Thing' is derived from the conceptions of 'unemployed' and 'instrument': so the mode of 'being-about . . .' which is *using* is primitive to the modes of 'being-about' which are knowing, classifying, and naming 'Things'.

(I may here interject that Heidegger seems to be confusing what is anthropologically primitive with what is logically primitive. It is perhaps a fact of human nature that I begin by being interested in things for what I can or can't do with them and only later do I want to know as a scientist what they are. But the former attitude involves equally with the latter the knowledge of things as having attributes and relations, though in infancy I restrict my interest to a few of those attributes and relations, namely those which bear on my business.

(I must leave till later my further and fundamental objection that all these so-called 'primitive' attitudes or ways of 'being-an-I' really involve *knowledge*, which knowledge necessitates universals and categories upon which the Analysis of *Dasein* throws—and can throw—no light at all.)

It is important to note that, in all the ways of being-about, being-in, being-with, and being-without that characterize a '*Dasein*', the *Dasein* has some sort of *understanding of* what it is being or doing. Not that it has scientific, 'thematic' *knowledge*—for this is a late product—but the moods, tenses, and inflections of its being-itself are 'illuminated' or 'transparent' to itself. If it were not so the Analysis of *Dasein* would have no self-evidence, and so would not be the proper approach to our ultimate problem.

The spatiality of the world is derived from such primitive attitudes as having-to-hand-convenient-for-using or not-having-to-hand; but apart from mentioning the similarity of Heidegger's treatment of Space and

later of Time with that of Bergson and some anthropologistic pragmatists,
I must pass quickly over this and several other important sections in which
the constituents and structure of the world we 'have' are derived or
analysed.

What in the end *is* a *Dasein?* What does 'sum' in 'Cogito ergo sum' ultimately denote? Behind the quesion 'What are the root types of my be-
haviour, my attitudes, my actions, and my passions?' lies the question
'What is it to *be* an *I* (*Dasein*)?'

The answer rings at first strangely. 'Dasein ist Sorge.' What I am is
Concern or Care (*cura*). Willing, wishing, wondering, reflecting, knowing, doing, with their 'accusatives', all are ways of 'caring' or 'caring
about' or 'caring for'.

Heidegger tells us that he came to this conception of Care as the abso-
lutely primitive Being that an 'I' as such has, through studying the Augustinian and other Christian philosophies of human nature; but I surmise,
too, that there are legacies in it of the characterization by Brentano and
Husserl of Consciousness as what has intentionality. For by 'Care' Heidegger does not mean any particular emotion of fearing, or being anxious,
or wishing, or any particular act of striving, or any particular inclination
or impulse, but the primitive sort of being in which all such emotions and
acts and states are founded; for they are all particular ways of 'caring'.

Next (what bears on the special problem of the *temporal* nature of an
'I'), what I am is not exhausted by what I have done and become up to
date; rather it is of the essence of my being what I am that there are potentialities in me; I *can* be what I am not yet; and what I can be belongs
just as intrinsically to my being as what I am already, i.e., that of my
being which I have already realized. Care is accordingly as essentially care
about what I might be as care about what I already am. This leads to an
analysis of what my Being as a *whole* is, i.e., the whole structure of which
what I am up to date and what I might be are integral moments. Now one
of the characteristics of my whole being is that *qua* Life it terminates in
Death—*terminates* in Death without finding its *completion* in it. So we
have to investigate what sort of a whole it is which has both termination
in Death and a completion (never fully realized) in being all that it has
the potentiality of being. In this whole belong conscience—the certainty
of what I might be—and the sense of sin or guilt—the certainty that I am
not what I might have been. (Here Heidegger is reviving important Augustinian theses which lead one to wonder if the second part of this work
will not be a sort of Eckhart philosophy in phenomenological clothing.)

But here, for the reviewer at any rate, the fog becomes too thick; and
the results of the analyses of our intrinsic temporality, of the several concepts of time, historical becoming, history, and the criticisms of the theories of Dilthey and Hegel must go unexpounded.

A word about the *method* of Phenomenology. It is its boast that it does not make and does not presuppose 'logical constructions' or 'theories' or 'systems'. 'Phenomenology makes no hypotheses.' It does not move by making deductions from axioms or inductions from observed and recorded facts. Its method is that of 'exemplary intuition', i.e., the inspection of individual examples *qua* exemplifications of Essences or Types—this of course in the region of consciousness. We intuit in this or that feeling of anger, act of choice, or imagination, that essential character lacking which the particular examined would be someting other than a case of being angry, choosing, or imagining.

So here Heidegger claims simply to be revealing, unpacking, or interpreting the essence of what we do and are. Accordingly, his sentences, which on first reading seem to be mere dogmatic assertions, have to be read as expressions of a Hermeneutic analysis to understand which is to see that it is true. He is simply telling us explicitly what we must have known 'in our bones' all the time. Similarly, e.g., Cook Wilson does not' tell us anything *new* about Conception, Opinion, or Belief; he is telling us something which we, when told, recognize that we knew implicitly from the start.

The dangers lie in the undue extension of this method; if, for instance, our interpreter has, without realizing it, a theory of knowledge, or a metaphysical system, he may easily come to interpolate into the interpretations that he gives something that could never have been intuited in the exemplary instance he is examining—since, even if it be true, yet it was never in the Essence of that example. Or else, under the same influence, he may omit to notice an integral element in that Essence. Thus I suspect that certain theories of human nature have been interpolated into Heidegger's analysis of it; and on the other side the basic place of knowing in being-in-the-world or in any experiencing of a Meaning has been forgotten. And so an anthropologistic Metaphysic seems to have been read out of our everyday experience, of which both the positive element of Humanism and the negative sceptical element of Relativism and Solipsism appear to be derived from views interpolated into and not won by the Phenomenological Method.

It remains to make a few tentative comments and criticisms upon the general idea, and especially the method, of this approach to the Hermeneutic of Being via the Hermeneutic of 'being-an-I' ('*Dasein*').

(1) In the first place it is taken for self-evident that some sort of *understanding* what I do and am belongs essentially to my doing what I do and being what I am. This doctrine is, I suppose, the same as that of Brentano and Husserl that in 'inner' or 'immanent perception' I have a source of self-evident positive judgments and that I have no other such source; so that any degree of '*Evidenz*' in any positive judgment that I make must

either be or be grounded in the self-evidence of 'inner perception'. But while there is no objection to the thesis that I can know my own experiences and the 'I' who has them, the assertion that this is all that I can know, or that if I can know anything else I can only know it if I first know my experiences and my 'I', is far from self-evident; indeed it seems to me to contradict itself. At any rate it presupposes a theory of knowledge and a metaphysic, and so a Phenomenology based on this theory is not presuppositionless. However it might still be the case that the analysis of what it is to be 'an I' and to experience my experiences was the best, though not the only, approach to the ultimate analysis of what Being as such is. 'I' might be the most accessible or the most transparent example of Being.

(2) Some would quarrel with the original assumption that there *is* a problem about the Meaning of Being. But as the (perhaps departmental) question of the relation between Being *qua* timeless 'subsistence' and existing *qua* existing in the world of time and space seems to me a real one, I do not take up this cudgel.

(3) But there is what I regard as a vital ambiguity present in that expanded theory of Phenomenology which makes it the logical '*prius*' of not only psychology but logic, metaphysics, and the mathematical and natural sciences. Accepting Brentano's improvement on the Locke-Hume theory of 'ideas' according to which the distinction was made between the act and the content (or immanent object) of a *Vorstellung*, the phenomenologists have very properly generalized the principle and find in every phenomenon of consciousness, i.e., in every intentional act or experience an act side and a content or Meaning side. Then, looking at the world, they see that every thing or event, every relation or universal, every conceivable 'It' can be regarded as the objective correlate or content to an appropriate act of consciousness—knowing, perhaps, or surmising, or being vexed at, or wanting, or being interested in.

And as it is the proper business of phenomenology to analyze states and acts of consciousness, everything is in this way drawn into its net; for anything and everything is or has a Meaning-for-me, and the meaning of the act or acts in which it has its Meaning-for-me is the proper subject matter of the science of intentionality.

But while it is a dangerous metaphor to speak of acts having 'meanings' or of things as being the 'meanings of acts', it is a fatal error to speak of a thing known as the correlate of a knowing-act as if that implied that we could get to the heart of the thing by analyzing our experience of knowing it. A twin is a correlate to a twin but operations upon the one are at most operations upon the other one's twin, not operations upon the other one himself.

And this leads to dangerous results in the practice of the phenomenological method; it leads to them here in *Sein und Zeit*. For the presence of *knowledge* of some reality (which is surely present in any and every conscious experience) though it is not explicitly recognized is surreptitiously imported as well into such terms as 'understanding' and 'illumination' as into the countless nursery terms which Heidegger is trying to build up into a new philosophical vocabulary.

For instance, the general characterization of our conscious being as a 'being-in-the-world' surely implies that *underlying* our other reactions and attitudes there is *knowledge*. We 'have' or are 'in-the-world' only if we know that at least one 'something' exists. Similarly the attempt to derive our knowledge of 'things' from our practical attitude towards tools breaks down; for to use a tool involves knowledge of what it is, what can be done it, and what wants doing.

And if we like to call things that we know 'correlates of acts of knowing', we must at least recognize that the analysis of what those things are is not in the least degree forwarded by an analysis of our acts of knowing them, but only by getting to know still more about the things themselves.

This ambiguity is especially well concealed, equally deeply involved, in the conception of Meaning. The thing which I know and which I signify with such symbols as sentences is in one sense of the word the 'Meaning' of my sentences: but it is not (except *per accidens*) an *Erlebnis* or an act of consciousness; nor is it anything constituted by an act of consciousness. Only in another sense of the word is 'Meaning' something derivative from a state or act of consciousness—namely when it is not the thing symbolized by a symbol but the fact that this symbol symbolizes that thing. Certainly a symbol symbolizes because we choose that it shall, so its meaning (i.e., meaningfulness) is the product of an act of consciousness, but the origin of the functioning of a symbol is no more the origin of the thing which it is its function to symbolize than the forest in which a sign-post grew is the parental home of the town to which the sign-post points.

And I stress these arguments against the Husserl–Heidegger treatment of Meaning for two connected reasons:

(a) I think it can be shown that Husserl's theories of Meaning (*Sinn* and *Bedeutung*) are primarily developments of Brentano's theory of 'ideas' (*Vorstellungen*). A Meaning is, at the start, just the intentional 'accusative' of an act of 'having an idea'; later the term also covers the intentional 'accusatives' of acts of Judging, so that propositions as well as concepts are Meanings. Now (as Representationism always ends in Subjectivism) this theory has in the end to say that the world of things and events *as I apprehend it* must be just a tissue of Meanings, which Meanings must be the contribution of acts of consciousness.

(b) I think, too, that it can be shown that the only reason why Heidegger's Hermeneutic of '*Dasein*' takes or promises to take the form of a sort of anthropologistic Metaphysic (smelling a little oddly both of James and of St. Augustine) is because Heidegger presupposes that the Meanings which his Hermeneutic is to unravel and illuminate must be in some way man-constituted.

But though I deplore the damage wrought upon his Metaphysics by the presuppositions which Heidegger has unconsciously inherited, I have nothing but admiration for his special undertaking and for such of his achievements in it as I can follow, namely the phenomenological analysis of the root workings of the human soul.

He shows himself to be a thinker of real importance by the immense subtlety and searchingness of his examination of consciousness, by the boldness and originality of his methods and conclusions, and by the un-flagging energy with which he tries to think beyond the stock categories of orthodox philosophy and psychology.

And I must also say, in his behalf, that while it is my personal opinion that *qua* First Philosophy Phenomenology is at present heading for bank-ruptcy and disaster and will end either in self-ruinous Subjectivism or in a windy mysticism, I hazard this opinion with humility and with reserva-tions since I am well aware how far I have fallen short of understanding this difficult work.

Sein und Zeit, it is worth mentioning, is most beautifully printed and the pages have generous margins.

5. KARSTEN HARRIES

Fundamental Ontology and the Search for Man's Place

IN THE *Investigations* Wittgenstein remarks that philosophical problems have the form "I don't know my way about." [1] Not that all problems having this form are therefore philosophical—to have lost one's way in some strange city hardly suffices to make one a philosopher. But why not? Is it perhaps because in such cases our disorientation is only superficial? In a deeper sense we still know our place and what to do: thus we could ask someone for help or look for a map. The problem poses itself against a background of unquestioned ways of doing things on which we can fall back in our attempt to discover where we are and where we should go. Philosophical problems have no such background. They emerge only when man has begun to question the place assigned to him by nature, society, and history and to demand more secure foundations than established practice can provide.

The development of Heidegger's thought can be understood as a continuing search for such foundations. Questioning had led the young Heidegger from faith to theology, loss of faith from theology to philosophy. Unable to deny Nietzsche's proclamation of the death of God, Heidegger was forced to struggle with the disintegration of an order that with this death had lost founder and foundation.[2]

A third of this article was taken over, with minor changes, from an earlier essay, "The Search for Meaning," in *Existential Philosophers: Kierkegaard to Merleau-Ponty*, ed. G. A. Schrader, Jr. (New York, 1967), pp. 162–208, though the present article reflects a somewhat different reading of *Being and Time*.

1. *Philosophical Investigations*, trans. G. E. M. Anscombe (New York, 1953), par. 123.
    2. See *Die Selbstbehauptung der deutschen Universität* (Breslau, 1933), p. 12.

In such early works as the dissertation [3] and his *Habilitationsschrift* [4] this struggle lets Heidegger adopt what appears to be a quite traditional transcendental approach: the need for foundations, no longer satisfied by God or a transcendent realm of true being, leads to a search for the structures constitutive of the objects of experience, to an inquiry into the being or the logos of phenomena, to phenomenology understood as transcendental ontology. In *Being and Time* this search takes a new turn. Ontology is shown to be itself in need of a foundation. Heidegger's "fundamental ontology" addresses itself to this need. Yet in the end it, too, fails to provide the foundation promised by the term. The transcendental approach turns against itself; instead of leading us to secure ground, it only gives greater urgency to the demand for such a ground and returns us to the question: what is man's place?

In order to show the priority of the question of Being Heidegger considers the crisis prevailing in the positive sciences. Mathematics, physics, biology, history, theology—all were then caught up in a questioning of their own basic concepts (*SZ* 9–10).[5] Especially the ongoing revolution in physics suggested to Heidegger the need to give science a foundation in ontology. This suggestion should not seem surprising. Consideration of that other crisis which gave birth and shape to modern science shows that this science had its origin not so much in new observations as in a new way of mathematically projecting nature (*SZ* 362). Descartes's ontology of extended substance helped to provide research still uncertain of how to proceed with a foundation. Heidegger terms such ontology "productive logic," productive "in the sense that it leaps ahead, as it were, into some area of Being, discloses it for the first time in the constitution of its Being, and, after thus arriving at the structures within it, makes these available to the positive sciences as transparent assignments for their inquiry" (*SZ* 10–11). Kant's *Critique of Pure Reason* offers another example. Heidegger understands it as an ontological inquiry into the being of "Nature" that exhibits the foundations on which "the ontical inquiry" of the natural sciences rests. The search for foundations thus leads Heidegger, as it did Husserl, to transcendental philosophy: ontology is understood as the inquiry that moves beyond ontical description, description of what as a matter of fact is the case, to an exhibition of the *categories*, the structures that ground these phenomena and make them possible.

But if ontology is thus more fundamental than the positive sciences, it is itself in need of a foundation. To return to the Cartesian example: what

---

3. *Die Lehre vom Urteil: Ein kritisch-positiver Beitrag zur Logik* (Leipzig, 1914).
4. *Die Kategorien-und Bedeutungslehre des Duns Scotus* (Tübingen, 1916).
5. Page references are to *Sein und Zeit*, 7th ed. (Tübingen, 1953), abbreviated *SZ*. Translated by J. Macquarrie and E. Robinson as *Being and Time* (New York, 1962).

right does Descartes have to insist on the adequacy of an understanding of nature that reduces its being to extended substance? Any such ontology "remains itself naive and opaque if in its researches into the Being of entities it fails to discuss the meaning of Being in general" (*SZ* 11). Descartes was of course quite aware of the need to give a foundation to his ontology of nature. He sought that foundation in an interpretation of the essence of human being as thinking substance. That interpretation rests on a twofold abstraction: first, the self is disengaged from the world and transformed into a mere spectator of what is; it is then further purified by being brought to the realization that the body and the senses are not essential to its being. This angelically pure self is made the measure of what presents itself to us. Using that measure the world of the senses is judged to be no more than perspectival appearance. If we want to do justice to the being of nature we have to use descriptions from which all those aspects which presuppose a particular point of view have been eliminated. The form of such description is provided by mathematics.

Has Descartes done justice to the essence of human being and thus provided his ontology of nature with the necessary foundation? How adequate is the access to beings offered by the interpretation of the self as thinking substance? To answer such questions a more careful analysis of man's being is necessary. But consideration of the *Meditations* can help us to understand Heidegger's claim that "*fundamental ontology*, from which alone all other ontologies can take their rise, must be sought in the *existential analytic of Dasein*" (*SZ* 13). Traditional ontology must lack a foundation as long as it seeks to exhibit the structures constitutive of the things man encounters, while taking for granted a particular interpretation of that encounter, which gives priority to detached observation, without questioning the adequacy of that interpretation. Fundamental ontology attempts to meet this deficiency by giving more careful attention to the many different modes in which man exists and encounters things. Its goal is the exhibition of the structures constitutive of human being (*Dasein*). These structures are the "existentialia" of *Being and Time*. One has to guard against an interpretation that sees in Heidegger's existentialia a particular kind of categories, i.e., those categories constitutive of the substance man. The fundamental role of existential analysis is overlooked by such an interpretation. Categories are related to existentialia as ontology is related to fundamental ontology.

Fundamental ontology investigates the existential structure of human being. What then is man? Whatever he may be, this much is certain: man is a being in the world. But so are other things such as trees or houses. Is man then one of many things in the world? Is he in the world as matches are in a box? Within limits this comparison is of course correct: it describes the way my body is in a room. But man is more than just another thing. For things to be given at all there must be a being to whom they are given. This much is right about the idealist's claim that objects can be only for a subject.[6] Instead of being just another thing in the world, man is the being to whom the world, including all the things within it, can reveal itself.

The difficulty with talk about subject and object is that it tends to take the self out of the world, placing it before the world as a spectator stands before a picture in which he has no place. But to be a self is to experience the things of the world from within the world. Man, Heidegger insists, does not happen to be in the world; his being is essentially a being in the world. Thus it cannot be identified with the subject of traditional philosophy. If one had to use the language of subject and object, it would be more correct to identify man's being with the relation holding between subject and object than with either subject or object (SZ 132). Still, such formulations fail to do justice to what Heidegger has in mind. His own term "being-in" is more suggestive in that it emphasizes that human being is essentially a dwelling in and being familiar with the world.

To make the encounter between man and things possible, there must be something like a distance separating the two. Things can present themselves only as other than the self. The other supplies the dimension in which alone things can appear. But what is this "other" which is presupposed by experience? Perhaps this is a meaningless question, for to give an answer would seem to make this other into something, into some definite object, while it is the condition of all objectivity. Thus it cannot be anything; it must be nothing. The projection of man into nothing is another expression for the being-in of Dasein.[7]

Yet the expression is misleading in that it gives too much substantiality to Dasein. It suggests that Dasein is something which then projects itself into a nothingness, whatever this might mean. What Heidegger wants to suggest is rather that Dasein is nothing apart from this projection. A questioning that discovers meanings only in facts must find such formulations meaningless. Dasein is indeed not a fact, but a nothingness; a relation, a gap, an in-between. But only as such a nothingness can it be the place where beings disclose themselves. Dasein is the place of this disclosure.

One of Heidegger's favorite metaphors, likening man's being to a forest clearing (Lichtung) suggests this. One may object to the philosopher's

6. See SZ 230. "Being (not entities) is something which 'there is' only in so far as truth is. And truth is only in so far and as long as Dasein is." This perhaps puzzling passage, which suggests that entities may transcend Dasein while being does not, rests on Heidegger's understanding of being as presence to Dasein. If we are to speak of the being of entities, these entities must already have been understood in some sense. Such understanding, however, in no way creates these entities.

7. See Was ist Metaphysik?, 5th ed. (Frankfurt, 1949) (What is Metaphysics?" trans. R. F. C. Hull and A. Crick, in Existence and Being [Chicago, 1949].

use of such blatantly metaphorical language. But the metaphor deserves careful consideration. A clearing is a gap within the forest that permits light to enter and allows things to be seen with a clarity that the darkness of the forest does not allow. Heidegger's metaphor thus joins a distance with a light metaphor. The latter two metaphors have long governed epistemological speculation, which has tended to take for granted that the model provided by vision is adequate to understanding. But how adequate is it? What do we mean when we speak of "the light of the intellect" or place the subject at a distance from the object? By calling attention to its metaphorical status, the term "clearing" not only puts itself into question; it also calls our attention to the metaphorical basis of traditional epistemology and thus invites a questioning and rethinking of too easily taken-for-granted concepts.

If fundamental ontology must take the form of an analytic of Dasein, how do we find proper access to this analytic? How can the one-sidedness of traditional ontology be avoided? Nothing that has been said so far has seriously put into question its spectatorial stance. But how warranted is that stance? Can a static metaphor like "clearing" do justice to man's being? Is man's being not essentially a being on the way, a caring and looking ahead, a seizing and discarding of possibilities? To guard against the temptation of reading unwarranted preconceptions into what is to be analyzed, Heidegger insists that we "choose such a way of access and such a kind of interpretation that this entity can show itself in itself and from itself. And this means that it is to be shown as it is *proximally and for the most part*—in its average *everydayness*" (SZ 16–17). This turn away from the spectatorial stance of traditional ontology to the everyday may remind us of the anti-Cartesianism of Wittgenstein's *Investigations*. Yet the italicized words introduce an important and too often overlooked caveat: they indicate the brackets which enclose the entire first part of *Being and Time*. Is it clear that "average everydayness" gives us adequate access to what is? Do we discover here something like a foundation? As long as these questions are not answered, the analysis can only be *"provisional"* (SZ 16).

Following the guiding thread of "average everydayness" we are forced to reject the starting point of traditional philosophy. Our first, and still our most usual encounter with things is not at all a detached observing of the facts around us. Rather we find ourselves involved with things and with other persons. Our understanding is inseparably tied to what we are up to, to our cares and concerns. When a philosopher pauses and gropes for an example of what he means by an object and finally comes up with the chalk he was holding or the blackboard on which he was writing, he easily overlooks that chalk and blackboard were given to him in a quite

different manner when he was using them than they are given to him now
that he has stopped writing and made them the objects of his reflections.
Such detachment represents an artificial and derivative mode of encounter.
"Proximally and for the most part" things are known in their use. The
dislocation that is part of the theoretical attitude changes this. Now things
become mere objects, facts. The use that is made of things becomes accidental. In the former case, when an entity is given as a thing to be used,
Heidegger speaks of it as "ready-to-hand," in the latter case, as "present-
at-hand." "Readiness-to-hand" and "presence-at-hand" are the most basic
categories advanced in *Being and Time*. And following the guiding thread
of "average everydayness," readiness-to-hand is given priority.[8]

A second example may help to show how much is at stake here. Take
an apple tree, blooming in some peasant yard. The peasant, anticipating
the harvest, looks at it with very different eyes from the artist who discovers color values and the excitement of a net of crisscrossing gnarled
branches. A boy might see yet another thing, perhaps a tree to climb or
a branch to swing from; or he may anticipate what the tree will be to him
in the fall, not a bearer of the harvest, but a seducer, beckoning him to
climb the fence and to pilfer some of the fruit.

What is the real tree? Or is this perhaps a question that already implies
a commitment to a particular and indeed derivative attitude? The real
tree—that would presumably be the tree freed from subjectivistic interpretations contributed by different individuals. Thus to get at the real tree
we would have to detach it from different contexts of interpretation. This
is the point of the reduction of being, first to presence-at-hand, and then
to objectivity. Against the claims of such reductive ontologies, Heidegger
insists on a more fundamental approach that lets us be open to the many
different ways in which the tree reveals itself and recognizes the artificial-
ity and derivative status of an understanding of being that reduces it to
presence-at-hand.

"Proximally and for the most part" things are given to us as meaningful. For the peasant the tree is not simply one tree among others, just one
more thing in his world; it is irreplaceable. Perhaps he does not even no-

8. One may well wonder how adequate the attempt to divide beings in this way
is. Where, for example, do aesthetic phenomena fall? In *Being and Time* they receive
little attention. The suggestion that "the Nature which 'stirs and strives'" can be
understood as readiness-to-hand cannot convince, which is not to dispute the claim
that it cannot be discovered as pure presence-at-hand (SZ 70). As becomes clear in
subsequent works, to do justice to aesthetic phenomena we have to abandon the guiding thread that "average everydayness" provides. See especially "Der Ursprung des
Kunstwerkes," *Holzwege* (Frankfurt, 1950) ("The Origin of the Work of Art,"
trans. A. Hofstadter, in *Poetry, Language, Thought* [New York, 1971]). That this
guiding thread is very much conditioned by our historical situation is suggested by
Heidegger's admission that readiness-to-hand may have "nothing to contribute: to
an interpretation of the primitive world" (SZ 82).

tice its quiet presence in the backyard; perhaps it is taken so much for granted that it is noticed only on certain occasions when it seems to demand attention. Such attention will not be a detached contemplating, but a caring for the tree: it requires pruning; the apples have to be picked; or the splintered branches left by the last storm have to be sawed off cleanly. In such care the tree reveals itself. At the same time this care binds the peasant and the tree into a larger order which includes fields and village, home and church, family and neighbors. Caught up in that order he knows his place and what is to be done. He understands the meaning of life. But what is it that he understands? What could he answer if someone were to ask him? No doubt, such an itinerant philosopher would be disappointed. What would we say? The meaning of our place in the world does not disclose itself in clear and distinct ideas. There is only a feeling, a mood.

We started with the question: what is man's place? The search for a foundation that would establish what is to be done led to the much simpler and more specific question: what is the foundation on which the positive sciences rest? It now appears that this foundation is in the end nothing other than ordinary experience and that science must be understood as a particular and derivative way in which man relates to things. Presupposed is the transformation of readiness-to-hand into presence-at-hand and the reduction of presence-at-hand to objectivity. But if "average everydayness" offers us the foundation we are looking for, do we not have to reconsider the claim that philosophy is privileged as the inquiry into foundations? Has traditional philosophy, searching for more secure foundations, led us to a clearer recognition of our place? Has it not by surrendering that ground which "average everydayness" provides misled us and compounded rather than remedied the problem of loss of place?

An affirmative answer is suggested by such traditional problems as the problem of the reality of things without me, the problem of solipsism, and the problem of nihilism or the loss of value. Heidegger's analysis suggests that such problems are not to be solved, but to be dissolved by showing that they rest on a one-sided and reduced understanding of human being. There is no need to prove that an isolated subject can break out of its isolation and make contact with independently existing things. The conception of the self as subject, which is presupposed by attempts to prove the reality of things without me, is itself deficient. "The 'scandal of philosophy' is not that this proof has yet to be given, but that *such proofs are expected and attempted again and again*" (SZ 205). Similarly, being-with-others is constitutive of human being. "So far as Dasein *is* at all, it has Being-with-one-another as its kind of Being" (SZ 125). There is no need of proof.

The problem of nihilism or the loss of value is given only cursory attention in *Being and Time*. There is a hint that talk about value has its origin in the reduction of being to presence-at-hand. Again there is the suggestion that we do not need and cannot supply proofs that would establish beyond the realm of facts a realm of values that can endow our life with significance. "Proximally and for the most part" we find ourselves in meaningful situations. Only when the context of care, in which things are encountered in terms of the projects in which man is engaged, is bracketed, do we encounter something as a brute fact. The Cartesian view of the subject is the result of such bracketing. It has its origin in a revolt on the part of the self against all ties of care that bind it to the world. "With this revolt all beings become objects. As objective, beings are drowned in the immanence of subjectivity. The horizon no longer possesses a light of its own." [9] The transformation of the self into a detached subject lets the world lose its meaning. As detached subject, man is no longer claimed. Nothing matters. But how, if nothing matters, is it possible to act at all?

How can man act, if besides the realm of facts that simply "are" there is not also a realm of meaning? If there were only facts life would be reduced to absurdity. To defeat this absurdity traditional philosophy resorts to values. The lack discovered in the world of facts is remedied by pasting value labels on these facts (*SZ* 150). Value theory is thus, according to Heidegger, an attempt to restore to the world the meaning lost in the reduction of being to presence-at-hand. Values are only the objectified traces of meanings that are inseparable from "average everydayness."

To illustrate "average everydayness" I chose as my example a peasant. Although Heidegger likes to choose similar examples, such a choice may seem anachronistic in a world where the peasant is doomed to extinction, to be replaced by the farmer who will exploit the soil in the way an engineer forces a river to turn turbines that will yield electricity. The example betrays a certain nostalgia, a desire to discover man's place in an urban world marked by mobility and anonymity. It is indeed not difficult to discover such a longing in Heidegger's works. In a posthumously published interview we find Heidegger still insisting that only an individual who has his roots in a particular landscape and tradition is capable of truly significant work.[10] Heidegger liked to think of himself as someone who still belonged to the earth, more at home in a tavern, talking to peasants about the weather or the illness of some animal, than amidst the chattering

9. *Holzwege*, p. 241.
10. "Nur noch ein Gott kann uns retten," Spiegel Gespräch mit Martin Heidegger am 23. September 1966, *Der Spiegel* (1976), no. 23, p. 209.

crowd attending professional conferences and social gatherings.[11] Still, one is not quite convinced by this show of earthiness. It seems to betray not so much a peasant turned thinker as a very modern dissatisfaction with the modern world. There is in Heidegger much of the old *Wandervogel* spirit, which led young men and women to escape from "the walls of the grey cities," armed with lute and song, in search of a Germany even the romantics had failed to find. Heidegger's vision of the peasant, secure in the knowledge of his place in the world, may seem attractive, but do we not also know that we cannot make it our own, that to do so is not so much an expression of a will to affirm oneself as it is a flight from the present?

The question points to a difficulty in *Being and Time*, a difficulty that gains central importance in subsequent works. In the first part of *Being and Time* Heidegger seems to give priority to readiness-to-hand, which is taken to describe the being of things as they are encountered "proximally and for the most part." Presence-at-hand is discussed as a deficient mode of being, to be accounted for by calling attention to the dislocations and reductions it presupposes. Unfortunately in our world the distinction is not so easily drawn. What we encounter "proximally and for the most part" includes technological equipment. Such equipment is ready-to-hand; yet it presupposes science, which in turn rests on the reduction of being to objectivity and on the dislocation of the self that is inseparable from that reduction. Heidegger later came to see that technological equipment cannot be understood as just another, perhaps more complex, tool. With technology the ontology of objectivity, which, on Heidegger's account, has to uproot and dislocate the individual, has entered everyday existence. To what extent is it still possible for us to take a step back from traditional ontology and undo its reduction of being to presence-at-hand? Has that reduction not become part of our common sense?

A more fundamental question must be raised, directed not so much against Heidegger as against interpretations that take for granted that Heidegger gives priority to readiness-to-hand. Are such interpretations compatible with what Heidegger actually says in *Being and Time*? To be sure, following the guiding thread of "average everydayness" we have to grant that the kind of being that belongs to the entities we encounter "proximally and for the most part" is indeed readiness-to-hand, and that to insist that there is "some world-stuff which is proximally present-at-hand in itself" which is then "given subjective coloring" is to distort the phenomena (*SZ* 71). Theoretical knowledge must be understood as derived from and founded in more engaged modes of understanding. "To lay bare what

11. "Warum bleiben wir in der Provinz?" *Der Alemanne, Zu neuen Ufern, Kultur-beilage* (7 March 1934), p. 1.

is just present-at-hand and no more, cognition must first penetrate *beyond* what is ready-to-hand in our concern. *Readiness-to-hand is the way in which entities as they are 'in themselves' are defined ontologico-categorically"* (*SZ* 71).

But what does Heidegger mean when he speaks of "entities as they are 'in themselves' "? Is this to suggest an unconditional priority for readiness-to-hand? The very next sentence forces us to question this: "Yet only by reason of something present-at-hand, 'is there' anything ready-to-hand." We seem to be moving in a circle: presence-at-hand is said to have its foundation in readiness-to-hand, which in turn 'is given' only "by reason" of presence-at-hand. If by moving from readiness-to-hand to presence-at-hand we lose important dimensions of experience, everyday familiarity with things is said by Heidegger to numb us and to let us overlook what things are. In *Being and Time* Heidegger not only shows that dislocation threatens a loss of meaning, but also that such dislocation makes things visible.

A basic challenge, not only to the priority of readiness-to-hand, but to any attempt to take too seriously the guiding thread of "average every-dayness," is posed by Heidegger's association of everydayness with inauthenticity. Consider his claim that "proximally and for the most part" language is idle talk. The term "idle talk" is somewhat unfortunate in that it suggests a particular misuse of language, perhaps what Wittgenstein meant by an "idling" of language. But when Wittgenstein likens the way philosophers use language to "an engine idling" he has in mind language that no longer functions as a part of a language-game, where "language-game" is understood as "the whole, consisting of language and the actions into which it is woven." [12] Heidegger is thinking of a much more fundamental phenomenon. "Idle talk" refers precisely to language that does function as part of a language-game which in its entirety is taken for granted. We say what one says, do what one does. The language of the everyday is idle talk. "Idle talk is the kind of Being that belongs to Being-with-one-another itself" (*SZ* 177). But if so, are we not, when following the guiding thread of everyday experience and discourse, in danger of taking as fundamental a mode of encounter that, according to Heidegger, seems adequate only "because it is insensitive to every difference of level and of genuineness and thus never gets to the 'heart of the matter' " (*SZ* 127)? If everyday language is idle talk, how can we claim that the guiding thread of the "proximally and for the most part" leads us to anything like firm ground?

But unlike Wittgenstein, who is claiming that in leading us back from philosophical to ordinary language he is "clearing up the ground of language," Heidegger does not claim anything of the sort. Quite the contrary: he insists that the analyses of the first part of *Being and Time* have

12. *Philosophical Investigations*, pars. 132 and 7.

only a preparatory and provisional character (*SZ* 16–17). They are not yet authentically ontological and cannot claim primordiality. In the beginning of the second part, this provisional character of the preceding analyses is reemphasized. "One thing has become unmistakable: *our existential analysis of Dasein up till now cannot lay claim to primordiality*. Its forehaving never included more than the *inauthentic* Being of Dasein, and of Dasein as *less* than a *whole*" (*SZ* 233). How then do we gain a more primordial understanding and thus a more secure foundation? What guiding thread should we follow once we have abandoned "average everydayness"? The last sentence quoted offers a hint: we have to consider the authentic Being of Dasein and we have to understand Dasein as a whole.

If inauthenticity characterizes everydayness, authentic existence must be sought beyond the usually accepted and taken for granted. Authenticity requires a questioning leave-taking from the security offered by what one says and does. We must lose our usually taken-for-granted place in the world if we are to see and act for ourselves. The mood that effects such displacement and allows for the possibility of authentic existence is anxiety. Anxiety reveals the groundlessness of human existence.

"Proximally and for the most part," man finds himself in meaningful situations. He answers the question, what is man's place? simply by living, and he possesses something like a foundation in submitting to what one generally says and does. But there are moments when a suspicion seizes man that in the end all such saying and doing counts for nothing, that what the world considers important is of no account, that all finite being is but an island in an emptiness which in the end will submerge all. Heidegger, acknowledging his debt to Kierkegaard, understands anxiety as the mood that discloses the nothingness behind all phenomena. As long as man is able to remain within the domain of the everyday, faithfully following the route prescribed to him, anxiety remains submerged. But someone who has spent his life as a loyal employee or a faithful spouse may suddenly realize that all the things which he has taken so seriously have not really touched him. As the world of the everyday fades in insignificance a curious calm fills him. For a moment at least he feels free of it, alone with himself and with the surrounding emptiness.

Such a mood is always attended by a certain uneasiness, which has little in common with fear. Fear is part of the everyday. To fear is to face the possible loss of something which is taken to matter. Anxiety precludes fear, for in anxiety persons or things that normally claim our attention and care no longer do so. A kind of vertigo seizes the individual. Nothing is stable, nothing offers man a place to stand or a sure sign by which to orient himself. In anxiety displaced man understands his utter insecurity and homelessness.

If anxiety lets man withdraw from his engagement with other things and persons into his own being, it is only this withdrawal which makes it possible for him to assume a position over against the world and to open himself to what is. Only by opening himself to the meaning of nothingness can man gain an understanding of the meaning of Being; only where there is a willingness and the strength to endure anxiety can Being reveal itself. Anxiety opens us to the mystery that there is something rather than nothing. Thus looking at a gnarled tree in the fog, we may for a moment lose the myopic vision of the everyday and understand the meaning of Being.

But what if, instead of hearing the mysterious call of Being, anxiety lets us sense the groundlessness and contingency of our own being and of the being of all things and lets us turn away in nausea? The strength to face anxiety is a strength to face an abyss which threatens all meaning. Where this strength is lacking all that remains is a covering up of anxiety, and, if man is essentially subject to anxiety, this covering up must also be a covering up of man's own being: man turns to average everydayness and discovers here something like a ground. Instead of listening to the voice of nothingness within him, he lets others tell him his place and who he is. He escapes from the burden of having to be himself by escaping to the safety of the "they." It is reassuring to know that one is doing only what everyone is doing. Yet such reassurance is bought at the price of authenticity. To be authentic is to possess oneself as one really is. The covering up of anxiety precludes such possession. And yet, what does man lose when his anxiety is hidden? After all, does one not do what is expected? One has attended the right schools, married the right person, and associates with the right people. One is successful, one is loyal to one's friends, one believes in God. So what is it that has been lost? Nothing! And yet to have lost this nothing is to have lost oneself.

Man's tendency to flee from anxiety forces us to understand inauthenticity as the usual mode of human being. With the attempt to establish everydayness as a foundation inauthenticity triumphs over philosophy.

Heidegger insists that we gain a "primordial" understanding of Dasein only if we understand Dasein as a whole. "If the Interpretation of Dasein's Being is to become primordial, as a foundation for working out the basic question of ontology, then it must first have brought to light existentially the Being of Dasein in its possibilities of *authenticity* and *totality*" (*SZ* 233). Given the guiding thread of "average everydayness" this may well seem an impossible demand. As a being who is always ahead of himself in anticipation, care, and concern, is man not essentially incomplete? "But have we not at the very outset of our Interpretation renounced the possibility of bringing Dasein into view as a whole. Everydayness is precisely that Being which is 'between' birth and death" (*SZ* 233). Is man ever given to himself as a whole? Is he not always confronted by the task of having to be himself and thus incomplete? This openness is constitutive of Dasein. Where this openness has disappeared man can no longer be; he completes himself only in death. In contemplating the possibility of his completeness, man necessarily faces the possibility of his not being. The demand to "bring to light" the being of Dasein in its "totality" forces us thus to understand Dasein as being-towards-death. Anticipating his own death man recognizes himself as a whole and at the same time faces the groundlessness of his being. This last possibility, which cannot be surpassed, reveals the meaning of his being-in-the-world. Not that this meaning is readily accepted. Anxious about anxiety we seek refuge in inauthenticity. We want to forget death. Of course, we cannot but admit that one dies; we know that we, too, shall have to die someday. But not yet; death is still far away, far enough at any rate to permit us to raise some screens to hide this last inescapable possibility, which nobody can take from us, which more than any other reveals to us how inescapably this life is our own, how alone each one of us is in the face of death.

Anxiety can lead man to himself; it can also lead him away from himself. Authenticity and inauthenticity have their ground in anxiety, which confronts man with the possibility of either gaining or losing himself. This twofold possibility should not be interpreted as confronting us with a clear decision, which can settle the matter once and for all. In every situation the authenticity of man's being is at stake. Human existence is essentially caught in the tension between authenticity and inauthenticity. Even when one pole seems to have suppressed the claims of the other, the voice of the latter has not been silenced altogether. We are either tempted to surrender our autonomy and to seek safety in the community and the familiar world or we are called out of the world to that silence we carry within ourselves. We stand between the voices of temptation and conscience, where Heidegger understands conscience as the call with which man calls himself, lost in inauthenticity, back to himself. The call of conscience, as Heidegger analyzes it, is the warning call of man's care for his being.

What does the call of conscience tell the individual? What message does it convey? What indeed can man tell himself? The voice of conscience is silence (SZ 273). This silence does not point to a specific place the individual should occupy, but leads back to the groundlessness of human being, to an acknowledgment of what Heidegger terms guilt, of man's inability to secure his being and his place.

Conscience demands to be heard. Such hearing is more than passive receptivity; it implies a response. Hearing the voice of conscience man can respond by running away, obedient to the call of temptation, or he can summon the strength to place himself under his own truth which calls in conscience. The voice of conscience discloses to man his essential being. The authentic response to such disclosure is the resolve to be oneself in

the face of the essential precariousness and groundlessness of human existence.

Such a view of authentic existence may suggest a heroic nihilism, a faith
in the meaning of life in spite of, or perhaps rather because of a lucid
awareness of the nothingness that governs human existence and that dooms
man and all his projects to establish a secure dwelling place for himself to
certain defeat. Perhaps this attempt to salvage victory from defeat, meaning from nothing, is peculiarly German. *Being and Time* reads in places
as if Heidegger has been inspired by the *Nibelungenlied*, as if its hero
were dark Hagen, who stands beyond good and evil, whose life is shad-
owed by death, who possesses the strength to accept the certainty of defeat, responding to it with an affirmation of the situation into which he
has been cast, and who discovers meaning in this affirmation.

In *Being and Time* Heidegger opposes the lucid awareness of the groundlessness of human existence, which characterizes authenticity, to the flight
to security, which is the mark of inauthenticity. This suggests that philosophy, at least to the extent that it is governed by the search for security,
must be understood as a phenomenon of inauthenticity. One could thus
argue with some plausibility that in *Being and Time* transcendental philosophy deconstructs itself: what started as an attempt to establish man's
place has yielded to a gesturing toward silence.

Such an interpretation, however, fails to do justice to Heidegger's understanding of authenticity. If man exists essentially with others and in the
world, must authentic self-affirmation not include an affirmation of oneself as part of a community and as engaged in the world? Heidegger takes
care to guard against an interpretation of authenticity which would demand that the self withdraw from the world. "Resoluteness, as *authentic
Being-one's-Self*, does not detach Dasein from its world, nor does it isolate
it so that it becomes a free-floating 'I'. And how should it, when resoluteness as authentic disclosedness, is *authentically* nothing else than *Being-in-
the-world?* Resoluteness brings the Self right into its current concernful
Being-alongside what is ready-to-hand, and pushes it into solicitous Being
with Others" (*SZ* 298). But if "idle talk is the kind of Being that belongs
to Being-with-one-another itself" (*SZ* 177), how can we separate inauthenticity and community? The unmediated opposition between authenticity and inauthenticity cannot be maintained. To want to be purely authentic is to be inauthentic in that our essential ties to the community and
the world have been covered up. Authentic being-with-others can only be
understood as an authentic way of taking up inauthenticity. "*Authentic*
existence is not something which floats above falling everydayness; existentially, it is only a modified way in which such everydayness is seized upon"
(*SZ* 179). The call of conscience establishes a distance between the self

and the world, but only to demand that we return to the world and engage ourselves in it. Such engagement, however, demands that we choose our place. But where should man stand? Is one place as good as another? In that case it would not matter what is done as long as it is done authentically. Form would have triumphed over substance. But we cannot settle for such an empty echo of Kantian autonomy. More is at stake in decision. We must choose and choice requires criteria. Given Heidegger's analysis, the authentic individual cannot cease struggling with the question, what is man's place? in spite of the fact that the analysis of guilt implies that there can be no final answer to this question. And yet, to say that there can be no final answer cannot mean that the attempt to find an answer is meaningless and that one answer cannot be recognized to be better than another. But how is such recognition possible?

In *Being and Time* this question receives no adequate answer, even if the analysis of authenticity demands such an answer. The attempt to establish the inherited past as the authority that assigns man his place proves insufficient. The voice of the past is too ambiguous. To meet this insufficiency Heidegger went on to develop his analysis of work, which lets man recollect the meaning of the earth as it establishes the world as an order that assigns him a place he can recognize as his own.[13] Such work is no longer the task of the philosopher. Unable to establish man's place, transcendental philosophy raises a demand that only poetry and myth can answer.

13. Cf. my "Heidegger as a Political Thinker," this volume, p. 304.

6. Ludwig Wittgenstein

On Heidegger on Being and Dread

Monday, December 30, 1929
(at Schlick's)

I CAN READILY THINK what Heidegger means by Being and Dread. Man has
the impulse to run up against the limits of language. Think, for example,
of the astonishment that anything exists. This astonishment cannot be expressed in the form of a question, and there is also no answer to it. Everything which we feel like saying can, a priori, only be nonsense. Nevertheless, we do run up against the limits of language.[1] This running-up against
Kierkegaard also recognized and even designated it in a quite similar way
(as running-up against Paradox).[2] This running-up against the limits of
language is *Ethics*. I hold that it is truly important that one put an end
to all the idle talk about Ethics—whether there be knowledge, whether

This text, "Zu Heidegger," is taken from *Ludwig Wittgenstein und der Wiener
Kreis: Gespräche, aufgezeichnet von Friedrich Waismann*, ed. B. F. McGuinness
(Frankfurt am Main, 1967), pp. 68–9, with the permission of Basil Blackwell. Trans-
lation by Michael Murray. Some of the commentary first appeared in "A Note on
Wittgenstein and Heidegger," *Philosophical Review* 80 (October, 1974), included
with permission of the editor.

1. See *Tractatus* 5.6, 5.62, 6.45, and "Lecture on Ethics," passim. (Footnotes to this
text are the editor's, and rely in part on those of B. F. McGuinness.)

2. See Kierkegaard, *Philosophical Fragments*, trans. D. Swenson and H. V. Hong
(Princeton, N.J., 1967). "But what is this unknown something with which the Reason
collides when inspired by its paradoxical passion . . .?" (p. 49). "[It is] the unknown.
. . . It is the limit to which the Reason repeatedly comes. . ." (p. 55). Note that
Kierkegaard's *The Concept of Dread* (1844) is the only significant philosophical
writing on Dread before Heidegger's *Being and Time*.

there be values, whether the Good can be defined, etc. In Ethics one is always making the attempt to say something that does not concern the essence of the matter and never can concern it. It is a priori certain that whatever one might offer as a definition of the Good, it is always simply a misunderstanding to think that it corresponds in expression to the authentic matter one actually means (Moore).[3] Yet the tendency represented by the running-up against *points to something.* St. Augustine already knew this when he said: What, you wretch, so you want to avoid talking nonsense? Talk some nonsense, it makes no difference! [4]

EDITOR'S COMMENTARY

This little known text was preserved thanks to the notebooks of Friedrich Waismann. In January, 1965, the editors of the *Philosophical Review*, with the approval of Wittgenstein's literary executors, published a truncated version of the original, along with an English translation by Max Black.[5] The passage was printed as a sequel to the English text of Wittgenstein's unpublished "Lecture on Ethics" written between September, 1929 and December, 1930. For reasons never explained the title of the Waismann entry—ON HEIDEGGER—as well as the key opening sentence, which announces Wittgenstein's discussion as provoked by a basic thought of Heidegger, were deleted from the original and omitted from the translation. Moreover, in this conversation, in the midst of the Vienna Circle, Wittgenstein claims to have understood and even agreed with that thought. In all probability Wittgenstein was referring to Heidegger's well-known inaugural lecture "What Is Metaphysics?" (1929).[6] But ever since Carnap's equally famous paper on "The Overcoming of Metaphysics" (1931) became the canonical refutation, Heidegger's lecture has provided

---

3. The exact wording is uncertain, though its sense is clear. He refers to Moore's *Principia Ethica* (Cambridge, 1903), §§5–14.

4. According to McGuinness, this was a favorite quotation of Wittgenstein's. Although the exact passage has not been found, he suggests *Confessions* I, iv: "*et vae tacentibus de te, quoniam loquaces muti sunt.*"

5. Vol. 74 : 3–27.

6. Delivered at the University of Freiburg, in July, and published by Friedrich Cohen (Bonn, 1929). English translation by R. F. C. Hull and Alan Crick in *Existence and Being*, ed. Werner Brock (Chicago, 1949). References are to the English translation, followed by the pages of the German text reprinted in *Wegmarken* (Frankfurt am Main, 1967). In his edition of the Waismann papers McGuinness refers this allusion to *Being and Time* (1927), pp. 186–87: "*That in the face of which one has Dread (Angst) is Being-in-the-world as such. What is the phenomenal difference between that in the face of which Dread dreads and that in the face of which fear is afraid? That in the face of which one has Dread is not any thing within the world. . . . The world as such is that in the face of which one has Dread.*" While this text is certainly relevant to Wittgenstein's remark, and to the subsequent ones on the limits of language (cf. the tractarian notion that the limits of my language are the limits of

many analytical philosophers with a supposed paradigm of the worst.[7] Perhaps this was sufficient reason for someone to sanitize the Wittgenstein text before publication. In any case, Wittgenstein's affinity for the Heidegger text would be less surprising, if we did not have the incomplete and one-sided account of Wittgenstein's work given by some Anglo-American interpreters.[8]

To some extent, of course, what Wittgenstein says in the passage is related to some propositions in the *Tractatus* (see 6.421, 6.44, 6.45), those whose significance Russell and Carnap never understood. More germane, though, is the roughly contemporary "Lecture on Ethics," which elucidates an experience very near to the one described by Heidegger:

> I believe the best way of describing [this experience] is to say that when I have it I wonder at the existence of the world. And I am then inclined to use such phrases as "how extraordinary that anything should exist" or "how extraordinary that the world should exist." [p. 8]

By 1929 Heidegger's preoccupation with the question of the meaning of Being is well known. In "What Is Metaphysics?" he expands the earlier analysis of Dread as Dread in the face of being-in-the-world—its meaning for fundamental ontology—into an ontological mood in which the Nothing that veils Being is revealed:

> Dread reveals Nothing. [p. 336/9]

> Nothing is neither an object nor anything that "is" at all. Nothing occurs neither by itself nor "apart from" what is, as a sort of adjunct. . . . It is in the Being (*Sein*) of what is that the nihilation of Nothing (*das Nichten des Nichts*) occurs. [p. 340/12]

> Only in the clear night of Dread's Nothingness is what-is as such revealed in all its original overtness: that it "is" and is not Nothing. [p. 339/11]

At the end of the lecture, Heidegger formulates what he regards as the most basic question of thought, "Why is there something and not rather Nothing?", one he repeats in the companion essay "On the Essence of

my world), it does not explain the precise relation between Dread (*Angst*) and Being (*Sein*). This problem was taken up directly in the lecture, and a second, closely affiliated text, *On the Essence of Reasons*, published in the same year in the *Jahrbuch für Philosophie und phänomenologische Forschung*, and separately by Max Niemeyer, (Halle). Bilingual edition, trans. T. Mallick (Evanston, 1969).

7. See A. J. Ayer, *Language, Truth and Logic* (London, 1936), pp. 43–44; W. V. O. Quine, *Word and Object* (Cambridge, Mass., 1960), p. 133; and George Pitcher, *The Philosophy of Wittgenstein* (Englewood Cliffs, N.J., 1964), pp. 201–03. All of these writers borrow their knowledge of Heidegger from Carnap.

8. For a forceful criticism of this account, see Allan Janik and Stephen Toulmin, *Wittgenstein's Vienna* (New York, 1973).

Reasons." In this Why there lies an implicit preconceptual, prior understanding of Being.[9] In the years following Heidegger develops this question at length in the *Introduction to Metaphysics*. Finally in a 1943 postscript to the original "What Is Metaphysics?" Heidegger declares:

> Man alone of all beings, when addressed by the voice of Being, experiences
> the marvel of all marvels: that what-is *is* . . . The clear courage for essential
> Dread guarantees that most mysterious of all possibilities: the experience of
> Being. [p. 335/103]

Both Wittgenstein and Heidegger insist that statements about Being
(Nothing) or the Good can make no sense on the purely logical, natural,
or ontic plane, and that such statements must therefore register as "nonsense," a "misuse of our language" ("Lecture on Ethics," pp. 8–9); "nonsensical" or at odds with "logic" ("What Is Metaphysics?" pp. 330–31,
356–57). Wittgenstein argues that the experience of Being cannot be formulated into a question, let alone answered. Heidegger seems to be saying
something similar when he suggests that this experience is precipitated by
special moods like dread, radical boredom, or joy. To be sure, Heidegger
expressly identifies the unique form of the question. But he insists that the
question is not answerable in the standard way—by appealing to some reason, cause, or being, even a highest being, as Leibniz does—and in this
sense Heidegger himself suggests the question cannot be answered.

For Heidegger, this basic ontological question, properly set forth, corresponds to Wittgenstein's astonishment at the world. Though Wittgenstein rejects a formulating of the question, he does say with Heidegger
that what one tries to say here is of the greatest importance: it is "what
is valuable," "what is really important," "the meaning of life" ("Lecture
on Ethics," p. 5) or "the revelation of what-is" ("What Is Metaphysics?"),
"the burning center of all questioning," and the happening of history on
which man's destiny depends.[10] At times Heidegger draws the distinction
between Being and beings as dramatically sharp as Wittgenstein does that
between value and fact, yet Heidegger rejects the value/fact bifurcation
as produced under the spell of traditional ontology. He seeks to transcend
it by rethinking the modes of the Being of things in the context of human
concerns and by exploring the possibilities of innovative speech. Wittgenstein, we could say, appreciated what the failure to speak Being *pointed to*
but he preferred the austere silence of letting it be contained as the unsaid
is contained in the said.[11]

9. *The Essence of Reasons*, pp. 114–15.
10. *An Introduction to Metaphysics*, trans. Ralph Manheim (New Haven, 1959),
pp. 42, 93, 143 (*Einführung in die Metaphysik* [Tübingen, 1953], pp. 82–93).
11. For Wittgenstein's views on what art might accomplish, see *Wittgenstein's
Vienna*, pp. 175, 191–97, and Paul Engelmann, *Letters from Ludwig Wittgenstein,
with a Memoir*, ed. B. F. McGuinness, trans. L. Furtmüller (Oxford, 1967).

7. Otto Pöggeler

Being as Appropriation

PART ONE

Being and Time

HEIDEGGER, in *Being and Time*, takes up Plato's question of what the expression "being" [*seiend*] actually means. In fact, he sees himself forced, first of all, to reawaken an understanding of the question of the meaning of Being (*SZ* 1 [1]). This question must be understood if one is to inquire after the Being of beings and the modes in which Being becomes materialized in other than a naive and short-sighted manner. "And precisely the ontological task of a nondeductive, constructive genealogy of the various possible modes of Being requires a preunderstanding of that which we actually mean by this expression: 'Being' " (*SZ* 11). The question of Being [*die Seinsfrage*] is not the "concern of a free-floating speculation on the most general generalities," but rather, is both the most fundamental question and the most concrete. If ontological research does not wish to remain suspended without a foundation, it must presuppose a clarification of this basic question (*SZ* 8ff.).

While the question of the meaning of Being still occupied a central position in the investigations of Plato and Aristotle, it was later forgotten. Being is held to be the most general and most empty concept and thus, an undefinable but yet self-evident concept. "Thus, that which, as something hidden, drove the philosophizing of the ancients to, and kept in, restless activity thereby achieved a crystal-clear self-evidence, such that whoever now asks about it [i.e., *die Seinsfrage*] is charged with a methodological error" (*SZ* 2). How did this come about?

Translated by Rüdiger H. Grimm in *Philosophy Today* [Celina, Ohio 45822] 19 (Summer, 1975) from "Sein als Ereignis," *Zeitschrift für philosophische Forschung* 13 (1959), omitting the introductory discussion. Reprinted with permission of the author and the editor.

1. SZ refers to the 7th ed. of *Sein und Zeit* (Tübingen, 1953) and the corresponding marginal pagination of *Being and Time*, translated by John Macquarrie and Edward Robinson (New York, 1962).

Metaphysics asks: what is Being? It inquires after the Being of beings. It orients itself toward the beings which it finds in the "world" and can thus represent them. Metaphysical thinking is, from the very beginning, representational [*vorstellendes*] thinking. It therefore has the temporal structure of a pure making-something-present." Beings, understood as that which actually is, are interpreted in terms of presence, "i.e. they are conceived as presence (οὐσία)" (*SZ* 26).

If the Being of beings is grasped as presence, it is understood with respect to a specific mode of time, the present (*SZ* 25). Metaphysics, however, does not further pursue the problem hidden in the fact that Being as presence is always already understood within the horizon of time. Metaphysics does not inquire after Being as such, but rather, forgets and disguises the whole question of Being. Even though Being, as presence, is, in a still hidden manner, thought in the light of time, ontology from its earliest beginnings seems to focus all its efforts on the attempt to keep the primordial characteristics of time out of consideration. Ontology supersedes time or levels it off to static time, i.e., eternity. The meaning of Being is then determined on the basis of this "frozen" time, but in such a way that this meaning is never considered by itself. Thus, the Being-question as the question of the meaning of Being itself never really becomes a problem. When Heidegger inquires after Being and time, he raises the question of Being itself. The delineation of the meaning of Being is no longer to be merely presupposed, but must be thought through in itself. In contrast to this, when Being in metaphysics is understood as presence, the temporal moment remains simply in the present and thus the meaning of Being remains that which is always left unthought.

With the question concerning Being and time, Heidegger addresses to metaphysics the decisive question: Is it possible or not to go behind the presupposed understanding of Being? Have metaphysics and its central discipline, the doctrine of Being, i.e., ontology, even gotten to their own ground if they presuppose that Being must be grasped as presence? If the answer is no, how is time to be thought of within a "fundamental ontological" investigation, if presence itself is to be thought of from the horizon of time? How is time, within whose horizon the meaning of Being is delineated, to be thought? When Heidegger speaks of Being and time, time does not mean something which stands alongside Being, which perhaps must be superseded if Being itself is to be expressed. Being and time are rather so intertwined that one can be understood on the basis of the other. Neither does time mean that time alongside of which space is situated, but rather, that primordial movement to which even space belongs, a movement which, as Being itself, releases beings from out of itself. That time which is meant in the title of *Being and Time* cannot be understood on the basis of traditional metaphysical thinking at all. Time has a fundamental ontological function in metaphysics, to be sure, since Being is understood, in a hidden manner, as presence from a temporal horizon. Yet, metaphysics obtains no knowledge or understanding of this ontological function, and has no insight into the ground of the possibility of this function. "On the contrary: Time itself is taken as a being among other beings, and the attempt is made to grasp time in its Being-structure within the horizon of that inexpressibly naive understanding of Being which is itself oriented toward time" (*SZ* 26). What time is, is read off from those beings which are themselves in time. In this manner, time itself is naturally not thought of in its Being.

Since Heidegger inquires after Being and time, he must show, in contrast to that manner in which the concept of time plays a role in traditional ontology, "that and how the central problematic of all ontology is rooted in the phenomenon of time, provided it be correctly viewed and correctly made explicit." He must critically detach himself from the traditional concept of time "which has persisted from Aristotle to Bergson, and even later" (*SZ* 18). Proceeding from the problematic of temporality, Heidegger raises Western metaphysics anew as something concerning which a decision must be made. The second part of *Being and Time*, which was planned but never published, was to have given the "principle characteristics of a phenomenological destruction of the history of ontology on the basis of the problematic of temporality." Heidegger had wanted to go back beyond Kant and Descartes to Aristotle, whose treatise on time was to have been treated as "a way of discriminating the phenomenal basis and the limits of ancient ontology" (*SZ* 39ff.).

How can the problematic of "Being and time"—that which is left unthought by metaphysics—be taken up? How can time be primordially intertwined with Being? Being is always the Being of beings and for this reason, the formulation of the question of *Being and Time* can be found via an explanation which interprets beings with respect to time. If Being is to be thought as fundamentally interconnected with time, then time must show itself when the Being of beings is questioned. Among the beings in question, one being assumes a privileged position: Dasein. By Dasein, Heidegger understands man as the "there," i.e., as the place of the disclosure of Being. It is Dasein which raises the question of Being. Therefore, Dasein which raises the question, must be disclosed in its Being if the question of Being itself is to become transparent. Dasein can ask about Being because it is distinct from other beings in that, in its Being, Dasein is concerned about this very Being. Since the essence of Dasein lies in "ek-sistence," in its being-able-to-be [*Sein-können*], understanding Being is a characteristic of the Being of Dasein. Thus, Dasein has not only an ontic priority—as being among beings—but also an ontological priority: Dasein is in itself ontological: it has an understanding of Being. This does not mean, to be sure, that Dasein immediately develops an ontology as a questioning after Being which is simply transparent to itself. Dasein's being-ontological is at first merely a preontological, unclear, and unconceptualized understanding of Being. However, Dasein not only understands itself in its Being, but also the Being of beings which are unlike Dasein. The soul of man, as metaphysical tradition says, is in a certain sense everything that is. Thus, Dasein becomes the ontico-ontological condition for the possibility of all ontologies (*SZ* 11ff.).

Dasein, as a privileged being, must first of all be explained in its Being, if ontology, the science of Being, is once more to be raised as a problem, and if access is to be gained to the question of Being and time. The Being of Dasein must show itself as primordial temporality in order that on the basis of the temporality of Dasein, that time, in whose light the meaning of Being comes to be determined, can be thought. That is why Heidegger, during the summer semester of 1923, entitles a lecture course "Ontology or Hermeneutics of Facticity," and the analytic of Dasein becomes for him the way to determine the meaning of Being. Heidegger forces into harmony here the metaphysical tradition, which thinks Being in a hidden manner in the light of time, and a nonmetaphysical and antimetaphysical tradition, which brings the temporality and historicity of man's factical ek-sistence into view. Or more precisely, Heidegger's thinking proceeds from that utmost tension which is indicated by the titles *Ontology or Hermeneutics of Facticity* and *Being and Time*. Since one was unable to relive the tension of this course of thought in the way that Heidegger did, his thinking was misunderstood on the one hand as a traditional, static ontology, and on the other hand as a historicism radicalized into an existentialism.

Since Heidegger poses the question of Being on the basis of man's understanding of Being, he, in a certain sense, led to transcendental philosophy. Husserl had radicalized phenomenology into a doctrine of transcendental constitution, and Heidegger places himself in the context of this school of thought. Husserl had attempted to open up for philosophical investigation that region of primordial origins in which the constitution of every being occurs. *Being and Time* is dedicated to Husserl: Heidegger takes over Husserl's orientation toward questions of origin, and in his analytic of Dasein inquires after the mode of Being of that transcendental ego which carries out the constitution of beings [*des Seienden*]. He grants Dilthey, as well as Husserl and Scheler that they, indeed, no longer grasp the person as something "thing-like", or as a substantial entity. And yet, Heidegger says, the actual mode of Being of the person has not yet been made properly clear and has always been covered up time and again by the traditional anthropological determinations (*SZ* 46ff.). Such determinations remain oriented within the traditional and inadequate conception of Being, even then and precisely then, when the person is no longer "reified" as a mere thing and is determined directly through "nothingness." The question of the mode of Being of that being "in which 'world' becomes constituted," is, as Heidegger wrote to Husserl, the central problem of *Being and Time*. "It must be shown that the mode of Being characteristic of human Dasein is totally different from that of all other beings, and that precisely this mode of Being, such as it is, contains the possibility of transcendental constitution." Heidegger's transcendental ego, however, is not the *cogito* of Descartes and not the pure consciousness of Husserl. Rather, it is "ek-sistence" taken as the essence of Dasein and characterized by Being-in-the-world, care, finitude, temporality, and historicity. "Transcendental constitution is a central possibility of the ek-sistence of the factical Self. . . ." [2]

In the *cogito sum,* the mode of Being of the *sum* must again become problematic, if the meaning of Being is to be successfully determined as no longer oriented toward "thing" and "substance." On the other hand, the mode of Being of the *sum* cannot be properly determined without a deepened determination of the meaning of Being. On the one hand Heidegger's "ontology" must not be understood on the basis of the pre-Kantian ontology, which was oriented toward things, but from the critical, transcendental-philosophical point of departure; on the other hand, Heidegger's transcendental philosophy is oriented from the very beginning toward that Being which supersedes beings to such an extent that it is "transcendence per se." Heidegger thus uses the term "transcendental philosophy" not only in Kant's sense, but also in the sense of the scholastic doctrine of transcendentals (*SZ* 38). In his Kant book (1929), he treats Kant's transcendental philosophy as metaphysics, i.e., ontology. He attempts to show, in the same sense in which he formulated the problematic of *Being and Time,* that the foundation of transcendental philosophy collapses and the abyss of metaphysics becomes revealed when the I think of the transcendental ego is seen in its primordial relationship to time. Thus, that which was left unthought by metaphysics is now finally allowed expression.

The fundamental ontology of *Being and Time* is concerned with that which metaphysics has left unthought and thus, with the ground [*Grund*] and the abyss [*Abgrund*] of all metaphysics and ontology. The structure of the first part of this work is determined by the attempt to tear thought away from its orientation toward things and to lead it back to its ownmost self and its temporality so that, through the clarification of transcendental constitution, it becomes possible to give a determination of the meaning of Being. In the first chapter, the basic structures of Dasein are outlined. Here it becomes clear also, why traditional and, in particular, our everyday thinking is oriented toward things that are present-at-hand. The sec-

2. See Walter Biemel, "Husserls Encyclopedias Brittanica Artikel und Heideggers Anmerkungen dazu," in *Tijdsschrift voor Filosophie*, 12 (Leuven/Utrecht, 1950), pp. 246ff.; see especially p. 274.

ond chapter shows that ek-sistence, in its essence, is temporal and historical, and thus makes transcendental constitution possible. In the third section, which was not published then, the temporality of Dasein, as that
being which understands Being, was to have been treated as the transcendental horizon of the question of Being, so that within this horizon, the
determination of the meaning of Being which was the main issue of these
investigations would have been made possible, and thus ontology would
have been brought back to its ground, i.e., its foundation, which had been
up to that point left unthought.

Since thought is placed in a primordial relationship to temporality and
historicity, this investigation can reach a ground only there, where it always already is, i.e., in history. Since there can be no radically new beginning on the basis of "the things themselves" (as Husserl had required),
Heidegger himself introduces the destruction of metaphysics, the return
to the primordially historical, into phenomenology. There can be no systematic presentation apart from such a destruction. Therefore, Heidegger
adds to the first, more systematic section of *Being and Time* a second,
more historical section. Yet, the basic issue here is not the juxtaposition of
the two sections, but rather their interdependence. The first section is
permeated with "historical" references; the second is concerned with a
"systematic" task.

I would like to attempt to establish the point of departure of *Being and
Time* somewhat more precisely by means of a few more references to the
published portion. The first section of this work gives a "preliminary
analysis of the fundamental characteristics of Dasein." The fundamental
structure of Dasein is described as Being-in-the-world. This structure is
then examined according to its various moments, and finally grasped in
its unity as care. Dasein is not to be thought of as a worldless subject,
from which (at least since Descartes) the attempt had to be made repeatedly to bridge the gap between it and the "world." Dasein, as Being-
in-the-world, is always already alongside of things. While Husserl's constitutive phenomenology attempted to clear the way to an absolute,
all-constituting ego, Heidegger posits, as the essence of man, the "there"
of that Being which makes human being possible in such a manner that
it always already places man in the totality of beings, as oriented toward
things. Phenomenological constitution is made possible by means of a
Being which is not at our disposal. Thus, phenomenology becomes ontology for Heidegger. Ontology no longer furnishes merely the guidelines
for phenomenological constitution, and no longer merely precedes phenomenology, as in Husserl. Phenomenology rather refers to the method,
whereas ontology designates the content of one and the same enterprise.

The tendency of metaphysics to trace everything back to an ultimate
ground is once more realized in Husserl. In the modern era, this ground
has been found in an unconditioned subjectivity. Heidegger breaks this

"will" toward an unconditioned subjectivity. Being, which is not at our disposal, places man into the totality of all beings, but in such a way that man comports himself to beings as beings, and thus is the clearing, the "there" of Being. The fact that Being is not at our disposal holds sway over man as his "dispositionality" [*Befindlichkeit*]. This reveals the fact that man finds himself [*sich befindet*] within the totality of all beings. This "dispositionality" also opens up access to nature thought of in a primordial manner or, as Heidegger later says, the "earth." The Self is understanding determined by mood, and not pure consciousness. The point of departure from pure consciousness stems from an unsurmounted Cartesian dualism; it cannot be completed by a consideration of man's "bodiliness" since man is neither body and soul, nor mind as a synthesis of both, but rather the factical Self. "The one-sided observations of somatology and pure psychology," observes Heidegger with regard to Husserl,[3] "are possible only by reason of the concrete whole of man which, as such, initially determines his mode of Being." Heidegger is concerned with the concrete wholeness of man when he determines Dasein as factical ek-sistence, as the unity of thrownness and project, or of moodedness and understanding. Dasein is just as little a worldless "I" or a pure consciousness as it is an isolated individual. Rather, it is always already with others, and even arises primarily in the "Anyone" [*das Man*].

Dasein is, however, not alongside of things and with other people in the sense that it conceives of them in a purely theoretical attitude as abstract entities, merely present-at-hand. Rather, everything is bound to a "for-the-sake-of-which" made possible by Dasein's being-able-to-Be. Thus, things are not primarily presented in the temporal mode of presence characteristic of what is present-at-hand, but enter into a more primordially thought temporal design [*Zeitspielraum*]. Being is no longer revealed by the *intuitus*, which is oriented toward seeing and directed toward the being-present of what is present-at-hand, nor even by Husserl's *intentio*, but by care. The intentional relationship becomes rooted in that achievement of Dasein which is concerned with the "meaningfulness" of things, and which thus is always factical. That which is in the world is, philosophically, not first discovered in its pure potentialities, in order afterwards to receive back its factical being in a colorless and totally empty realization. Rather, facticity—which is irreducibly unique and historical, and thus cannot be converted into an idea—has already entered into the world. Heidegger's historical conception of world is oriented toward the New Testament, toward Augustine and Dilthey, but not toward the Greek conception of the cosmos. Heidegger accuses the ontological tradition (which originated from Greek thought) of having passed over the

3. Ibid., p. 279.

phenomenon of the world—and explicitly in Parmenides—even at its very beginning and of continuing to pass it by (*BT* 100). In place of the un-recognized world-phenomenon, a distinct region of eternal entities arose. For this reason, "even the relationship to the world, in the sense of a dis-tinct comportment to this being, was interpreted as νοεῖν, as intuitus, as no-longer mediated perception or reason." [4] Heidegger wishes to turn this tradition of thought back to a more primordial experience when, in *Being and Time*, he begins with a clarification of the structure of Being-in-the-world.

The analysis of Dasein, furthermore, lets one grasp why the traditional understanding of Being is governed by an inadequate ontology of what is present-at-hand (*SZ* 130) and a logic (*SZ* 129) that is grounded therein. Because Dasein is Being-in-the-world, it is "proximally and for the most part fascinated by its world" (*SZ* 113). In this manner, Dasein does not take the world as such into view. Because it is a characteristic of Dasein that it is thrown in among beings it remains, as long as it is, "being thrown." It is cast into the swirl of that inauthentic understanding of Be-ing which arises from having fallen prey to beings. The constant danger of fallenness belongs to Dasein, which as Being-in-the-world is "in itself tempting" (*SZ* 177). As Being-in-the-world, Dasein not only falls prey to beings, but even understands itself on the basis of thinglike beings; it lifts these beings out of their movement and the ever-changing relationship to itself; it assures itself of them by going beyond things which are present and merely present-at-hand, to something eternally present and always present-at-hand. When Heidegger speaks of presence-at-hand, he does not wish to discuss primarily the question of the reality or the "independence from consciousness" of things, but rather, to point out that sudden change-over by which the original relationship to things becomes a mere seeing of something merely present-at-hand. This changeover is not only facti-cally present in our knowledge; it is the ideal of our traditional concep-tion of knowledge. "The idea of the *intuitus* has guided all interpretations of knowledge from the beginnings of Greek ontology until today, whether or not that *intuitus* can be factically reached" (*SZ* 358). Thus, since Descartes, mathematical thinking has been given a priority, because thinking was always oriented toward the eternally present. Mathematics, however, is concerned with that which is always present, always remains, and outlasts all change. And it is precisely mathematics which reveals the all-leveling changeover from our primordial relationship to things to a mere "presence-at-hand" in its final radicality (*SZ* 96).

It is precisely because Heidegger retrieves ek-sistence from fallenness that he can primordially unveil the temporality of ek-sistence. The second

---

4. *Vom Wesen des Grundes*, 4th ed. (Frankfurt, 1955), p. 41; *The Essence of Reasons*, trans. Terrence Malick (Evanston, Ill., 1969), p. 94.

section of *Being and Time* shows that the "essence," i.e., the ontological meaning, of Dasein lies in temporality, and that care as the articulated structural totality of the Being of Dasein is to be understood in terms of temporality. The result is a deeper understanding of the fact that Dasein is tempted to fall a prey to being, and thereby to become inauthentic. Inauthentic thought and behavior are oriented toward that which is in time, and in this manner are set in opposition to authentic thinking and behavior, which grasp themselves as the temporalization of time. The determination of Dasein in terms of temporality expresses a decision in regard to the metaphysical concept of time. This conception of time ultimately remains oriented toward that which is in time, and thus fails to grasp primordial temporality, the temporalization of time itself. Primordial temporality is historicity. Still, the temporality of the "common" conception of time; which is oriented toward what is in time, is equiprimordial with historicity and is, in a sense, thereby justified (*SZ* 377). Dasein, as the temporalization of time and thus as transcendental constitution, is only historical and world-founding insofar as it (as factical ek-sistence) is already in the world alongside beings that are in time. Everydayness and inauthenticity cannot simply, once and for all, be left behind. Dasein can only be authentic when it continually tears itself away from inauthenticity, which thus is always already presupposed.

The unfolding of the temporality of Dasein into the equiprimordial structures of historicity and inner-temporalizing shows the ontological direction of the analysis of Dasein, whose goal it is to reveal temporality as the horizon of the understanding of Being, and to gain a victory over the metaphysical understanding of Being. Yet even the analyses of the second section, such as those of death and conscience, which at first seem to be solely an ek-sistential appeal, serve primarily an ontological purpose, provided they are properly understood. They sharpen the insight that Dasein, as factical ek-sistence, is temporality rooted in moodedness or thrown project [*geworfener Entwurf*]. As understanding or as being-able-to-Be, Dasein is possibility, but it is authentically this possibility only when it constantly anticipates the utmost unsurpassable possibility. This utmost possibility is death. To die—"i.e., to feel death as present (Luther)"—deepens that possibility which Dasein is, to the utmost possibility which is boundless impossibility, namely, the impossibility of each and every mode of ek-sisting as a determinate being-able-to-be. That possibility which Dasein, as being-able-to-be, is springs from an ultimate impossibility of anticipating this utmost possibility as an anticipation of an ultmate impossibility, in that it gives Dasein to understand that it is "guilty."

Being guilty does not mean here the incurring of moral guilt but, quite formally, "being the ground of a negativity." With regard to its first aspect, this negativity arises from the fact that Dasein has not laid its own foundation, which is its thrownness, but must nevertheless accept this thrownness. Through the acceptance of this thrownness, Dasein must itself become this foundation, which yet is not Dasein itself but which Dasein must rather always first let be given to itself. It "has been released from its basis, not through itself but to itself, so as to be as this basis" (*BT* 284f.). When Dasein, as the understanding of Being, resolutely brings itself before Being, the access to Being shows itself as determined by a "not." Dasein is powerless before Being. Dasein is always already in debt to Being because Being proves itself to be the condition for the fact that Dasein is. This having-to-go-into-debt of Dasein appears in Heidegger's later works in a new fashion, as thinking is brought into a relatedness with thanks and thanksgiving. In *Being and Time* the concept of guilt does not, therefore, accentuate a "dark aspect" of Dasein, but is much more part of the attempt to find an ultimate foundation for thinking, as was attempted by Schelling in a similar, though metaphysically speculative, fashion. Schelling, after his *Investigations concerning the Essence of Human Freedom* thought he could go beyond Hegel's metaphysics by means of a more deeply laid foundation for metaphysics.

Yet, being-guilty as the basis of a negativity still has a second aspect, and Heidegger's analysis derives this aspect, too, from that type of thinking which the late Schelling attempted to develop under the heading of "positive philosophy." Dasein is not nugatory merely as a result in its concrete project insofar as this project is a distinct choice, which may choose one thing only while, at the same time, having to give up something else. Thrownness has always already marked off a region of possible choices. Dasein discovers its factical possibilities in resoluteness, and thereby its Being-in-position as a Being-in-a-position, i.e., as situation. Resolute ek-sistence is certain of its own truth only insofar as it takes note of the "situational" character of this truth. Ek-sistence should not become frozen in one determinate situation, but must leave itself free for a possible taking-back or a resolute repetition. The truth, in which ek-sistence stands, is thus always "located." Its light streams into the openness of a "there," which is distinguished by a situation, and therefore also by temporality and historicity. Being gives itself only into a bounded openness, and is to this extent characterized by a "not" [*Nicht*]. This limitation cannot be overcome by a speculative metaphysics of history.

The ontological aim of *Being and Time* is obvious throughout. This goal leaps into view if one casts only a first, superficial glance (and this, of course, without some sort of self-induced blindness) at the basic concepts, inasmuch as they are characteristic of Heidegger on the one hand, and of the metaphysical tradition on the other. In Heidegger, a radical isolation takes place which leads to an always factical ek-sistence. (This ek-sistence need not be a single individual, but may also be a community.) Within the metaphysical tradition, on the other hand, facticity is seen as mere realization. The irreplaceability of each Dasein does not come into view, and the situation, as historical localization, is left unconsidered. Metaphysics does not orient itself toward the openness of the future as a tensely drawn possibility, which arises out of an utmost impossibility, but rather toward "reality," which then is transcended toward a compelling, eternal necessity. If no eternal soul substance can be found in the Self, there is certainly still a pure subjectivity which remains constantly present-at-hand through all changes from subject to subject. The constant unrest in the being-able-to-Be of man's ek-sistence is stilled. Eternity, as continuously abiding presence, takes the place of temporality and historicity. Thus, in the search for something eternally certain and perpetually present-at-hand, which one can cling to, all sense of being threatened is left behind. Thinking steps out of primal uncanniness and makes itself at home in something eternally present-at-hand. Man's resting in this eternity overcomes all being-guilty and all negativity. Finitude enters into an endless being-with-itself.

Heidegger's exposition of the basic concepts of metaphysics finally focuses on the question of whether or not Being can be understood as continuous presence. Does not an understanding of Being which grasps Being as continuous presence shrink back from the actual task at hand, namely that of bringing the temporal character of this presence to expression? These questions were to have been worked out in the third and unpublished section of *Being and Time,* which had as its task the "explication of time as the transcendental horizon for the question of Being." The fact that Heidegger increasingly put off matters until they could be treated in this section and in the investigations which were to follow it indicates to what a great extent the whole work was directed toward this section. Thus, the discussion of the forgetting of the world by Western thought (100), the new determination of logos (160), the fuller development of the idea of phenomenology (357), ontology (230), and science (357), and the discussion of the problem of language are all postponed for later treatment. The "as" in "taking-something-as-something" and therewith presence-at-hand and readiness-to-hand are to be later clarified (333, 351, 360, 366, 436f.); everydayness is to be more deeply understood (372); the relationship of space and time worked out anew (368); and the question of how time has its own mode of Being is to be answered (406). The whole ek-sistential analysis demands a "renewed recapitulation within the framework of a fundamental discussion of the concept of Being" (333, 436). The published portion of *Being and Time* therefore quite concretely fails to hit the mark. For this reason, Heidegger states quite explicitly at the end of the published portion that what he has done is only a way, i.e., a way toward working out of the question of Being.

The working out of the question of Being is the attempt to inquire into the meaning of Being as such, whose characterization remains simply an unthought presupposition of metaphysics. In the introduction to *Being and Time*, Heidegger explicitly gives an "exposition of the question of the meaning of Being." All questioning, he says there, asks about something, namely, that which is asked about [*das Gefragte*]. It inquires after that which is asked about in that it asks something. It has in addition that which is interrogated [*das Befragte*]. That which is asked about is determined by that which is interrogated and is directed toward that which is to be found out by the asking [*das Erfragte*]. "Furthermore, in what is asked about there lies also that which is to be found out by asking; this is what is really intended" (*SZ* 5). In the question of Being, that which is asked about is Being. That which is interrogated are beings, and among these beings, one being, i.e., Dasein, in particular. That which is to be found out by the asking is the meaning of Being. The published portion of *Being and Time* gives an analysis of that which is interrogated, i.e., Dasein, but purely for the sake of that which is asked about, i.e., Being. Nevertheless, the investigation does not reach that which is to be found out by the asking, i.e., the meaning of Being. Thus, the investigation fails to reach its goal and is prematurely broken off.

This is not to say that the investigation was not leading up to that goal. To be sure, Heidegger does not ask about some Being-in-itself beyond the world—for in this case, Being would simply be a determinate being once more—but asks rather about the meaning of Being, and thus, he asks the question of how Being is revealed to man. To ask the question concerning the meaning of Being means to ask about a possible understanding of Being. "Meaning is that wherein the intelligibility of something maintains itself" (*SZ* 151). The meaning of Being means that horizon of understanding in which Being is revealed (not, however, an "ultimate meaning of Being"). Within this horizon, Being enters that primordially thought truth which Heidegger calls nonconcealment. Being—not beings—is only "insofar as truth is" (*BT* 230). Being "is" as truth, as the openness and intelligibility of beings, as that clearing in which beings may appear. The meaning, i.e., the truth and openness of Being, "is" only in the *Da* [i.e., there] of Dasein, which is nothing other than a realm of openness. The question of the meaning of Being and the question concerning Dasein's being-understanding aim, even though from different directions, at the same central point, in which the meaning of Being and Dasein's being-understanding are one. "But to lay bare the horizon within which something like Being in general becomes intelligible, is tantamount to clarifying

the possibility of having any understanding of Being at all—an understanding which itself belongs to the constitution of the being called Dasein"
(SZ 231).

The clarification of the understanding of Being is carried out in the
published portion of *Being and Time*. The Being of a being, i.e., the
meaning of the Being of Dasein, is determined so that Dasein may show
itself to be the place of the truth of Being, as the one who understands
the meaning of Being. Since Heidegger grasps Dasein primordially as the
temporalization of time, authentic ek-sistence is revealed as that place in
which Being can be temporal. Time is thus able to disclose itself as the
horizon for any and every understanding of Being. "The projection of
the meaning of Being in general can be carried out within the horizon of
time" (SZ 235). *Being and Time*, taken in its basic intention, aims at this
turning point in which the thinking of the temporality of Dasein enters
into time as openness, as the meaning or truth of Being. Yet precisely
there where Heidegger finished his preparations and arrived at his ownmost formulation of the question, he lacked the appropriate language in
which to express his basic intention. He thus broke off the attempt. Since
only the first two sections of *Being and Time* were published, there arose
the misunderstanding that the so-called "reversal" [*Kehre*] indicated a
turning away from an earlier (ek-sistentially philosophical) position to an
(ontologically historical) position which had been worked out later. A
glance at the course which Heidegger's thinking takes, however, makes it
quite plain that the published portion of *Being and Time* was already
thought out on the basis of the "self-reflective" consideration of the relationship of Being to beings or (as the case may be) of beings to Being.
Furthermore, the work itself shows that, from the very beginning, man's
ek-sistence enters into play only from a consideration of the "reversal."
Being and Time begins with an exposition of the question of the meaning
of Being; indications are constantly given that the analytic of Dasein is
on the way to a determination of the meaning of Being, and actually already presupposes a conception of this meaning and therefore is caught
up in a circle. The completion of the "reversal" is not turning to a new
position, but rather a return to the original point of departure and a return to that ground upon which this circle-of-thought has rested from the
very beginning. This ground is, of course, not only the basis of Heidegger's own thinking, but also that which was left unthought by metaphysics.

The Break

Why, we must ask, does Heidegger prematurely break off what was attempted in *Being and Time*, and how does he still manage to bring his

thought to its goal? In *Being and Time*, it is stated that "that which is to be found out by the asking," i.e. the meaning of Being, demands its own manner of being grasped, which manner may not be oriented toward beings (*SZ* 6). In the *Letter on Humanism*, then, Heidegger admitted, in retrospect, that the thinking of *Being and Time* denied to the "reversal" an appropriate language, because it could not be carried out within the language of metaphyics.[5] Metaphysics conceives of beings as beings; it inquires after the Being of beings, but not after Being itself. Metaphysics thus presupposes a determinate conception of the meaning of Being, merely insofar as it does not think through the character of that time in whose light Being becomes determined. Thus, the conceptual framework of metaphysics prevents the question of Being itself from being raised. In fact, this question simply fades away if the questioning does not give up the language of metaphysics. Heidegger has attempted to substantiate this thesis through a reflection on the thought of Ernst Jünger, a contemporary of Heidegger's on this path of thought.[6] Jünger believed himself to have gone beyond the "zero meridian" of nihilism, and yet his conceptual framework still remains within the sphere of metaphysics. If, however, the question concerning Being itself is the first and only fruitful step toward the overcoming of nihilism,[7] then the conceptual framework of classical metaphysics must be abandoned, since it does not allow this question to come into focus. After the failure of *Being and Time*'s endeavor, Heidegger still attempts to bring his questioning to its destination, in that he seeks radically to overcome metaphysics by a *return into the ground of metaphysics*.[8]

The question of the meaning of Being brings that which metaphysics leaves unthought and ungrounded, i.e., the abysslike ground of metaphysics, to expression. An excursus through the history of metaphysics (which the second portion of *Being and Time* was supposed to have attempted) must reveal the abysslike ground so that thought, by means of its own questioning, may return into it. Heidegger now considers above all the beginning, the completion, and the end of metaphysical thought, from the earliest Greek thought, to the philosophy of mediation of German Idealism, and to Nietzsche. Nietzsche is not treated as that existential thinker whose utterances must be held in suspension. Rather, Nietzsche is drawn quite close to Aristotle, and taken simply in his most

5. *Platons Lehre von der Wahrheit. Mit einem Brief über den 'Humanismus,'* 2nd ed. (Bern, 1954), p. 72; "Letter on Humanism," trans. Edgar Lohner, *Philosophy in the Twentieth Century*, vol. 3, ed. William Barret and Henry Aiken (New York, 1962), p. 280.

6. *Zur Seinsfrage* (Frankfurt, 1965); see especially p. 26; *The Question of Being*, trans. William Kluback and Jean T. Wilde (New Haven, 1958), p. 72.

7. See *Einführung in die Metaphysik* (Tübingen, 1953), p. 155; *Introduction to Metaphysics*, trans. Ralph Manheim (New Haven, 1959), p. 203.

8. Since the 5th edition (1949), *Was ist Metaphysik?* has been prefaced with an introduction bearing this title.

basic ideas. As a metaphysical thinker, Nietzsche thinks from the idea of
the eternal recurrence. Yet, as a "thinker of eternity," he is not the prelude to a philosophy of the future, but rather, the consistent end of the
metaphysical tradition. Metaphysics represents beings in their Being, but
in this representation it relates them to subjectivity. This subjectivism,
which was present from the very beginning in metaphysics, finds its radical completion in Nietzsche, who made the will to power the *essentia* of
all beings. Metaphysics thinks Being as perpetual presence: metaphysics
reaches its completion when Nietzsche determines the *existentia* of beings
to be the eternal recurrence of the same. Nietzsche's doctrine, as the doctrine of the eternal recurrence of all things, overthrows the metaphysics
of essences because now there can no longer be any essential difference
between beings. Thus, metaphysics ends with Nietzsche. Heidegger seeks
not only to bring metaphysics to this end, but even the whole of Western
history which, even in the phase of our scientific-technical organization, is
still determined by metaphysics. Heidegger understands the all-destroying
world wars of our time in the light of the final history of metaphysics. He
interprets metaphysics and its end with the help of the concepts and catch-
phrases of total war.

Nietzsche's attempt to overcome nihilism does not overcome nihilism at
all, but rather entrenches it all the more firmly. In a thought which thinks
from the viewpoint of the will to power and the eternal recurrence of the
same, Being cannot appear in its truth, cannot appear as that destining
[*Geschick*] which it, in fact, is but which is "not simply at our disposal."
As Heidegger stated in his Nietzsche lectures during the summer semester
of 1939, "In the eternal recurrence of the same, the final historical essence
of this last metaphysical explanation of beingness [*Seiendheit*]—i.e., as the
will to power—is conceived of in such a manner that the essence of truth
is denied any possibility of becoming that which is most questionable, and
the meaninglessness which is thereby placed into power unconditionally
determines the 'horizon' of our times and brings about its completion." [9]
The completion of meaninglessness reveals itself to the historical-technical
consciousness of our time not as the end, "but as the 'liberation' for a
steadily-increasing loss of Self, and ultimately, to an intensification of
everything." "One neither knows nor ventures that Other, which in the
future will be the One and Only, because it was already abiding in the
very beginning of our history, even though ungrounded: the truth of
Being, our standing in this truth, out of which world and earth alone
struggle to achieve their essence for man, and man, in this struggle experiences the reply of his essence to the God 'of' Being." Only in a new
experiencing of Being can nature and history find man and God in their
essence. Since the end of metaphysics forcibly brings about this new be-

9. *Nietzsche* (Pfullingen, 1961), vol. 2, pp. 27ff.

ginning, i.e., of a "standing in" truth insofar as essential thinking should continue to exist at all—thinking is obliged to repeat the first beginnings of thought, the earliest Greek thought, and redecide all those decisions on the basis of which metaphysics arose. Heidegger demands to go back into the ground of the first beginnings of thought. "What has been in the first beginnings of thought is thereby forced to rest upon the abyss of its ground, which has remained ungrounded up until now, and thus, for the first time, to become history."

This newly beginning thought, which arises from the end of metaphysics, raises once more the question which *Being and Time* had to leave unanswered. The completion of the reversal, toward which *Being and Time* not only tended but out of which this whole work was already conceived, cannot simply be considered a further carrying out of the point of departure of *Being and Time*. The "reversal," as Heidegger actually carries it to completion, is a turning away from this first point of departure, which still asked about the Being of beings in the metaphysical manner of questioning. Just as a skier does not make a turn arbitrarily or out of pure high spirits, neither does Heidegger arbitrarily break off the train of thought of *Being and Time* just when it is in full motion. An abyss had opened up before him, the abyss of the meaningless which had been revealed by Nietzsche's bringing metaphysical thinking to a close.

Thought cannot simply by-pass this abyss. Insofar as thought does not wish to carry out merely an underground restoration and ever again fall into the same abyss, it must itself enter this abyss. Thought must go through metaphysics to that which remains unthought in metaphysics; it must appropriate metaphysics before it can abandon it. That is why Heidegger asks the question: *What Is Metaphysics?* (1929), why he attempts an *Introduction to Metaphysics*,[10] which aims at a basic overcoming of metaphysics. Already the fact that Heidegger takes up the leading concepts of metaphysical thought in order to do away with them one after the other, indicates that he wishes to overcome metaphysics by appropriating it and thinking through it to that which it left unthought. Metaphysics is simultaneously ontology and logic. Already in his Kant book, Heidegger rejects formal and transcendental logic (in contrast to Husserl's efforts at that time). Formal logic, he says, must be deprived of its privileged position in metaphysics, which it has maintained since antiquity. The very idea of a formal logic is questionable. The idea of a transcendental logic is simply meaningless.[11] In the *Introduction to Metaphysics*, the heading "ontology," which was first adhered to, is rejected also. Heideg-

10. The lecture course given under this equivocal title during the summer semester of 1935 was published in 1953.

11. *Kant und das Problem der Metaphysik*, 2nd. ed. (Frankfurt am Main, 1951), pp. 200ff.; *Kant and the Problem of Metaphysics*, trans. James S. Churchill (Bloomington, Ind., 1962), pp. 229ff.

ger wishes to separate himself from other contemporary "ontological" efforts in philosophy (p. 31). The *Letter on Humanism* thus states that ontology—in keeping with its name—always thinks only the meaning of beings, and therefore not Being itself. Heidegger seeks first of all to establish a connection between the sciences and the wanting-to-have-an-awareness of Dasein. However, the sciences, which supposedly were to have been metaphysically grounded, finally become mere derivatives of a metaphysics which itself is to be overcome. This consideration, which takes up the wanting-to-have-an-awareness of Dasein on a new level, is placed in opposition to the sciences. The later Heidegger does not wish to have his thought understood as phenomenological research or even as philosophy. That is why he now seeks out art. Art emerges out of an inner necessity into the horizon of the thinker who prepares himself to think the truth of Being: primordial art, of whose end metaphysics speaks, sets the truth of Being into motion; it makes beings "more being" [*seiender*] by guarding Being in beings. The disclosure of the world, as it occurs in art and, above all, in poetry seems to be the only one which stands on that primordial level upon which thought, too, seeks to make itself at home. Thought itself has a hidden poetic character because it no longer is the metaphysical proposing presentation of beings in their Being as continuous presence, but reaches out into an open future, thereby bearing presence and absence simultaneously. At this point Heidegger comes close to early Greek aphoristic thinking as well as to the more recent Western 'sayings of the soul which should be sung rather than spoken'— an expression through which Nietzsche for some time laid himself open to the experience of the god Dionysus, who is simultaneously presence and absence.

Yet it is not a "poetry" beyond metaphysics which leads into the abyss-like ground of metaphysics, but rather the attempt to retrieve primordially the questions of metaphysics. Shortly after *Being and Time*, Heidegger attempts in the lecture *What Is Metaphysics?* and in the essay *The Essence of Reasons* to reflect upon the "Nothing" [*das Nichts*], and upon the Nothing between Being and beings, i.e., the ontological difference. In this way, Heidegger meets the demand which he himself had made in the analysis of guilt and conscience in *Being and Time*, namely, the demand to raise the problem of the ontological origin of Nothing (*SZ* 285ff.). Since Nothing is thought of as a "no" with regard to all beings, the question arises of why there are beings at all, rather than Nothing? Not only facticity of Dasein, but even the fact that there are beings as such is called into question in this metaphysically greatly expanded problem. When metaphysics asks something of this nature, it turns to a highest being as the ground of all other beings. In this fashion, however, metaphysics does not think Being as such. By including in his question a ". . . rather than Nothing" Heidegger cuts off the path to a highest, unquestionable Being.

He reduces this question to the question of the meaning, the truth or openness of Being itself. In the leading question of metaphysics—i.e., What are beings?—which asks about the Being of beings, the fundamental question is presupposed, in which the meaning of Being itself—that which is left unthought by metaphysics—is brought into question.

The meaning or the truth of Being, as that which metaphysics leaves unthought, is the abysslike ground of metaphysics. The truth of Being is that center in which Being and Dasein (which has an understanding of Being) come together, in which the "reversal" thus completes itself. That thinking which wishes to bring the abysslike ground of metaphysics to expression must enter into this center. Heidegger reflects upon this center when, in the two decades after the appearance of *Being and Time,* he makes the problem of truth and Being the foremost theme of his thought. The lecture *The Essence of Truth* and the essay *Plato's Doctrine of Truth* give some insight into his working on this theme. Heidegger reflects upon the unthought foundation of the Western conception of truth, that non-concealment which must ever again be wrested from forgottenness and hiddenness, and which thus first makes truth as the *adequatio* of thought and thing possible. Truth, which is thought of as a nonconcealment, is the happening of truth [*Wahrheitsgeschehen*], and in this happening prevails the temporality of Dasein and that time in which Being itself gives itself in its openness. We are concerned here not simply with the essence of truth in the sense of Dasein's standing-in-truth, but rather, concerned even more with the truth of Being taken as abiding Being, i.e., with truth as the openness of Being. In this way, the "reversal" is completed: Dasein as Being-in-the-world no longer stands at the center of these considerations, but rather Being in its meaning and its truth, and thus Being as that which makes "world" possible. Thought no longer moves from beings to Being, but rather from Being to beings.

If the relationship of Dasein to Being is determined by a double nothing then Being in its transition to beings is characterized by a double "superiority." There is, of course, no Being without beings—Being is the "granting" of beings—but yet, Being brings about in itself the difference between Being and beings. It releases beings out of itself into openness, and among these beings there is Dasein as the privileged place of Being's openness. However, for its part, Dasein, taken in itself, does not have Being at its disposal. To this a second aspect is to be added, namely, the place of the openness of Being is bounded by the fact that at each given time it "whiles" in a determinate way [*Jeweiligkeit*]: the openness or nonconcealment of Being takes place at each given time only upon a background of concealment. Being, which appropriates Dasein as the place of its disclosure, remains fundamentally not at Dasein's disposal, just as it ever again transcends the mode of abiding characteristic of Dasein.

Being, taken as the unavailable and at each time historical destining of

Being [*Seinsgeschick*], reveals itself in its meaning, or in its openness and truth, as the event of appropriation [*Ereignis*]. "Ereignis" does not mean here, as it still did within the terminology of *Being and Time*, a certain occurrence or happening, but rather Dasein's complete self-realization in Being, and Being's appropriation [*zueignen*] to Dasein's authenticity. The word 'Ereignis' cannot be made plural. It determines the meaning of Being itself. It is, as a *singulare tantum*, a key concept of thought like the Greek word *logos* or the Chinese word *tao*.[12]

Being as the event of appropriation: with this definition Heidegger's thinking has arrived at its goal. In the event of appropriation, time, in whose light Being has always been understood, though in a hidden manner, is simultaneously thought also. Heidegger's thinking returns to its own ground in that it brings the abysslike ground, that which was left unthought by metaphysics, to expression. Thus, the way of thought finds its course to the continually circumnavigated center. Thought gradually finds its genuine structure by thinking its only thought. As a carrying out of the question of Being, and thus as the carrying out to completion of thought's way, Heidegger's thinking strictly limits itself to adhering to that one and only thought "which one day will remain fixed like a star in the heavens of the world": "To approach a star, and only this . . ." [13]

PART TWO

In his confrontation with metaphysics, Heidegger raises the first and last questions of thought anew. Thus, that which was left unthought by metaphysics achieves expression. Heidegger seeks to think that which was left unthought by returning to the ground of metaphysics. He thinks Being in the sense of the appropriating event. This determination of the meaning of Being was thought through in 1936 but did not appear in an exact formulation until twenty years later.

Because Heidegger thinks the meaning of Being itself, he can take up the metaphysical question of the Being of beings, of Being in its various modes of realization. He seeks to secure beings in the truth of Being. In so doing, he cannot simply take over the logic of metaphysics, but must forcibly bring about a new decision concerning the *logos*.

Through the return to the ground of metaphysics, that which has been thought by metaphysics is posed anew as something which must be decided upon and, in this manner, can be primordially adopted. By means

12. See *Identität und Differenz* (Pfullingen, 1954), p. 25; *Identity and Difference*, trans. Joan Stambaugh (New York, 1969, p. 36).

13. *Aus der Erfahrung des Denkens* (Pfullingen, 1954), p. 7; The Thinker as Poet," trans. Albert Hofstadter, in *Poetry, Language, Thought* (New York, 1971), p. 4.

of a meditation which is focused on Being's history, Heidegger reflects upon the characterizations of the meaning of Being which, although prevailing in various phases of metaphysics, were not expressly put into question there. Thus, Heidegger seeks to place metaphysical thinking back upon that ground which itself has remained unthought, to incorporate his own thinking into that "happening" of the truth as it comes to us from our tradition.

I cannot go further into all these efforts of Heidegger's, of which at least some bits were made available in lectures and essays. Nevertheless, I still would like to attempt three things: First of all, I would like to reflect once more upon the course of Heidegger's thinking as a whole, to be able to more accurately grasp the central point and the inherently tense unity of Heidegger's thought, and thereby ward off some misunderstandings. Thus, I shall pay particular attention to what the word "ground" [*Grund*] means in the discussion of fundamental ontology and the return to the ground of metaphysics. Secondly, I would like to give at least a few indications of how Heidegger seeks to think that-which-is on the basis of the event of appropriation, and determine the *logos* which his thinking follows in so doing. Finally, I would briefly like to show how Heidegger's thought gains its cohesiveness by placing traditional, metaphysical thought back upon its ground, which has remained unthought.

The Ground

Heidegger's thinking grows out of a reflection upon metaphysics. But what is metaphysics? Metaphysics (ontology in the broader sense) seeks to determine beings in their Being, and to articulate Being according to its various modes of realization. This is why metaphysics asks the question: What are beings? At one point, metaphysics asks about beings as beings in general, or about beings as such; then it is general metaphysics (ontology in the narrower sense). Metaphysics, however, does not only inquire after those characteristics which can be discovered in every being, in beings as such, but it inquires also after that Being which makes a particular, individual being to be what it is. It is then special metaphysics (*metaphysica specialis*). Metaphysics, from the very beginning, asks about beings as beings only in such a manner, that it defines beings as a whole in terms of a privileged being—a highest or divine being. When, in the Christian faith, God was understood as the creator of mankind and the world, theological metaphysics was incorporated into the three parts of traditional *metaphysica specialis* (natural theology, psychology, cosmology).

Metaphysics asks about beings in such a way that it grounds the Being of beings in a highest being, and defines it in terms of this highest being. Metaphysics thinks beings in their Being, but does not determine this Being in its own proper meaning, but rather thinks it immediately in terms of a highest being, which for its part is determined in terms of a meaning of Being which is not thought in itself, as such. Being and beings are not kept apart in such a way that the meaning of Being could become problematic. The meaning of Being remains unthought; its meaning is merely presupposed. Metaphysics, as representative thinking, orients itself toward thinglike beings, which it finds present in the "world" as present-at-hand. It thus understands Being, and even the Being of the highest being, in terms of presence-at-hand or presence. Since it is never explicitly put into question, this understanding of the meaning of Being takes place only in a hidden manner in the light of time: presence [*Anwesenheit*] is thought of from the perspective of the temporal mode of the present time [*Gegenwart*]. It is for this reason that Heidegger asks: If Being is determined as presence, how then is time itself to be thought of which in a hidden manner is cothought with the notion of presence? "Through the question contained in the expression 'Being and Time,' that which was left unthought in all metaphysics is indicated." [14] The question about Being and time seeks to think that which metaphysics has always forgotten to think: the meaning of Being itself.

Heidegger finds an approach to that time in whose light the meaning of Being comes to be determined by examining the Being of that being which is characterized by an understanding of Being, in terms of temporality. That being which is so characterized is Dasein. Metaphysics can find no approach to the question of Being and time because it must interpret time in its Being in terms of a "now," precisely because it understands Being in terms of an inadequately thought-through temporal mode, namely, "the present time." Metaphysical thinking orients itself toward that which is present-at-hand within the world, and transcends this present-at-hand to something which is eternally present at hand or present. Thus, this sort of thinking must overlook that typical standing-out toward a future which is not simply at one's disposal which is characteristic of primordial temporality. Time is grasped as a succession of now-points which are present, were present, or will be present. Christian theology reveals a more primordial relationship to time and temporality, i.e., a relationship of standing-out toward a future which is not at one's disposal. Heidegger mentions frequently in *Being and Time* the impulses which he received from the theological thought. It is these impulses which have led him to that path which his questioning takes.

Heidegger asks about Dasein and its temporality merely for the sake

14. *Was heisst Denken?* (Tübingen, 1954), p. 42; *What is Called Thinking?*, trans. Fred D. Wieck and J. Glenn Gray (New York, 1968), p. 103.

of the question of Being. The privileged position which Dasein receives does not mean that a subjectification of all beings is to be undertaken. Of course, Heidegger's thought remains separated by an abyss from that kind of metaphysics which, by means of a transcendental reflection, believes itself capable of defining the "gradation" of beings with respect to Being. But precisely because Heidegger reflects upon the fact that we can approach beings which are not like Dasein merely through that openness which Being receives in our understanding of it, is it that these beings can "speak" to man in their total otherness and foreignness, without immediately being anthropomorphically misinterpreted. The analysis of Dasein should not be understood as giving support to modern anthropologism in any way. In such anthropologism, man is put into the position of the highest being. Everything which is is delivered over to man. Beings are only insofar as they are for man and given over to him. Everything revolves around man and seems to be connected with him. Man, made thusly dependent upon himself, becomes understood as "nihilistic" in the sense of "merely temporal" and "finite." As a matter of fact, *Being and Time* has been misinterpreted as just such an anthropologism. One was thus forced to regard the thought of the later Heidegger as a turn to a completely different position. In Heidegger's later thinking, the foundation upon which everything is founded is supposed to be no longer resolute ek-sistence, but rather, a mythologized Being.

Yet, neither Dasein nor Being is an ontic fundament, an ultimate ground in the sense of metaphysics. Thus, it is meaningless to say that Heidegger has changed his view by substituting one fundament (Being) for another (man). Dasein is the "there," the place of the truth of Being, and therefore by no means "something" different from Being. And yet, there actually is an equivocation in Heidegger's earlier speaking about a fundamental ontology supposedly to be discovered through the analysis of Dasein. It sometimes appears as if the analysis of Dasein were not only the way to the working out of the question of Being, but even prior—if not superior—to it, its "fundament." [15] These various "tensions" which are found in Heidegger's course of thought are obviously not to be simply explained away, for then Heidegger's thought could not be regarded as an authentic "searching for the way." One must bear in mind, however, that Heidegger constantly calls attention to the fact that the analysis of Dasein must already presuppose a clarification of the meaning of Being, and that this analysis must be repeated after the clarification of the meaning has appeared to be successful. Thus, there can be no talk of a one-sided grounding of the question concerning Being through a clarification of man's understanding of Being. Furthermore, Heidegger explicitly puts

15. See *SZ*, pp. 13ff.; *Kant und des Problem der Metaphysik*, pp. 200ff.; *Kant and the Problem of Metaphysics*, pp. 229ff.

the equivocation which is inherent in his speaking about fundamental ontology into question at the end of *Being and Time:* "Can one," he asks,
"provide ontological grounds for ontology, or does it also require an
ontical foundation? and which being must take over the function of providing this foundation?" (*SZ* 436)

It is a characteristic of metaphysics that it presupposes an ontic foundation for ontology, and lets the meaning of Being be determined from the
perspective of a particular being. In contrast to this, Heidegger cuts off
the path to a highest being, which is no longer questioned in its Being,
with the question: "Why is there anything at all, and not simply Nothing?" In this way, thought enters into the happening of truth, in which
the meaning of Being itself becomes revealed. Since Heidegger pays particular attention to the temporal character of this happening of truth, to
to the concurrence of concealment and nonconcealment, he succeeds in
determining the meaning, and therefore the truth, of Being, by explicitly
discussing the temporal moment which, as presence, remains hidden in the
traditional understanding of Being: Being as the event of appropriation.

That which was left unthought by metaphysics, not merely the Being
of beings, but the meaning of Being itself, comes to be thought. In this
way, metaphysics comes to its "ground." What the word "ground" may
mean here is explained by Heidegger where he rethinks the fundamental
concepts of metaphysics: identity, difference, and ground. Heidegger does
not simply ask what identity, difference, and ground have to say about
beings, but asks rather, how they belong to Being itself, Being as the event
of appropriation. The identity of Being is "self-sameness" [*Selbigkeit*],
and not equivalence [*Gleichheit*]. Identity articulates beings in their essence in such a manner that this essence remains a "determining characteristic" [*Eigentum*] of the event of appropriation. The essence of, e.g.,
technology or poetry, is not the transtemporal validity of an eternally
present, unchanging idea, but rather that destined [*geschickt*], historical
essence which is not simply at our disposal. This essence reveals itself each
time in a strict, but still temporal commitment when Dasein accepts the
destining of Being [*Seinsgeschick*], and as the "there" of Being is "identical" with it. Beings can then be understood in their Being as beings. If
beings are understood in their Being, the difference between Being and
beings is broken open. This difference [*Unterschied*], the ontological difference [*Differenz*], constitutes the center of that thinking which, as
meta-physics, transcends beings to Being. Heidegger seeks to show how
this difference is at the same time the carrying-out of "overcoming" or
transcendence, as well as "arrival" or presence. Just as Heidegger thinks
transcendence from the perspective of Dasein, as the act in and through
which Dasein's understanding being-able-to-Be supersedes beings and in
which this being simultaneously arrives at a new truth before Dasein's attuned moodedness, he also thinks the transition of Being to beings as the

simultaneous arrival of beings in the unconcealment of Being. The carrying out of the difference—the happening of truth—is thought of as the carrying out of the event of appropriation. In contrast to what is the case in metaphysics, Heidegger no longer grounds the transcendence from beings to Being in a highest being which grounds itself and everything else, i.e., a *causa sui*. If Being is conceived of as a "ground," it not only grounds beings, but must itself be grounded in a highest being. In this way, metaphysics becomes onto-theo-logy: it thinks Being on the basis of the divine as the ground (*logos*) of all beings. Being and beings are then not kept sufficiently distinct, so that Being cannot reveal itself in its meaning and be determined as the event of appropriation. Being itself does not become a problem here. Even the highest being is understood as something eternally present-at-hand, because the understanding of Being has oriented itself above all toward beings which are simply encountered, toward things present-at-hand. Even if, in a new approach, thinking is grounded in an ultimate "I think," even then this "I think" is, in turn, understood from the perspective of eternal presence as a "pure, primordial, unchanging consciousness," which in every consciousness remains the same and thus is its ground.

Metaphysics, as the science of grounds, comes to completion in the technique of an absolute knowing, which makes available an ultimate ground. In contrast to this, thought (in Heidegger's sense) remains directed toward historical Being, which is nondeterminable and not simply at our disposal, and which is thought as the "destining of Being" [*Seinsgeschick*], as the event of appropriation. The meaning of Being as the "ground" which remained unthought in metaphysical thinking, can perhaps be thought of as an "abysslike ground, but in the final analysis cannot really be thought of as a "ground" at all. The discussion of ground is given up after having been explicitly worked out. Because the event of appropriation is just itself, and nothing more, it is without a "why?" which asks about grounds or reasons. "It remains," Heidegger says at the conclusion of his lecture on *The Principle of Sufficient Reason*, "just play: the highest and the most profound play. But this 'just' is everything, the one, the only." [16]

Being as the event of appropriation is neither an ultimate ground nor a highest being, but this is *not* so precisely because it is the "granting" of beings [*das Geben vom Seienden*], because it is the "it grants" itself. The "it grants" [*es gibt*] is not a "ground for the world": neither is it the power over its "granting": it is not God, who "creates" beings. Being as the event of appropriation gives beings into openness, and allows them to reveal themselves as the Being "of" beings.

Being as nondeterminable, historical destining of Being which is not

16. *Der Satz vom Grund* (Pfullingen, 1957), p. 188. See also my book, *Der Denkweg Martin Heidegger* (Pfullingen, 1963).

simply at our disposal grants at any given time the clearing in which beings become manifest. It thus makes possible the "bursting open" of the
world as a historical world (history to be taken here in the sense in which
it is not limited only to man). Since Heidegger seeks to develop a primordial concept of world (world as "Fourfold"), he overcomes the
forgetfulness-of-the-world characteristic of Western ontology which had
already been discussed in *Being and Time* (100). Being, as the Being of
beings, itself becomes a "derivative" of world. The more Heidegger enters
into his own thinking, the more he leaves metaphysical concepts behind.
He even drops the fundamental concept "Being," because it is a specifically
metaphysical concept. He is able to drop this concept because that which
metaphysics thought under this heading is the event of appropriation, when
it is rethought by means of a reflection on the meaning of Being.

That Which Is

When Heidegger seeks to think Being in its meaning, when he seeks to
think the event of appropriation, this does not mean that he rejects the
question of the Being of beings. Rather, this whole question becomes fruitful in a totally new fashion when the meaning of Being is thought of as
the event of appropriation. Heidegger's overcoming of metaphysics still
maintains a positive attitude toward metaphysical questions. That thinking
which on its "forest trails" [*Holzwege*] abruptly becomes confronted
with that which was never before trodden, i.e., the question of the meaning of Being, reaches this question in that it comes out of metaphysics and
thinks back through metaphysics to that which metaphysics left unthought. This thinking ever again travels along those paths which metaphysics has opened up for it; it takes up the metaphysical question concerning the Being of what is. "Does the soul speak? Does the world speak?
Does God speak?" These questions conclude the prose piece *Der Feldweg*
(1953). "Everything addresses renunciation toward the Self-same. Renunciation does not take. Renunciation grants." The questions of *metaphysica specialis* about the soul, the world, and God are once more
brought back into the question about "that which is the Same," about Being. Thus, these questions can become fruitful in a new sense. The extent
to which Heidegger has always borne these questions with him is shown
by a mere glance at the course his thought has taken.
    At the end of his Duns Scotus book, Heidegger—addressing himself to
the scholasticism and mysticism of the middle ages and to Hegel—calls
for a "philosophy of the living spirit, of active love, of the worshipful in-
timacy with God [*Gottinigkeit*]." The sharpest possible distinction between theology and metaphysics follows immediately upon this leap into

the theological metaphysics of the West. He appeals to Luther, who in the name of a "theology of the cross" rejected the "theology of glory," which—in its metaphysics understood as theodicy—calls evil good and good evil (as Luther says in the twenty-first thesis of the Heidelberger Disputation). When thought sees itself thrown back upon itself, it must come to grips with Nietzsche who, as the "last German philosopher who passionately sought God," expresses the fate of the West in his declaration: "God is dead!" Only in this way can thought, with Hölderlin, enter inquiringly the level of the holy, in which the Divine, God or gods, have the abode where they can appear. Inasmuch as this thought abandons the God of the philosophers as a dead, merely being, and "defined" God, it perhaps come closer, as Godless thinking to the "godly God." It holds true for this thinking that "Whoever has experienced theology in its own roots, the theology of the Christian faith as well as that of the philosophers, prefers today to remain silent about God within the realm of thought." [17]

Nature is to be thought primordially as "earth," so that it can be torn free from both the one-sided objectivization of science, and from technology with its one-sided interest in permanent availability and usefulness. Thus, nature can be experienced anew on the basis of the event of appropriation. Man is no longer thought of as a "subject,' but rather as the one who has to carry out the event of appropriation. The work of art, the thing, the language are thought from the viewpoint of the event of appropriation.

The Being of that which is is not simply understood from the perspective of continuous presence, from the "idea," thought of statically, or with reference to an unchanging universal. Rather, it is asked if the Being or the essence of beings is not to be properly understood as a "historical abiding" [*Wesen*], from the perspective of the event of appropriation. That thinking which orients itself toward "seeing," which represents beings as beings with respect to a Being or essence which is continuously present, is transformed into an explaining thinking which grasps the essence of beings as historical abiding, or as the "place" which at any given time it always gains through the event of appropriation. If truth is to be thought of as a happening, then representational thought must make a fundamental change. It can no longer orient itself simply toward the temporal mode of the present, but rather, must "stand-out" toward time more primordially. Heidegger has brought this fundamental change in thought to completion by conceiving of ontology as phenomenology, but phenomenology as hermeneutics, and then by going back from hermeneutical thought to a thinking which follows a *logos* that remained concealed in metaphysics, and

---

17. *Identität und Differenz*, pp. 51, 71; *Identity and Difference*, pp. 54, 72.

was not primordially developed either in theological or historical hermeneutics.

The character of Heidegger's thought has been variously misunderstood. It is believed that talk about Being must be completely empty, if Being is not grounded in a being. It was said that ontology was to be placed upon an ontic foundation, e.g., God, or at least an eternal world or man himself. As a matter of fact, that thinking which Heidegger himself characterizes as "preparatory" is marked by a certain "emptiness" or formalism (e.g., within the analysis of Dasein, Heidegger distinguished between "existential" and "existentiell"). In fact, however, the relationship to beings is already posited along with the thinking of Being. The early Heidegger therefore spoke of the formal-indicative nature of his concepts. The formalism of these "indications" is not that of an empty, self-sufficient form which is separated from its content. Rather, the relationship to the fulfillment through the content is already posited in the form, but held back and in suspension, so that the formality is maintained. The form is not an empty shell, but rather always ready to make the leap to the concrete through a content. This fulfillment is held back, however, because it is irreducibly factical. That for which resolute Dasein resolves itself, "which" reveals itself in Being as the event of appropriation, remains open, since thought can neither posit it nor derive it without destroying the character of the event of appropriation.

It has been further said of Heidegger's "ontology" that it fails to achieve its sought-after formalism, since it springs from a particular-historical understanding. However, this abstract alternative, namely that between the ontological-universal and the ontic-historical, also fails to do justice to his formal-indicative conceptuality.

When Heidegger, in *Being and Time*, brings a particular structure to light, it appears to be a phenomenon in the sense of Kant's "condition for the possibility of experience," or Plato's *eidos*. The provisional conception of phenomenology, as Heidegger develops it at the beginning of *Being and Time*, must lead one to hold Heidegger's investigations to be eidetic investigations in the sense of Husserl's phenomenology. Nevertheless, whoever understands *Being and Time* in this fashion must be shocked when Heidegger, in this work, quotes Count York's statement to the effect that, with regard to the inner historicity [*Geschichtlichkeit*] of self-consciousness, a systematization which is separated from historiography [*Historie*] is simply inadequate (SZ 401f.). If, however, the meaning of the Being of Dasein lies in its factical ek-sistence, which properly speaking is historicity, then for such a Dasein no purely unhistorical possibilities can be in actual fact essential. The universality of formal-indicative concepts is only a certain sort of "universality," which always aims toward its fulfillment in that which at any given time is historical. For this reason,

Heidegger had already proposed the destruction of systematization in *Being and Time*. For the same reason, Heidegger later attached the analyses of *Being and Time* to that region of history where they belong. Thus, it is shown by the lecture *"What Is Philosophy?"* for instance, how that moodedness which as a rule (and thus in a certain universality) determines man is capable of being grasped only with the perspective of a basic mood [Grundstimmung], which at each given time is characteristic for an epoch.

The meaning of the Being of Dasein, as grasped through the existential analysis, can just as little be made into an "idea," as the meaning of Being can be determined on the basis of a statically thought idea. The universal, binding character of Heidegger's thought does not come about through the contemplation of something which is always, ideally present, but rather, because it "stands out" toward a destining which at any given time makes our historical abiding possible. The identity of this abiding, which achieves only a certain "universality," is derived from the event of appropriation. The enduring of the destiny, however, is only then binding, and not simply arbitrary, when it thinks from what has been into the future. This thought moves within the circle of historical understanding, and for this reason must seek, in a never-ending motion, to get behind those presuppositions which it has always already made for itself. It "grounds" itself by moving back and forth in this circle. Of course, it must allow the ultimate "ground" upon which it rests to be historically handed over to it, as something which is not simply at its disposal. It can never (as in Hegel) supersede this immediacy in an all-grounding dialectic. The final paradox of this thought's circular but never ultimately terminated movement lies in this, that the emergence of the historicity of thought itself happens historically.

Since Heidegger moves within the circle of historical understanding, he must make the initial presupposition of this understanding, i.e., language, a theme for reflection. And thus, it is not an uncritical aspect of thought which manifests itself in his "etymologizing," but rather a critical aspect: the attempt to put into language those very presuppositions which thought makes when it speaks. Hamann, in his metacritique, once objected against Kant, that the highest and final purification or critique of reason, namely the purification of language, could never be achieved. According to Hamann, language is the organon and criterion of reason: and yet language is historical. However, since Heidegger pays particular attention to the incorporation of thought into historical language, one may also characterize his thought as "metacritical," at least insofar as it can be measured against critical theory at all.

Of course, one does not recognize the metacritical character of Heidegger's thought in its necessity if one simply keeps staring at his often noted etymologies, or dismisses Heidegger's thinking as "mere" poetry.

It is even possible to gain access to Heidegger's methodological procedure through the Western tradition of thought (and not just exclusively from early Greek aphoristic thought). Heidegger attempts a topology,[18] i.e., a saying of the place, and thus a thinking of the truth, of Being, where he analyzes such guide words and guiding principles as *"physis," "logos,"* "Nothing is without ground," or "man dwells poetically." If we call these guide words and guiding principles *"loci"* or *"topoi,"* we gain a second meaning for the word "topology," a meaning which Heidegger himself, however, does not consider. We may thus connect Heidegger's thinking with a tradition which was once of utmost importance. In his attempt to make a science out of philosophy, Aristotle distinguished "Topics" or "Dialectics" from "Apodictics" as the properly rigorous method of philosophy. Even Vico still made mention, though with somewhat different intentions, of the priority which "Topics" has over "critical theory," i.e., over the exact methodology of our era. The Christian dogmatists (e.g., Melanchthon) utilized most decisively and for the longest time, the term *"loci"* because they were striving for a systematization while still having to heed the irreducible historicity of faith. Heidegger's latest endeavors of thought, too, form a topology, i.e., they are designations of the place, or sayings of the place of Being's truth, with the help of a selection of loci or a collection of the guiding concepts and principles of Western thought. Modern philosophy, linguistics, and research into the history of concepts all, in their own particular ways, attempt something similar. Furthermore, the methodically developed limitation to only exemplary guide words and guiding concepts is today a necessity. We have only to consider Dilthey's work, which remained fragmentary, to see that the traditional methods of research in the human sciences are no longer adequate for historical reflection.[19]

The later Heidegger, of course, rejects any attempt at constructing "methods" in order then to reflect upon them. He does not even wish explicitly to propose that manner in which the event of appropriation needs thought as the hermeneutical circle itself. Instead, he wishes in his thought to turn more primordially back to and to dwell in the hermeneutical relationship itself, in which the meaning of Being is "announced" to Dasein, which already has an understanding of Being (SZ 37). We have seen already that even the formal-indicative concepts are not to be thought of as universal forms, through which representational thought gets a grip upon beings, but rather a guidance toward the happening of truth. The guiding words upon which the later Heidegger reflects are to be understood as clues and indications, which are addressed to questioning thought

---

18. *Aus der Erfahrung des Denkens*, p. 23; "The Thinker as Poet," p. 12.
19. See my essay, "Dichtungstheorie und Toposforschung," *Jahrbuch für Aesthetik und allgemeine Kunstwissenschaft* 5 (Cologne, 1960), pp. 89–201.

so that it may enter more purely into the event of appropriation. Thus, as a thought which "explains" it may gather together everything which is into the event of appropriation.

Hanging-Together

To determine Being in its meaning as the event of appropriation, to secure beings as beings in the truth of Being, i.e., the event of appropriation, to attain the "*logos*," i.e., the language which is capable of properly responding to the event of appropriation: this is what Heidegger attempts. That destiny, as which Being itself prevails, which is not at our disposal and cannot be conceptually determined, is to be experienced as such. This experiencing should neither be covered over by a dialectic, in the sense of a metalogic (Hegel), nor should this experiencing be altogether avoided, as is the case when thought, confronted with the traditional conceptual forms, yields to the historical representation of the past, thereby failing to do justice to historicity (Dilthey). This experiencing can be authentically endured only if thought goes through metaphysics and overcomes it, both as ontology and logic, from the "ground" on upwards.

On the basis of its understanding of Being as continuous presence, traditional ontology grasps the Being of beings as a continuously present, ideal something. Heidegger seeks to ground this ontology through the return to a mode of thought which thinks Being's historical abiding from the event of appropriation. In the same way, he seeks to go back through traditional logic (and not merely to bypass it) to a more primordial *logos*. The young Heidegger wrote: "What is logic? Already here we are faced with a problem, the solution of which is reserved for the future." Then as thinking became the endurance of a future which was not at one's disposal, Heidegger held that the whole idea of logic was dissolved in the swirl of a more primordial questioning.[20] But Heidegger is concerned precisely with giving that thought which springs from the event of appropriation a "logical" and not simply a rhapsodic form. For this reason he seeks, by means of a reflection upon the fundamental principles of logic, to go back to the ground of traditional logic and thus discover the *logos* of his own thinking. Naturally it goes without saying that through this return to the "ground" of metaphysics, traditional logic and contemporary logic just as little lose their rights, within their own limits, as do the demonstrations of unchanging essences. The rather uncautious

20. See "Neuere Forschung über Logik" in *Literarische Rundschau*, vol. 38, ed. J. Sauer (Freiburg, 1912), p. 466. See also *Was ist Metaphysik?*, 7th ed. (Frankfurt am Main, 1955), p. 37; "What Is Metaphysics?" trans. R. F. C. Hull and Allan Crick, in *Existence and Being*, ed. Werner Broch (Chicago, 1967), p. 343.

polemic which prevails today between "hermeneutical" philosophy and logical positivism serves only to obliterate the fact that a fruitful dialogue between those who are attempting to construct a "hermeneutical" logic (Lipps) and the representatives of logical positivism is more than possible.

True, in his own thinking, Heidegger never made the possible positive meanings of "idea" or "logic" thematic, at least in the classical sense of these words. His thinking complies only with the free-floating structure of a whole, the moment we eliminate those one-sided formulations and directions of questioning which grew out of the attempts at a break-through and out of those polemical arguments which, to be sure, are oc-casionally necessary. Thus, one might pose the question, whether or not the experience of a continuously present idea as well as logic, and con-nected with it the whole of classical metaphysics, are to be considered a derivative or even degenerate mode of thought, or if they should not rather be considered a mode of thinking that, within certain limits, does in fact do justice to primordial phenomena.

If the answer to this question is to be other than a merely traditional or positivist-pragmatic presupposition, it must be arrived at through a think-ing which enters into dialogue with that which metaphysics has left un-thought. Only such a debate over Being preserves the possibility of re-appropriating that which metaphysics has in fact thought. Heidegger him-self does not think that which metaphysics has left unthought exclusively in terms of the event of appropriation, but also attempts, by means of his ontological-historical reflections, to raise anew the question concerning those particular articulations of the meaning of Being which dominated certain phases of metaphysics, even though they were not explicitly thought through in themselves. The understanding of Being as Idea, *ener-geia*, objectivity, will to power, etc., must be thought through on the basis of what was not thought in it, i.e., time as the horizon of the under-standing of Being. In this manner, thought, as it has been understood up until now, is to be placed back onto its own ground.

Heidegger, however, does not think that which metaphysics left un-thought by placing himself at the "end" of history and making the law of a self-contained system into the law of history, and thus superseding history (Hegel). Much more, Heidegger's thinking places itself into his-tory in the full knowledge that it itself is finite and historical. The reflec-tion which brings to completion the step backwards into that which has always at any given time been left unthought does not itself arrive at a final end or absolute completion.

Heidegger thinks his single thought, in that he goes back to what meta-physics left unthought, and thus frees himself for a thought yet to come. His thinking is a *way of thinking* and not simply a way which Heideg-ger brings to completion, but rather a way by means of which metaphysics goes beyond itself. The necessity of Heidegger's thought grows out of the fact that it must bring into language that which thought, up to now, has left unthought. This thought gains its binding character in that it is concerned with the whole of the Western tradition, which determines us all. The dialogue with Heidegger must gain its rigor from this binding character, from the relationship to the Same.

8. STANLEY ROSEN
Thinking about Nothing

IN THE COURSE of this short essay, it will not be possible to review, let alone comment on, all aspects of Heidegger's doctrines concerning *Nicht, Nichtigkeit,* and *Nichts.* The inseparability of these doctrines from the central concern with *Sein* makes them coextensive with Heidegger's career as a thinker. For this very reason, however, it is possible to discuss some of the crucial aspects of the question of Being and Nothingness. As Heidegger himself says, every great thinker has just one thought. His greatness consists in the degree to which he thinks that thought through to completeness. We can hope for neither greatness nor completeness. But the central and comprehensive nature of the *Seinsfrage* enables us to gain one or two purchases upon matters of decisive importance. Wherever one reaches out, so to speak, one always touches the same spot.

My procedure in "reaching out" will be to give virtually no summaries of Heideggerean texts, which I shall scarcely mention until the last section of this paper. My primary audience is the analytical philosopher, or better, the contemporary representative of the European tradition combining "common sense" and mathematical rationalism. I assume in this reader only sympathy and fair play. I shall try to persuade him that the question Heidegger raises, even though he does not answer it, and to some degree may not have formulated it correctly, is worth asking and taking seriously. My paper is thus concerned primarily with the development (I almost wrote "analysis") of a problem rather than with the translation of Heidegger's baroque texts into acceptable academic English. I write neither as an analyst nor a Heideggerean, but (if one may hope for anything) as a philosopher.

Suppose, then, that someone asks us what we are thinking about, and we reply, "Oh, nothing." This is, surely, a rather common occurrence. Sometimes we mean by "nothing" nothing in particular, and this in turn can mean either that we are daydreaming or letting "all kinds of things" (perhaps even "everything") pass through our minds. Or else it can mean that, in the usual sense of the term, we are not thinking at all. How often have we been moved to say, "My mind is a complete blank"? Underlying both these meanings is the not-so-tacit assumption that to think is to think *something*. Thus, for example, in a daydream, if I think about "all kinds of things," I do so by means of specimens, groups, or processes which, however fluid, are sufficiently identifiable to articulate the flow of consciousness in a way that can be described. The fact that my day-dream lacks logical structure, or is not directed by fixed processes of thought, that it lacks a definite purpose, all this is beside the point. I can't "let my imagination go" if I let go of every definite thing. For this would be to let go of my imagination, and that is quite another matter. Even when using "think" in a very informal and extended sense, so as to include dreaming, imagining, musing, and the like, we regard it as reasonable to be asked *what* we are thinking about. If we cannot answer the *what?* with sufficient definiteness to employ names or equivalent verbal descrip-tions, then we confess: "My mind is a complete blank."

Of course, this confession need not be literally true. There may be all kinds of colors, fluid shapes, even sounds and blurred fragments of thought in our "stream of consciousness." Still, we believe that *this* is not what we were asked. This is not what it means to think. We could direct our attention, say, to colors or shapes present in any given memory of a state of consciousness. Or we could perhaps report directly on what is going on "inside one's mind" (an expression not to be taken too seriously): "I see a red patch, a grid pattern," and so on. Then we would, albeit in a rather loose sense of the term, be thinking, because thinking is *about* something. If someone were to demand of us that we not think "about" anything, but think nothing, we might be able to comply, by ceasing to think. We should not, however, be likely to say that, in ceasing to think about anything, we were in fact thinking something called "nothing." I doubt that anyone except for the Heideggerean adept, or the mystic, would be much moved by the command to "bethink nothing" or "Noth-ingness." In short, this is the point at which something odd *may* take place, provided that we are not too stiff-necked to deviate from our ac-customed ways of analyzing what it means to think.

In the previous paragraph, I used the expression "to bethink Nothing-ness." I shift from "nothing" to "Nothingness" in order to bring out that the command is not to fail to think about this or that, but to think the "ground" of the absence of this and that, the origin of each instance of nothing, so to speak. The difference between the two cases may be at least suggested as follows: we can count an instance of nothing: not this, not that. But we cannot count Nothingness, because it is not an instance. The "-ness" form, which signals an abstract noun, and so presumably a countable unit, is here quite misleading, albeit not completely so, as I shall eventually indicate. Here, let us defend the contention that, in saying "Nothingness," there is no mention of "something" in terms of which to count. Of course, and this is crucial to the understanding of Heidegger, we might try to count Nothingness as that unit (remember the "-ness") which is contrasted to everything whatsoever, or to Being. But Being is itself not this or that: quite literally, it is *nothing*. The attempt to count Being succeeds only in counting a being: this or that unit. Consequently, Being is indistinguishable from Nothingness, at least so far as counting is concerned. If to think is to think something, this is because to be is to be countable; or so we might well wish to argue. Since we cannot think, that is, think about, Nothingness, one of two alternatives seems to be forced upon us. Either there is "no such thing" as Nothingness, or we need a new kind of thinking for this radically peculiar case, which we might call *bethinking*. To "bethink" is not to think about, but in a sense hard to define precisely, to *be* what one thinks. This is a very poor explanation, since I used the word "what" where it is surely inappropriate. Second, I used the verb "to be." How can one "be" Nothingness? We can at least give a hint concerning this second question. If Being and Nothingness are the same, then (it might be held) the bethinking of Nothingness is the assimilation of the thinker into the sameness of Being and Nothingness. Is this not, after all, what the mystic claims to do?

Well, the reference to the mystic may tilt the balance so far as my analytical reader is concerned. He may prefer to reject the remarks about bethinking as nonsense, and choose the first alternative. I might mention to him in passing that a man as rational as Aristotle said more than once: the mind becomes "somehow" what it thinks. But this, of course, assumes that there is something to think about. Now a further problem arises. How are we going to carry out our intention to assert the first alternative? It cannot be right to say that "there is no such thing as Nothingness" for at least two reasons. First, as far as it goes, it constitutes at least a verbal admission of a Heideggerean thesis, though a relatively trivial admission. But second, the alternative emerges from the view that to be is to be something, or to be countable. Note that this definition is circular, since it defines "to be" by use of the verb "to be." However, we assume that this difficulty could be overcome. The more important point is that the negation of a thing must itself be a definite thing or a definite negation: it must stand to the thing as *non-p* stands to *p*. As one might put it, the *p* in "*p*" and "*non-p*" must have the same sense. The assertion that "Nothingness" is "no (such) thing," i.e., "not any thing," is true enough on Heideggerean grounds but dubious otherwise, since it seems to grant the thinghood of what is negated in the expression "Nothingness." The usual way in which this old puzzle (going back to Plato) is today avoided is by introducing the language of set theory and mathematical logic. In the Platonic puzzle, to deny the thinkability or speakability of Nothingness (τὸ μηδαμῶς ὄν) is to think and speak it. The contemporary resolution of the puzzle is to reinterpret "Nothingness" as "not any thing" in the sense of the negation of the existential quantifier (7 (Ǝx)). This is, of course, a modified development of Plato's own resolution, since it rests upon the assumption that to be is to be countable, i.e., "quantifiable" (or "the value of a variable").

In a recent volume of essays devoted to Plato, we find two treatments of this puzzle. According to the first, Nothingness (the author's term is "Nothing") is a "subject-excluder," not a subject: "expressions such as 'nothing' were coined to block gaps that would otherwise be filled by references to one or more of whatever sort of thing is in question. It becomes baffling if we insist that if Nothing can be spoken of it must conform to the rules for those subjects of discourse that it is designed to displace. . . . For this is to require that if Nothing is to be mentionable it must establish its credentials as a logical subject, identifiable and de-scribable: we must be able to say that it is a so-and-so, and which so-and-so it is." [1] Very sensible, one is inclined to reply. But does it really serve to clear up the question of Nothingness? Only if we assume in advance that the "sense" of Nothingness is purely syntactical. For whatever reason sensible men may have devised the expression "nothing," our question is not with *any* "sort of thing" whatever. The passage just cited is repre-sentative of analytical replies that beg the question. And one may profit-ably ask at this point: is the question in fact meaningless? Is the expression "Nothingness" nothing other than a misformed or misconceived version of a "subject-excluder"? What is "excluding"? More sharply put, to say "there are no so-and-so's" is to employ negation. But how can we ex-plain negation? Surely not on the basis of truth tables, since these make use of falsity, which contains the idea of negation. The sense of "no" in "there are no so-and-so's" is derived in part from the kind, form, or property defining the *set* of so-and-so's, and thus from the connections between this set and others, as well as from the "fit" between language and sets. The negation in any definite case depends finally upon the capacity to think every individual object whatsoever as either a member or not a member of the given set. We may pick out those objects which are members by definition, one-to-one correlation, and so on, but none of these devices accounts for the root ideas in the failure of an object to be a member of a set. Stated simply, "not to be a member" requires us to think of both nothing and everything. But these notions cannot be con-structed from finite units, because they are not themselves sums of finite

1. G. E. L. Owen, "Plato on Not-Being," in *Plato I: Metaphysics and Epistemology,* ed. G. Vlastos (New York, 1971), p. 246.

units. An excessive dependence upon the concept of quantification makes it impossible to provide a satisfactory explanation of "one" or unity. And this in turn rules out a rational distinction between the unity of a whole and that of a sum.

It would take me too far afield to discuss the problem of unity in detail. Suffice it to say that, in terms of quantification theory and the principles of analysis, what counts as a unit is purely arbitrary, or at the convenience of the analyst.[2] I shall have occasion to add a remark about this point in the next section. Meanwhile, let us emphasize that "everything" and "nothing" are concepts underlying quantifications of units that cannot themselves be explained on the basis of such quantificational operations. To say this is in no way to confuse "nothing" for "something" in the sense of a physical object, or some favored abstract object. It is to take "nothing" for what it must be in analytical philosophy: a concept. But the sense of the concept cannot be derived from its reference, since it has none.

According to the early Wittgenstein, for example, the negation sign in a proposition corresponds to "nothing in reality."[3] A proposition "p" is negated, not by 'non' or ' 7 ' but by "what is in common to all the signs of this notation which deny p."[4] Wittgenstein makes use in these two passages of both "nothing" and "all," the latter functioning in the context like "everything." Neither term is intelligible in terms of what *is* the case. In other words, Wittgenstein does not tell us what it means to "deny" p. For example, we might say that q stands for the conjunction of propositions corresponding to the facts that, taken together, exclude the possibility of the fact expressed by p. But how do we explain that q contradicts p without at the same time explaining that contradiction contains negation as an essential ingredient? Since there is nothing in reality to which the negation sign corresponds, how did it come to our attention, or better, how did we associate a concept with it? If the fact that p is not the case is equivalent to the fact that q is the case, then the assertion of q is part of an explanation why p does not obtain, but it is not the whole of that explanation. We must first notice the absence of p. It is all very well to talk of "inferring" non-p from q; the question is how this is done. No manipulation of present items will produce by itself an absence.

2. See W. V. O. Quine, *Word and Object* (New York, 1960), p. 22: "considered relative to our surface irritations, which exhaust our clue to an external world, the molecules and their extraordinary ilk are thus much on a par with the most ordinary physical objects"; and p. 23: "we have no reason to suppose that man's surface irritations even unto eternity admit of any one systematization that is scientifically better or simpler than all possible others." This is the "scientific" foundation for the rejection of the distinction between essential and accidental properties (p. 199) and the dissolution of problems by avoiding usage that engenders them (p. 261).

3. *Tractatus* 4. 061.

4. Ibid. 5. 512.

This point is sufficiently important that it deserves an extended example. To say that negation corresponds to nothing in reality is an inference from the assertion that reality consists of definite, countable objects. If a term has a reference, this reference must consist of such countable objects. In this case, "nothing" can have a sense if and only if it has no reference. Yet that sense is intelligible only with respect to the concept of a thing or object ("not any thing"). How then do we determine the reference of a predicate in a false assertion? It is essential to try to answer this question *before* having recourse to the canonical notation of the predicate calculus. For the point is that the use of this calculus already presupposes that we know how to use "not." The problem is "removed" by analysis, but the analysis makes use of the problematic concept. To say falsely that a so-and-so is such-and-such is to misidentify a specific property. This seems to mean that the reference of a term can be something other than (and even contradictory to) its actual or normal reference. When someone mistakenly predicates F of a, it is fair to say that, in this case, he does not know what he is talking about. If another observer, with access to the original, corrects the initial assertion by saying truly that "not Fa," he correctly refers to the property represented by F as absent from the term represented by a, but he is not presumably referring to absence simply (or to Nothingness) as present. The initial speaker was erroneously referring to the absent property as present in a. Presumably he was led to do so by misidentifying a present property. In other words, he took the present property, not as itself, and not even as absent, but as something else. The reference of his predication is not the present property. But it cannot be the intended and absent property since, if it were, we could not distinguish in a stable and effective manner between true and false predication. An evidently false predication could be certified as true on the grounds that the reference was correctly intended by the speaker. In our example of the two observers, the distinction is artificially preserved by the *deus ex machina* of the second speaker, who is assumed to have access to the original. But no explanation is given of the mechanism of misidentification in the first case, or of how the second speaker certifies his access to the original, for that matter. And it is upon these two factors that the analysis of "not" depends.

The distinction between a true and a false predication cannot be allowed to turn upon the intention of the speaker, as perhaps all parties to the dispute would agree. Nor is it permissible to relegate the problem of how we come to make a false predication to psychology or epistemology, as extralogical or extrasemantical. The construction of our logic, as I have already emphasized, is itself dependent upon our understanding of how to use "not." If the function of "not" within the logic falsifies the process by which we actually employ it in thinking and speaking, then a problem has been "avoided" at the cost of explaining how we think. It would make more sense to say that "not" points to Nothingness, or that it functions semantically to designate an absence of reference. To do so, however, is to transform it into a concept, the concept of the null set. This is the procedure followed by the second essay on Plato of the two noted above. The second author proceeds more technically than the first: "Logical orthodoxy finds a way of removing the apparently referential status of 'nothing' . . . by parsing" the propositions in which it occurs into $not\text{-}(\exists x)$ (Fx). Furthermore, "this orthodoxy makes $(\exists x)$ (. . . (x)) a certain predicate of predicates of individuals. It is a predicate, here applied to the predicate F, which we may roughly equate with the higher-level notion of *instantiation* . . . On this account, $not\text{-}(\exists x)$ (. . . (x)), like $(\exists x)$ (. . . (x)), will also be a higher-level predicate or predicate of predicates of individuals. It will be the compound predicate of predicates, noninstantiation. And whether a man knows it or not, what he is thinking about and struggling for an account of when he thinks about *nothing* is precisely what this compound second-level predicate of first-level predicates stands for," namely, "a third-order statement of the existence of a second-level concept" which, of course, is itself, as a subject of thought, a concept, the concept *nothing*, "even if nobody thinks about this concept." [5]

This is brisk stuff, but the net import is to interpret Nothingness in terms of a concept with sense but no reference, i.e., the null set. The second-level concept of a first-level concept of no extension "is a property-like account of *nothing*. Its extensional counterpart would be *the extension of the concept 'concept with no extension'* or $\{\{\Lambda\}\}$, the unit set of the null set. Both relate to *nothing* as applied within the domain of individuals. . . . " [6] The property to which the author refers is not of Nothingness, but of the concept *nothing*. The author does not notice that he has made no actual reference to nothing (as he calls what I designate by "Nothingness") because he assumes from the outset that a concept is called for. The concept of a concept lacking in extension itself has extension, as the author's symbolism shows: it is precisely a *unit set*. So, strictly speaking, he does not interpret Nothingness as a concept lacking in reference. But this is, I think, a technical error on his part, to which he was led by his initial understanding of *nothing* as a property of individuals. Since a property must inhere in individuals, it must be a unit. But a unit is present, not absent, or else it cannot be counted. In other words, the author has been misled by the doctrine of referentiality. According to this doctrine, there must be something to which to refer. The

5. D. Wiggins, "Sentence Meaning, Negation, and Plato's Problem of Non-Being," in Vlastos, *Plato I*, pp. 273ff.

6. Ibid. p. 274.

unit must have positive identity. If this positive identity cannot be an orthodox object, then we must find a concept to do objective duty. This assumed solution corresponds to the assumed nature of the problem: the "apparently referential status" of *nothing*. But such an appearance has been imported into the problem by the set theoretician. Nothingness appears to refer only when it is misconstrued as a faulty logical subject. What {{Λ}} represents, stated crudely, is a construction (surely not a natural entity) by the intellect of a consequence of Nothingness, a radicalized conception of negation in the logic of quantification. But negation has still not been explained.

Anyone who wishes to take seriously the problem of Nothingness must reconcile himself to a willing suspension of belief in the world of concepts, objects, quantifiers, and the like. This in turn means that the problem cannot be cleared up by an application of the sense-reference distinction. Since Nothingness is not a concept, not merely can it have no reference, but, strictly speaking, it cannot have a sense. The set-theoretical approach just looked at is oriented in terms of reference or extensionality. This orientation in turn is defined with respect to objects. The intelligibility of a concept having no objects, the null set, depends upon, and is defined in terms of, concepts having objects, just as negation is defined in terms of affirmation. The sense of a concept is itself defined as that part of the meaning which enables us to determine its reference.[7] Therefore, even if we accept the Fregean schematism for the analysis of language, we shall remain squarely within the ontological framework of Platonic-Aristotelian rationalism, with one major exception. We agree that to be is to be something, i.e., countable, but we are no longer talking about things, beings, or ὄντα. We are now, in describing things, talking about concepts. This is the Kantian heritage of modern set theory and analytical philosophy. And this is how we come to talk about the null set, or the unit set containing the null set, instead of at least attempting to think (or bethink) Being and Nothingness.

FREGE ON EXISTENCE

In the previous section, I have tried to show the plausibility of Heidegger's (or anyone else's) inquiry into Nothingness. This inquiry originates in the simplest reflection upon ordinary experience. There is no question

7. See M. Dummett, *Frege* (London, 1973), p. 91. This formulation might be challenged, and was, by the anonymous reviewer in the TLS, 30 November 1973. But if references determine senses, and there is no reference, how do we arrive at a sense for the null set? Maybe this is another reason why Wiggins speaks of the unit set containing the null set (although the main reason is that *nothing* is for him a predicate of predicates, whereas the null set is a predicate).

here of mysticism or melodrama. And the inquiry cannot be pursued exclusively, or primarily, by means of contemporary analytical techniques. The very formulation by analysts of the "apparent puzzle" of Nothingness (or nothing) is a mistake. On the other hand, we can only gain by thinking through the analytical resolution of the problem of Nothingness, as well as its treatment of negation. I rather suspect that we learn more about Nothingness through a careful inspection of ostensibly clear but actually muddled analytical arguments than we do by attempting to assimilate, or duplicate, Heidegger's famous existential encounter with Nothingness. In any case, I shall turn to that encounter in the next section of this paper. I want now to add some arguments against rejecting the whole "speculative" inquiry into Nothingness on the basis of Frege's analysis of existence. The crucial point in my argument is as follows. If concepts exist (if the reference of a predicate is a concept), then surely we shall be populating the universe with an apparently unending supply of entities, and entities that are self-contradictory in the sense that they must be both eternal and invented by man, or that give rise to contradictory linguistic situations, and so on. But if concepts do not exist, or if the reference of a predicate is to be explained semantically rather than ontologically, then the capacity to "refer" to countably distinct semantical entities becomes inexplicable. It is worth remarking at the outset that the latter problem does not arise from a false view that language, if it means anything at all, must be about objects. Instead, it arises from the false view that to exist is to be, or to count as, an object.

We begin by considering briefly the Fregean thesis that it is impossible meaningfully to deny the assertion that "A exists." [8] Frege wishes to show the correct analysis of existence statements. In assertions of the form just cited, whatever value one gives to A must exist or be experienceable, i.e., subsumable under one or more concepts. Frege thus equates the meaning of "exists" with "is experienceable." It therefore makes no sense to say that something that one has experienced has not been experienced. On the other hand, if one asserts that "the object of representation B is experienceable," this may be negated, since there is obviously a difference between an experienced representation and the possibility of its referring to a real object. We may note also that, on Fregean grounds, it is impossible to put *Nothing* into the slot marked (or filled) by A, since *Nothing* is to be explained via the negation of the existential quantifier ($7\,(\exists x)$), where x presumably ranges over some definite set of entities. We have seen already that this interpretation fails to meet the issue raised by the expression "Nothingness," since (a) a negative quantifier contains negation as an unexplained term; (b) the restriction to a set is

8. "Dialog mit Punjer über Existenz," in *Schriften zur Logik und Philosophie aus dem Nachlass*, ed. G. Gabriel (Hamburg, 1971), pp. 17ff.

impossible in the case of Nothingness, which, if it "negates" at all, negates all sets, and not just their members; and (c) a negative quantifier is a concept, and hence something countable. I do not know what sense it would make to talk about quantifying over quantifiers. But it would make less sense to deny that there "are" quantifiers (note again, this is not to suggest that quantifiers are objects: to take it that way is to beg the question at issue). No matter how we analyze the "are" in this case, if we do not simply dissolve the concepts of quantification and negation, we are left with countable items. And if nothing countable is left, then we are face to face with Nothingness.

To return to "A exists": for Frege, only definite or countable instances can be the values of the variable A. Furthermore, Frege seems to claim that "exists" or "is" adds no information to the mere assertion of some value for A.[9] One might object that, as so stated, this erases the difference between "exists" and "does not exist" in such ordinary uses as "The largest number does not exist." As already noted, however, Frege analyzes such statements in such a way as to show that no objects (numbers) fall under the concept "largest number." The assertion that "A exists" is understood to say that there is at least one thing such that it falls under the concept, or bears the predicate, A. If A is a proper name, e.g., Pegasus, we can perhaps follow Quine's suggestion and speak of the concept "Pegasizing" or the predicate "pegasizes."[10] The example is especially useful because it shows how, on the assumption that concepts exist, one must give "eternal" status to what are obviously inventions of the human imagination. But I want to look at another side of the issue. Let me try to bring out the fact that, despite Frege's analysis of "being," his position amounts finally to the Aristotelian contention that there is no contrary to being (i.e., in Frege's case, to being a predicate). I think this will have several interesting consequences.

In the statement "Pegasus does not exist," we are saying on Fregean lines, not that there is no concept "Pegasus," but that there is not at least one object falling under the concept "Pegasizing." If it were the case that we could say "the concept 'Pegasus' does not exist," what would the statement mean? The closest I can come to thinking of a Fregean analysis is this: for all predicates, there is at least one, Pegasus, such that there is not at least one object falling under it. But this, of course, simply tells us something about the reference of the concept, not its sense. For Frege, a concept can have sense without reference. And so, his argument against saying "A does not exist" surely applies to an effort to deny the sense of the concept "Pegasizing." In other words, it is not concepts which possess contraries, but existence statements. If concepts exist,

9. Ibid., pp. 16f., 19.
10. Quine, *From a Logical Point of View* (Cambridge, Mass., 1963), p. 8.

"negative" concepts do not. But if concepts do not exist, then how can we think, mention, and count them? Even on the alternative that concepts are semantical expressions that cannot or ought not to be said to exist, it remains true that there is no contrary to a concept. And this is the same as the Platonic-Aristotelian doctrine that there is no contrary to "man," "horse," or "flower." Thus, for example, "not-man" means approximately "something-other-than-man." There are, of course, contrary predications of man, etc. But predication is explained in terms of the primary sense of "being," *ousia*, in which properties do or do not inhere. I shall come back to this in a moment. Meanwhile, we note that Frege goes the Greeks one better. He transforms the predicables into pseudo-*ousiai*. This, however, has odd consequences.

To continue, the correct analysis of "not-man" is not the negation of a concept, but also not the negation of an essence or *ousia*. This shows us the link between the classical tradition and the interpretation of "not" in contemporary quantification theory. In the latter case, just as *nothing* means $7 (\exists x) (\ldots (x))$, so "this is not a man" is analyzed as $(\exists x)$ $(Tx \mathbin{\&} 7 Mx)$, where $7 Mx$ means, not the negation of the concept, but the negation of the x picked out by the quantifier. We thus reach the result that, for the Greeks, what "is" in the proper sense of the term has no contrary. If to be is to be experienceable, or thinkable, or nameable, then "what is" cannot not be. One may, of course, destroy a man, a horse, or some other "object" or being. But one cannot destroy the *ousia* "man," etc. What is the situation in Frege? Concepts replace *ousiai*, and these may not be destroyed. Hence they must exist or "be" forever. And since what exists can be counted or quantified, concepts must be able to stand in for objects in higher-level quantification. Regular objects (but not the pseudoobjects of higher-level quantification) can be destroyed, with no damage to the correlative concept. And this fact allows us to insist that the ontological status of the object is inferior to that of the concept. On the other hand, objects are fundamental to the intelligibility of concepts. Even empty concepts are explained relative to the existence of concepts having objects. Shall we say that objects possess existential and epistemological priority over concepts? I do not believe that this distinction between ontological on the one hand and existential and epistemological on the other is a coherent one. Yet something like it must be drawn.

In any case, I am not now concerned with the question, interesting as it is in its own right, as to which is fundamental, the concept or the object. My point is that *quantification and negation bifurcate here*. Negation is the denial of existence, which in turn means to exclude objects from falling under a concept (and so with pseudoobjects in higher-level quantification). The operation of negation or exclusion does not touch the existence of the concepts in question. They simply *are*. I note in passing that the destruction of an object is not the same as the exclusion of an object from its concept. The exclusion or inclusion of objects from or in concepts is the contemporary analogue to the Platonic doctrine of the interweaving of forms or "greatest genera" discussed in the *Sophist*. The key point here for us is that things, in this doctrine, "are" by virtue of sharing in the form or genus *ousia*. For Plato as well as for Frege, this is an "empty predicate" in the sense that it does not tell us anything about some *other* property of a thing. What it does is to distinguish everything that exists from imaginary combinations of predicates which do not exist. On the Fregean doctrine, this exclusion seems to be impossible, because any conceivable thing or property can be transformed into a predicate, e.g., "Pegasus," which must then refer to an existing concept, a concept, however, which cannot exist (except in higher-level predication) because it is not an object.

So the main point is as follows. The verb "is" in the sense of "exists," has a function in classical philosophy that we may insist plays its role in Frege's doctrine, whether he honors it or not, and that cannot be explained by the notions of identity or predication, since these may both be denied or negated. But the "is" in the expression "concepts are" (or "exist") does not predicate, and it does not link two distinct properties to the same object. If it merely points out the existence of the object, as in $A=A$ (which cannot be denied in nondialectical logic), that is the same as saying that a given concept is the same as itself, or that it *is* what it is, which is again not a predication of a distinct property to a distinct object. The "identity" of a concept with itself is a property, if at all, of the *being* of the concept, i.e., the existent concept. Since the "is" in the assertion that there are concepts is distinct from quantification (as one could also say, because it belongs to all concepts), what we are here concerned with is the ontological "is" par excellence. This "is" is as unanalyzable as "true," which, according to Frege, belongs trivially to every assertion. In fact, although I shall not press the point, I suggest that "true" is intelligible only because it points toward the Being which is also pointed out by the ontological "is." To say that neither term adds information of a predicative nature is just another way of saying that both point, not simply to Being, but to Nothingness.

A failure to take seriously the ontological "is" (and so the unanalyzed function of "true"), a failure that is the consequence of an orientation by extensionality, reference, or modern quantification theory, and so finally a kind of "objectivism," leads very soon to the disintegration of objects into a contingent collocation of predicates, which collocation has in each case been "constructed" at the convenience of the analyst. The essence or *ousia* of the object is discarded, and in that sense "negated."

Curiously enough, this result follows from an obscurity intrinsic to the Platonic-Aristotelian doctrine of knowing. The obscurity in question has been partially concealed by Heidegger, thanks to his choice of terms to describe the Greek conception of Being. I clarify the issue here, in order to show how it strengthens his own criticism of Western rationalism in both its ancient and contemporary forms. According to Heidegger, this rationalist tradition defines Being as *parousia* or "presence" (*Anwesenheit*). To be present is of course to present oneself to an audience. In this case, beings are the consequence of the presentation of Being before man, who sees only the interaction of the presentation and his own activity of seeing. The result is perspectivism or subjectivism (exactly as in the case of Quine, cited above, note 2). Being is concealed beneath beings.

If we take Aristotle (where the point is more sharply drawn than in Plato) as a representative of this tradition, the situation is somewhat different. Whereas "being" (or perhaps Being) is equated with *ousia*, the term *parousia* is reserved for the property "present in" *ousia*, and to which there corresponds an affirmative predication. The absence of a property in *ousia*, to which a negative predication corresponds, is called an *apousia*.[11] Discursive thinking, then, picks out the presence or absence of properties in *ousia*, but it does not and cannot say anything of *ousia* itself. The *ousia*, which is interpreted by Aristotle as *eidos* and by Plato as *idēa*, *eidos*, and *genos* (but never as a semantic predicate), is ostensibly present or accessible to us via intellectual intuition. (In the later Platonic dialogues, nothing is said of intellectual intuition, but this only deepens the mystery of the visibility of the forms or genera.) Yet whatever we say of *ousia* must be couched in discursive speech, and so through predication. The merits in translating *ousia* as though it were the same as *parousia* are outweighed by the disadvantage, from Heidegger's own standpoint, of obscuring the invisibility of the visible. *Ousia* is unspeakable and unthinkable, at least so far as *dianoia* (the discursive or calculative thinking) is concerned. It therefore becomes impossible to explain what we mean by intellectual intuition. Each such explanation, just as in the case of an ostensible explanation of the content of an intuition, is in fact an explanation of something else. The "presence" of *ousia* is, then, indistinguishable from its "absence." As we might put this, Being is indistinguishable from Nothingness.

But the practical consequence within the tradition is the disappearance of essence.[12] A thing or object can then be identified only on the basis of

11. Aristotle, *Metaphysics* Γ, 1011b13ff.

12. See Quine, *From a Logical Point of View*, p. 22: "Meaning is what essence becomes when it is divorced from the object of reference and wedded to the word." This in turn leads to the abandonment by Quine of meanings. Cf. p. 48: meanings are replaced by significances of linguistic form. For a different view on essences by a linguistic philosopher, see S. Kripke, "Naming and Necessity," in *Semantics of Natural Language*, ed. Donald Davidson and Gilbert Harman (Holland, 1972).

what counts as a satisfactory analysis. Since "satisfactory" is itself defined on the basis of human intentions, the very notion of definite things or Fregean objects is necessarily jeopardized from within by the dissolution of Nothingness. In the language of analysis, objects become the objects of intentions, and efforts like that of Quine to reduce intentional idiom and restrict science to direct quotation about the physical nature of organisms seem to dissolve in self-contradiction.[13] This is the price one pays for the failure to take seriously the question of Nothingness.

Before closing this section, I should like to make one more point. It is senseless in the Fregean universe to say that *omnis determinatio negatio est*. A determination is a property of an object, whereas a negation is a syntactic or logical operation with no reference to objective reality. But basically the same situation holds in the Platonic-Aristotelian teaching. Stated with maximum simplicity, analytical rationalism attempts to exclude nonbeing from being. Science rests upon the distinctness and definiteness of its objects.[14] To say that a given object is intrinsically a negation, or both itself and its opposite, is to render it unstable. The sharp distinction between one object and another is destroyed. But this means that the analytical tradition cannot account for the fact that each thing is *nothing* but itself, something upon which the tradition itself insists, thereby invoking a sense of the negative that has nothing to do with quantification. All the analyst can do at this point is to imitate Voltaire in his manner of attacking religion: we are regaled with irony and laughter. Now I like a good joke as well as the next man, but the practitioner of analytical irony must understand that he has accomplished nothing of a philosophical nature by his irony. However odd it may sound to Aristotelian ears, the difference between one genus and another cannot be explained by means of differences falling within a genus. We begin to see the problem clearly, not by talking it away, nor by chanting the magic formula against a *metabasis eis allo genos*, but by taking seriously this fact: *nothing* distinguishes one genus from another. And this *nothing* is not a logical subject; on the contrary, it gives logical subjects their being.

To summarize: the assertion that a concept cannot be negated is in effect the same as the assertion that Being has no contrary. But this separation of Being from Nothingness amounts to a hypostasizing of Nothingness in the form of the *concept* of negation. Since the concept of negation applies to objects rather than to concepts, the latter neither are nor are not. But this "is and is not" is precisely the sameness of Being and Nothingness addressed by Heidegger. It is a nonquantifiable Being underlying all senses of "is" and so of "not." Differently stated: analyti-

13. See *Word and Object*, p. 221.
14. See B. Russell, "The Philosophy of Logical Atomism," in *Logic and Knowledge*, ed. R. C. Marsh (London, 1956), p. 204.

cal philosophy founders upon the issue of the existence of concepts. The problem takes a more fruitful shape if we agree that concepts are human constructions, whereas forms, essences, or beings are not. On the other hand, we gain nothing, or lose as much as we gain, by the distinction noted, unless we supplement the doctrine of predication with some other account of thinking, being, and not-being.

HEIDEGGER'S ENCOUNTER WITH NOTHINGNESS

Thus far I have tried to derive the problem of Nothingness from a consideration of certain weak spots in analytical philosophy. It would be perhaps too cryptic, but not wrong, to summarize my remarks thus far as follows: the analytical tradition suffers from the root defect of Platonism, the hypostasizing of Nothingness. Now I shall consider Heidegger himself a bit more closely. My purpose is not in the least to provide a resumé of all that he says concerning Nothingness. Such resumés exist, and may be easily consulted by the novice.[15] Instead, I shall choose some representative passages from pivotal Heideggerean texts, in order to show that his treatment of Nothingness is also marked by a kind of "Platonism." This will lead me to some general observations, which may be summarized in these conclusions. A "scientific ontology" is altogether impossible, because all talk of "Being" in quasimathematical or discursively analytical terms is both self-contradictory and misses the mark at which it ostensibly aims. If a "scientific" or "logical" account of Being were at all possible, it would have to be Hegelian, or employ a dialectico-speculative logic. But Hegelian ontology is also impossible, because it conceptualizes Nothingness. It does not follow from this that we are free to dispense with the question of Being and Nothingness, however. Every careful, serious, and self-conscious attempt to philosophize leads us sooner rather than later to this question. One can have nothing but disdain for fashionable efforts to conceal the question, however understandable is the origin of these fashions. And finally, if one cannot resolve the question "logically," then perhaps it is best to return to Plato after all—not to his logic, however, but to his myths. I do not mean by this that we should jettison logic, but that we must continuously refresh and repair it. The human condition, if I may use that hackneyed phrase, is necessarily to think the unthinkable. To turn away from that task is to cease to exercise what I should not hesitate to call the divine mandate or categorical imperative of self-consciousness.

I began this essay with an illustration of the fact that, under all ordinary

15. For a survey, see W. J. Richardson, *Heidegger: Through Phenomenology to Thought,* 3rd ed. (The Hague, 1974).

circumstances, when someone asks us "what" we are thinking, if we cannot reply, we admit that we have not been thinking. In a very specific sense, Heidegger may be said to accept this analysis of thinking about nothing. Heidegger's famous discussions concerning the encounter with Nothingness, in *Sein und Zeit*, make this quite clear.[16] Let me state the point as simply as possible. The encounter with Nothingness, or, in its initial form, with nothing (*nichts*), does not occur via thinking in the traditional sense of thinking something (a *Seiendes*). Instead, it occurs via a mood or "existential attunement" of *Dasein* (literally, "there-being" but rendered for all practical purposes by "man" or "concrete individual"). This mood is dread or anxiety (*Angst*); at least, that is the example Heidegger chooses. As everyone presumably knows by now, existential anxiety does not itself answer to the question "what?" by naming a thing, state, process, or future event. Heidegger turns away from thinking to the experience of moods because, at least in *Sein und Zeit*, he does not reject the traditional view (as transmitted by Husserl) that to think is to think something. Since Being and Nothingness are not something, not this or that, whereas thinking is thinking this or that, we cannot *begin* to think about Being and Nothingness by thinking about them directly (or finally, "about" them at all).

We begin the presentation of the problem with Being (and this is crucial for understanding Heidegger's "Platonism": Nothingness must be approached via Being). Being is "strict transcendence" of all beings or things (*SZ* 4). If it should be possible to think Being at all, then we shall require a new kind of thinking, a kind that is not thing-oriented, and which must therefore reply "nothing" to the question "what?" As is evident from the entire existential analysis of *Sein und Zeit*, the move from beings to Being, the transition across the "ontological difference," presupposes the most extensive application of the thinking of things: this, that, and such-and-such. We require an elaborate discursive or analytical, and in this crucial sense traditional, preparation for the new kind of thinking. But an essential element in that preparation is the encounter with nothing through anxiety rather than thinking.

Whereas anxiety, in the special Heideggerean sense, is not thinking, the sense of the experience is accessible (or at least is presented) only through discourse of a traditional kind. To go directly to the nerve of the analysis, anxiety arises only within a world that is already a web of articulations or senses, a web spun by the finite *Dasein* in its finite speeches, deeds, desires, and so on. We experience anxiety with respect to this world as such (*SZ* 187), or with respect to ourselves as "being-in-the-world as such" (*SZ* 186). The "as such" points to the definiteness of the notion of

16. *Sein und Zeit*, 7th ed. (Tübingen, 1953) (hereafter abbreviated *SZ*), paragraphs 40 and 58 et passim.

"world" or of "being-in-the-world" that allows us to think it as the "be-fore what" (*wovor*) of our anxiety. There is, then, a kind of "what" in the experience of nothing, which enables us to move beyond mood, at-tunement, or "experience" in some precognitive, prelogical sense, to the exposition of *Sein und Zeit*, which identifies "nothing" as Nothingness (*das Nichts*). "Nothing" becomes ontologically meaningful only by what looks initially like reification into *the* Nothing, i.e., Nothingness or *das Nichts*. Differently stated, in *Sein und Zeit*, Nothingness is indis-tinguishable from, if not identical with, the world "as such." We can no more think "the world as such" than we can think Nothingness, at least in a way traditional enough to eventuate in ontological assertions (how-ever surprising their content). Every effort to think the world as such results in thinking some aspect of the world: this or that. One might perhaps call this the noetic version of Aristotle's logical rejection of a *summum genus*. There is, however, at least an initial plausibility in the claim that we experience Nothingness via anxiety. Even if one prefers to make a Freudian interpretation of the phenomenon, it is not uncommon.

We must emphasize, as has been apparent from what preceded, that by "Nothingness," Heidegger does not mean "absolute vacuousness" or *nihil absolutum*. Anxiety detaches *Dasein* from its existential connections with things in the world by emptying these of meaning, not by erasing or obliterating them (*SZ* 343). Heideggerean "negation" is thus an existen-tial version of logical or Platonic negation. It attaches a "non-" to a *p*. The "total negation" of anxiety, so to speak, brackets the world with a "non" or deprives it of sense. This is Heidegger's existential version of the phenomenological *epochē*. The "disconnecting" of the significance of the world is an encounter with the world as such. But it does not (as in the case of Husserl) take us outside the world. Heidegger's "transcen-dence" is an *immanent transcendence*. Anxiety reveals us as finite beings-in-the-world, for whom the world, and so we ourselves, are marked by *Nichtigkeit* (*SZ* 308; cf. 187f., 330). The Nothingness is that of the world as such, i.e., not of nothing whatsoever, but of everything.[17]

This is a point that, so far as I know, holds good throughout Heideg-ger's published work.[18] Indeed, it is intensified after *Sein und Zeit* by the identification of Nothingness with Being.[19] In one striking phrase among many, man, as the shepherd of Being, is "the place-holder of Nothing-ness."[20] So then, we move from beings via anxiety to Nothingness, and

17. In addition to *Sein und Zeit*, see *Nietzsche*, vol. 2 (Pfullingen, 1961), p. 50.
18. For relevant passages, see Richardson, and H. Feick, *Index zu Heideggers "Sein und Zeit*," 2nd ed. (Tübingen, 1968).
19. "Was ist Metaphysik?" in *Wegmarken* (Frankfurt, 1967), pp. 11f.; *Nietzsche*, vol. 2, pp. 51, 337, 383; *Zur Seinsfrage* (Frankfurt, 1956), pp. 37f. See also Richard-son, pp. 204, 474 et passim.
20. *Holzwege* (Frankfurt, 1952), p. 321.

thus to Being. The pivotal experience is not thinking, but we can think, and therefore talk, about it. Our thinking and talking may gear us up for authentic resolution and activity, or (as Heidegger puts it from the mid-thirties on) it may prepare us for the authentic "letting things be" of the enlightened thinker. Then again, we may or may not receive a new "gift" of Being from the Nothingness which is, as it were, the "visible" side of Being, the side turned toward man as thinking animal. We may or may not learn a new kind of thinking appropriate to Being and Nothingness, rather than to this and to that. What interests me now is just the fact that we are able to think about nothing. And for Heidegger, this means thinking about Nothingness, namely, *the* Nothingness that is not detached from, but belongs to, Being.[21]

The shift from "negativity" (*Nichtigkeit*) or "nothing" (*nicht*) to Nothingness (*das Nichts*) looks, then, like a hypostasizing of Nothingness. It was pointed out by the Eleatic Stranger in Plato's *Sophist* that, when Parmenides warns us not to say "the altogether not" (τὸ νηδαμῶς ὄμ), he contradicts himself by the very utterance of the prohibition. We have already seen the inadequacy of the analytical resolution of this problem. Putting to one side the article required by Greek grammar, it is obvious that Parmenides prohibits mention, or is interpreted in the *Sophist* as prohibiting mention, of Nothingness in a sense other than Heidegger's. Strictly speaking, the prohibited Nothingness would seem to have no sense at all. Thus Heidegger, in rejecting the *nihil absolutum*, is actually obeying the injunction of Parmenides. The article in *das Nichts* is not a mere grammatical appendage, but answers to the "what" in the "before what" (*wovor*) of the anxiety described in *Sein und Zeit*. *Das Nichts* is the Nothingness "of" (subjective and objective genitive) Being. And this is Platonism. We attempt to suppress or discard the *nihil absolutum*, but succeed in doing so only by making Nothingness the same as Being. However, in thereby succeeding in our effort to talk "about" (or be-speak) Nothingness, we contradict ourselves, since whatever we say is predicative, or a bespeaking of this or that. And this contradiction leads to Hegel. But I am moving a bit too quickly. Heidegger's treatment of Nothingness is neither completely Platonic nor completely Hegelian. The question is whether *Heideggerean* thinking does not succumb to "nihilism," or the failure of western metaphysics to think Being as distinct from beings.[22]

Let us recapitulate in the light of this question. Since it is meaningful to prohibit reference to the altogether not or *nihil absolutum*, it must be meaningful to refer to it. And yet, to "what" are we "referring"? Certainly not the null set or the unit set containing the null set. The turn

21. *Nietzsche*, vol. 2, p. 51.
22. Ibid., pp. 337ff. et passim.

away from this Nothingness to another is a turn from this to that, at least in speech. The turn away from the *nihil absolutum* takes place *within* the horizon of the Nothingness that "is and is not." Since Heidegger's Nothingness, because it is the same as Being, and so other than the *nihil absolutum*, has the Platonic attribute of definiteness or finitude, why can we not describe it in the language of predication? Have we not just done so? And since we distinguish the *nihil absolutum* from *das Nichts*, do we not think *both*? As I have already suggested, my own view is this: Heidegger's ontology does indeed terminate in a self-contradiction. At this point, Heidegger has two choices: either to return to Hegel's logic of contradiction, or to abandon ontology. In fact, he chose the latter. This is the sum and substance of the famous "turn" (*Kehre*) in Heidegger's thinking. But Heidegger did not abandon the *Seinsfrage*, and it remains the case that he must give an account of the thinking that "bethinks" Being and Nothingness while rejecting the *nihil absolutum*. Of course, as Heidegger regularly insists, his task is to pose the question, not answer it. He is "on the way toward" the bespeaking of Being, *unterwegs zur Sprache*. Nevertheless, questioning is, if not asserting, accompanied by a good deal of asserting.

To take the example noted above, Heidegger, if I am not mistaken, never disowns his initial view of Being as finite. Therefore Nothingness must be finite as well. And this is also obvious from the distinction between *das Nichts* and the *nihil absolutum*. But if *das Nichts* is *finite*, it must be a countable unit. Is not finitude then a *property* of an in-itself inaccessible *ousia*? Looking at the matter in this way, we are led to ask whether every predicative assertion is not the picking out of a property of *Sein-Nichts* (as it might be written), the inaccessible *ousia*, in just the way that, for Aristotle, every *parousia* inheres in a definite (but unspeakable) *ousia*. One can understand Heidegger's desire to think the inaccessible *ousia* rather than its *par-* (or *ap-*) *ousiai*. But in a fundamental sense, Heidegger has said nothing since the abandonment of the project begun with *Sein und Zeit*. The point can be made by approaching from the side of the *nihil absolutum*. The distinction between it and *das Nichts* means that the former is drawn into our thinking, in exactly the way that Hegel assimilates into the thinking of Absolute Spirit the *nihil* indicated in the phrase *creatio ex nihilo*. But this makes *Sein-Nichts* both finite and infinite (as is already signaled in the expression "is-and-is-not"). We are not underway toward a postlogical thinking, but in the midst of Hegel's dialectico-speculative logic.

When Hegel says "*the* Absolute," he means "the identity of identity and difference" or the identity-within-difference of finitude and infinity. This is not the place to expound Hegel's logic.[23] But it has to be said that

23. For some discussion, see my *G. W. F. Hegel* (New Haven and London, 1974).

the instability of predicative discourse, studied earlier with respect to negation, existence, and quantification, is still present in Heidegger. If one likes, one may call this instability the "potentiality" of the *Augenblick* or moment of genuine decision. Still, a choice has to be made. In my view, the choice is between a Hegelian logic or Platonic myth. Heidegger's *Sprache* seems to me to be neither the one nor the other. It makes positive assertions which are self-contradictory, but it neither softens these assertions into myth nor treats them dialectically. Heidegger rejects both myth and logic. But even if it were held that Heideggerean thinking is a kind of mythical (or "poetic") thinking, I should reply that, as is clear from Plato, myth requires logic as much as logic requires myth. Philosophical thinking, all fashions aside, is both mythical and logical. There is no trace of a logic in Heidegger. Perhaps this is because he identifies logic with predication. He rather paradoxically requires a thinking of finitude which is itself neither purely finite nor purely infinite. It cannot be purely finite, since then it would be subject to the axiom that to be is to be countable, as well as to the principles of identity, contradiction, and excluded middle. But it cannot be purely infinite, since it would then lack articulation: it would not "uncover" the true Being, except in some voiceless "illumination" of the void. The only alternative is that Heidegger's new thinking must be both finite and infinite. And this raises the issue of Hegel.

To say this, of course, is not to suggest that Hegel resolved the problem of Being and Nothingness. On the contrary, I am not even convinced that Hegel correctly formulated the issue, since he begins (like Heidegger) from a Kantian orientation toward concepts or the Concept. That is, he assimilates Nothingness into Being, but transforms Being into Thinking (to put the point simply). The reflexive self-grasping of thinking is the Concept. But Nothingness is not a Concept. I will try to fill out this opinion by way of a conclusion to my paper. In Hegel's logic, each finite statement finally implicates every genuinely distinct finite statement, since each is a manifestation of a total or unified process. The process, or *Sein-Nichts*, is revealed by the complete logical analysis of the "implication" (not deductive inference) of finite statements of each other. Language thus "uncovers" or "discovers" the Whole (a thesis also held by Heidegger, although in somewhat different form). Language, on these assumptions (common to Hegel and Heidegger), replaces, or fulfills the task assigned by others to, intellectual intuition. If we turn to a deeper stratum of Platonism than is contained in the "logical" discussions, wholes, as opposed to sums of units, are accessible to direct intellectual intuition. An essential ingredient in Heidegger's criticism of the Platonic doctrine of Ideas is his tacit rejection, exactly as in the case of Kant and Hegel, of a nondiscursive but cognitive intuition. Kant, Heidegger, and Hegel, are all within the tradition stemming from the "logical" branch of Platonism. But this tradition arrives at the rejection of the visibility of *ousia*, or the replacement of the pure receptivity of *nous* by the activity of *Bewusstsein, Geist,* or *Dasein.* It results in conceptual thinking, whether that phrase is used or not. I am aware that Heidegger would reject this formulation of his teaching. Heidegger regularly claims that he wishes to overcome the "subject-object" distinction that characterizes the conceptual thinking ultimately derived from Platonic perspectivism ("what" a thing looks like to the knower). Nevertheless, Being-in-the-world is an "existentialized" version of Hegel's Concept and Kant's transcendental ego. The fact that in his later thinking Heidegger shifts his emphasis from man to Being is irrelevant to the point. Or rather, it confirms the point: as available to thinking, Being is a gift *to man,* or *perspectival.* This is Heidegger's "Nietzscheanism." One may call it historicism or radical subjectivism as one pleases; labels add nothing and take nothing away. Being as thought is a Being within thinking, a Being that gives itself to thinking *as* thinkable. This is what I mean by Heidegger's "conceptualism." *Es gibt Sein.* But the giving is a reflexive act; it does not come from "outside." Thus Heidegger retains his earliest conviction of the finitude of Being. And so he is unable to explain how he rejects the *nihil absolutum* that lies beyond *Sein-Nichts.*

Plato never says anything on this crucial point of how we are aware of the *nihil absolutum.* Whenever he addresses himself to this issue, he simply transforms it into a question of negation and predication. If we make use of a genuinely Platonic thought, however, we may say that the *nihil absolutum* is present in the Whole as the limit or boundary of form. It "gives" itself to us "from outside," or from "beyond being" (ἐπέκεινα τῆς οὐσίας). In so giving itself, it defines or gives beings as well. We can "see" this, but can say nothing of a "scientific" or non-self-contradictory nature about it. This is an admittedly cryptic formulation of why I deny that language replaces intellectual intuition. On the contrary, language is guided by intellectual intuition, and the key to this is ourselves as thinking. For thought can never be grasped in logical or conceptual structure. If thought "gives" or "produces" concepts, it is not itself a concept. This is perhaps Hegel's central error.

I can suggest one other way of putting this point. The Hegelian claim to have replaced intellectual intuition by discourse amounts to the claim that essence shows itself totally within its appearing determinations. Essence both is-and-is-not its determinations. It "is" them because it is not some other hidden or separate *ousia.* It is "not" them because it cannot be equated with the "sum" of its finite determinations, especially because these, as finite, are self-contradictory (as is best seen in genesis or *Werden,* which is simultaneously coming to be and passing away). We can restate this as the claim by Hegel to have explained the identity-within-difference of finitude and infinity. That assertion stands up only if Hegel has explained everything (including Nothingness). But how would one confirm that this has been accomplished, except by *seeing* that it is so, that there is nothing more to explain? Is not this "seeing of nothing" a step outside the circular process of the self-confirming Concept?

Especially in the United States, but not only here, we live in an age that has little patience for speculations like the ones I have introduced in the preceding paragraphs. This is easy to understand. Men prefer to do things rather than to sit back and watch; or at least those who do things tend to set the pace. To "accomplish something" is a phrase that already gives the palm to technological thinking. Those who in the last analysis do not care to do anything but prefer to watch, should not complain about this. It gives them something to see.

Hermeneutics and Language

9. PAUL RICOEUR

The Task of Hermeneutics

I WILL ADOPT the following working definition of hermeneutics: hermeneutics is the theory of the operation of understanding in its relations to the interpretation of texts. My guiding idea will be that of the actualization of discourse as a text, and all of the second lecture will be devoted to elaborating the categories of the text. Thus the way should be prepared for an attempt to resolve the central aporia presented in this first lecture—the disjunction, destructive in my eyes, between explanation and understanding. The search for a conplementarity between these two attitudes, which hermeneutics with a semantic origin has tended to dissociate, will epistemologically express the reorientation of hermeneutics by the notion of text.

The historical survey of hermeneutics I propose here converges on the formulation of an aporia which is the same one which has prompted my own research. Therefore the presentation which follows is not neutral in the sense that it is meant to be free of presuppositions. Even hermeneutics itself puts us on guard against the illusion of such a claim to neutrality.

I see the recent history of hermeneutics as dominated by two preoccupations. The first is to progressively enlarge the goal of hermeneutics in such a way that all the *regional* hermeneutics are included in a *general* hermeneutics. But this movement from regional to general hermeneutics cannot be brought to its fulfillment unless at the same time the properly epistemological preoccupations of hermeneutics—I mean its effort to constitute itself as scientific—are subordinated to the ontological preoccupations where "understanding" ceases to appear as a simple mode of "know-

Translated by David Pellauer in *Philosophy Today* [Celina, Ohio 45822], 17 (Summer, 1973) and reprinted with permission of the author and the editor. This is the first of two lectures presented at Princeton Theological Seminary in May, 1973. The second lecture is mentioned but not included.

ing" in order to become a "way of being" and of relating itself to beings and to being. So the movement of generalization is accompanied by a movement of radicalization by which hermeneutics becomes not just general but also fundamental hermeneutics.

FROM REGIONAL HERMENEUTICS TO GENERAL HERMENEUTICS

The First "Place" of Interpretation

The first "locality" which hermeneutics undertakes to present is surely that of language and more particularly written language. It is important to recognize the contours of this first place, since my own enterprise in the second lecture could appear as an attempt to "re-regionalize" hermeneutics by means of the notion of text. There is question therefore of specifying why hermeneutics has a privileged relation to questions about language. We can begin, it seems to me, with a noteworthy characteristic of natural languages which calls for a work of interpretation at the most elementary and banal level of conversation. This characteristic is polysemy, the trait that our words have more than one signification when they are considered outside of their use in a determinate context. I will not be concerned here with the economic reasons which justify recourse to a lexical code which presents such a unique characteristic. What counts for the present discussion is that the polysemy of words calls forth as its counterpart the selective role of contexts in determining the current value of words in a given message, addressed by a specific speaker to a hearer in a particular situation. Sensitivity to context is the necessary complement and the unavoidable counterpart of polysemy.

But the use of contexts in turn brings into play an activity of discernment which takes place in a concrete exchange of messages between interlocutors and whose model is the language game of question and answer. This activity of discernment is properly called interpretation. It consists in recognizing which relatively univocal message the speaker has constructed upon the polysemic base of the common lexicon. To produce a relatively univocal discourse with polysemic words and to identify this intention of univocity in the reception of messages is the first and the most elementary work of interpretation. It is within this very large circle of exchanged messages that writing carves out a limited domain which Dilthey, to whom I shall return in more detail shortly, calls "expressions of life fixed by writing." These call for a specific work of interpretation for reasons which we will discuss in the second lecture, which belong precisely to the actualization of discourse as text. Let us provisionally say that in writing the conditions of direct interpretation through the question and answer game, therefore through dialogue, are no longer fulfilled.

Specific techniques are required to raise to discourse the series of written signs and to discern the message across the superimposed codifications proper to the actualization of discourse as text.

Schleiermacher

The true movement from regional to general hermeneutics begins with the effort to disengage a general problem from the activity of interpretation which is undertaken in each instance although the texts may differ. The recognition of this central and unifying problematic was the work of Schleiermacher. Before him there was a philology of classical texts, principally those of Greco-Latin antiquity, and an exegesis of sacred texts, the Old and New Testaments. And in each of these two domains the work of interpretation varied according to the diversity of the texs. A general hermeneutics requires therefore that we transcend particular applications and discern the operations common to the two great branches of hermeneutics. But in order to do this, we must not just rise above the particularity of rules and recipes among which the art of understanding was scattered. Hermeneutics was born from this effort to raise exegesis and philology to the rank of a *Kunstlehre*, that is, to a "technology" or "technique" which would not be limited to a simple collection of unrelated operations.

Now this subordination of the particular rules of exegesis and philology to the general problematic of understanding constituted a revolution like the one that Kantian philosophy had achieved elsewhere, principally in relation to the natural sciences. In this respect, we can say that the philosophical horizon closest to hermeneutics is Kantian. The general spirit of critical philosophy, as we know, is to invert the relation between a theory of knowledge and a theory of being. We must measure the capacity for knowledge before raising the question of the nature of being. And it is understandable that it was in a Kantian climate that the project to relate the rules of interpretation, not to the diversity of texts and things in these texts, but to the central operation which unifies the diversity of interpretation could be formed. If Schleiermacher himself was not conscious of carrying out in exegesis and philology the sort of Copernican revolution that Kant carried out in the order of the philosophy of nature, Dilthey was perfectly aware of it in the neo-Kantian climate at the end of the 19th century. But this required an insight of which Schleiermacher had no idea—the inclusion of the exegetical and philological sciences within the historical sciences. It is only within this insight that hermeneutics can appear as a global response to the great lacuna of Kantianism, and also recognized clearly by Cassirer: that in a critical philosophy there is an unbridgeable gap between physics and ethics.

But there was not only question of filling a lacuna in Kantianism, there was also question of profoundly revolutionizing the Kantian concept of the subject. Because it limited itself to investigating the universal conditions for objectivity in physics and ethics, Kantianism could only bring to light an impersonal mind, bearer of the conditions of the possibility of universal judgments. Hermeneutics could not add to Kantianism without taking from Romantic philosophy its most fundamental conviction, that the spirit is the unconscious creator at work in individual geniuses. Schleiermacher's hermeneutical program carried the double mark of both Romanticism and critical philosophy. It was Romantic in its appeal to a living relation to the process of creation, critical in its wish to elaborate the universally applicable rules of understanding. Perhaps all hermeneutics is forever marked by this double filiation to Romanticism and critical philosophy. The proposals to battle against misunderstanding in the name of the famous adage, "There is hermeneutics wherever there is misunderstanding," is critical; and the proposal to "understand an author as well as and even better than he understood himself," is Romantic.

We must understand that it is an aporia as well as a first sketch which Schleiermacher gave to his descendents in the notes on hermeneutics which he never succeeded in turning into a complete work. Schleiermacher struggled with the problem of the relation between two forms of interpretation: "grammatical" interpretation and "technical" interpretation. This is a constant distinction in his work, but its meaning changed over the years. Before Kimmerle's edition of Schleiermacher's *Hermeneutics* in 1959, we did not know of the notes from 1804 and the following years. This is why everyone credited Schleiermacher with advocating a psychological interpretation, which in the beginning was actually on an equal footing with grammatical interpretation.

Grammatical interpretation was concerned with the characteristics of discourse that were common to a culture. Psychological interpretation was concerned with the singularity, the genius, of the author's message. Now, even if these two forms of interpretation are equally valid, we cannot practice them at the same time. As Schleiermacher says: to consider the common language is to forget the writer; to understand an individual author is to forget his language, which is just passed over. Either we perceive the common or we perceive the particular. The first type of interpretation is called "objective" since it deals with the distinctive linguistic characteristics of the author, but it is also called "negative," since it simply indicates the limits of understanding. Its critical value bears only on errors concerning the meaning of words. The second type of interpretation is called "technical," doubtless because of the very project of a *Kunstlehre,* a technology. The real project of hermeneutics is accomplished in this second type of interpretation. It is a question of reaching the subjectivity of him who speaks, language being forgotten. Language here becomes an instrument at the service of individuality. This type of interpretation is also called "positive" because it reaches the act of thinking which produces the discourse.

Not only does one type of interpretation exclude the other, each requires distinct talents, as the respective excesses of each reveal. An excess of the first gives pedantry; an excess of the second, nebulousness. It is only in the later texts that the second type of interpretation prevails over the first, and that the divinatory character of interpretation emphasizes its psychological character. But even then psychological interpretation—this term replaces that of technical interpretation—is never limited to an affinity with the author. It implies critical motives in the activity of comparison; an individuality can only be grasped through comparison and contrast. Thus the second type of hermeneutics also includes technical and discursive elements. We never directly grasp an individuality, but only its differences from another and from ourselves. The difficulty in arbitrating between the two hermeneutics is thus complicated by the superimposing on the first pair of oppositions ("grammatical" and the "technical") a second pair of oppositions ("divination" and "comparison"). Schleiermacher's famous *Discourses* witness to this extreme perplexity on the party of the founder of modern hermeneutics. I propose to show in the second lecture that this perplexity can be overcome only if we make clear the relation of a work to the subjectivity of the author and if we shift the emphasis in interpretation from pathetic investigation of submerged subjectivities to the meaning and the reference of the work itself. But first we must push the central aporia of hermeneutics further by considering the decisive enlargement which Dilthey accomplished in subordinating the philological and exegetical problematic to the historical problematic. This enlargement, in the sense of a greater universality, prepares for the displacement of epistemology toward ontology, in the sense of a greater radicality.

Dilthey

Dilthey is at the critical turning point in hermeneutics where the scope of the problem is magnified but is still presented in terms of the epistemological debate characteristic of the whole neo-Kantian epoch.

The necessity to incorporate the regional problem of interpretation into the larger field of historical knowledge imposed itself on a mind anxious to account for that great success of German culture in the 19th century, the discovery of history as a science of the first rank. Between Schleiermacher and Dilthey were the German historians of the 19th century, Ranke, Droysen, etc. The text to be interpreted from then on was historical reality itself and its interconnections (*Zusammenhang*). But before we ask how to understand a text from the past, a prior question comes up—how to conceive historical continuity. Before the coherence of the text comes that of history, considered as the great document of man, as the most fundamental expression of life. Dilthey is above all the interpreter of this pact between hermeneutics and history. What we today call "historicism" in a pejorative sense expresses a cultural fact, the transfer of our interest from humanity's main works to the historical interconnections which carry them. The discrediting of historicism was not just a result of the puzzles it raised, but of another cultural change which took place more recently and which makes us give preference to the system over change, to synchrony over diachrony. We will see in the remaining lectures how much the structural tendencies of contemporary literary criticism express both the failure of historicism and the deeper subversion of its problematic.

But even though Dilthey brought to light for philosophical reflection the great problem of the intelligibility of the historical as such, he was inclined by a second major cultural fact to seek the key to a solution not in the domain of ontology but in the reformation of epistemology. The second cultural fact to which we allude is represented by the growth of positivism as philosophy, if we thereby understand, in general terms, the demand that the mind take as its model for all intelligibility the sort of empirical explanation current in the natural sciences. Dilthey's times were those of the complete refusal of Hegelianism and an apologetic for experimental knowledge. Thus the only way of doing justice to historical knowledge seemed to be to give it a scientific dimension, comparable to the dimension which natural sciences had conquered. So it was in order to reply to positivism that Dilthey undertook to endow the cultural sciences with an epistemology and a methodology just as respectable as those belonging to the natural sciences.

On the basis of these two great cultural facts, Dilthey posed his fundamental question: how is historical knowledge possible, or more generally, how are the sciences of the spirit possible? This question brings us to the threshold of that great opposition which runs through all of Dilthey's work, the opposition between the explanation of nature and the understanding of history. This opposition is pregnant with consequences for hermeneutics, thus cut off from naturalistic explanation and forced into the realm of psychological intuition.

Dilthey sought the distinctive trait of understanding in psychology. Every science of the spirit—and by this Dilthey meant every knowledge of man implying some historical relation—presupposes a primordial capacity to place oneself into the psychical life of others. In natural knowledge, in effect, man only reaches those distinct phenomena whose fundamental thingness escapes him. In the human order, on the contrary, man knows man; no matter how foreign the other man may be to us, he is not alien in the sense of the unknowable physical thing. The difference of status between the natural thing and the spirit therefore requires the difference of status between explanation and understanding. Man is not radically foreign to man because he gives signs of his existence. To understand these signs is to understand man. The positivistic school completely ignores the difference in principle between the physical and psychic worlds.

Someone might object that the spirit, the spiritual world, is not necessarily individual. Did not Hegel witness to a sphere of the spirit, the "objective" spirit, the spirit of institutions and cultures, which can in no way be reduced to a psychological phenomenon? But Dilthey still belonged to that generation of neo-Kantians for whom the pivot point of every human science was the individual, considered, it is true, in his social relations, but fundamentally singular. This is why the sciences of the spirit as fundamental sciences need psychology, the science of the individual acting in society and in history. Reciprocal relations, cultural systems, philosophy, art, and religion are all constructed on this basis. More precisely, and more epoch-making, it is as activity, as free will, as initiative and enterprise that man seeks to understand himself. Here we recognize the firm purpose to turn away from Hegel, to leave the Hegelian concept of the *Volksgeist* and thus to stand again with Kant, but, as we said earlier, to stand at the place where Kant had stopped.

The key to this critique of historical knowledge which defaulted to Kantianism is found in the fundamental phenomenon of an "internal connection" or "inner connection" by which the life of another person lets itself be discerned and identified in its manifestations. Because life produces forms and exteriorizes itself in stable configurations, the knowledge of others is possible. Feeling evaluation, rules for willing, etc., tend to be deposited in an acquired structure offered for others to decipher. The organized systems that culture produces in the form of literature constitute a second-order stratum built upon the primary phenomenon of the teleological structure of the productions of life. We know how Max Weber in his turn undertook to resolve the same problem with his concept of ideal types. Both men struggled with the same problem, how to conceptualize the fluctuating experiences of life that are in opposition, or so it seemed, to the regularity of nature. An answer is possible because spiritual life fixes itself within structured wholes capable of being understood by another person. From 1900 on Dilthey depended upon Husserl to give consistency to this notion of "interconnection." Husserl, at that time, was establishing that psychic life was characterized by intentionality, the property of intending a meaning capable of being identified. Psychic life itself could not be reached, but one could grasp what it intended, the objective and identical correlate in which psychic life transcended itself.

This concept of intentionality and of the identical character of the intentional object allowed Dilthy to reinforce his concept of psychic structures through the Husserlian notion of meaning.

What happens in this new context to the hermeneutical problem we got from Schleiermacher? The passage from understanding, defined largely as the capacity to transpose oneself into someone else, to interpretation, in the precise sense of understanding the expressions of life fixed by writing, brings up a twofold problem. On the one hand, hermeneutics completed empathetic psychology by adding a supplementary stage to it. On the other hand, empathetic psychology gave a psychological inflection to hermeneutics. This explains why Dilthey retained from Schleiermacher the psychological side of his hermeneutic in which he recognized his own problem, understanding through transference into another person. Considered from the first point of view, hermeneutics consists of something specific; it intends to reproduce an interconnection, a structured whole, by taking hold of a category of signs, signs which have been fixed by writing or by any other process of inscription equivalent to writing. It is then no longer possible to grasp the psychic life of others in its immediate expressions. We must reproduce or reconstruct it by interpreting the objectified signs. Distinct rules are required for this *Nachbilden* because of the investing of expression in objects. As with Schleiermacher, philology, that is, the explication of texts, furnishes the scientific step for understanding. For both thinkers, the essential role of hermeneutics consists in "theoretically grounding, against the constant intrusion of Romantic arbitrariness and sceptical subjectivity, the universal validity of interpretation, the basis of all certitude within history." Thus hermeneutics constitutes the objectified layer of understanding, thanks to the essential structures of the text.

But the counterpart of a hermeneutical theory founded upon psychology is that psychology remains its final justification. The autonomy of the text, which will be at the center of our reflections in subsequent lectures, can only be a provisional and superficial phenomenon. This is precisely why the question of objectivity for Dilthey remains both an unavoidable and an insolvable problem. It is unavoidable because of the claim to respond to positivism by an authentically scientific conception of understanding. This is why Dilthey never ceased to refine and perfect his concept of "reproduction," making it more suitable for the needs of objectification. But the subordination of the hermeneutical problem to the psychological problem of understanding others condemned it to look for the source of all objectification beyond the field of interpretation. For Dilthey, objectification begins very early, beginning with interpretation of oneself. What I am for myself can only be grasped through the objectifications of my life. Self-knowledge is already an interpretation which is not easier than any other interpretation, and probably more difficult, for I only understand myself through the signs I give of my life and which are not returned to me by others. All self-knowledge is mediated through signs and works. This is how Dilthey responded to the *Lebensphilosophie* so influential in his day. He shared this philosophy's conviction that life is essentially creative dynamism. But against the "philosophy of life," he held that this creative dynamism cannot know itself but can only interpret itself through the detour of signs and works. There was thus in Dilthey's thought a fusion between the concept of dynamism and that of structure—life appears as a dynamism that structures itself. This is how the later Dilthey attempted to generalize the concept of hermeneutics, tying it ever more firmly to the teleology of life. Acquired meanings present values, and distant ends constantly structure the dynamic of life according to the three temporal dimensions of past, present, and future. "Man instructs himself only by his actions, by the exteriorization of his life and by the effects these produce on others." He only learns to know himself through the detour of understanding, which is always an interpretation. The only truly significant difference between psychological interpretation and exegetical interpretation lies in the fact that life's objectifications tend to be deposited and sedimented in a stable acquisition which takes on all the appearances of Hegel's objective spirit. If I can understand worlds which have disappeared, it is because each society has created its own instruments for understanding in creating the social and cultural worlds in which it understands itself. Universal history thus becomes the hermeneutical field. To understand myself is to make the greatest detour, that of the great memory which retains what has become significant for men as a group. Hermeneutics is the merging of the individual with the knowledge of universal history, it is the universalization of the individual.

Dilthey's work, more than Schleiermacher's brings to light the central aporia of a hermeneutics which places understanding the text under the law of understanding another person who expresses himself there. If this enterprise remains fundamentally psychological, it is because it takes as the final interpretation not *what* a text says, but *who* expresses himself there. At the same time, the object of hermeneutics is continuously removed from the text, from its meaning and its reference, toward the life that is expressed here. Gadamer has presented well this latent conflict in Dilthey's work (*Wahrheit und Methode*, pp. 205–08). The conflict is finally between a philosophy of life with its deep irrationalism and a philosophy of meaning which makes the same claims as the Hegelian philosophy of the objective spirit. Dilthey transformed this difficulty into an axiom: "Life contains the power to transcend itself in significations." Or as Gadamer says, "Life exegetes itself, it has a hermeneutical structure." But this hermeneutics of life is a history and this is incomprehensible. The passage from psychological understanding to historical understanding presupposes in effect that the interconnection of life's works is no longer lived or experienced by anyone. This is its objectivity. And this is why we can ask if, in order to think about the objectifications of life and to treat them as given, it is not necessary to put the whole of speculative idealism at the root of life, finally to think of life as spirit (*Geist*). If not, how are we to understand that in art, religion and philosophy life expresses itself most completely by most objectifying itself? Is it not because here the spirit is most at home? And is this not to admit that hermeneutics is only possible as sensible philosophy through what it has borrowed from Hegelian concepts? It is then possible to say of life what Hegel said of the spirit: "Here life grasps life."

It is still true, however, that Dilthey perfectly caught sight of the kernel of the problem, that life only grasps life through the mediation of unities of meaning that are raised beyond the historical flux. Dilthey caught sight of a mode of transcending finitude without complete transcendence, without absolute knowledge—of interpretation. In this way he indicated the direction in which historicism could be conquered by itself, without invoking any triumphant coincidence with some absolute knowledge. But, to continue this work it is necessary to renounce linking hermeneutics to the purely psychological notion of transference into an alien psychic life. It is necessary to unfold the text, no longer backwards toward its author, but forward toward its immanent meaning and toward the sort of world which it discovers and opens up.

FROM EPISTEMOLOGY TO ONTOLOGY

Since Dilthey, the decisive step was not to improve the epistemology of the sciences of the spirit, but to question its fundamental postulate, that these sciences can be rivals of the natural sciences by means of an appropriate methodology. This presupposition, which dominates Dilthey's work, implies that hermeneutics is one kind of "theory of knowledge," and that the debate between explanation and understanding can go on within the limits of the *Methodenstreit* so dear to neo-Kantians. It is this presupposition of hermeneutics understood as epistemology that is essentially called into question by Heidegger and later by Gadamer. Their contributions cannot therefore be taken as the simple prolongation of Dilthey's enterprise. Rather they must be seen as an attempt to dig beneath the epistemological enterprise in order to disclose its ontological conditions. If we can place the first movement, from regional hermeneutics to general hermeneutics, under the aegis of a Copernican revolution, we must place the second, which we are now undertaking, under the aegis of a second Copernican reversal, which will relocate the questions of method within fundamental ontology. We must not expect therefore from either Heidegger or Gadamer a perfecting of the methodological problematic coming out of the exegesis of sacred or profane texts, by philology, psychology, the theory of history, or the theory of culture. On the contrary, there is a new question. Instead of asking, "How do we know?", the question will be, "What is the mode of being of that being who only exists through understanding?"

Heidegger

With Heidegger, the question of *Auslegung*, exposition or interpretation, coincides so little with that of exegesis that it is joined from the introduction of *Being and Time* to the "forgotten question of being." What we are interrogating is the meaning of being. But in this question we are guided by that which is sought. The theory of knowledge is inverted from the beginning by a questioning which precedes it and which depends upon the manner in which a being encounters being, even before it opposes itself to it as an object in face of a subject. Even if *Being and Time* puts the accent on Dasein (that being-there which we ourselves are) more than the later works of Heidegger, this Dasein is not a subject for whom there is an object, but a being within being. Dasein denotes the "place" where the question of being arises, the place of manifestation. The centrality of Dasein is just that of a being which understands being. It is part of its structure as a being to have an ontological preunderstanding of being. Hence to show the constitution of Dasein is not at all "to ground by derivation" as in the methodology of the human sciences, but to disengage "the fundamental structure by exhibition" (§ 3). An opposition is thus created between the ontological foundation, as we just said, and epistemological grounding. This would be just an epistemological question if the problem was that of basic concepts which regulate regions of particular objects, the nature-region, life-region, language-region, history-region. Certainly science itself moves toward such an explication of its fundamental concepts, particularly where there is a crisis of foundations. But the philosophical task of grounding is something else. It aims at disengaging the fundamental concepts which "determine the preliminary understanding of a region, furnishing the base for all the thematic objects of a science and which thereby orient all positive research." What is at stake in hermeneutical philosophy will thus be "the exposition of that being relative to its constitution of being." This exposition will add nothing to the methodology of the sciences of the spirit. Rather it will dig below that methodology to reveal its foundations: "thus in history what is philosophically prior is not the theory of the formation of concepts about historical matters, not the theory of historical knowledge or even the theory of history as the object of historical science, but the interpretation of historical being relative to its historicity." Hermeneutics is not a reflection on the sciences of the spirit, but an explication of the ontological ground on which these sciences may be built. From this comes what appears to me to be the key sentence: "It is within hermeneutics thus understood that is contained what we must name 'hermeneutics' in a derivative sense: the methodology of the historical sciences of the spirit."

This first inversion found in *Being and Time* calls for a second. For Dilthey the question of understanding was tied to the problem of other minds. The possibility of reaching a foreign psyche through transference dominated all the sciences of the spirit, from psychology to history. It is noteworthy, that in *Being and Time* the question of understanding is freed entirely from the problem of communication with another person. There is a chapter which is called *Mitsein*, being-with, but it is not within this chapter that we find the question of understanding, as one might expect from a Diltheyan approach. The foundations of the ontological problem are to be sought in the domain of the relation with the world and not in the domain of relation with another person. It is in relation to my situation, in the fundamental understanding of my position within being, that understanding in its principle sense is implied. It is not without interest to recall the reason why Dilthey proceeded as he did. It was beginning from a Kantian argument that he posed the problematic of the human sciences. The knowledge of things, he said, leads to something unknown, the thing itself. But in the case of psychic life, there is no thing-in-itself. What another is, we are ourselves. Knowledge of a psychic life therefore has an undeniable advantage over knowledge of nature. Heidegger, who had read Nietzsche, was no longer so innocent. He knew that the other, just as much as myself, is more unknown to me than any phenomenon of nature can be. Here dissimulation is undoubtedly thicker than anywhere else. If there is a region of being where inauthenticity reigns, it is within the relation of each person to every other possible person. This is why the great chapter on being-with is a debate with the "they," as the home and privileged location for all dissimulation. It is thus not surprising that it is not by a reflection on being-with, but on being-in that the ontology of understanding begins. Not being-with another—which would duplicate our subjectivity—but being-in-the-world. This placement of the philosophical locus is just as important as the transfer from the problem of method to the problem of being. The question about the "world" replaces the question about "others." In making understanding "worldly," Heidegger "depsychologizes" it.

This displacement has been completely misunderstood by those so-called existentialist interpretations of Heidegger that have especially flourished in the Anglo-Saxon world. They have taken the analyses of care, anxiety, being-toward-death in the sense of a refined existential psychology. They do not notice that these analyses belong to a meditation on the "world-hood of the world" and that they essentially are aimed at destroying the claim of a knowing subject to be the measure of objectivity. What we must take over from this claim about the subject is the conditions for dwelling in the world in terms of which there is a situation, understanding, and interpretation. This is why the theory of understanding must be preceded by the recognition of a grounding relation which assures the anchorage of every linguistic system, and therefore of books and texts, in something which is not in primordial terms a phenomenon of articulation or of discourse. We must first find ourselves (for better or worse), find ourselves "there" and feel ourselves (in a certain manner), before orientating ourselves. If *Being and Time* exploits the depths of certain feelings such as fear and anxiety, it is not to "do existentialism," but in order to disengage by these revelatory experiences a tie to reality more fundamental than the subject-object relation. Through knowledge we already and always have objects before us. The mood of the situation precedes this being in face of, by situating us.

And so arises understanding. But it is not yet a fact of language, writing, or text. Understanding itself must first be described, not in terms of regarding or of discourse, but as a power of being. The first function of understanding is to orient us in a situation. Understanding is not addressed therefore to grasping a fact but to the apprehension of a possibility and our utmost potentialities. We must not lose sight of this point when we draw the methodological consequences of this analysis: to understand a text, we shall say, is not to find an inert meaning which is contained therein, rather it is to unfold the possibility of being which is indicated by the text. Thus we will be faithful to the Heideggerian understanding which is essentially a "project" or, in a more paradoxical fashion, a "project" of a prior "being-thrown." Here again the "existentialist" tone is deceiving. "Projecting has nothing to do with comporting oneself toward a plan that has been thought out, and in accordance with which Dasein arranges its being; on the contrary, any Dasein has, as Dasein, already projected itself and as long as it is, it is projecting" (SZ, p. 185).[1] What is important here is not the existential moment of responsibility or of free choice, but the structure of being which makes choice problematic. The "either-or" is not first, but derived from the structure of "being-thrown."

It is thus only in the third position in the triad, situation-understanding-interpretation, that the ontological moment enters which interests the exegete. But before the exegesis of texts comes the exegesis of life and world.

---

1. *Sein und Zeit*, 7th ed., trans. J. Macquarrie and E. Robinson (New York, 1962).

Interpretation is first an explication, a "development" of understanding, a development which "does not transform understanding into something else but makes it become itself" (*SZ*, p. 185). All return to the theory of knowledge is thus forbidden. What is explicated is the hermeneutical "as" (*als*) which is attached to the articulations of experience. "Explication does not make the *as* appear; it only gives it an expression" (*SZ*, p. 186).

But if the analytic of Dasein does not expressly aim at the problems of exegesis, it does provide a meaning for what could appear to be a failure on the epistemological level, in that it relates this apparent failure to a more primitive ontological structure. This failure is what has often been spoken of in terms of a *hermeneutical circle*. In the human sciences, as has often been noticed, subject and object are mutually implied. The subject contributes to the knowledge of the object and in return is determined in its own subjectivity by the hold which the object has on it even before the subject has come to know the object. Stated in the terminology of subject and object, the hermeneutical circle can only appear as a vicious circle. It is the function of a fundamental ontology to disclose the underlying structure which accounts for what in methodological analysis appears as a vicious circle. It is this structure which Heidegger calls "preunderstanding." But we would be entirely mistaken if we tried to describe preunderstanding in terms of a theory of knowledge, that is once again, in the categories of subject and object. The relations of familiarity which we can have, for example, with a world of tools, can give us a first glimpse of what the preliminary having (fore-having) from which we derive a new usage of things might mean. This anticipatory character belongs to the manner of being of every being which has historical understanding. Thus it is in terms of the analytic of Dasein that we must understand the proposition that "the interpretation of something, as this or that is grounded essentially on a fore-having, fore-sight, and fore-conception" (*SZ*, p. 191). The role of presuppositions in textual exegesis is thus nothing more than a particular case of this general law of interpretation. Transposed into the theory of knowledge and measured by the claim of objectivity, preunderstanding received the pejorative connotation of being a prejudgment. But on the contrary, for fundamental ontology, prejudgment is only understood on the basis of the anticipatory structure of understanding. The famous hermeneutical circle is henceforth no more than a shadow of this anticipatory structure seen from a methodological point of view. Whoever has understood this knows that "what is decisive is not to get out of the circle but to get into it in the right way" (*SZ*, p. 190).

As you will have noticed, the principal weight of this meditation does not bear on discourse nor on writing. Heidegger's philosophy—or at least that of *Being and Time*—is so little a philosophy of language that the question of language is only introduced after the questions of situation, understanding, and interpretation. Language, in the period of *Being and Time*, remains a second level of articulation, the articulation of interpretation in "statements" (*Aussage*, § 33). But the connection of the statement to understanding and interpretation makes us see that its first function is not communication with another person, nor attribution of predicates to logical subjects, but "pointing-out," "showing," "manifestation" (*SZ*, p. 192). This supreme function of language reminds us of its connection to the ontological structures which precede it: "That language only now becomes a theme of our examination," says Heidegger in § 34, "indicates that this phenomenon has its roots in the existential constitution of Dasein's disclosedness" (*SZ*, p. 203). And later: "Discourse is the articulation of intelligibility" (ibid). Thus we must replace discourse within the structures of being, and not the latter within discourse: "Discourse is the way we articulate significantly the intelligibility of being-in-the-world" (*SZ* p. 204).

In this last remark we find the passage to the later philosophy of Heidegger which will ignore Dasein and begin immediately with language's power of manifestation. But it follows from *Being and Time* that "saying" (*reden*) appears as superior to "speaking" (*sprechen*). "*Saying*" designates the existential constitution and "speaking" its worldly aspect which falls into the empirical. This is why the first determination of "saying" is not to say something, but the pair, "hearing"-"keeping silent." Here again Heidegger inverts our ordinary, and even our linguistic, tendency to make the operation of speaking primary (locution, interlocution). To understand is to hear. In other words, my first relation to speech is not that I produce it but that I receive it: "Hearing is constitutive of discourse" (*SZ*, p. 206). This priority of hearing marks the fundamental relation of speech to the opening to the world and to the other. Its methodological consequences are considerable: linguistics, semiology, and philosophy of language are all tied firmly to the level of speaking and do not reach the level of saying. In this sense fundamental philosophy no more ameliorates linguistics than it adds to exegesis. While speaking forces us back to the speaking man, discourse forces us back to things said.

At this point one will no doubt ask: Why do we not stop here and simply proclaim ourselves Heideggerian? Where is the famous aporia previously announced? Have we not eliminated the Diltheyan aporia of the theory of understanding, condemned by turns to being opposed to naturalist explanation and to struggling with it as to which is more objective or more scientific? Have we not transcended this aporia by subordinating epistemology to ontology? In my opinion the aporia is not resolved, it is only transferred elsewhere and thereby even aggravated. It is no longer *in* epistemology—between two modes of knowing—but *between* ontology and epistemology taken as wholes. With Heidegger we can move backwards to the ground but any return from ontology to the epistemological question about the status of the human sciences is impossible. This situation is the most unhappy that one can think of, for a philosophy which breaks the dialogue with these sciences is left with only itself. Moreover, it is only on the way back that we can prove the claim that questions of exegesis and of historical criticism in general are "derivative" questions. As long as we have not proceeded to this derivation, the very surpassing of these questions in favor of the questions of grounding remains unquestionable. Have we not learned from Plato that the ascending dialectic is the easiest one and that it is on the way back of the descending dialectic that the true philosopher declares himself? To me the unanswered question in Heidegger is, "How are we to account for any *critical* question within the framework of a fundamental hermeneutics?" However it is in the movement of return that the affirmation that the hermeneutical circle (in the sense of the exegetes) is "grounded" in the structure of anticipation of understanding at the fundamental ontological level can appear and attest to itself. But ontological hermeneutics seems incapable, for structural reasons, of unfolding this problematic of return. Even in Heidegger this question is abandoned as soon as it is asked. We read in *Being and Time:* "In the circle is hidden a positive possibility of the most primordial kind of knowing. To be sure, we genuinely take hold of this possibility only when, in our interpretation, we have understood that our first, last, and constant task is never to allow our fore-having, fore-sight, and fore-conception to be presented to us by fancies and popular conceptions, but rather to make the scientific theme secure by working out these fore-structures in terms of the things themselves" (*SZ*, p. 153).

Here therefore is posed in principle the distinction between anticipation according to the things themselves and an anticipation which only comes from fancies (*Einfälle*) and popular conceptions (*Volksbegriffe*). But how can Heidegger go any further when he immediately declares that "the ontological presuppositions of historiographical knowledge transcend in principle the idea of rigor held in the most exact sciences," and he then avoids the question of the rigor proper to the historical sciences themselves? The concern to ground the circle more deeply than any epistemology can prevents Heidegger from repeating the epistemological question after the ontology.

Gadamer

This aporia becomes the central problem of the hermeneutical philosophy of Hans-Georg Gadamer in *Wahrheit und Methode* (1960). This Heidelberg philosopher proposes to take up again the question of the human sciences by means of the Heideggerian ontology and more precisely by means of its inflection in the latest works on philosophical poetics. The basic experience around which his whole work is organized, is that of the scandal for the modern consciousness of the "alienating distanciation" (*Verfremdung*) which seems to him to be the presupposition of these sciences. Alienation is in effect much more than a sentiment or a mood, it is the ontological presupposition which supports the objectivity of the human sciences. The methodology of these sciences inevitably implies, in Gadamer's eyes, the taking of a distance—which in its turn expresses the destruction of the primordial relation of participation (*Zugehörigkeit*) without which there exists no relation to the historical as such. This debate between alienating distanciation and the experience of participation is carried on by Gadamer within the three spheres of hermeneutical experience: the aesthetic sphere, the historical sphere, and the sphere of language. In the aesthetic sphere, the experience of being grasped always precedes and makes possible the critical exercises of judgment for which Kant wrote the theory under the title of the judgment of taste. In the historical sphere, the consciousness of being carried by traditions which antedate me is what makes possible all exercise of a historical methodology at the level of the human and social sciences. Finally, in the sphere of language, which in a certain way overlaps the other two spheres, the co-belonging to things articulated by the great voices of the creators of discourse precedes and makes possible every scientific treatment of language as an available instrument and every claim to dominate the structure of the text in our culture by objective techniques. Thus a single thesis runs through the three parts of *Wahrheit und Methode*.

Gadamer's philosophy expresses the synthesis of the two movements we have described from regional hermeneutics to general hermeneutics and from the epistemology of the human sciences to ontology. The expression of the hermeneutical experience expresses well this synthetic character. But furthermore, Gadamer notes with regard to Heidegger the attraction of a return from ontology back to epistemological problems. It is in this light that I will speak of Gadamer here. The title of his work also confronts the Heideggerian concept of truth with the Diltheyan concept of method. The question is to what extent the work earns the right to be called "truth *and* method," or whether it should not be called "truth *or* method." If Heidegger escapes any debate with the human sciences by a supreme movement of transcendence, Gadamer achieves a better debate just because he takes Dilthey's question seriously. The section of his work devoted to the historical consciousness in this respect is very significant. The long historical review which Gadamer imposes on himself before presenting his own ideas attests that hermeneutical philosophy ought first to recapitulate the struggle of Romantic hermeneutics against the *Auf-klärung*, that of Dilthey against positivism, and that of Heidegger against neo-Kantianism. Without a doubt the declared intention of Gadamer is not to fall back into the same old rut of Romanticism. Romanticism, he declares, only inverted the theses of the *Aufklärung*, without succeeding in displacing the problematic itself or changing the terrain of the debate. This is why the romantic philosophy attempted to rehabilitate prejudg-ment, which is a category of the *Aufklärung*, and which continues to reinstate critical philosophy, that is, a philosophy of judgment. Romanti-cism conducted its struggle on a terrain defined by its adversary on the role of tradition and authority in interpretation. But it is a question of knowing whether the hermeneutics of Gadamer has truly gone beyond the Romantic point of departure of hermeneutics, and if his affirmation that "the being man finds his finitude in the fact that he first of all finds himself in the middle of traditions" (p. 260) can escape the interplay of the reversals in which he sees philosophical Romanticism enclosed in the face of the claims of every critical philosophy. Dilthey is reproached for having remained a prisoner of a conflict between two methodologies and for "not having known how to break away from the traditional theory of knowledge" (p. 260). His point of departure remains the consciousness of self as master of itself. With Dilthey subjectivity remains the last refer-ence. A certain rehabilitation of prejudgment, authority, and tradition is thus directed against the reign of subjectivity and interiority, that is, against the criteria of reflexive philosophy. This antireflexive polemic con-tributes to giving this plea the appearance of a return to a precritical posi-tion. However provoking—not to say provocative—this plea might be, it holds to the reconquest of the historical dimension over the reflexive mo-ment. History precedes me and my reflection, I belong to history before belonging to myself. Now Dilthey could not understand this because his revolution remained an epistemological one and because his reflexive cri-terion prevailed over his historical consciousness. At this point Gadamer is heir to Heidegger. It is from him that Gadamer receives the conviction that what we call prejudgment expresses the structure of anticipation of human experience. At the same time philological interpretation must be made a derivative mode of fundamental understanding.

This theory of historical consciousness marks the summit of Gadamer's reflection on the foundation of the sciences of the spirit. This reflection is placed under the title of the *Wirkungsgeschichtliches Bewusstein:* word by word, the consciousness of the history of effects. This category no longer comes from the methodology of historical inquiry but from the reflexive consciousness of his methodology. It is the consciousness of be-ing exposed to history and its action in such a way that one cannot ob-jectify this action on us because it is a part of the historical phenomenon itself. We read in the *Kleine Schriften*, p. 158: "By that I mean that we cannot extricate ourselves from historical becoming, or place ourselves at a distance from it, in order that the past might become an object for us. . . . We are always situated in history. . . . I mean that our consciousness is determined by a real historical becoming such that consciousness is not free to situate itself over against the past. On the other hand, I mean that it is always a question of newly becoming conscious of the action which is thus exercised on us, such that everything past which we have just experienced constrains us to take it totally in hand, to assume its truth in some way. . . ."

I wish to pose my own problem beginning from this concept of historical agency: How is it possible to introduce a particular critical moment into a consciousness of belonging, expressly defined by the refusal of distanciation? This can only occur, I think, to the degree that this historical consciousness does not limit itself to repudiating distanciation, but also sets out to assume it. Gadamer's hermeneutics contains a series of decisive suggestions which will become the point of departure for my own reflections in my second lecture. First, in spite of the great opposition between participation and alienating distanciation, the efficient consciousness of history contains within itself an element of distance. The history of effects is precisely the history which takes place under the condition of historical distance. It is the proximity of the distant, or to say the same thing differently, efficacity at a distance. There is therefore a paradox of otherness, a tension between the near and the distant essential to any historical consciousness.

Another index of the dialectic of participation and distanciation is furnished by the concept of a "fusion of horizons." In effect, according to Gadamer, if the condition of the finitude of historical knowledge excludes every transcendent point of view, every final synthesis in a Hegelian manner, that finitude is not such that I am enclosed in a point of view. Where there is a situation, there is a horizon capable of being narrowed or enlarged. We owe to Gadamer this very fruitful idea that communication at a distance between two consciousnesses differently situated takes place through a fusion of their horizons, that is, from the blending of their intentions about the distant and the open. Once again a factor of distanciation among the near, the far, and the open is presupposed. This concept means that we do not live within closed horizons nor within a unique horizon. To the extent that the fusion of horizons excludes the idea of a total and unique knowledge, the concept implies the tension between the self and the alien, between the near and the far, and therefore the play of difference is included in the coming together.

Finally, the most precise indication in favor of a less negative interpretation of alienating distanciation is contained in the philosophy of language

achieved by Gadamer's work. The universal "linguisticality"—this word
more or less translates Gadamer's *Sprachlichkeit*—means that my participation in a tradition or traditions passes through the interpretation of
signs, works, and texts, in which cultural heritages are inscribed and offered for our deciphering. Certainly the whole of Gadamer's meditation
on language is turned against the reduction of the world of signs to instruments which we can manipulate at will. All of the third part of
Wahrheit und Methode is a passionate apology for the "dialogue which
we are" and the preliminary understanding which support us. But linguistic experience only exercises its mediating function because the partners in a dialogue both efface themselves before the things said, which,
in a way, guide the dialogue. Now, where is this reign of the thing said
over the partners more apparent than when *Sprachlichkeit* becomes
Schriftlichkeit, or in other words, when mediation through language becomes mediation through a text? Then that which makes us communicate at a distance is the "issue" of the text, which no longer belongs to
either its author or its reader.

This last expression, the "issue" of the text brings me to the threshold
of my own reflections and it is this threshold which I will cross in the
second lecture.

10. Hans-Georg Gadamer

The Historicity of Understanding as Hermeneutic Principle

THE HERMENEUTIC CIRCLE AND THE PROBLEM OF PREJUDICES

Heidegger's Disclosure of the Fore-Structure of Understanding

HEIDEGGER went into the problems of historical hermeneutics and criticism only in order to develop from it, for the purposes of ontology, the fore-structure of understanding.[1] Contrariwise, our question is how hermeneutics, once freed from the ontological obstructions of the scientific concept of objectivity, can do justice to the historicity of understanding. The way in which hermeneutics has traditionally understood itself is based on its character as art or technique. This is true even of Dilthey's extension of hermeneutics to become an organon of the human sciences. It may be asked whether there is such a thing as this art or technique of understanding—we shall come back to the point. But at any rate we may enquire into the consequences that Heidegger's fundamental derivation of the circular structure of understanding from the temporality of Dasein has for the hermeneutics of the human sciences. These consequences do not need to be such that a theory is applied to practice and the latter now be performed differently, i.e., in a way that is technically correct. They

Reprinted with permission from the English translation of *Truth and Method* (New York, Seabury Press, 1975; and London, Sheed and Ward, 1975), pp. 235–51, 258–67; based on the 2nd ed. of *Wahrheit und Methode: Grundzüge einer philosophischen Hermeneutik* (Tübingen, 1965).

1. *Being and Time*, trans. J. Macquarrie and E. Robinson (New York, 1962), pp. 312f.

could also consist in a correction (and purification of inadequate manners) of the way in which constantly exercised understanding understands itself—a procedure that would benefit the art of understanding at most only indirectly.

Hence we shall examine once more Heidegger's description of the hermeneutical circle in order to use, for our own purpose, the new fundamental significance acquired here by the circular structure. Heidegger writes: "It is not to be reduced to the level of a vicious circle, or even of a circle which is merely tolerated. In the circle is hidden a positive possibility of the most primordial kind of knowing. To be sure, we genuinely take hold of this possibility only when, in our interpretation, we have understood that our first, last, and constant task is never to allow our fore-having, fore-sight, and fore-conception to be presented to us by fancies and popular conceptions, but rather to make the scientific theme secure by working out these fore-structures in terms of the things themselves." [2]

What Heidegger works out here is not primarily a demand on the practice of understanding, but is a description of the way in which interpretation through understanding is achieved. The point of Heidegger's hermeneutical thinking is not so much to prove that there is a circle as to show that this circle possesses an ontologically positive significance. The description as such will be obvious to every interpreter who knows what he is about. All correct interpretation must be on guard against arbitrary fancies and the limitations imposed by imperceptible habits of thought and direct its gaze "on the things themselves" (which, in the case of the literary critic, are meaningful texts, which themselves are again concerned with objects). It is clear that to let the object take over in this way is not a matter for the interpreter of a single decision, but is "the first, last, and constant task." For it is necessary to keep one's gaze fixed on the thing throughout all the distractions that the interpreter will consantly experience in the process and which originate in himself. A person who is trying to understand a text is always performing an act of projecting. He projects before himself a meaning for the text as a whole as soon as some initial meaning emerges in the text. Again, the latter emerges only because he is reading the text with particular expectations in regard to a certain meaning. The working out of this fore-project, which is constantly revised in terms of what emerges as he penetrates into the meaning, is understanding what is there.

This description is, of course, a rough abbreviation of the whole. The process that Heidegger describes is that every revision of the fore-project is capable of projecting before itself a new project of meaning, that rival projects can emerge side by side until it becomes clearer what the unity of meaning is, that interpretation begins with fore-conceptions that are

2. Ibid., p. 153.

replaced by more suitable ones. This constant process of new projection is the movement of understanding and interpretation. A person who is trying to understand is exposed to distraction from fore-meanings that are not borne out by the things themselves. The working-out of appropriate projects, anticipatory in nature, to be confirmed "by the things" themselves, is the constant task of understanding. The only "objectivity" here is the confirmation of a fore-meaning in its being worked out. The only thing that characterizes the arbitrariness of inappropriate fore-meanings is that they come to nothing in the working-out. But understanding achieves its full potentiality only when the fore-meanings that it uses are not arbitrary. Thus it is quite right for the interpreter not to approach the text directly, relying solely on the fore-meaning at once available to him, but rather to examine explicitly the legitimacy, i.e., the origin and validity, of the fore-meanings present within him.

This fundamental requirement must be seen as the radicalization of a procedure that in fact we exercise whenever we understand anything. Every text presents the task of not simply employing unexamined our own linguistic usage—or in the case of a foreign language the usage that we are familiar with from writers or from daily intercourse. We regard our task as rather that of deriving our understanding of the text from the linguistic usage of the time of the author. The question is, of course, to what extent this general requirement can be fulfilled. In the field of semantics, in particular, we are confronted with the problem of the unconscious nature of our own use of language. How do we discover that there is a difference between our own customary usage and that of the text?

I think we must say that it is generally the experience of being pulled up short by the text. Either it does not yield any meaning or its meaning is not compatible with what we had expected. It is this that makes us take account of possible difference in usage. It is a general presupposition that can be questioned only in particular cases that someone who speaks the same language as I do uses the words in the sense familiar to me. The same thing is true in the case of a foreign language, i.e., that we all think we have a normal knowledge of it and assume this normal usage when we are reading a text.

What is true of the fore-meaning of usage, however, is equally true of the fore-meanings with regard to content with which we read texts, and which make up our fore-understanding. Here too we may ask how we can break the spell of our own fore-meanings. Certainly there can be no general presupposition that what is stated in a text will fit without fracture my own meanings and expectations. On the contrary, what another person tells me, whether in conversation, letter, book, or whatever, is generally thought automatically to be his own and not my opinion; and it is this that I am to take note of without necessarily having to share it. But this presupposition is not something that makes understanding easier, but harder, in that the fore-meanings that determine my own understanding can go entirely unnoticed. If they give rise to misunderstandings, how can misunderstandings of a text be recognised at all if there is nothing else to contradict? How can a text be protected from misunderstanding from the start?

If we examine the situation more closely, however, we find that meanings cannot be understood in an arbitrary way. Just as we cannot continually misunderstand the use of a word without its affecting the meaning of the whole, so we cannot hold blindly to our own fore-meaning of the thing if we would understand the meaning of another. Of course this does not mean that when we listen to someone or read a book we must forget all our fore-meanings concerning the content, and all our own ideas. All that is asked is that we remain open to the meaning of the other person or of the text. But this openness always includes our placing the other meaning in a relation with the whole of our own meanings or ourselves in a relation to it. Now it is the case that meanings represent a fluid variety of possibilities (when compared with the agreement presented by a language and a vocabulary), but it is still not the case that within this variety of what can be thought, i.e., of what a reader can find meaningful and hence expect to find, everything is possible, and if a person fails to hear what the other person is really saying, he will not be able to place correctly what he has misunderstood within the range of his own various expectations of meaning. Thus there is a criterion here also. The hermeneutical task becomes automatically a questioning of things and is always in part determined by this. This places hermeneutical work on a firm basis. If a person is trying to understand something, he will not be able to rely from the start on his own chance previous ideas, missing as logically and stubbornly as possible the actual meaning of the text until the latter becomes so persistently audible that it breaks through the imagined understanding of it. Rather, a person trying to understand a text is prepared for it to tell him something. That is why a hermeneutically trained mind must be, from the start, sensitive to the text's quality of newness. But this kind of sensitivity involves neither "neutrality" in the matter of the object nor the extinction of one's self, but the conscious assimilation of one's own fore-meanings and prejudices. The important thing is to be aware of one's own bias, so that the text may present itself in all its newness and thus be able to assert its own truth against one's own fore-meanings.

When Heidegger showed that what we call the "reading of what is there" is the fore-structure of understanding, this was, phenomenologically, completely correct. He also showed by an example the task that arises from this. In *Being and Time* he gave a concrete example, in the question of Being, of the general statement that was, for him, a hermeneutical problem. In order to explain the hermeneutical situation of the question of being in regard to fore-having, fore-sight, and fore-conception, he critically applied his question, directed at metaphysics. Here he was actually doing simply what the historical, hermeneutical consciousness requires in every case. Methodologically conscious understanding will be concerned not merely to form anticipatory ideas, but to make them conscious, so as to check them and thus acquire right understanding from the things themselves. This is what Heidegger means when he talks about "securing" our scientific theme by deriving our fore-having, fore-sight, and fore-conceptions from the things themselves.

It is not, then, at all a case of safeguarding ourselves against the tradition that speaks out of the text but, on the contrary, of keeping everything away that could hinder us in understanding it with respect to its matter. It is the tyranny of hidden prejudices that makes us deaf to the language that speaks to us in tradition. Heidegger's demonstration that the concept of consciousness in Descartes and of spirit in Hegel is still influenced by Greek substance ontology, which sees Being in terms of what is present and actual, undoubtedly goes beyond the self-understanding of modern metaphysics, yet not in an arbitrary, willful way, but on the basis of a fore-having that in fact makes this tradition intelligible by revealing the ontological premises of the concept of subjectivity. On the other hand, Heidegger discovers in Kant's critique of "dogmatic" metaphysics the idea of a metaphysics of the finite which is a challenge to his own ontological scheme. Thus he "secures" the scientific theme by framing it within the understanding of tradition and so putting it, in a sense, at risk. This is the concrete form of the historical consciousness that is involved in understanding.

This recognition that all understanding inevitably involves some prejudice gives the hermeneutical problem its real thrust. By the light of this insight it appears that historicism, despite its critique of rationalism and of natural-law philosophy, is based on the modern Enlightenment and unknowingly shares its prejudices. And there is one prejudice of the Enlightenment that is essential to it: the fundamental prejudice of the Enlightenment is the prejudice against prejudice itself, which deprives tradition of its power.

Historical analysis shows that it is not until the Enlightenment that the concept of prejudice acquires the negative aspect we are familiar with. Actually "prejudice" means a judgment that is given before all the elements that determine a situation have been finally examined. In German legal terminology a "prejudice" is a provisional legal verdict before the final verdict is reached. For someone involved in a legal dispute, this kind of judgment against him affects his chances adversely. Accordingly, the French *préjudice*, as well as the Latin *praejudicium*, means simply "adverse effect," "disadvantage," "harm." But this negative sense is only a consecutive one. The negative consequence depends precisely on the positive validity, the value of the provisional decision as a prejudgment, which is that of any precedent.

Thus "prejudice" certainly does not mean a false judgment; integral to this concept is that it can have a positive and a negative value. This is due clearly to the influence of the Latin *praejudicium*. There are such things as *préjugés légitimes*. This seems a long way from our current use of the word. The German *Vorurteil*, like the English "prejudice" and even more than the French *préjugé*, seems to have become limited in its meaning, through the Enlightenment and its critique of religion, and have the sense simply of an "unfounded judgment." It is only its having a basis, a methodological justification (and not the fact that it may be actually correct) that gives a judgment its dignity. The lack of such a basis does not mean, for the Enlightenment, that there might be other kinds of certainty, but rather that the judgment does not have any foundation in the facts themselves, i.e., that it is "unfounded." This is a conclusion only in the spirit of rationalism. It is the reason for the discrediting of prejudices and the claim by scientific knowledge completely to exclude them.

Modern science, in adopting this principle, is following the rule of Cartesian doubt of accepting nothing as certain that can in any way be doubted, and the idea of the method that adheres to this requirement. In our introductory observations we have already pointed out how difficult it is to harmonize the historical knowledge that helps to shape our historical consciousness with this ideal and how difficult it is, for that reason, for the modern concept of method to grasp its true nature. This is the place to turn these negative statements into positive ones. The concept of "prejudice" is where we can make a beginning.

The Discrediting of Prejudice by the Enlightenment

If we pursue the view that the Enlightenment developed in regard to prejudices we find it makes the following fundamental division: a distinction must be made between the prejudice due to human authority and that due to overhastiness. The basis of this distinction is the origin of prejudices in regard to the persons who have them. It is either the respect in which we hold others and their authority that leads us into error, or else it is an overhastiness in ourselves. That authority is a source of prejudices accords with the well-known principle of the Enlightenment that Kant formulated: Have the courage to make use of your own understanding. Although this distinction is clearly not limited to the role that prejudices play in the understanding of texts, its chief application is still in the sphere of hermeneutics. For the critique by the Enlightenment is directed primarily against the religious tradition of Christianity, i.e., the Bible. By treating the latter as an historical document, biblical criticism endangers its own dogmatic claims. This is the real radicality of the modern Enlightenment as against all other movements of enlightenment: it must assert itself against the Bible and its dogmatic interpretation. It is, therefore, particularly concerned with the hermeneutical problem. It desires to understand tradition correctly, i.e., reasonably and without prejudice. But there is a special difficulty about this, in that the sheer fact of something being written down confers on it an authority of particular weight. It is not altogether easy to realize that what is written down can be untrue. The written word has the tangible quality of something that can be demonstrated and is like a proof. It needs a special critical effort to free oneself from the prejudice in favor of what is written down and to distinguish here also, as with all oral assertions, between opinion and truth.

It is the general tendency of the Enlightenment not to accept any authority and to decide everything before the judgment seat of reason. Thus the written tradition of Scripture, like any other historical document, cannot claim any absolute validity, but the possible truth of the tradition depends on the credibility that is assigned to it by reason. It is not tradition but reason that constitutes the ultimate source of all authority. What is written down is not necessarily true. We may have superior knowledge: this is the maxim with which the modern Enlightenment approaches tradition and which ultimately leads it to undertake historical research. It makes the tradition as much an object of criticism as do the natural sciences the evidence of the senses. This does not necessarily mean that the "prejudice against prejudices" was everywhere taken to the extreme consequences of free thinking and atheism, as in England and France. On the contrary, the German Enlightenment recognised the "true prejudices" of the Christian religion. Since the human intellect is too weak to manage without prejudices it is at least fortunate to have been educated with true prejudices.

It would be of value to investigate to what extent this kind of modification and moderation of the Enlightenment prepared the way for the rise of the romantic movement in Germany, as undoubtedly did the critique of the Enlightenment and the revolution by Edmund Burke. But none of this alters the fundamental facts. True prejudices must still finally be justified by rational knowledge, even though the task may never be able to be fully completed.

Thus the criteria of the modern Enlightenment still determine the self-understanding of historicism. This does not happen directly, but in a curious refraction caused by romanticism. This can be seen with particular clarity in the fundamental schema of the philosophy of history that romanticism shares with the Enlightenment and that precisely the romantic reaction to the Enlightenment made into an unshakeable premise: the schema of the conquest of mythos by logos. It is the presupposition of the progressive retreat of magic in the world that gives this schema its validity. It is supposed to represent the progressive law of the history of the mind, and precisely because romanticism has a negative attitude to this development, it takes over the schema itself as an obvious truth. It shares the presupposition of the Enlightenment and only reverses the evaluation of it, seeking to establish the validity of what is old, simply because it is old: the "Gothic" Middle Ages, the Christian European community of states, the feudal structures of society, but also the simplicity of peasant life and closeness to nature.

In contrast to the Enlightenment's belief in perfection, which thinks in terms of the freedom from "superstition" and the prejudices of the past, we now find that olden times, the world of myth, unreflective life, not yet analyzed away by consciousness, in a "society close to nature," the world of Christian chivalry, all these acquire a romantic magic, even a priority of truth. The reversal of the Enlightenment's presupposition results in the paradoxical tendency to restoration, i.e., the tendency to reconstruct the old because it is old, the conscious return to the unconscious, culminating in the recognition of the superior wisdom of the primeval age of myth. But the romantic reversal of this criterion of the Enlightenment actually perpetuates the abstract contrast between myth and reason. All criticism of the Enlightenment now proceeds via this romantic mirror image of the Enlightenment. Belief in the perfectibility of reason suddenly changes into the perfection of the "mythical" consciousness and finds itself reflected in a paradisic primal state before the "fall" of thought.

In fact the presupposition of a mysterious darkness in which there was a mythical collective consciousness that preceded all thought is just as dogmatic and abstract as that of a state of perfection achieved by a total enlightenment or that of absolute knowledge. Primeval wisdom is only the counterimage of "primeval stupidity." All mythical consciousness is still knowledge, and if it knows about divine powers, then it has progressed beyond mere trembling before power (if this is to be regarded as the primeval state), but also beyond a collective life contained in magic rituals (as we find in the early Orient). It knows about itself, and in this knowledge it is no longer simply "outside itself."

There is the related point that even the contrast between genuine mythical thinking and pseudomythical poetic thinking is a romantic illusion that is based on a prejudice of the Enlightenment: namely, that the poetic act, because it is a creation of the free imagination, is no longer in any way bound within the religious quality of the myth. It is the old quarrel between the poets and the philosophers in the modern garb appropriate to the age of belief in science. It is now said, not that poets tell lies, but that they are incapable of saying anything true, since they have an aesthetic effect only and merely seek to rouse through their imaginative creations the imagination and the emotions of their hearers or readers.

The concept of the "society close to nature" is probably another case of a romantic mirror image, whose origin ought to be investigated. In Karl Marx it appears as a kind of relic of natural law that limits the validity of his socioeconomic theory of the class struggle. Does the idea go back to Rousseau's description of society before the division of labor and the introduction of property? At any rate, Plato has already demonstrated the illusory nature of this political theory in the ironical account he gives of a "state of nature" in the third book of the *Republic*.

These romantic revaluations give rise to the attitude of the historical science of the nineteenth century. It no longer measures the past by the yardsticks of the present, as if they represented an absolute, but it ascribes their own value to past ages and can even acknowledge their superiority in one or the other respect. The great achievements of romanticism—the revival of the past, the discovery of the voices of the peoples in their songs, the collecting of fairy tales and legends, the cultivation of ancient customs, the discovery of the world views implicit in languages, the study of the "religion and wisdom of India"—have all motivated the historical research that has slowly, step by step, transformed the intuitive revival into historical knowledge proper. The fact that it was romanticism that gave birth to the historical school confirms that the romantic retrieval of origins is itself based on the Enlightenment. The historical science of the nineteenth century is its proudest fruit and sees itself precisely as the fulfillment of the Enlightenment, as the last step in the liberation of the mind from the trammels of dogma, the step to the objective knowledge of the historical world, which stands as an equal besides the knowledge of nature achieved by modern science.

The fact that the restorative tendency of romanticism was able to combine with the fundamental concern of the Enlightenment to constitute the unity of the historical sciences simply indicates that it is the same break with the continuity of meaning in tradition that lies behind both. If it is an established fact for the Enlightenment that all tradition that reason shows to be impossible, i.e., nonsense, can only be understood historically, i.e., by going back to the past's way of looking at things, then the historical consciousness that emerges in romanticism involves a radicalization of the Enlightenment. For the exceptional case of nonsensical tradition has become the general rule for historical consciousness. Meaning that is generally accessible through reason is so little believed that the whole of the past, even, ultimately, all the thinking of one's contemporaries, is seen only "historically." Thus the romantic critique of the Enlightenment ends itself in enlightenment, in that it evolves as historical science and draws everything into the orbit of historicism. The basic discrediting of all prejudices, which unites the experiential emphasis of the new natural sciences with the Enlightenment, becomes, in the historical Enlightenment, universal and radical.

This is the point at which the attempt to arrive at a historical hermeneutics has to start its critique. The overcoming of all prejudices, this global demand of the Enlightenment, will prove to be itself a prejudice, the removal of which opens the way to an appropriate understanding of our finitude, which dominates not only our humanity, but also our historical consciousness.

Does the fact that one is set within various traditions mean really and primarily that one is subject to prejudices and limited in one's freedom? Is not, rather, all human existence, even the freest, limited and qualified in various ways? If this is true, then the idea of an absolute reason is impossible for historical humanity. Reason exists for us only in concrete, historical terms, i.e., it is not its own master, but remains constantly dependent on the given circumstances in which it operates. This is true not only in the sense in which Kant limited the claims of rationalism, under the influence of the sceptical critique of Hume, to the a priori element in the knowledge of nature; it is still truer of historical consciousness and the possibility of historical knowledge. For that man is concerned here with himself and his own creations (Vico) is only an apparent solution of the problem set by historical knowledge. Man is alien to himself and his historical fate in a quite different way from that in which nature, which knows nothing of him, is alien to him.

The epistemological question must be asked here in a fundamentally different way. We have shown above that Dilthey probably saw this, but he was not able to overcome the influence over him of traditional epistemology. From his starting point, the awareness of "experience," he was not able to build the bridge to the historical realities, because the great historical realities of society and state always have a predeterminant influence on any "experience." Self-reflection and autobiography—Dilthey's starting points—are not primary and are not an adequate basis for the hermeneutical problem, because through them history is made private once more. In fact history does not belong to us, but we belong to it. Long before we understand ourselves through the process of self-examination, we understand ourselves in a self-evident way in the family, society, and state in which we live. The focus of subjectivity is a distorting mirror.

The self-awareness of the individual is only a flickering in the closed circuits of historical life. That is why the prejudices of the individual, far more than his judgments, constitute the historical reality of his being.

PREJUDICES AS CONDITIONS OF UNDERSTANDING

The Rehabilitation of Authority and Tradition

This is where the hermeneutical problem comes in. This is why we examined the discrediting of the concept of prejudice by the Enlightenment. That which presents itself, under the aegis of an absolute self-construction by reason, as a limiting prejudice belongs, in fact, to historical reality itself. What is necessary is a fundamental rehabilitation of the concept of prejudice and a recognition of the fact that there are legitimate prejudices, if we want to do justice to man's finite, historical mode of being. Thus we are able to formulate the central question of a truly historical hermeneutics, epistemologically its fundamental question, namely: where is the ground of the legitimacy of prejudices? What distinguishes legitimate prejudices from all the countless ones which it is the undeniable task of the critical reason to overcome?

We can approach this question by taking the view of prejudices that the Enlightenment developed with a critical intention, as set out above, and giving it a positive value. As for the division of prejudices into those of "authority" and those of "overhastiness," it is obviously based on the fundamental presupposition of the Enlightenment, according to which a methodologically disciplined use of reason can safeguard us from all error. This was Descartes's idea of method. Overhastiness is the actual source of error in the use of one's own reason. Authority, however, is responsible for one's not using one's own reason at all. There lies, then, at the base of the division a complete antithesis between authority and reason. The false prejudice for what is old, for authorities, is what has to be fought. Thus the Enlightenment regards it as the reforming action of Luther that "the prejudice of human prestige, especially that of the philosophical [he means Aristotle] and the Roman pope was greatly weakened." The Reformation, then, gives rise to a flourishing hermeneutics, which is to teach the right use of reason in the understanding of transmitted texts. Neither the teaching authority of the pope nor the appeal to tradition can replace the work of hermeneutics, which can safeguard the reasonable meaning of a text against all unreasonable demands made on it.

The consequences of this kind of hermeneutics need not be those of the radical critique of religion that we found, for example, in Spinoza.

Rather the possibility of supernatural truth can remain entirely open. Thus the Enlightenment, especially in the field of popular philosophy, limited the claims of reason and acknowledged the authority of Bible and Church. We read in, say, Walch, that he distinguishes between the two classes of prejudice—authority and overhastiness—but sees in them two extremes, between which it is necessary to find the right middle path, namely a reconciliation between reason and biblical authority. Accordingly, he sees the prejudice from overhastiness as a prejudice in favor of the new, as a predisposition to the overhasty rejection of truths simply because they are old and attested by authorities. Thus he discusses the British freethinkers (such as Collins and others) and defends the historical faith against the norm of reason. Here the meaning of the prejudice from overhastiness is clearly reinterpreted in a conservative sense.

There can be no doubt, however, that the real consequence of the Enlightenment is different: namely, the subjection of all authority to reason. Accordingly, prejudice from overhastiness is to be understood as Descartes understood it, i.e., as the source of all error in the use of reason. This fits in with the fact that after the victory of the Enlightenment, when hermeneutics was freed from all dogmatic ties, the old division returns in a changed sense. Thus we read in Schleiermacher that he distinguishes between narrowness of view and overhastiness as the causes of misunderstanding. He places the lasting prejudices due to narrowness of view beside the momentary ones due to overhastiness, but only the former are of interest to someone concerned with scientific method. It no longer even occurs to Schleiermacher that among the prejudices in the mind of one whose vision is narrowed by authorities there might be some that are true—yet this was included in the conception of authority in the first place. His alteration of the traditional division of prejudices is a sign of the fulfillment of the Enlightenment. Narrowness now means only an individual limitation of understanding: "the one sided preference for what is close to one's own sphere of ideas."

In fact, however, the decisive question is concealed behind the concept of narrowness. That the prejudices that determine what I think are due to my own narrowness of vision is a judgment that is made from the standpoint of their dissolution and illumination and holds only of unjustified prejudices. If, contrariwise, there are justified prejudices productive of knowledge, then we are back with the problem of authority. Hence the radical consequences of the Enlightenment, which are still contained in Schleiermacher's faith in method, are not tenable.

The distinction the Enlightenment draws between faith in authority and the use of one's own reason is, in itself, legitimate. If the prestige of authority takes the place of one's own judgment, then authority is in fact a source of prejudices. But this does not exclude the possibility that it can also be a source of truth, and this is what the Enlightenment failed to see when it denigrated all authority. To be convinced of this, we only have to consider one of the greatest forerunners of the European Enlightenment, namely Descartes. Despite the radicalness of his methodological thinking, we know that Descartes excluded morality from the total reconstruction of all truths by reason. This was what he meant by his provisional morality. It seems to me symptomatic that he did not in fact elaborate his definitive morality and that its principles, as far as we can judge from his letters to Elizabeth, contain hardly anything new. It is obviously unthinkable to prefer to wait until the progress of modern science provides us with the basis of a new morality. In fact the denigration of authority is not the only prejudice of the Enlightenment. For, within the Enlightenment, the very concept of authority becomes deformed. On the basis of its concept of reason and freedom, the concept of authority could be seen as diametrically opposed to reason and freedom: to be, in fact, blind obedience. This is the meaning that we know, from the usage of their critics, within modern dictatorships.

But this is not the essence of authority. It is true that it is primarily persons that have authority; but the authority of persons is based ultimately, not on the subjection and abdication of reason, but on recognition and knowledge—knowledge, namely, that the other is superior to oneself in judgment and insight and that for this reason his judgment takes precedence, i.e., it has priority over one's own. This is connected with the fact that authority cannot actually be bestowed, but is acquired and must be acquired, if someone is to lay claim to it. It rests on recognition and hence on an act of reason itself which, aware of its own limitations, accepts that others have better understanding. Authority in this sense, properly understood, has nothing to do with blind obedience to a command. Indeed, authority has nothing to do with obedience, but rather with knowledge. It is true that authority is necessary in order to be able to command and find obedience. But this proceeds only from the authority that a person has. Even the anonymous and impersonal authority of a superior that derives from the command is not ultimately based on this order, but is what makes it possible. Here also its true basis is an act of freedom and reason, which fundamentally acknowledges the authority of a superior because he has a wider view of things or is better informed, i.e., once again, because he has superior knowledge.

Thus the recognition of authority is always connected with the idea that what authority states is not irrational and arbitrary, but can be seen, in principle, to be true. This is the essence of the authority claimed by the teacher, the superior, the expert. The prejudices that they implant are legitimized by the person himself. Their validity demands that one should be biased in favor of the person who presents them. But this makes them then, in a sense, objective prejudices, for they bring about the same bias in favor of something that can come about through other means, e.g., through solid grounds offered by reason. Thus the essence of authority belongs in the context of a theory of prejudices free from the extremism of the Enlightenment.

Here we can find support in the romantic criticism of the Enlightenment; for there is one form of authority particularly defended by romanticism, namely tradition. That which has been sanctioned by tradition and custom has an authority that is nameless, and our finite historical being is marked by the fact that always the authority of what has been transmitted—and not only what is clearly grounded—has power over our attitudes and behavior. All education depends on this, and even though, in the case of education, the educator loses his function when his charge comes of age and sets his own insight and decisions in the place of the authority of the educator, this movement into maturity in his own life does not mean that a person becomes his own master in the sense that he becomes free of all tradition. The validity of morals, for example, is based on tradition. They are freely taken over, but by no means created by a free insight or justified by themselves. This is precisely what we call tradition: the ground of their validity. And in fact we owe to romanticism this correction of the Enlightenment, that tradition has a justification that is ouside the arguments of reason and in large measure determines our institutions and our attitudes. It is even a mark of the superiority of classical ethics over the moral philosophy of the modern period that it justifies the transition of ethics into "politics," the art of right government, by the indispensability of tradition. In comparison with it the modern Enlightenment is abstract and revolutionary.

The concept of tradition, however, has become no less ambiguous than that of authority, and for the same reason, namely that it is the abstract counterpart to the principle of the Enlightenment that determines the romantic understanding of tradition. Romanticism conceives tradition as the antithesis to the freedom of reason and regards it as something historically given, like nature. And whether the desire is to be revolutionary and oppose it or would like to preserve it, it is still seen as the abstract counterpart of free self-determination, since its validity does not require any reasons, but conditions us without our questioning it. Of course, the case of the romantic critique of the Enlightenment is not an instance of the automatic dominance of tradition, in which what has been handed down is preserved unaffected by doubt and criticism. It is, rather, a particular critical attitude that again addresses itself to the truth of tradition and seeks to renew it, and which we may call "traditionalism."

It seems to me, however, that there is no such unconditional antithesis between tradition and reason. However problematical the conscious restoration of traditions or the conscious creation of new traditions may be, the romantic faith in the "growth of tradition," before which all reason must remain silent, is just as prejudiced as and is fundamentally like the Enlightenment. The fact is that tradition is constantly an element of freedom and of history itself. Even the most genuine and solid tradition does not persist by nature because of the inertia of what once eixsted. It needs to be affirmed, embraced, cultivated. It is, essentially, preservation, such as is active in all historical change. But preservation is an act of reason, though an inconspicuous one. For this reason, only what is new, or what is planned, appears as the result of reason. But this is an illusion. Even where life changes violently, as in ages of revolution, far more of the old is preserved in the supposed transformation of everything than anyone knows, and combines with the new to create a new value. At any rate, preservation is as much a freely chosen action as revolution and renewal. That is why both the Enlightenment's critique of tradition and its romantic rehabilitation of tradition fall short of true historical being.

These thoughts lead to the question of whether in the hermeneutic of the human sciences the element of tradition should not be given its full value. Research in the human sciences cannot regard itself as in an absolute antithesis to the attitude we take toward the past as historical beings. In our continually manifested attitude toward the past, the main feature is not, at any rate, a distancing and freeing of ourselves from what has been transmitted. Rather, we stand always within tradition, and this is no objectifying process, i.e., we do not conceive of what tradition says as something other, something alien. It is always part of us, a model or exemplar, a recognition of ourselves which our later historical judgment would hardly see as a kind of knowledge, but as the simplest preservation of tradition.

Hence in regard to the dominant epistemological methodologism we must ask if the rise of historical consciousness has really detached our scientific attitude entirely from this natural attitude to the past. Does understanding in the human sciences understand itself correctly when it relegates the whole of its own historicity to the position of prejudices from which we must free ourselves? Or does "unprejudiced science" have more in common than it realizes with that naive openness and reflection in which traditions live and the past is present?

At any rate, understanding in the human sciences shares one fundamental condition with the continuity of traditions, namely, that it lets itself be addressed by tradition. Is it not true of the objects of its investigation—just as of the contents of tradition—that only then can its meaning be experienced? However much this meaning may always be a mediated one and proceed from a historical interest, that does not seem to have any relation to the present; even in the extreme case of "objective" historical research, the proper realization of the historical task is to determine anew the meaning of what is examined. But the meaning exists at the beginning of any such research as well as at the end: as the choice of the theme to be investigated, the awakening of the desire to investigate, as the gaining of the new problematic.

At the beginning of all historical hermeneutics, then, the abstract antithesis between tradition and historical research, between history and knowledge, must be discarded. The effect of a living tradition and the effect of historical study must constitute a unity, the analysis of which would reveal only a texture of reciprocal relationships. Hence we would do well not to regard historical consciousness as something radically new —as it seems at first—but as a new element within that which has always made up the human relation to the past. In other words, we have to recognise the element of tradition in the historical relation and enquire into its hermeneutical productivity.

The Hermeneutic Significance of Temporal Distance

Let us consider first how hermeneutics sets about its work. What follows for understanding from the hermeneutic condition of belonging to a tradition? We remember here the hermeneutical rule that we must understand the whole in terms of the detail and the detail in terms of the whole. This principle stems from ancient rhetoric, and modern hermeneutics has taken it and applied it to the art of understanding. It is a circular relationship. The anticipation of meaning in which the whole is envisaged becomes explicit understanding in that the parts, that are determined by the whole, themselves also determine this whole.

We know this from the learning of ancient languages. We learn that we must "construe" a sentence before we attempt to understand the individual parts of the sentence in their linguistic meaning. But this process of construing is itself already governed by an expectation of meaning that follows from the context of what has gone before. It is also necessary for this expected meaning to be adjusted if the text calls for it. This means, then, that the expectation changes and that the text acquires the unity of a meaning from another expected meaning. Thus the movement of understanding is constantly from the whole to the part and back to the whole. Our task is to extend in concentric circles the unity of the understood meaning. The harmony of all the details with the whole is the criterion of correct understanding. The failure to achieve this harmony means that understanding has failed.

Schleiermacher differentiated this hermeneutic circle of part and whole in both its objective and its subjective aspect. As the single word belongs within the total context of the sentence, so the single text belongs within the total context of a writer's work, and the latter within the whole of the particular literary genre or of literature. At the same time, however, the same text, as a manifestation of a creative moment, belongs to the whole of its author's inner life. Full understanding can take place only within this objective and subjective whole. Following this theory, Dilthey speaks then of "structure" and of the "centering in a midpoint," from out of which there follows the understanding of the whole. In this he is applying to the historical world what has always been a principle of all textual interpretation: namely, that a text must be understood in terms of itself.

The question is, however, whether this is an adequate account of the circular movement of understanding. Here we must go back to the result of our analysis of Schleiermacher's hermeneutics. We may set aside Schleiermacher's ideas on subjective interpretation. When we try to understand a text, we do not try to recapture the author's attitude of mind but, if this is the terminology we are to use, we try to recapture the perspective within which he has formed his views. But this means simply that we try to accept the objective validity of what he is saying. If we want to understand, we shall try to make his arguments even more cogent. This happens even in conversation, so how much truer is it of the understanding of what is written down that we are moving in a dimension of meaning that is intelligible in itself and as such offers no reason for going back to the subjectivity of the author. It is the task of hermeneutics to clarify this miracle of understanding, which is not a mysterious communion of souls, but a sharing of a common meaning.

But even the objective side of this circle, as Schleiermacher describes it, does not reach the heart of the matter. We have seen that the goal of all communication and understanding is agreement concerning the object. Hence the task of hermeneutics has always been to establish agreement where it had failed to come about or been disturbed in some way. The history of hermeneutics can offer a confirmation of this if, for example, we think of Augustine, who sought to relate the Christian Gospel to the Old Testament, or of early Protestantism, which faced the same problem or, finally, the Age of the Enlightenment, when it is almost like a renunciation of agreement to seek to acquire "full understanding" of a text only by means of historical interpretation. It is something qualitatively new when romanticism and Schleiermacher ground a universal historical consciousness by no longer seeing the binding form of tradition, from which they come and in which they stand, as the firm foundation of all hermeneutical endeavor.

One of the immediate predecessors of Schleiermacher, Friedrich Ast, still had a view of hermeneutical work that was markedly concerned with content, in that, for him, its purpose was to establish harmony between the world of classical antiquity and Christianity, between a newly discovered genuine antiquity and the Christian tradition. This is something new, in comparison with the Enlightenment, in that this hermeneutics no longer accepts or rejects tradition in accord with the criterion of natural reason. But in its attempt to bring about a meaningful agreement between the two traditions to which it sees itself as belonging, this kind of hermeneutics, is still pursuing the task of all preceding hermeneutics, namely to achieve in understanding agreement in content.

In going beyond the "particularity" of this reconciliation of the ancient classical world and Christianity, Schleiermacher and, following him, nineteenth-century science, conceive the task of hermeneutics in a way that is formally universal. They were able to harmonize it with the natural sciences' ideal of objectivity, but only by ignoring the concretion of historical consciousness in hermeneutical theory.

Heidegger's description and existential account of the hermeneutic circle constitutes in contrast a decisive turning point. The hermeneutic theory of the nineteenth century often spoke of the circular structure of understanding, but always within the framework of a formal relation of the part and the whole or its subjective reflex, the intuitive anticipation of the whole and its subsequent articulation in the parts. According to this theory, the circular movement of understanding runs backwards and forwards along the text and disappears when it is perfectly understood. This view of understanding culminated logically in Schleiermacher's theory of the divinatory act, by means of which one places oneself entirely within the writer's mind and from there resolves all that is strange and unusual about the text. As against this approach, Heidegger describes the circle in such a way that the understanding of the text remains permanently determined by the anticipatory movement of fore-understanding. The circle of the whole and the part is not dissolved in perfect understanding but, on the contrary, is most fully realized.

The circle, then, is not formal in nature; it is neither subjective nor objective, but describes understanding as the interplay of the movement of tradition and the movement of the interpreter. The anticipation of meaning that governs our understanding of a text is not an act of subjectivity, but proceeds from the communality that binds us to the tradition. But this is contained in our relation to tradition, in the constant process of education. Tradition is not simply a precondition into which we come; rather, we produce it ourselves, inasmuch as we understand, participate in the evolution of tradition, and hence further determine it ourselves. Thus the circle of understanding is not a "methodological" circle, but describes an ontological structural element in understanding.

The significance of this circle, which is fundamental to all understanding, has a further hermeneutic consequence that I may call the "foreconception of completion." But this, too, is obviously a formal condition of all understanding. It states that only what really constitutes a unity of meaning is intelligible. So when we read a text we always follow this complete presupposition of completion, and only when it proves inadequate, i.e., the text is not intelligible, do we start to doubt the transmitted text and seek to discover in what way it can be remedied. The rules of such textual criticism can be left aside, for the important thing to note is that their proper application cannot be detached from the understanding of the textual content.

The anticipation of completion that guides all our understanding is, then, always specific in content. Not only is an immanent unity of meaning guiding the reader assumed, but his understanding is likewise guided by the constant transcendent expectations of meaning which proceed from the relation to the truth of what is being said. Just as the recipient of a letter understands the news that it contains and first sees things with the eyes of the person who wrote the letter, i.e., considers what he writes as true, and is not trying to understand the alien meanings of the letter writer, so we understand texts that have been handed down to us on the basis of expectations of meaning which are drawn from our own anterior relation to the subject. And just as we believe the news reported by a correspondent because he was present or is better informed, we are fundamentally open to the possibility that the writer of a transmitted text is better informed than we are, with our previously formed meaning. It is only when the attempt to accept what he has said as true fails that we try to "understand" the text, psychologically or historically, as another's meaning. The anticipation of completion, then, contains not only this formal element that a text should fully express its meaning, but also that what it says should be the whole truth.

We see here again that understanding means, primarily, to understand the content of what is said, and only secondarily to isolate and understand another's meaning as such. Hence the first of all hermeneutic requirements remains one's own fore-understanding, which proceeds from being concerned with the same subject. It is this that determines what unified meaning can be realized and hence the application of the anticipation of completion.

Thus the meaning of the connection with tradition, i.e., the element of tradition in our historical, hermeneutical attitude, is fulfilled in the fact that we share fundamental prejudices with tradition. Hermeneutics must start from the position that a person seeking to understand something has a relation to the object that comes into language in the transmitted text and has, or acquires, a connection with the tradition out of which the text speaks. On the other hand, hermeneutical consciousness is aware that it cannot be connected with this object in some self-evident, unquestioned way, as is the case with the unbroken stream of a tradition. There is a polarity of familiarity and strangeness on which hermeneutic work is based: only this polarity is not to be seen, psychologically, with Schleiermacher, as the tension that conceals the mystery of individuality, but truly hermeneutically, i.e., in regard to what has been said: the language in which the text addresses us, the story that it tells us. Here too there is a tension. The place between strangeness and familiarity that a transmitted text has for us is that intermediate place between being an historically intended separate object and being part of a tradition. The true home of hermeneutics is this intermediate area.

It follows from this intermediate position in which hermeneutics operates that the work of hermeneutics is not to develop a procedure of understanding, but to clarify the conditions in which understanding takes place. But these conditions are not of the nature of a "procedure" or a method, which the interpreter must of himself bring to bear on the text, but rather they must be given. The prejudices and fore-meanings in the mind of the interpreter are not at his free disposal. He is not able to separate in advance the productive prejudices that make understanding possible from the prejudices that hinder understanding and lead to misunderstandings.

This separation, rather, must take place in the understanding itself, and hence hermeneutics must ask how it happens. But this means it must place in the foreground what has remained entirely peripheral in previous hermeneutics: temporal distance and its significance for understanding.

This point can be clarified by comparing it with the hermeneutic theory of romanticism. We shall recall that the latter conceived understanding as the reproduction of an original production. Hence it was possible to say that one should be able to understand an author better than he understood himself.

That subsequent understanding is superior to the original production and hence can be described as superior understanding does not depend so much on the conscious realization that places the reader on the same level as the author (as Schleiermacher said), but denotes rather an inevitable difference between the interpreter and the author that is created by the historical distance between them. Every age has to understand a transmitted text in its own way, for the text is part of the whole of the tradition in which the age takes an objective interest and in which it seeks to understand itself. The real meaning of a text, as it speaks to the interpreter, does not depend on the contingencies of the author and whom he originally wrote for. It certainly is not identical with them, for it is always partly determined also by the historical situation of the interpreter and hence by the totality of the objective course of history. A writer like

Chladenius, who does not yet see understanding in terms of history, is saying the same thing in a naive, ingenuous way when he says that an author does not need to know the real meaning of what he has written, and hence the interpreter can, and must, often understand more than he. But this is of fundamental importance. Not occasionally only, but always, the meaning of a text goes beyond its author. That is why understanding is not merely a reproductive, but always a productive attitude as well. Perhaps it is not correct to refer to this productive element in understanding as "superior understanding." For this phrase is the application of a principle of criticism from the age of the Enlightenment on the basis of the aesthetics of genius. Understanding is not, in fact, superior understanding, neither in the sense of superior knowledge of the subject because of clearer ideas, nor in the sense of fundamental superiority that the conscious has over the unconscious nature of creation. It is enough to say that we understand in a different way, if we understand at all.

This concept of understanding undoubtedly breaks right out of the circle drawn by romantic hermeneutics. Because what we are now concerned with is not individuality and what it thinks, but the objective truth of what is said, a text is not understood as a mere expression of life, but taken seriously in its claim to truth. That this is what is meant by "understanding" was once self-evident (we need only recall Chladenius).

But this dimension of the hermeneutical problem was discredited by historical consciousness and the psychological turn that Schleiermacher gave to hermeneutics, and could only be regained when the impasses of historicism appeared and led finally to the new development inspired chiefly, in my opinion, by Heidegger. For the hermeneutic importance of temporal distance could be understood only as a result of the ontological direction that Heidegger gave to understanding as an "existential" and of his temporal interpretation of the mode of being of Dasein.

Time is no longer primarily a gulf to be bridged, because it separates, but it is actually the supportive ground of process in which the present is rooted. Hence temporal distance is not something that must be overcome. This was, rather, the naive assumption of historicism, namely that we must set ourselves within the spirit of the age, and think with its ideas and its thoughts, not with our own, and thus advance towards historical objectivity. In fact the important thing is to recognise the distance in time as a positive and productive possibility of understanding. It is not a yawning abyss, but is filled with the continuity of custom and tradition, in the light of which all that is handed down presents itself to us. Here it is not too much to speak of a genuine productivity of process. Everyone knows that curious impotence of our judgment where the distance in time has not given us sure criteria. Thus the judgment of contemporary works of art is desperately uncertain for the scientific consciousness. Obviously we approach such creations with the prejudices we are not in control of, pre-suppositions that have too great an influence over us for us to know about them; these can give to contemporary creations an extra resonance that does not correspond to their true content and their true significance. Only when all their relations to the present time have faded away can their real nature appear, so that the understanding of what is said in them can claim to be authoritative and universal.

It is this experience that has led to the idea in historical studies that objective knowledge can be arrived at only when there has been a certain historical distance. It is true that what a thing has to say, its intrinsic content, first appears only after it is divorced from the fleeting circumstances of its actuality. The positive conditions of historical understanding include the self-contained quality of a historical event, which allows it to appear as a whole, and its distance from the opinions concerning its import with which the present is filled. The implicit prerequisite of the historical method, then, is that the permanent significance of something can first be known objectively only when it belongs within a self-contained context. In other words, when it is dead enough to have only historical interest. Only then does it seem possible to exclude the subjective involvement of the observer. This is, in fact, a paradox, the epistemological counterpart to the old moral problem of whether anyone can be called happy before his death. Just as Aristotle showed what a sharpening of the powers of human judgment this kind of problem can bring about, so hermeneutical reflection cannot fail to find here a sharpening of the methodological self-consciousness of science. It is true that certain hermeneutic requirements are automatically fulfilled when a historical context has become of no more than historical interest. Certain sources of error are automatically excluded. But it is questionable whether this is the end of the hermeneutical problem. Temporal distance has obviously another meaning than that of the quenching of our interest in the object. It lets the true meaning of the object emerge fully. But the discovery of the true meaning of a text or a work of art is never finished; it is in fact an infinite process. Not only are fresh sources of error constantly excluded, so that the true meaning has filtered out of it all kinds of things that obscure it, but there emerge continually new sources of understanding, which reveal unsuspected elements of meaning. The temporal distance which performs the filtering process is not a closed dimension, but is itself undergoing constant movement and extension. And with the negative side of the filtering process brought about by temporal distance there is also the positive side, namely the value it has for understanding. It not only lets those prejudices that are of a particular and limited nature die away, but causes those that bring about genuine understanding to emerge clearly as such.

It is only this temporal distance that can solve the really critical questions of hermeneutics, namely of distinguishing the true prejudices, by which we understand, from the false ones by which we misunderstand. Hence the hermeneutically trained mind will also include historical consciousness. It will make conscious the prejudices governing our own understanding, so that the text, as another's meaning, can be isolated and valued on its own. The isolation of a prejudice clearly requires the suspension of its validity for us. For so long as our mind is influenced by a prejudice, we do not know and consider it as a judgment. How then are we able to isolate it? It is impossible to make ourselves aware of it while it is constantly operating unnoticed, but only when it is, so to speak, stimulated. The encounter with a text from the past can prove this stimulus. For what leads to understanding must be something that has already asserted itself in its own separate validity. Understanding begins, as we have already said above, when something addresses us. This is the primary hermeneutical condition. We now know what this requires, namely the fundamental suspension of our own prejudices. But all suspension of judgments and hence, a fortiori, of prejudices, has logically the structure of a question.

The essence of the question is the opening up, and keeping open, of possibilities. If a prejudice becomes questionable, in view of what another or a text says to us, this does not mean that it is simply set aside and the other writing or the other person accepted as valid in its place. It shows, rather, the naiveté of historical objectivism to accept this disregarding of ourselves as what actually happens. In fact our own prejudice is properly brought into play through its being at risk. Only through its being given full play is it able to experience the other's claim to truth and make it possible for he himself to have full play.[3]

The naiveté of so called historicism consists in the fact that it does not undertake this reflection, and in trusting to its own methodological approach forgets its own historicity. We must here appeal from a badly understood historical thinking to one that can better perform the task of understanding. True historical thinking must take account of its own historicity. Only then will it not chase the phantom of an historical object which is the object of progressive research, but learn to see in the object the counterpart of itself and hence understand both. The true historical object is not an object at all, but the unity of the one and the other, a relationship in which exist both the reality of history and the reality of historical understanding. A proper hermeneutics would have to demonstrate the effectiveness of history within understanding itself.

3. Translator's note: In this passage the author plays on the German expressions *ins Spiel bringen, auf dem Spiele stehen,* and *sich ausspielen.*

11. RONALD BRUZINA

Heidegger on the Metaphor and Philosophy

IT IS AN EASY CHARGE TO MAKE against the philosophy of Martin Heidegger that it plays too loosely with the meanings of words. Instead of clarifying basics unambiguously, his writings deliberately introduce and exploit shifts of meaning and unexpected associations. The metaphorical element of language becomes with him all-pervasive, and instead of being an aid to more logical analysis, quite crowds it out. His thought in the end is word play and, in far too great a part, metaphor play; and it is obvious that he has opted for poetry against serious and positive philosophic explanation.

It need not be with disapproval, however, that one takes Heidegger's work to be dominantly metaphorical. One could see it as a charging of the philosophic scene with new ways of understanding things, offering material to others for more careful elaboration, organization, and explication. A fairly recent study of Heidegger's "aesthetics," for example, speaks admiringly and positively of the metaphorical weight of his "Origin of the Work of Art": [1]

> In such passages as these Heidegger's language exhibits a lyricism and degree of metaphorical statement rarely found in the writings of professional philosophers. He is in fact approaching the limits of meaningful expression.[2]

Indeed, it is not on whether the characterization of Heidegger's work as metaphorical is or is not fair that readers divide into followers and an-

Reprinted from *Cultural Hermeneutics* 1 (1973), with permission of the editors and D. Reidel Publishing Company.

1. "Der Ursprung Des Kunstwerkes," in *Holzwege* (Frankfurt, 1950).
2. Eugene F. Kaelin, "Notes toward an Understanding of Heidegger's Aesthetics," in *Phenomenology and Existentialism*, ed. Edward N. Lee and Maurice Mandelbaum (Baltimore, 1967), p. 82.

tagonists; but rather on the question what to make of it as philosophy. Metaphorical it is, but as *philosophy* is it illumination or nonsense, and in what proportion?

Much can be said about this either way, has been, and will be. But this is not the subject for consideration here, simply because I do not see it to be an issue that reaches the heart of Heidegger's project. It remains on the periphery, not taking Heidegger's own claims and disclaimers seriously, and not following Heidegger in the direction he quite clearly shows he is going. What is at issue, then, is not the question whether valid philosophy is to be drawn from metaphorical utterance, or indeed whether valid philosophy can be or is developed *in* metaphorical discourse. This way of framing the question presupposes the validity and at least potentially explicit clarity of "the metaphor" as a categorical concept. Heidegger, on the other hand, is calling for a questioning of the very designation "metaphor," and he does so because he finds the metaphor holds a paradoxical place in the philosophic account of discourse. The peculiarity is this: Philosophy's account of discourse is to be an account of the discourse of philosophy itself, that is, the elucidation and validation of philosophic discourse itself. The metaphor, however, is at one and the same time both defined against philosophic discourse and inescapably used within it; the metaphor is both assigned an accessory status, if admitted at all, and yet is the very type of expression within which meaningful characterization for fundamental elements first arises. Metaphor is both excluded from and grounding for rational explication. As such the metaphor shows the existence of paradox, not simply with regard to itself, but with regard to the very constitution of philosophic reason and philosophic discourse. In the end, Heidegger's call for serious consideration of the metaphor is a call for serious consideration of the character of the field of philosophic reason.

Two of Heidegger's works in particular provide an exposition of Heidegger's movement within this theme of the metaphor and philosophy. *On the Way to Language* [3] is particularly significant precisely as a 'monograph' on language. At the same time, *The Principle of Reason* [4] offers clearer lessons on some elements involved in a reflection on language. I would like to suggest a joint reading of the two, following a strategy of thinking involving several tactics. Let me indicate these tactics in a few words and then go on to elaborate them in an actual study of certain passages.

3. *Unterwegs zur Sprache* (Tübingen, 1959); English translation by Peter D. Hertz, *On the Way to Language* (New York, 1971). (References to this work will take the following form: *US*—the original German Text; *WL*—the English translation. I shall give page references to both even where I supply a translation of my own. Unless otherwise stated, the translation given will be Hertz's.)

4. *Der Satz vom Grund* (Tübingen, 1957).

One tactical exercise, the most obvious, offers explicit criticism of the metaphor as a designation for certain kinds of expressions inasmuch as this designation necessarily presupposes certain schemata of distinctions which are paradigmatically metaphysical. A second movement does not address the concept of the metaphor directly but has to do with the character of that type of discourse philosophy deems most appropriate for knowledge, namely, the assertive proposition. These first two tactical exercises therapeutically clear the area for a third, namely, reflection on the kinship of poetry and thought.

Such are the elements of a movement that I suggest will assist in reading Heidegger on the question of language and rational inquiry. Let me begin, now, to explicate them one by one.

Heidegger's most explicit remarks on the metaphor occur within two contexts, one in *The Principle of Reason*, and the other in *On the Way to Language*. In each case the justice of designating a particular expression under consideration "metaphorical" is shown to be dependent upon the acceptance of a certain schema of distinctions. Take *The Principle of Reason* first. Heidegger is here reflecting on the Leibnizian principle, "Nothing is without reason." He does so in two stages (Chapters 1-5 and 6ff., respectively), elaborating on layers of meaning he finds in the statement of the principle by shifting the accentuation of the words in it. This accentuation shift occurs in Chapter 6 in this form: Nothing *is* without *reason* (Nichts *ist* ohne *Grund*.) Heidegger points out, now, that we could say the shift in *heard* emphasis gives us a new way of *seeing*. And this way of speaking introduces the matter of the metaphorical.

We would very likely say more carefully that we gain a new way of *understanding* the statement through a shift in the way it is heard, or in the way it is read. Neither auditory nor visual experience *is* understanding itself, so that thought can be termed hearing or seeing only in a *transferred* sense, i.e., in a *metaphorical* sense. ($\mu\epsilon\tau\alpha$-$\psi\omega\rho\epsilon\tilde{\iota}\nu$ = *trans-ferre*). But now, this designating of the use of the term "seeing" or "hearing" for "understanding" as a *transferred* meaning obviously presupposes certain distinctions and divisions. Specifically one must first suppose the validity of a distinction between the sensible and the supersensible orders of cognitive activity: understanding is achieved in reason, sensing in the senses. One must further accept a division of the sensible into differentiations by organ: seeing is done by the eye, hearing by the ear. Only within a schema of this kind can the designation *metaphorical* have validity as characterizing the use of "seeing" for "understanding" or "thinking." It is at once obvious that the schema is a metaphysical one, and that consequently the validity of the designation metaphorical for this instance of a way of speaking has a metaphysical schema as its basis. Heidegger's own words make the point in the clearest terms, and because much will be drawn from them, I should like to quote them at some length.

> Because our hearing and seeing are never reception on the mere sense-level, it remains inappropriate to state that thinking can be taken as listening and as seeing only in a transference, viz., a transference of the sensible in question into the non-sensible as two self-subsisting domains. The establishment of this divorce of the sensible and nonsensible, of the physical and the non-physical, is a fundamental trait of what, named metaphysics, gives authoritative determination to Western thought. Once it is recognized that this distinction between the sensible and the non-sensible is insufficient, metaphysics loses the rank of the authoritative determinant for the course of thinking.
>
> Once, then, metaphysics is seen as restricted, the notion of metaphor as authoritative falls as well. In particular it provides the criterion for our notion of the essence of language. Metaphor is so often used in this way as a means for interpreting the works of poetry and the images of art in general. Only within metaphysics is there the metaphorical.[5]

On the Way to Language, now, offers further illustration of how terming a particular expression "metaphorical" presupposes the distinctions that constitute the metaphysical perspective. At the same time we shall come closer to seeing the point of the last paragraph just cited, to the effect that the concept of the metaphor sees the standard for our understanding of the nature of language.

In the essay "The Nature of Language" ("Das Wesen der Sprache"), Heidegger draws significance for a reflection on language from various lines of poetry that speak of language. At one point (*US,* pp. 205–07, *WL,* pp. 99–100) Heidegger quotes Hölderlin, who offers expressions in which words are said to be "the flowers of the mouth." Now, Heidegger's remark is that "we stay bogged down in metaphysics if we were to take the name Hölderlin gives here in the expression 'words, like flowers' as being a metaphor." (*WL,* p. 100) [6] This remark, however, comes at the end of a long passage detailing the schema within which words are given a philosophically proper characterization. Against this schema, the likening of words to flowers becomes a crossing over into an improper category to compose a characterization.

Heidegger has little trouble marshaling evidence for both identifying the schema in question and highlighting its status as fundamental.

> Language confronts us . . . as speaking activity, as activation of the speech organs: mouth, lips, tongue. Language shows in speaking as a phenomenon occurring in man. That language has long since been experienced, conceived,

---

5. *Der Satz vom Grund* (hereafter cited as *SG*), pp. 88–89.
6. *US,* p. 207.

and determined in this way is attested by the names Western languages have given themselves: γλῶσσα, lingua, langue, language. [*WL*, p. 96] [7]

Aristotle follows this same orientation in the opening passage of his treatise *On Interpretation*.

> Spoken words are the symbols of mental experience and written words are the symbols of spoken words. Just as all men have not the same writing, so all men have not the same speech sounds, but the mental experiences, which these directly symbolize, are the same for all, as also are those things of which our experience are the images. [16a] [8]

Here two orders of distinction are in play. One defines the sign character of language, viz., the distinction between sign and signified, while the other provides the ontological order in terms of which this distinction can be applied to some instance of signification. This latter order gives us once again the same basic distinction set that Heidegger speaks of in the passage on the metaphor from *The Principle of Reason*, viz., the distinction between sensible and nonsensible, physical and mental. At the same time it brings in the Platonic distinction between reality and image or representation. Putting all this together, then, the analysis of language comes to be patterned in one basic way, namely, with phonic reality on one side and mental intention on the other, while this intention relates to a thing referred to in some kind of signifying representational way, according to which truth is attained (*US*, p. 204, *WL*, p. 97).

There are a number of ways to take Heidegger's contention that the designation of certain expressions as metaphorical involves us in metaphysics. He might be saying, for example, that some set of distinctions is presupposed by any particular instance of the designation of an expression as metaphorical, and that some such schema may be metaphysical. But this would be a trivial observation, and he has more in mind than that. He is talking about *philosophy* of language and its project of *explaining the nature of language*. He is talking about the effort to come to a *rationally analyzed understanding* of the phenomenon of language. He seems to mean that such an effort at philosophical scientific comprehension *cannot help*

---

7. *US*, p. 203.
8. I quote here the Edgehill translation from *The Basic Works of Aristotle*, ed. Richard McKeon (New York, 1941). In "Das Wesen der Sprache," pp. 203–04 (*WL*, p. 97), as well as in "Der Weg zur Sprache," p. 244 (*WL*, p. 114), Heidegger offers a rendering in German that attempts to be sensitive to those nuances of the Greek wording lost in standard translation. His reading is considerably richer than the one given here, but this one better illustrates the conceptual schema drawn out of Aristotle's words as determinative for the philosophy of language. Heidegger's interpretation finds more than that schema in Aristotle's sentences, but precisely as the unthought element against that thought out and tradition-sanctioned schema.

but imply a general metaphysical schema in virtue of which certain kinds of expression *do not count as explanatory*, namely, such expressions as "words, flowers of the mouth." But once again, that a particular attempt at explanation inevitably implies some metaphysical schema is no new thesis for philosophical consideration, and any claim made for or by Heidegger that his thinking is radically different cannot justify itself if that is all it amounts to.

What, then, is Heidegger after? What Heidegger is getting at when he says such things as "Only within metaphysics is there the metaphorical" shows up better in what I have referred to as the second movement of his philosophic strategy, namely, in his remarks on the character of that type of discourse deemed most appropriate for philosophic knowledge. Here we find not comments on the metaphor itself, but comments on *assertion discourse* and *rational account*, i.e., *ratio*.

To extract sentences from a whole context is nowhere more falsifying a procedure than in the attempt to give an account of Heidegger's thought. This is particularly true when the point one wishes to bring forward from his writings entails rejecting some characterization of the manner of his thinking that is likely to be applied to it. In other words, it is difficult to say *positively* what Heidegger is doing by citing statements in which he says only what he is *not* doing. These negative statements only make their point in a whole passage by exemplification, not by statement.

For example, in "The Way to Language," in the very last paragraphs, after pages of worded reflections on language, after eminently "Heideggerian" "enigma-sentences," and in particular in the midst of some pointed "summary statements," Heidegger simply says: "*Die Sage* [a word which here "names" something essential of language, "Saying"] does not let itself be captured in any assertive statement"; and a few lines later: "This sounds like an assertive statement. If we take it as only that, then it does not say what is to be thought." [9] Now, to grasp the way Heidegger's words *are* to be taken would require careful notice of how language is being used here, in terms of the particular words themselves. But I am not at the point of doing that now. What I want to do here is simply to underline a certain characterization of a type of discourse which is traditionally taken as proper to rational explication, and which Heidegger asks us to recognize as such in order to preclude it as an appropriate understanding of what *his* wording aims to be.

Let me cite another passage of this kind from *On the Way to Language*. At one point, Heidegger is turning over in his reflections a line from Stefan George's poem, "The Word" ("*Das Wort*"):

9. *US*, p. 266, my translation (*WL*, p. 134).

So I renounced and sadly see:
where word breaks off no thing may be. [*WL*, p. 60] [10].

He remarks that a paraphrase as to the content of the line (he gives several possibilities) is not at all the way to gain understanding of the meaning. By rewriting it as an unpoetical statement, "we would have reduced poetry to the subsidiary status of being documentary confirmation for thought, as well as taken thought too lightly. Indeed we would already have forgotten the whole point, namely, to have an experience with language." [11] Later he adds: " . . . we must be careful not to force the vibration of the poetic saying into the rigid groove of an univocal statement, and so destroy it." (*WL*, p. 64) [12]

Heidegger is definite about one thing here. Wording taken as *assertive statement discourse* is *not* what he understands *his* language to be aiming for, nor is it what language as such in any primary sense should be taken to be when it is a matter of thinking in a truly fundamental way. This disavowal can be found in any of Heidegger's later writings, but what is not found is an explicit examination of the disavowed type of discourse precisely as constituting the base category for determining that other type of language known as the *metaphor*. Heidegger clearly understands it this way, but he has not done a thorough exposition of this point. It remains implied, not explicit. And it has an effect upon what he has to say about the relationship of poetry to thought, as we shall later show.

What is needed, then, is clarification of the assertive statement (*Aussage*) as defining a primary type of discourse on the basis of which other types are determined. There are two ways of doing this, one by drawing material from Heidegger's treatment of another related topic, namely, the epistemological and ontological meaning of reason (*ratio*), the other by taking up some recent reflections by various authors on the distinction between the metaphorical and the literal. I wish to try to represent concisely as much of both as can be illuminating to the main theme of this paper, how in Heidegger's thinking the designation "metaphorical" is to be interpreted as indicative of a deep problematic character for the enterprise of rational philosophy as such.

(a) In the course of the essay, "The Nature of Language," Heidegger makes one small aside that tells us where to go for complementary reflection on his part. Heidegger is carefully reading George's poem "The Word" to find help in it for understanding language. He has indicated that this help is not to come by way of transposing the meaning of the poem into paraphrastic statement. It is to offer assistance precisely to

10. *So lernt ich traurig den verzicht:*
     Kein ding sei wo das wort gebricht. [*US*, p. 162ff.]
11. *US*, p. 166, my translation (*WL*, p. 63).
12. *US*, p. 167.

thinking *while remaining poetry*, and not through transposition into assertive discourse. The situation is one of poetry and thought as subsisting in a kind of communal situation.

> Poetry and thought, each needs the other in its neighborhood, each in its fashion, when it comes to ultimates. In what region the neighborhood itself has its domain, each of them will define differently, but always so that they will find themselves within the same domain. But because we are caught in the prejudice nurtured through centuries that thinking is a matter of *ratio*, that is, of calculation in the widest sense, the mere talk of a neighborhood of thinking to poetry is suspect.
>
> Thinking is not a means to gain knowledge. Thinking cuts furrows in the soil of Being [*WL*, p. 70, translation slightly modified] [13]

Transposition from the poetic to the propositional statement is not what constitutes thinking for Heidegger with regard to the meaning of the poem. But this is precisely where Heidegger *departs* from the traditional understanding of philosophy as rational thought; for Heidegger sees the tradition as establishing propositional discourse, assertion or statement discourse (of the sort 'S is p'), *as the proper mode of articulation*. Correlative to *ratio*, reason, rational account, etc., is the *proposition*, for in the propositional statement is articulated the structure and identity of elements whose detailing and relating constitute *knowledge*. This whole situation, now, is the theme of study in Heidegger's *The Principle of Reason*, which should here have to read through if my exposition of the general topic of this paper were to be more fully elaborated. Let me however simply quote one passage from the last summary chapter of the book.

The Principle of Reason is a long reflection on the Leibnizian principle, *Nihil sine ratione*. Leibniz characterizes this statement as *principium reddendae rationis sufficientis*. Heidegger has several questions to ask about this formula in order to explicate its import. In sum these questions amount to asking (1) why must reasons be given, and (2) to or for whom (or what). To the first part of this question, Heidegger finds Leibniz's answer to be, simply, that reasons must be given because that is what constitutes truth.

> Truth is for Leibniz always . . . *propositio vera*, a true proposition, that is, a correct judgment. Judgment is *connexio praedicati cum subjecto*, the binding of the predicate with that of which it is predicated. What gives binding force as the unifying unity of subject and predicate is the ground [*Boden*], the reason [*Grund*], of the judgment. This is what justifies the connection. The reason [*Grund*] accounts for the truth of the judgment. Account in Latin is *ratio*. The basis [*Grund*] of the truth of judgment is given as *ratio*.[14]

13. *US*, p. 175.
14. *SG*, p. 193.

To the second part of the question to whom or to what must reasons be given, Heidegger finds the reply to be this:

> To man who determines objects by way of judgment-representation. Represent: *repraesentare*—to make something present to man. Since Descartes, followed by Leibniz and the whole of modern thought with him, man is experienced as the I (ego) that relates itself to the world in such a way that it poses the world before and against itself in correct syntheses of representation, that is, in judgments. Judgments and statements are correct, i.e., true when the basis or reason [*Grund*] for the connection of subject and predicate is given, rendered, for and by the representing I (ego). . . . Only when the reason or basis [*Grund*] of the judgment-synthesis is properly given by and for the I (ego), does what is represented come to stand securely as Gegenstand, that is, as object for the representing subject[15]

Now, it is obvious that the way Heidegger understands the proposition is bound up with the German philosophic tradition. But at the same time, this does not as such invalidate a more general claim that, in one way or another, the proposition is the mode of articulation that philosophy in principle sets itself up in, when it proposes to be rational analysis and reflection. Reason as definition, explanation, theoretic explication, theoretic conceptualization, and so forth, is in principle and by aim this kind of discourse. But how this kind of discourse determines the basis for the designation "metaphorical" is not yet clear. What is needed is some analysis of that against which the metaphorical is distinguished, and then reflection to see whether this other category of expression is to be identified with rational philosophic discourse.

(b) Whatever a particular author's conclusions regarding the nature of metaphor, I think it can be quite fairly stated that, at least as a matter of *fact*, the analysis leading to the conclusion works on the basis of a concept of the literal or proper meaning of an expression. To demonstrate this would mean examining a large number of treatments of the metaphor, but in summary let me do it this way. The conclusions reached by authors tend to follow one of four lines of argument:

(1) The literal meaning of metaphorical expressions is nonsense. Hence the metaphor has no cognitive but only emotive value.

(2) The metaphorical expression can be reinterpreted as having literal meaning in one way or another, e.g., most commonly as an implied comparison or analogy. It thus has cognitive value, but this is emotively enhanced, not constituted, by the device of transfer of predication. (This is generally taken as Aristotle's position.)

(3) The metaphorical does indeed have cognitive value, but not because it can be reduced to literal statement. On the contrary, its cognitive import and force lies in contravening the norms of literal statement. Meta-

15. *SG*, p. 194–95.

phor gains its meaningfulness as a unique form of language from the tension produced by our recognizing in it an incompatibility of literal meanings (thus Monroe Beardsley),[16] or because it recommends a new application of words against their normal (literal) use (Max Black).[17] In either case, the metaphor offers a new way of looking at things. It is creative and seminal.

(4) The metaphor is the basic form of language. All language is metaphorical. Literal meaning is really metaphorical meaning under another guise, or forgotten as metaphorical.

Now in all these cases, including the last one, the point of the argument is quite clearly parasitic upon the concept of the literal. Only because there is some notion of a literally meaningful expression, however it may be put, is there a conclusion regarding this other form of expression, the metaphor, even where (as in the last two types of argument) this conclusion allows for the metaphor a kind of meaningfulness beyond that of literal expression.

I wish to look a little more closely at some elements of consideration in the last two positions sketched in order to focus on this concept of the literal. In the first place, to think of any expression as having "literal" meaning is to think of it with some restriction on the range of its use. An expression, for example, the word "tree," is used literally in cases where we are dealing with a certain kind of relatively large woody-stemmed plant. It is not used for animals or men, and hence is restricted as to the groups of thing to be dealt with in using it. But a second restriction enters when it is not only *groups* of things to which certain expressions are related by common usage, but when *orders* of groups of things are distinguished. Thus, if one speaks of a "family tree," one can mean *literally* a tree planted in some property shared by a whole family in common possession. But one would be using the expression *nonliterally* to mean a system of *relations* involving lines of descent, by blood or marriage. "Relation," then, is excluded from the literal meaning of the expression "tree" because "relation" belongs to another *order* of phenomena, rather than being simply another *group* of entities of the same undifferentiated order.

Now, if one were content to discriminate between a literal, or proper, usage of an expression and a metaphorical, or transferred, usage only on the basis of a distinction of groups of entities, one would have a one-level language, one in which, say, "beastly ambition" or "oaken resolution" would not only be literal but would not even occur. These expressions require a system of differentiation of *orders* of phenomena such that meaningful transference can be identified as such and permitted, namely, the basic distinctions between "spiritual," or "abstract," and "material," or

16. *Aesthetics* (New York, 1958), pp. 134–44.
17. "Metaphor," in *Philosophy Looks at the Arts,* ed. Joseph Margolis (New York, 1962), pp. 218–35.

"concrete." In fact, one finds the ranges of possible metaphorical, i.e., transfer-, usage, to be generated precisely by the basic Aristotelian distinctions (e.g., the categories and the ultimate genera of substance, not to mention most importantly the division of his treatise according to orders of subject matter, such as logic, physics, study of the soul, study of being, etc.). But that expressions be designated metaphorical or literal in common understanding because of implied acceptance of this system of distinctions does not get to the most fundamental point, namely, that the literal/ metaphorical distinction is required by the *positing of rational knowledge* as the aim of thought.

A claim of immense implication is involved in this last point, and for its demonstration more than just a summary presentation would be needed. Yet this is the claim that Heidegger charges the history of Western philosophy with necessarily implying in its very origin, and he need only turn to Husserl to find it brilliantly exemplified and justified. Put simply, Heidegger's charge is this: that the moment of the birth of thought as pursuit of rational knowledge is the moment of the positing of the ideal of a type of meaning and expression that, among other ways of putting it, implies the distinction between a direct and proper sense and an oblique or transferred sense. Let me expand first on this notion of "rational knowledge."

Following Heidegger's reading of the history of philosophy, which concurs here with Husserl's, knowledge taken as rational grasp is *account*, i.e., *ratio*, that is, adequately and explicitly articulated differentiation by complete essential (i.e., universal and constant) notes. Now, the first thing to be made clear about this principle is that it proposes an *ideal to be striven after*, an ideal that makes rational knowing a *project* rather than a fully gained reality. It is an implied *motive*, not a description of the actual. This, at least, is how Husserl sees the matter, beginning with its birth among the Greeks down to our own day.[18] But now as to its explication for our study, the first thing to be said is simply that obviously *not just any kind* of articulation will do as rational grasp. It must be one that respects and reveals *essential differences*. It aims at specification and distinction, not mixture and fusion. Indeed, mixture and fusion could not even be recognized without specification and distinction. Consequently, rational account, necessarily opting for the *clear differentiation* of meaning, must necessarily as well see itself as aiming for an articulation in *proper* expression rather than in transferred, that is, literal language rather than metaphorical.

One last point remains to be made in this portion of the study, and it is simply this. Rational account is preeminently *self*-accounting. Rational ac-

18. See Edmund Husserl, *The Crisis of European Sciences and Transcendental Phenomenology*, trans. David Carr (Evanston, 1970), especially parts 1 and 2 and appendix 4.

count must specify *itself* as well as those objects other than itself which it turns toward to explain, i.e., give an account of. (Thus Plato's "ideas," Aristotle's studies in logic and first philosophy, and so on, down to Husserl's phenomenology.) And the first job of this self-specification is the *placing* of itself in the proper *order* of reality. If, then, rationality identifies essentially in any way with the "spiritual," be this termed only the "conceptual" as distinct from the "perceptual," or if you wish the "mental" as against the "bodily," the "abstract" as against the "concrete" or "sensible," and so on, then not only does the project of rational inquiry imply the distinction between literal and metaphorical meaning, but it brings with it in principle a basic metaphysics, namely, the basic schema of distinctions that Aristotle after Plato so brilliantly and problematically articulated for us.

At this point, now, we return to the comment of Heidegger's (see above, p. 187): "Only within metaphysics is there the metaphorical." To which need only be added that for Heidegger Western philosophy is a long sequence of variations and reformulations of one basic metaphysical schema. This, then, is what Heidegger is after in his dismissal of the accusation that his way of putting things is metaphorical. He does not accept that as a just charge because it cannot be made by critics, or acknowledged by himself, without admitting the basic schema of differentiation and assignation he sees constitutive of the Western philosophic tradition, particularly in its establishment of *ratio* as the consummative action of thought. Rational philosophic thought is a project that constitutes itself by defining a schema of basic distinctions in terms of which are determined both its own validity as truth-tending and the orders of phenomena of which it would ideally render a full finished account, including itself. Heidegger is trying to realize a thinking that does not follow this schema of things, a radically "other" thinking which would nonetheless be genuine thinking. Something of what this would be can be seen by trying to grasp now what is involved in the third tactical movement I spoke of earlier, namely, reflection on (and within) the kinship of poetry and thought.

I want to prelude consideration of some of the things Heidegger says about thinking and poetry with a few last points of reflection regarding the distinction of the literal and the metaphorical, particularly in relation to the last two types of theory sketched above on pages 192–93. If I am correct in what I have just elicited as filling out the background behind Heidegger's dismissal of the designation metaphorical for characterizing his philosophic language, then one would be led to conclude that a watershed in the character of language lies in the moment when rational inquiry as pretending to epistemic truth begins. At that point, and at that point only, language enters the field of distinction between literal and metaphorical, whereas before it is *neither*. At that point, and at that point only, poetry comes to be thought to have a special character that distinguishes it from prose, whether narrative or scientific, whereas before composed language does not have to fit into one or the other of such philosophic provinces. That is, when thinking begins becoming rational in the manner in which it is practised dominantly in the history of philosophy, including the present day, at that same time formal composition by a speaker begins becoming that other kind of self-conscious art known as poetry in this same intellectual tradition.[19]

This would imply, then, that meaningful expression is, in its deepest character, beyond the distinction between literal and metaphorical; and this foundational trait of language is touched and aimed at by the third and fourth theories mentioned above. According to the third, metaphorical language has its meaningfulness in the juncture of incompatible literal senses, leading us to see the things spoken of in new ways out of those incompatible senses. Indeed, new literal senses can be thus generated. But this is possible not because the sense is *literal*, but because sense is not primordially literal. At the same time, this is not an indication that all language is metaphorical, which can make sense only within opposition to a literalness, as in the fourth theory, but rather that all language as such is not originally disposed and operative in a schema of disjunctions appropriate for the project of rationally explicit articulation. Language at an origin level is fluid, creative, exploratory, multiple. The world of such language is not a world of spiritual and material, supernatural and natural, abstract and concrete, supersensible and sensible. Expressions used are not yet assigned to one or the other of such metaphysical dichotomies of order, and consequently they are *neither* literal *nor* metaphorical, nor are they a mixture of both.[20] Distinction between types of discourse does not

19. The sort of studies that help to explicate what would lie behind this thesis can be found, for example, in Eric Havelock, *Preface to Plato* (New York, 1967), and Bruno Snell, *The Discovery of the Mind*, trans. by T. G. Rosenmeyer (New York, 1960). Out of the studies like these it can be seen how the transition from oral to written composition, from tribal to intensely personal witness, forms a whole with the birth of philosophy and scientific rationality.

20. This is the basis for arguing against the thesis of Max Müller and others, that all abstract words like "concept" or "spirit" got their "spiritual" meaning by transfer from an original material meaning, e.g., "get hold of," "breath." The point is that their meaning would not have been originally simply material or simply "mental." Nor of course would it have been *both*. It was a third type of sense, neither only one, nor a mixture of two. See Snell, *The Discovery of the Mind*, chap. 1, for a study that shows this type of sense in Homeric Greek. Owen Barfield in "The Meaning of the Word 'Literal,'" in *Metaphor and Symbol*, ed. L. C. Knights and Basil Cottle (London, 1960), pp. 48–63, draws close to this, especially in the discussion (p. 61), but is still captured by a terminology that dichotomizes. The point I am insisting upon here is also the import of Beda Alleman's defense of the "absolute metaphor" in modern poetry in "Metaphor and Antimetaphor," in *Interpretation: The Poetry of Meaning*, ed. Stanley R. Hopper and David L. Miller (New York, 1967), pp. 103–23, esp. pp. 114–21.

lie in the predominance of expressions in the literal mode as against the metaphoric, as those who study prescientific writings or living oral traditions might show us. The myth, for example, would not be metaphoric explanation and therefore insufficient explanation and impure *ratio*. It is not explanation at all, its value and sense do not lie in an approximateness to literal and true account-rendering.

Heidegger, it seems to me, is trying to achieve thinking in a mode of language of this nonmetaphysical, submetaphysical kind, and to treat his wording as "metaphorical" implies that one simply misses that point. Understanding language is not analyzing language and offering explanations in either new or old conceptualities. To offer this is to fail to catch on to a language itself. Instead, thinking language is to be simply experiencing language in a wholly unique way. One is to proceed by simply "letting oneself go in the way-making movement [of language] instead of trying to represent language [conceptually]." [21] This is the overall point of the two principle essays of *On the Way to Language*, "The Nature of Language," and "The Way to Language." And this is the point of maintaining a closeness to poetry in that thinking. Let me expand on this a little.

If we look up passages in which Heidegger says something about thought and poetry, we would quickly find apparent inconsistency. In the long series of Heidegger's writings since 1930, we find now poetic wording (*dichten, Dichtung*) given a primacy, now thinking (*denken*), and sometimes the two are treated as equally fundamental. Sometimes again they are deeply different, sometimes they seem to be unified. No clear *position* seems to result. By this time we should be ready to recognize that Heidegger is not attempting to formulate a position, but rather to execute a movement. If we realize now that this "movement" he executes is not only always *in language*, but also in a highly original and strange kind of wording, then we are close to seeing that this very *immersion in a wording movement* constitutes thinking. Listen to a few sentences torn out of *On the Way to Language*, on thinking and poetry.

From "The Nature of Language":

But what am I saying? Is there thinking, too, going on in a poem? Quite so— in a poem of such rank thinking is going on, and indeed thinking without science, without philosophy. [*WL*, p. 61] [22]

Poetry moves in the element of saying, and so does thinking. When we reflect on poetry, we find ourselves at once in that same element in which thinking moves. . . . But—no matter how we call poetry and thought to mind, in every case one and the same element has drawn close to us—saying —whether we pay attention to it or not. (*WL*, p. 83) [23]

21. *US*, p. 262, my translation (*WL*, pp. 130–31).
22. *US*, p. 164.
23. *US*, pp. 188–89.

Poetry and thinking are modes of saying. The nearness that brings poetry and thinking together into neighborhood we call Saying (*die Sage*).
(*WL,* p. 93)[24]

And from "The Way to Language":

We might perhaps prepare a little for the change in our relation to language. Perhaps this experience might awaken: All reflective thinking is
poetic, and all poetry a thinking. The two belong together by virtue of that
Saying (*Sagen*) which has already bespoken itself to what is unspoken because it is thought as thanks. (*WL* p. 136, translation slightly modified.) [25]

Poetry and thought both seem here to be placed within "Saying," even
while some distinction remains for them. But the distinction that ordinarily is assigned here is one that, across the contrast of the literal and the
metaphorical, implies a metaphysical schema. In trying to neutralize that
schema, Heidegger is at the same time trying to find a way to follow
poetry and thought as simply worded articulation. To do so, and to insist
that this following of wording *is* understanding, would be to reach an
appreciation of language itself. But, then, what sense is there to talk of a
distinction here between thinking language and poetic language?

The answer is simple—None . . . *if* for individuals raised in a scientific
age and a philosophic tradition wherein the distinctions and divisions between the rational and the aesthetic, the literal and the poetic, the rational
and the emotive, is so deep and so strong, *if* for such human beings it
were possible to achieve that kind of "primitive" or "primordial" wording.
But no one of us is free from these constraints, not even Heidegger or
the poets he reads. Heidegger's thinking must therefore proceed *from
within* this situation of distinction and division *toward* the "other" worded
"Saying" he tries to find, promote, and follow, for example, in his reading of the sayings of early Greek philosophy. Heidegger has to proceed
from within thought and *from within* poetry in their established separate-
ness *toward* overcoming that dichotomy, *toward* a wording that is simply
wording and no longer exposition, critique, definition, explanation, and
the like, *toward* a wording which, in his words, would be, simply, language as "the Saying" (*die Sage, Sagen*).

Now I think the continual reference in Heidegger to thinking as distinct in some way from poetry, though close to it, and the continuing inconsistency in the way this relationship is formulated result from the fact
that Heidegger only gradually sees the implication of his questioning of
the literal/metaphorical distinction. By the time he writes "The Way to
Language," the import of questioning this metaphysically governed dis-

24. *US,* pp. 199–200.
25. *US,* p. 267.

tinction becomes clearer as a questioning of a thought/poetry distinction as well, even if something of that distinction remains.

At the same time, this ambivalence, viz., between a thought-poetry distinction and a thought-poetry unitary "Saying," accurately reflects the actual character of Heidegger's own thinking, namely, as proceeding from within Western metaphysics toward "something else." Heidegger's writings are precisely ambivalent. On the one hand, they offer incisive and illuminating critical statements regarding philosophic theses from other philosophers, ancient and modern. They give helpful comments on situations in the present-day world, e.g., his remarks on technology and superpower culture. At the same time, however, we find attempts at an articulation completely alien to this kind of critical or descriptive or explanatory statement: Heidegger's networks of word play, such as, for example, those involving *Denken, Ereignis,* or *Gestell.* Leading from one to the other are statements of negation: For example, warning that some formulation is *not* to be taken as a statement, insisting that metaphysical schemas must be neutralized and set out of play in one's thinking, denying the relevance of the designation "metaphorical," and so on. The situation seems to be, then, one in which rational explication turns upon itself within its own schema of determination and affirms a closure for its field of competence in negating its own performance, in order to allow another way of moving to work which in no way is to be recuperated in terms of that negated field and schema of performance. The difficulty is that affirmation of closure and annulment of rational procedure is not done once and for all, and thereafter the "other way" takes over completely. Heidegger does not realize his "other thinking" except by proceeding "outward from within rational exposition," to paraphrase Wittgenstein in the *Tractatus.*[26] Heidegger's thinking, in its attempt to proceed otherwise, nonetheless always begins from within Western rationality, from within the distinctions and performances he wishes to negate.

Thus it is that Heidegger's writing is thinking and not poetry, while aiming to be simply "Saying." Thus it is that his words are to be taken literally in his rejections of the metaphysical schema he literally affirms as dominating Western mind, while those words work toward a worded thinking that offers nothing of literal explication. Thus it is, finally, that Heidegger's wordings deny the appropriateness for themselves of the designation "metaphorical," while attempting to actualize a type of meaningful articulateness that philosophy maintains surreptitiously within itself, in the very category of the metaphorical. The weight of Heidegger's considerations only bears down upon the philosophic enterprise to call it

26. "4.114 [Philosophy] must set limits to what can be thought; and, in doing so, to what cannot be thought. It must set limits to what cannot be thought by working outwards through what can be thought." *Tractatus Logico-Philosophicus,* trans. D. F. Pears and B. F. McGuinness (London, 1961).

into question if the metaphor, in its definition and placement by philosophy as opposed to a proper mode of expression, the literal, in fact functions deep within philosophy at the level of foundations or origins. And, indeed, this is how modern reconsiderations of metaphor see it, as for example, in the case of the last two theories mentioned above (pp. 192–93). Neither merely emotive nor simply abbreviated statement of literal analogy or comparison, the metaphor is something deeply necessary to the generation of philosophic insights and terminology. In these reconsiderations the metaphor is cognitive in a creative, originative way, yet precisely as not reducible to the literal. Here is the very paradox that Heidegger's way of thinking forces us to recognize as indicative of limitation in the self-constitutive field of philosophic reason. Having to face this paradox, philosophic reason finds itself unable to account for itself precisely by virtue of the distinctions and characterizations that make it possible to begin and proceed. The metaphor is not proper philosophic expression, yet the metaphor, inexplicably, generates philosophic expression. This, at least, is the lesson suggested in Heidegger's remarks with regard to language, thinking, and the metaphor.

History of Philosophy

12. GEORGE VICK

Heidegger's Linguistic Rehabilitation of Parmenides' "Being"

IT IS A fairly well-known fact that Martin Heidegger has defended Parmenides' account of Being,[1] but the strategy of his complex semantic and etymological arguments for the meaningfulness of Parmenides' type of discourse on Being is unknown to the great majority of philosophers in Britain and America—indeed is virtually unnoted even within the phenomenological-existential school (in part, perhaps, because of the abstruse character of both his thought and language).[2] Furthermore, the fact that Heidegger has corrected what is ordinarily taken as an essential part of Parmenides' theory (i.e., his monism) has scarcely been recog-

Reprinted with revisions from the *American Philosophical Quarterly* 8 (April, 1971), with permission of the editor.

1. The Parmenidean fragments with which Heidegger is most concerned are those making up Parmenides' Way of Truth, especially fragments 2, 3, 6, and 8, as ordered in Hermann Diels–Walther Kranz, *Die Fragmente der Vorsokratiker*, 9th ed. (Berlin, 1960). Many English translations are available, though none truly adequate from a Heideggerian point of view. Among them are G. S. Kirk and J. E. Raven, *The Presocratic Philosophers* (Cambridge, 1963), and Leonardo Taran, *Parmenides* (Princeton, 1965).

2. These arguments are found primarily in the most systematic work of Heidegger's later period, his *Einführung in die Metaphysik* (Tübingen, 1953) in which his summer lectures at Freiburg in 1935 were revised and published. See especially chaps. 2 and 3. Page references to this work will be given first to the English translation by Ralph Manheim, *An Introduction to Metaphysics* (New Haven, 1974)—designated as *IM*, then to the German text—designated as *EM*. The other major discussions by Heidegger of Parmenides are in *Was Heisst Denken?* (Tübingen, 1954), translated by J. Glenn Gray as *What is Called Thinking?* (New York, 1968); see part 2, lectures 5 through 11, and "Moira (Parmenides VIII, 34–41," in *Vorträge und Aufsätze* (Pfullingen, 1954), translated by David Krell and Frank Capuzzi in *Early Greek Thinking* (New York, 1975).

nized, nor is note taken of the way in which Heidegger's correction makes what remains of Parmenides' theory more defensible. In the following pages I shall attempt to set forth and explain Heidegger's strategy (including a reason why it has been useful for him to couch his argument in language that is so abstruse). I will then go on to show the way in which his correction of Parmenides' theory strengthens its claim to being true.

Admittedly, Heidegger is himself a highly controversial figure. There is very likely no contemporary European philosopher who is more disliked in Britain and America. Yet he is unquestionably the predominating figure in philosophy in Europe, his thought being as influential on the Continent as that of Wittgenstein in Britain and America (and in Germany itself more dominant, perhaps, than that of Hegel in the 1830's). It is this man who now maintains quite simply that of all those thinkers who have arisen in the West from early Greece until today, there has been none greater than Parmenides. For the past 2500 years, Heidegger claims, Western thought has been in a progressive decline from the peak it once reached in Elea.[3]

The reason for Heidegger's claim is his belief that Parmenides uncovered what is meant by the most important, but hidden and misunderstood, words in human language, that is (in English) the word "is" and its substantive counterpart, "Being." Heidegger claims that the understanding of these words is almost entirely lost today—with the result that, for most people, what Nietzsche said of "Being" is, in fact, true.[4] For them, it is the "last cloudy streak of evaporating reality." [5] It is not astonishing, then, to Heidegger, that various empiricists and nominalists have been able to argue that "Being" is a meaningless term, or that readers have been found to agree that when something is said to be or exist, there is nothing expressed which the word "Being" could properly denote.

THE ATTACK ON "BEING"

The modern rejection of "Being" has taken at least three different forms. Foremost in Heidegger's mind has been the criticism posited by Hegel,

---

3. For Heidegger's assessment of the value of Parmenides' thought, see *IM*, pp. 95–97; *EM*, pp. 73–74; especially: "These few words [of Parmenides' Way of Truth] stand there like Greek statues of the early period. What we still possess of Parmenides' didactic poem fits into a thin brochure, but this little brochure is one which might perfectly well replace whole libraries of supposedly indispensable philosophical literature. Anyone living today who knows the measure of such thinking must lose all desire to write books. . . . Actually Heraclitus . . . says the same as Parmenides. He would not be one of the great Greeks if he had said something different."

4. *IM*, pp. 35–37, 50–51. *EM*, pp. 27–28, 38–39.

5. Friedrich Nietzche, *The Twilight of Idols.*

who did not actually claim that all talk of Being, or even that of Parmenides, is entirely devoid of meaning, but only that taken by itself Being is, of all categories, the broadest and, therefore, empty.[6] What Hegel meant was that when, in abstracting from the concrete characteristics ("determinations") which are possessed by an object, we arrive at progressively broader categories, and finally at the broadest, Being, we do so only at the price of leaving out an increasing amount of content (or "determinations") until we arrive, finally, at one (Being) from which every "determination" is absent.

Better known to most readers in Britain and America, however, is the attack which has traditionally been raised by nominalists and empiricists who, since Hume, have claimed that aside from certain relations among "ideas" (or certain conventions of language), we can be aware only of what has been originally furnished in experience and that the only content furnished by experience are particulars (whether these are taken to be particular "impressions" or "sense data" or "things"). Hence, they argued, if our words are to signify anything more than mere relations between ideas they must ultimately signify only particulars. In this view, then, the words "being" and "existence" could ultimately signify nothing except particulars (either singly or in their various groupings), for above and beyond them there would simply be no content which "being" or "existence" could signify. There would be no sense, then, in speaking of Being if one meant by this word anything more than particular sense objects.[7]

But the most ardent opponents of Heidegger's own efforts to restore the meaningfulness of "Being" were the Logical Positivists. And while the foundations of their general theory of meaning were most often empiricist in nature, their special attack on the word "Being" was formulated in terms of, and presumably rested upon, considerations of a peculiarly logical sort.

Their attack was set forth in a relatively explicit form in Carnap's "The Overcoming of Metaphysics Through Logical Analysis of Language" and Ayer's "Demonstration of the Impossibility of Metaphysics" (although the foundations of their position are to be found in Russell's criticism of existence as a predicate of individuals, in his Theory of Descriptions).[8] In brief, their argument was that the use of the word "Being" as a substantive rests on a mistaken belief that there is some property of things which

6. G. W. F. Hegel, Science of Logic, vol. 1 (New York, 1929), chap 1.
7. See David Hume, Treatise of Human Nature, bk. 1, pt. 2, sect. 6.
8. Rudolf Carnap, "The Overcoming of Metaphysics" Erkenntnis 2 (1932), reprinted in this volume, pp. 23–34; A. J. Ayer, "The Impossibility of Metaphysics," Mind 43 (1934), pp. 335–45; Bertrand Russell, "The Philosophy of Logical Atomism," The Monist 27–28 (1918–19), pp. 495–526, especially lectures 5 and 6; also Introduction to Mathematical Philosophy (London, 1919), chap. 16.

could be called their "Being," much as one might speak of their color or shape. This belief arises, they held, because we have mistakenly assumed that existential statements assert something of subjects (i.e., that they exist), instead of recognizing that they assert something only of "predicates" or "incomplete symbols" (i.e., that they apply to something). To "assert existence," then, would properly mean only that a certain predicate applies to something, not that a particular subject enjoys or possesses some property called "existence" or "Being."

Up to this point the Positivist attack followed faithfully the line taken by Russell in his theory of Descriptions, but beyond this point it becomes somewhat clouded, in that it did not make clear precisely why existential statements could not affirm existence, or being, of a subject. That is, it did not make clear whether the reason was to be found in the nominalist and empiricist presuppositions which usually underlay the Positivists' general theory of meaning, or in considerations of a more peculiarly logical, and a prioristic character, such as had been offered by Russell. A clue is to be found, however, in the fact that Carnap spoke of the idea that existence cannot be anything asserted about a subject, as a "logical rule," and presumably for this logical rule he would give, not empirical, but logical, reasons.[9] If so, then they were very likely the logical reasons which had led Russell to formulate the rule in the first place, and which were, namely, that if there were in the world of actual things anything which could be called existence, then "existence" would be a predicate which could not conceivably be false, in that it would be impossible for it not to apply to every individual of which we might speak. Such a predicate, Russell held, would be in the strict sense meaningless, and use of it "characteristic of a mistake."[10] Hence, the Positivist's argument may have rested ultimately on Russell's presuppositions (1) that no object can be spoken of unless it exists, and (2) that the possibility of applying a predicate falsely is a necessary condition for its being meaningful.

THE MEANINGFULNESS OF "BEING"

Against the first and second of these attacks, which is to say, the Hegelian and empiricist arguments, Heidegger has developed extensive counter-arguments (which we shall analyze at some length). But to the Russellan-

_____

9. Carnap, p. 28. An empiricist basis for Carnap's attack on the meaningfulness of "Being" could be found in the reductionism that he espoused at this point, in which the meaning of every word is to be derived through reducing it to words appearing in "observation sentences." The same type of reductionism is spelled out by Ayer in terms of "ostensive definition" of propositions. See Carnap, sect. 2; Ayer, section entitled "Formulation of a Criterion of Significance."

10. Russell, "Philosophy of Logical Atomism," questions and answers at the end of lecture 5.

Positivist argument against existence as a predicate, he has not replied explicitly. Yet his thought does furnish us with at least the basis for two counterarguments. By raising the question (in the beginning of his *Introduction to Metaphysics*), why is there something rather than nothing, Heidegger brings to mind the possibility that existent things might not have been; and, of course, in light of the possibility that a designated thing might not have been, the fact that it is (as G. E. Moore has insisted) is significant, and a sentence expressing this fact, meaningful.[11] (A reply of this sort would challenge the second of Russell's presuppositions, by claiming, in effect, that even if a predicate were not, in fact, able to be applied falsely to a subject, the fact that it could be disjoined from the subject in our thinking of a situation contrary to fact is sufficient to render the predicate meaningful.)

But in addition, Heidegger had already implicitly denied the premise on which is based Russell's other presupposition, that if existence were a predicate, it could not apply falsely to any object of which we might speak, which is to say the presupposition that unless an object exists, it cannot be spoken of. For Heidegger had insisted that we can speak of non-being, of absence or void, and that such non-being is, indeed, very important in our experience.[12] (In doing this, Heidegger has offered what is in effect a rather dramatic, and highly controversial, variant of the Meinongian thesis that the extension of what exists is less than that of what we can intend; or if you will, that of all objects, existent objects are only a portion.) [13] And, in turn, to defend the meaningfulness of discourse about what is called "nothing" (against the attack of Carnap and others), Heidegger has proposed the thesis that if in particular systems of logic such discourse is not meaningful, it may be because the presuppositions of these systems embody a metaphysical position in which a stance has already been taken on the relation between being and nothing, whereas, Heidegger maintains, such a stance is precisely the sort of thing which his own inquiry into the meaning of "Being" would bring into question.[14]

But it is not for his still rather implicit response to the Russellian type of argument that Heidegger's defense of the meaningfulness of "Being" is most interesting. Others have developed, or are developing, appropriate counterarguments here in a more systematic and satisfactory fashion. The particular genius of Heidegger's defense of "Being" is to be found, rather, in his strategy against the Hegelian and empiricist attacks.

11. *IM*, p. 1; *EM*, p. 1. G. E. Moore, "Is Existence a Predicate–" *Proceedings of the Aristotelian Society*, supplementary vol. 15 (1936), pp. 175–88.

12. *IM*, pp. 22–29; *EM*, pp. 17–22. Also *Sein und Zeit*, 7th ed. (Tübingen), pp. 186–89; translated as *Being and Time* (New York, 1962), pp. 230–34.

13. Alexis von Meinong, "Theory of Objects," in Roderick Chisholm, ed., Realism and the *Background of Phenomenology* (Glencoe, 1960), pp. 76–117, especially pp. 78–86.

14. *IM*, pp. 25–26; *EM*, pp. 19–20.

Against the Hegelian attack, Heidegger has employed arguments that are largely semantic and etymological. But against the empiricist attack his strategy seems not to have proceeded altogether through what we would ordinarily call "direct argumentation." Instead, it would appear to consist at least in part of something far more subtle and indirect, that is, in the deliberate use of a calculated abstruse form of discourse, for whose understanding the reader would be required to find, in his own experience that which Heidegger refers to by the word "Being" (or *Sein*). (There are obvious similarities to Joyce's technique in *Ulysses* and *Finnegan's Wake*, in that both Heidegger and Joyce employ a deliberately difficult form of discourse in order to require the reader to break through his habitual understanding of language, and to turn anew to experience in order to find there the elusive meaning. But whereas Joyce would require the reader to turn from his habitual understanding of written signs to the hearing of spoken signs, Heidegger would require him to go beyond, to find the signified experience which alone could give to Heidegger's marks or sounds the role of signs.)

Through the use of this strategy, Heidegger would lead the reader to become aware in his own experience of what is meant by "Being" (or, more exactly by the various Greek expressions of "Being" which he explores at length), hence to find Being in an experience whose possibility the empiricist could not reject a priori without showing himself to be, in the final instance, arbitrary.[15] This is to say that Heidegger would lead the reader to recognize an experience of Being whose possibility the empiricist could not exclude without showing an essentially arbitrary notion of the limits of experience, a notion which the empiricist could not, then, defend on experimental grounds, but could at best advocate as a convention or set of rules within which he prefers to operate (and it would be, of course, a convention which could only appear unrealistic to someone possessing the kind of experience which it, the convention, would ex-

---

15. In this paper, I shall follow ordinary usage of the word "mean" in that at times we shall say that a word means what it is used to refer to (although perhaps at other times it may be said to mean without being used to refer to anything). I use the word "experience" to indicate "givenness," in this case, the givenness of Being. For what I believe are the same or related uses of "experience" and "given" in Heidegger's work, see *IM*, pp. 61, 92; *EM*, pp. 46, 70; also *What Is Called Thinking?*, pp. 110, 237; and Heidegger's *Time and Being*, trans. Joan Stambaugh (New York, 1972), pp. 1–24, in particular, pp. 5, 6, 8, 13, and 17. Despite the difficulties involved in what analysts call the "theory-ladenness" of experience or the given (or datum), words of this sort seem indispensable, and Heidegger's account of thinking, giving, presencing, and opening, most illuminative of them. See *IM* or *EM*, chap. 4, sect. 3; *What Is Called Thinking?*, part 2, lectures 5–11; and in *Time and Being* the lectures "Time and Being" and "The End of Philosophy and the Task of Thinking." (I disagree, of course, with Stambaugh's opinion on the appearing of Being and on onto-theology in her introduction to *Time and Being*, p. x.)

clude). And, of course, the experience which Heidegger had presupposed that his reader must become aware of in order to understand what he, Heidegger, was to say is the experience of Being which he believes belonged to the early Greeks, and, above all, to Parmenides. It is this experience which Heidegger believes to have emerged into language in Parmenides' "Way of Truth."

But although there were to be two different strategies involved, the scene of their deployment was to be largely the same. For it was through the same exegesis of the meaning of certain Greek words (especially *physis* and *ousia*) that Heidegger would both formulate his semantic and etymological attack on the Hegelian thesis, and, at the same time, attempt to lead the reader to an experience of Being of a pre-Socratic, Parmenidean sort. For only if the reader were actually to find in his experience something answering to the words which Heidegger was to use in his exegesis of early Greek expressions for Being, would the reader be likely to comprehend the force of Heidegger's argument against Hegel.

Heidegger's semantic argument is of an extreme sinuosity. Perhaps, he argues, the emptiness which very well may be present in the modern understanding of *das Sein* (Being) derives in part from the fact that the word is a verbal substantive, formed by placing a particle before the infinitive form, an act which would seem to stabilize the emptiness of detail, or indefiniteness, from which any use of the infinitive must suffer. This indefiniteness would itself consist in the fact that in employing any infinitive form (e.g., "to run") we necessarily lose the definiteness of tense, person, and mood to be found in other forms (e.g., "he runs" or "they ran" or "you would have been running"). In place of this definiteness we have a form which is by contrast only a kind of schema. It is capable of being used in abstract discourse to represent what can be expressed through all the other more definite forms, but only through not possessing any of the specific determination through which the other forms express their more definite meanings.[16]

Heidegger then proceeds to show that although Being is almost always expressed through a linguistic form which by its very nature must be relatively vague and empty, the content of experience which is expressed through this form is highly determinate hence in no way vague or empty. The first argument he offers is unusually indirect: the grammatical term for the kind of form the infinitive is, is "mood" or in Latin, *modus*. (Thus, we speak of the "infinitive mood" or *modus infinitivus*). But Heidegger observes the Greek for *modus* was *enklesis* and *enklesis* originally meant a kind of tipping over, or inclination to the side. Likewise, the same root meaning was, according to Heidegger, possessed by the Greek word

16. *IM*, pp. 55-56, 65, 67-69; *EM*, pp. 42-43, 49-50, 51-53.

ptosis, which came to designate the case of a noun, but which was first used by grammarians to designate any kind of inflection of a basic form (any deviation or declension), not only in substantives but also in verbs.[17]

The implication is, then, that expressing the meaning of any verb through a particular mood, or any other particular form must have been recognized by the Greek grammarians who chose to employ the words *enklesis* and *ptosis*, as a kind of falling away from the fullness of the verb's root meaning. For example, to say "I am" or "they would walk" must have been recognized as falling away in some manner from the fullness of what is there to be said.[18] In the Greek experience of what is expressed through forms of the verb "to be," there must, then, have been a fullness of meaning that is falling away from in its particular verbal expressions. This view is, of course, almost the opposite of Hegel's position that the immediate with which experience starts is a bare or empty datum which acquires meaning only through being interrelated into the elaborated whole of experience.[19]

Underlying these diverse positions are sharply opposed notions of the nature of what we might call "immediate experience" (that is, experience prior to our conscious activity of interrelation). For Hegel, the immediate experience is a bare minimal content which can have meaning only to the extent that it is interrelated with other factors. The immediate datum of experience is called by Hegel a kind of "abstraction," for only in and through the mind's active interrelating of the datum with other factors would the complex fullness or density which Hegel refers to as "concrete" be found.[20] Heidegger's reconstruction of the early Greek view is very different. Underlying the use of any particular *ptosis* or *enklesis* (e.g., "I am," or "you were"), hence, prior to any subsequent interrelating of what is expressed through particular *ptoses* or *enkleses*, there must be an underlying awareness of a fullness from which particular uses of the verb decline or fall away. What is originally understood is not a part which is then synthesized into a whole, but a unity which is somehow "fallen away" from in our use of particular forms.

To show that there is a unity underlying particular forms of the verb "to be," Heidegger argues first in an etyomological way, by pointing out that the verb "to be" in most European languages is made up of parts derived from three different linguistic roots:

1. The oldest, the actual radical word is *es*, Sanskrit *asus*, life, the living, that which from out of itself stands and which moves and rests in itself: the self-standing (*Eigenständig*). To this radical belong in Sanskrit the verbal formations *esmi, esi, esti, asmi*, to which correspond the Greek *eimi* and

17. *IM*, pp. 58–59; *EM*, p. 45.
18. *IM*, pp. 64–65, 67–68; *EM*, pp. 49–50, 51–52.
19. Hegel, "With What Must Science Begin," pp. 79–92.
20. Ibid.

einai, the Latin *esum* and *esse*. Sunt, sind, and sein belong together. It is noteworthy that the *"ist"* has maintained itself in all Germanic languages from the very start (*estin, est* . . .).

2. The other Indo-European radical is *bhu, bheu*. To it belong the Greek *phuo*, to emerge, to be powerful, of itself to come to stand and remain standing. Up until now this *bhu* has been interpreted according to the usual superficial view of *physis* and *phyein* as nature and "to grow." A more fundamental exegesis, stemming from preoccupation with the beginning of Greek philosophy, shows the "growing" to be an "emerging," which in turn is defined by presence and appearance. Recently the root *phy-* has been connected with *pha- phainesthai*. *Physis* would then be that which emerges into the light, *phyein* would mean to shine, to give light and therefore to appear. (See *Zeitschrift fur vergleichende Sprachforschung*, vol. 59.)

From this stem come the Latin perfect, *fui, fuo*; similarly our German *"bin," "bist,"* wir *"birn,"* ihr *"birt"* (which died out in the fourteenth century). The imperative "bis" (*"bis mein Weib"* [be my wife]") survived longer.

3. The third stem occurs only in the inflection of the Germanic verb *"sein"*: *was*; Sanskrit: *vasami*; Germanic: *wesan*, to dwell, to sojourn; to *ves* belong: *festia, fasti*, Vesta, *vestibulum*. The German forms resulting from this stem are *"gewesen," "was, war, es west, wesen*. The participle *"wesend"* is still preserved in *an-wesend* (present) and *ab-wesend* (absent). The substantive *"Wesen"* did not originally mean "whatness," quiddity, but enduring as presence, presence and absence. The *sens* in the Latin *prae-sens* and *ab-sens* has been lost. Does *Dii consentes* mean those gods who are present together? [21]

Here, Heidegger says, a crucial question arises: How and wherein do the three stems come together? For them to have merged into the one verb "to be" (*Sein*), Heidegger argues, there must have been an implicit, or underlying, understanding of Being sufficiently determinate to bring together these originally diverse stems.[22]

Furthermore, some understanding of the original fullness at the root of our usages of the verb "to be" must be retained by us—despite the modern charge that "Being" is an empty word. For when we recognize that some things are, or are not, we must, Heidegger insists, sufficiently understand Being to differentiate between it and non-being. We must know what "Being" means.

But how are we to determine whether a thing, presumed to be at some place and time, is or is not, if we cannot clearly differentiate in advance between

21. *IM*, pp. 71–72; *EM*, pp. 54–55. A related and etymologically more amplified discussion of these roots is found in Johannes Lohmann, "M. Heidegger's Ontological Difference and Language," in *On Heidegger and Language*, ed. and trans. J. Kockelmans (Evanston, 1972) especially pp. 325–27, where to the roots mentioned above are added *stá-* (to stand) and *gene-* (to be brought about, bring about).

22. *IM*, pp. 72–73; *EM*, pp. 55–56. Cf. Lohmann, pp. 303–63.

Being and non-being? How are we to make this crucial distinction unless we definitely know the meaning of what we are differentiating: namely non-being and Being. How can each and every existent be existent for us unless we understand "Being" and "non-being" beforehand? [23]

And again, in using a particular form of the verb "to be," we must know the complex fullness lying at its root sufficiently well to know in what way we are to decline from it, that is, in order to know which particular form to use (e.g., "you are" as opposed to "you would have been"), or how, through using the same form, to express different but related meanings.

We say: "God is." "The earth is." "The lecture is in the auditorium." "This man is from Swabia." "The cup is of silver." "The peasant is to the fields." "The book is mine." "Red is the port side." "There is famine in Russia." "The enemy is in retreat." "The plant louse is in the vineyard." "The dog is in the garden." "Uber allen Gipfeln/ist Ruh."

In each case the "is" is meant differently.

"God is"; i.e., he is *really present*. "The earth is"; i.e., we experience and believe it to be *permanently* there; "the lecture is in the auditorium"; i.e., it *takes place*. "The man is from Swabia"; i.e., *he comes from there*. "The cup is of silver"; i.e., *is made of* . . . "The peasant is to the fields"; he has gone to the fields and *is staying there*. "The book is mine"; it *belongs to me*. "Red is the port side"; i.e., it stands for port. "The dog is in the garden; i.e., he is running around in the garden. "Over all the summits/is rest"; that is to say? ? ?

In each one of these meanings we say the "is" without, either before or afterward, effecting a special exegesis of "is," let alone reflecting on being. The "is," meant now so and now so, simply wells up as we speak. Yet the diversity of its meanings is not arbitrary diversity.[24]

—For, as Heidegger suggests, and attempts later to show (in his protracted derivation of becoming, appearing, thinking, and the "ought" from the root meaning of "Being), the "is" conceals "within itself the multiplicity whose concentration enables us to make manifold existents accessible to us, each *as* it is."

Heidegger's thought at this point is essentially Platonic. Far from accepting the conceptualist claim that our awareness of the universal is the result of an activity of synthesizing elements that are first apprehended as particular, Heidegger insists that an understanding of the universal is presupposed in order for us to recognize elements apprehended in particulars

---

23. *IM*, p. 77; *EM*, p. 59. Here and elsewhere Heidegger's word *seiendes* is translated as either "thing" or "existent" instead of Manheim's "essent."
24. *IM*, pp. 89–91; *EM*, pp. 68–69.

as pertaining to the universal, that is, for us to pass in the first place from the particular to the universal.

> By way of an example, we substitute for the universal concept "Being" the universal concept "tree." If we wish now to say and define what the essence of tree is, we turn away from the universal concept to the particular species of tree and the particular specimens of these species. This method is so self-evident that we almost hesitate to mention it. Yet the matter is not as simple as all that. How are we going to find our famous particulars, the individual trees *as such*, as trees; how shall we be able even to *look for* trees, unless the representation of what a tree in general is shines before us? [25]

Hence, Heidegger reasons that it is only on the basis of our recognition of a root meaning of Being that we are able then to recognize particular things as being in ways corresponding to the various *enkleses* and *ptoses* of the verb "to be" ("they are," or "it was to have been," etc.). This recognition will occur, he suggests, only if the "is," or Being, conceals within itself the multiplicity whose concentration enables us to recognize things which are as being in precisely those ways in which they are.[26] Some grasp of the original fullness at the root of our usages of the verb "to be" must, therefore, be retained by us. Yet this retention will most often be highly implicit. For according to Heidegger, even in pre-Socratic Greece, it was only in certain pieces of discourse that the awareness lying at the root of our use of "to be" was anywhere near well expressed. (This occurred, of course, preeminently in Parmenides' poem.) [27]

But it is important to remember that the relation between the refracted, diminished meaning conveyed through the various *enkleses* of any verb, and the fullness which lies at the root of our usage of the verb, was itself identified by the Greek grammarians, not as that of a part to the whole, but as a kind of falling away or tipping over to the side. For this fact has allowed Heidegger to ask the question, from *what* was the *enklesis* recognized as falling away or tipping over? [28] The most obvious answer is, from the understanding which lies at the root of our uses of the verb, hence from whatever is implicitly apprehended which we begin to express in using a particular form of a verb, such as, say, "I run." (In Platonic terms, the implicit understanding would in this case be of the form "running," and would in some way include all of its possible partial instantiations.) But the more important reply, for Heidegger, is that what every *enklesis* of any verb must be at least implicitly recognized as falling away from is preeminently uprightness or erectness itself. This is very important be-

25. *IM*, p. 80; *EM*, pp. 60–61.
26. *IM*, pp. 91–92; *EM*, pp. 69–70.
27. *IM*, pp. 95–98; *EM*, pp. 73–74.
28. *IM*, pp. 59–60, 64; *EM*, pp. 45–46, 49.

cause according to Heidegger, the early Greek understanding of Being was itself expressed in terms (especially "*physis*" and "*ousia*") that are in direct relation to uprightness or erectness.[29] Because this fact and these terms are so important, it will be well for us to attend carefully to Heidegger's unusual exegesis of them.

Physis, Heidegger claims, originally meant standing-forth, or coming-to-stand in the sense of arising-from-itself (*zum Stande Kommen, in-sich-aus-sich-hinausstehen*).[30]

What does the word *physis* denote? It denotes self-blossoming emergence (e.g., the blossoming of a rose), opening up, unfolding, that which manifests itself in such unfolding and perseveres and endures in it; in short, the realm of things that emerge and linger on. According to the dictionary *phyein* means to grow or make to grow. But what does growing mean? Does it imply only to increase quantitatively, to become more and larger?

Physis as emergence can be observed everywhere, e.g., in celestial phenomena (the rising of the sun), in the rolling of the sea, in the growth of plants, in the coming forth of man and animal from the womb. But *physis*, the realm of that which arises, is not synonymous with these phenomena, which today we regard as part of "nature." This opening up and inward-jutting-beyond-itself [*in-sich-aus-ich-hinausstehen*] must not be taken as a process among other processes that we observe in the realm of the existent. *Physis* is being itself, by virtue of which existents become and remain observable.

Physis means the power that emerges and the enduring realm under its sway. This power of emerging and enduring includes "becoming" as well as "being" in the restricted sense of inert duration. *Physis* is the process of a-rising, of emerging from the hidden, whereby the hidden is first made to stand.[31]

On the other hand, *ousia* meant remaining-in-standing, or not falling away (*im Stand bleiben*).[32]

But all the definitions of being that we shall now list are grounded in, and are held together by, that wherein the Greeks unquestionably experienced the meaning of being, and which they called *ousia*, or more fully *parousia*. The usual, unthinking translation of this word as "substance" misses its meaning completely. For *parousia* we have in German a corresponding term —*An-wesen* (presence), which also designates an estate or homestead, standing in itself or self-enclosed. In Aristotle's time *ousia* was used both in this sense and in the sense of the fundamental term of philosophy. Something is present to us. It stands steadily by itself and thus manifests itself. It is. For the Greeks "Being" basically meant this standing presence.[33]

29. Ibid.
30. *IM*, pp. 59–60, 14; *EM*, pp. 46, 11.
31. *IM*, pp. 14–15; *EM*, pp. 11–12.
32. *IM*, pp. 60, 64; *EM*, pp. 46, 48.
33. *IM*, p. 61; *EM*, p. 46. See also *IM*, p. 194, or *EM*, p. 148, for the degeneration of the original meaning of *ousia*.

(It is especially at this point that Heidegger requires of the reader that he become aware in his own experience of the standing-forth of what is, and of the active exclusion from within standing-forth of any falling-away. Only if the reader is able to do this will he apprehend the force of Heidegger's argument.) Together, *physis* and *ousia* expressed an awareness of standing-forth as intrinsically not a falling away.

> "Being" meant for the Greeks: permanence in a twofold sense:
>   1. standing-in-itself [*In-sich-stehen*] in the sense of arising [*Ent-stehen, standing-out-of*] (*physis*),
>   2. but, as such, "permanent" (standing), i.e., enduring (*ousia*).[34]

Hence, the meaning at the root of the particular *enkleses*, or fallings-away, which constitute modes of the verb "to be," is itself a standing-forth into uprightness which is, in itself, an opposition to falling-away.

Because, then, what is expressed through any *enklesis*, or by any particular form, of a verb was recognized as a falling-away or tipping-over from uprightness, it must in some, albeit very implicit, way have been recognized as declining from the root understanding of Being.[35] That is to say that underlying the falling-away from the root meaning of any verb that occurs in using any particular form of the verb is a falling-away from the root meaning of "to be."

The tension between the understanding which lies at the root of our use of any verb and the impoverished or "falling-away" forms in which this meaning is expressed, is obviously especially acute in the case of our uses of the verb "to be" itself. (And when the particular form of "to be" is the emptiest or least determinate *enklesis* of all, the infinitive that is stabilized into the substantive *Sein*, the falling-away of what is expressed from what lies at the root of our use of the expression is extreme.) Hence, the implication of Heidegger's thought is that language, which proceeds always through one or another particular form (and discursive thought, which is in some way parallel to language), must necessarily involve a departure from an original, albeit highly implicit, apprehension of Being.

It is evident that Heidegger does not presuppose our ability to *find* what is spoken of as "standing-forth" and "not falling-away" (or "permanent enduring").[36] In effect, he presupposes that it is available to our awareness as a kind of "content" or even "referent"—that the word "*physis*" can function to make us aware of what could be called the "essence" of standing-forth, which is to say, of something recognizable as sufficiently

---

34. *IM*, pp. 63–64; *EM*, p. 48.
35. *IM*, pp. 59–60, 65; *EM*, pp. 46, 49–50.
36. It is to be noted that Heidegger speaks of the Greek *experience* of Being, e.g., *IM*, pp. 61, 92, 204; *EM*, pp. 46, 70, 155. See also "original experience of truth" in *IM*, p. 192; *EM*, p. 147; and "the Greek experience of . . . duration" in *What Is Called Thinking?*, p. 237.

identical to serve as an unequivocal basis for our several uses of the words "to stand-forth" or "to be," and to which, then we can in some sense "refer" (as, indeed, we can refer to anything that is sufficiently identical to be identified in this or in any other fashion.) More precisely, he presupposes that we are always at least implicitly aware of this "factor" whenever we use forms of the verb "to be." [37] But now, in his exegesis of *physis* and *ousia*, he would have us turn our attention toward it directly, in order to enter into a more explicit consciousness of it.

To accomplish this, he would have us undo or break back through the accumulated habits of thought and language which, he maintains, have covered over, or concealed, the fact of the emerging or standing-forth of what is. (Later on in his *Introduction to Metaphysics*, he describes the process by which, he believes, the pre-Socratic awareness of *physis* or Being has degenerated into our present situation: with Plato, it became necessary to ignore the standing-forth of what is, to focus, instead, upon the "what," or *eidos*, which stands forth; with Aristotle it became necessary to be concerned, not so much even with the patterns which stand forth, as with the correspondence of our own acts of judgment to these patterns, or to external things, viewed now primarily as criteria of the correctness of our thought; and with Kant, almost the last vestige of our consciousness of *physis* disappeared, as things themselves came to be thought of, not as standing-forth, but as posited or synthesized by our own thinking. Yet interesting and suggestive though it may be, it is not so much Heidegger's account of this process of degeneration which is important to us here, as it is the recovery of the awareness of *physis* which he attempts.)

As I have indicated, his technique for turning us toward a more explicit consciousness of *physis* would appear to consist at least in part in a deliberately original and difficult use of language, a use so strange as to require us to find new paths back from signifying words to signified experience. (I shall not attempt to illustrate the strangeness of his language through quoting particular passages, for his effect is achieved cumulatively.) To understand the tortuous passages in which he goes on to develop the meaning of "*physis*" in conjunction with that of *ousia, phainesthai*, and *logos*, we are required to run the gamut of our experience in order to seek out here and there what he could possibly mean, until at last we find the referent to which these unorthodox phrases, these strange descriptions, can apply.[38]

---

37. *IM*, pp. 76–79, 91–92; *EM*, pp. 58–60, 69–70.
38. Note especially the demands made upon both language and the reader by Heidegger's development of the meaning of *physis* in contrast to that of *phainesthai* (and the German *scheinen*), *IM*, pp. 98–115; *EM*, pp. 75–88.

THE MEANING OF "BEING"

But we should not imagine that in directing our attention to *physis*, or standing-forth, we should be knowing something different from what we know when we direct our attention to *ousia*, or permanent endurance (remaining-in-standing.) For we shall not fully arrive at what Heidegger regards as the pre-Socratic understanding of "Being" unless we come to recognize the unity of that in reference to which we would understand the words "standing-forth" (*physis*) and "permanent enduring" (*ousia*). Only then would we apprehend the intrinsically permanent character of standing-forth, or, if you will, recognize that standing-forth is itself intrinsically permanent in the sense that it intrinsically excludes not standing-forth or falling-away. This is to say, that only if we recognize that it is by virtue of *what* it is that standing-forth or *physis* excludes from itself any not-having-been or not-going-to-be, we will arrive at the Parmenidean understanding of Being to which Heidegger would lead us. Only then could we see (as Parmenides put it)

> . . . how Being, without having begun, is without destruction, complete (*voll-standig*, full-standing), alone, without tremor and not needing to be finished; neither was it before, nor will it be in the future, for being present, it is entire, unique, unifying, united, gathering itself in itself from itself (cohesive, full of presentness).[39]

But what we have seen, thus far, of Heidegger's exegesis of *physis-ousia* could lead to a very false impression if it were not pointed out that he has sharply turned away from what is usually regarded as an essential part of Parmenides' theory. His departure is a major one, and consists in the fact that the Being which Heidegger would lead the reader to become aware of would not rule out the possibility of multiplicity and change, nor, then, systematically require us to devalue our sense experience. But let me explain.

Heidegger distinguishes between things-which-are, or what in English we might call "existents" (*Seienden*), and the Being through which they are (*das Sein*). According to Heidegger, things which are, such as trees, men, thoughts, etc., truly are, but they are not thereby identical with what is meant by "Being." The relation between a thing and "its" being (between it and Being) is not one of identity. A more linguistic way of putting Heidegger's point would be that when we say that a particular thing is, what is denoted by our word for the thing is not identical with

39. *IM*, p. 96; *EM*, p. 73.

what is expressed (at least imperfectly, in a falling-away fashion) through our use of the word "is," nor, then, with what is denoted by the word "Being," where "Being" is taken as denoting what is, in Heidegger's sense, "declined" from in the existential uses of "is." (It is well to remember here that Heidegger has given the basis for a defense of the supposition that the existential "is" does express something which can be referred to, or denoted.)

This distinction was at least anticipated in Heidegger's early work, *Sein und Zeit*, and was insisted upon in his slightly later *Vom Wesen des Grundes*, where it was given the name of the "ontological difference." [40] But no real justification for it was to be found until the appearance of his *Introduction to Metaphysics*, and even there it is not spelled out in so many words. But the entire "Platonic" argument that we have noted against reducing the meaning of "Being" to that of particular forms of the verb "to be" is tantamount, at the same time, to an argument against reducing the meaning of "Being" to particular things. The diversity of the particular things which we say are is as undeniable as that of the senses in which we say they are; and no more than the latter can they be identified with the unitative Being which stands at the root of the various senses in which we say that these diverse things are. From Being, both these various senses and the diverse things which through them are said in different ways to be, must be seen as declining, tipping-over, falling-away into non-identity.

Furthermore, in the latter half of the *Introduction, das Sein* is distinguished, not so much from particular *Seienden*, as from certain "modes" which are analyzed as being ways of declining, or tipping-over, or departing, from Being.[41] They are: becoming, appearing, thinking, and the "ought" (to some extent they circumscribe the ways in which the particular uses of "is" or other forms of "to be," which we have mentioned earlier, depart from the root meaning of "Being" to which Heidegger has sought to lead the reader). The reason why Heidegger dwells at length upon these is to show Being through its contrast with them, but the point that is important to us, here, is that once again, and in a new manner, he has recognized something distinct from Being:

> Being is delimited over against becoming, appearance, thought, the ought—these are not something that has just been dreamed up. They represent powers that dominate and bewitch the existent, its disclosure and configuration, its closing and disfigurement. Becoming—is it nothing? Appearance—is it nothing? Thought—is it nothing? The ought—is it nothing? By no means.
>   But if all that is opposed to Being in the distinction is nothing, then it is

---

40. Heidegger, *Being and Time*, pp. 32–35, 67ff.; *Vom Wesen des Grundes* (Halle, 1931), p. 5.
41. See *IM*, pp. 93–95, 199–204; *EM*, pp. 71–73, 152–56.

existent [an existent], and ultimately more so than what is regarded as being such in the restricted, current view of Being. But in what sense of Being are becoming and appearing, are thinking and the ought existent? Certainly not in the sense of the Being from which they are distinguished. But this sense of "Being" has been the current one ever since antiquity.

Then the sense of "Being" that has been accepted up until now does not suffice to name everything that "is."[42]

What is denied here is the unqualified identification which Parmenides makes, or seems to make, of Being (or, to translate his Greek more accurately, of Is or the Is) with the entire range of what is, an identification which implies that nothing but Is itself is or can be. The identification is, of course, the basis for the almost invariably monistic reading of Parmenides' Way of Truth. For Parmenides surely did say that the Is itself is one and undivided. Also, it is on the basis of this identification that change would be excluded, not merely from what is called "Being" or the "Is," but from everything. Heidegger's distinction would break up this monolithic, changeless block.

To be sure, Is or Being, according to Heidegger's exegesis of *physis* (as *ousia*), would exclude from itself any coming to be or passing away, and also any internal division (although this last is not so clearly brought out). But the unity, and the beginninglessness and endlessness, which enter into what Is is, which is to say, into the identity of Is, would not enter into the identity of what is distinguished from Is, that is, into the identity of the multiple and changing things which, only for a while, and in declining or falling-away modes, "are."

Instead, the Heideggerian Is would be similar to the Heraclitean *Logos* or Fire, in and through which things change, but which throughout their change, remains constant. That is, through Is, things would be, in their tipping-over modes of becoming, appearing, thinking and the ought (and in the various more detailed forms corresponding to different *enkleses* or *ptoses* of "to be"), but throughout, Is would itself stand forth, upright, undeclining, not falling-away.[43]

But as I have indicated, most philosophers do not seem to be aware of the implication of Heidegger's distinction for Parmenides' doctrine. They fail to recognize the way in which his distinction would obviate what has been, after all, the chief motive for rejecting the Is (that is to say, the beginningless, endless Is). There can be no question, I think, but that this motive is to be found in the belief that accepting the Is would require us systematically to reject our experience of multiplicity and change. Surely, the arguments of a merely logical sort that have been raised since Aristotle against Parmenides' doctrine do not supply the reason for our rejection so

42. *IM*, pp. 203–04; *EM*, p. 156.
43. *IM*, p. 136; *EM*, p. 104.

much as they attempt to correct a body of reasoning which, if left unanswered, would leave us with the uncomfortable feeling that our option
for the commonsense world is at odds with ways of reasoning in which
we ordinarily place some confidence. This is to say that the arguments
which are put forth against Parmenides ordinarily follow, rather than precede, the conviction that he is wrong; and that they are meant to explain
how he went wrong, rather than to prove the fact that he did so. The
conviction that Parmenides' doctrine is mistaken rests on another basis,
and I submit that this basis is in fact most often the conviction that a doctrine which would require us to reject wholesale the truth value of our
experience must be mistaken.

It is precisely this sort of rejection which we should no longer have to
make if the Is were understood in keeping with Heidegger's distinction
between the Is and things which, in their various declining ways, "are."

(It is, of course, true that Heidegger did not merely distinguish Being
from becoming, appearing, and thinking; by an ingenious argument, he
also undertook to derive these from Being, and in such a way as to present them as modes in which Being might seem to show itself as a process
of becoming, that is, as a continuous "unfolding," "unveilment," or emergence. For in his account of what is meant by *physis* or standing-forth,
he argues that it is expressed fully only as a standing-forth-into-the-light,
as emergence into openness or unconcealment, into the *aletheia* which
has come to be translated as "truth." And standing-forth-into-the-light, he
attempts to show, is at the root of what is expressed by the words "appear," or *scheinen, phainesthai*. Thus, Being would necessarily give rise to
appearance; to stand-forth would be to stand-forth-into the light, into
unconcealment.[44] Furthermore, emergence into unconcealment would itself occur in, and in a sense be, the ordering and distinction, the gathering-
together through setting-apart, through which things emerge into apprehension as what they are, e.g., as sea, as earth, as animal, etc., which is to
say that it would be what Heidegger interprets as that which Heraclitus
meant by *logos*, which he maintains has come to be called "thinking." [45]
It is on this basis that Heidegger is able to say that Parmenides and Heraclitus spoke the same truth.[46] But it is also on the basis of this derivation
that the not-having-been that is presupposed by becoming, by passing

44. *IM*, pp. 98–115, especially pp. 98–103; *EM*, pp. 75–88, especially pp. 75–78.
Heidegger also speaks of *physis* and *aletheia* as inclining, not always to truth or unconcealment, but to deception and concealment. See *IM*, pp. 104–15; *EM*, pp. 79–88.
See also *Time and Being*, "The End of Philosophy . . . ," pp. 67–73, where Heidegger rejects his earlier translation of *aletheia* as "truth" in his pursuit of *aletheia* as
the opening of the Self-concealing, or of What conceals itself in the unconcealment
of the modes of existents which, in the final lines of our present essay, we view as
belonging to, but not finally identical with, Being.

45. *IM*, pp. 115–96, especially 115–35; *EM*, pp. 88–149, especially 88–104.

46. *IM*, pp. 97, 136–45, 199–206; *EM*, pp. 74, 104–11, 152–57.

from concealment into unconcealment, might seem to enter into the identity of what is meant by "Being." [47]

But if so, then this part of Heidegger's thought might seem to conflict with the interpretation which we have given of his Being as an Is from within which all not-being would be excluded. Yet it may be possible to integrate these apparently divergent lines of thought. First, it could be suggested that through the process of Being, that is, appearing-*logos*, things stand forth from concealment, but that the process itself does not emerge from concealment, in the sense of having once not been. When Heidegger speaks of emergent appearing, or Being, as having its origin in concealment, he could, then, be interpreted as meaning, not that Being once was not, or did not stand forth, but that at all times, or perpetually, Being is emergence from non-being and concealment.[48] These last would not be temporally prior to Being, or the Is, but perpetually cotemporal. They would belong to the essence of Being, as the origin from which Being would be a perpetual passage. Against this interpretation, however, is the fact that Heidegger has insisted, in speaking of Parmenides, that when "looking toward" Being from "within" Being, i.e., when considering it in itself, we must exclude from our view of it all coming-to-be and passing-away, as "incommensurate" with Being.[49] Hence it would seem very difficult, finally, to interpret Heidegger as viewing Being in itself as a perpetual coming-to-be or emergence, for to view it thus would not exclude all coming-to-be. There is, however, another solution, which I should like to propose: let us recall that Being, for Heidegger, must not finally be identified with the appearing and *logos* which are derived from it. For him, the "unity" of appearing and *logos*, or of becoming and the ought, with Being is not a strict identity, but a "belonging" in which that which necessarily arises from out of Being is yet set off from it by an inevitable otherness or "departure." [50] In more linguistic terms, we could say that when "is" is said of things which, through appearing, come to be, the "is" falls short of expressing the full or un-self-contradictory meaning of "is" from which all not-being is absent.[51] An origin in concealment and not-being would, then, belong to Being, not as viewed in itself, but as viewed through or in its manifestation in the declining modes of things which, precisely because of their non-identity with Being, can be only through being brought out of the concealment of an original not-being.)

47. Moreover, they might seem to enter into the essence of Being, not merely as its *terminus a quo*, but also as its *terminus ad quem*, if we keep in mind that Heidegger has said that, as *physis*, and thus as appearing, Being tends not only to disclosure or openness, but also to concealment (see note 44).
48. *IM*, p. 114; *EM*, p. 87. Cf. *Time and Being*, p. 5.
49. *IM*, p. 96; *EM*, p. 74.
50. *IM*, pp. 94, 103, 105, 108–10, 135–39; *EM*, pp. 72, 78, 80, 82–84, 103–06.
51. See our previous discusison of *enklesis*.

13. Hubert Dreyfus & John Haugeland
Husserl and Heidegger: Philosophy's Last Stand

INTRODUCTION

In this paper we will attempt partially to trace and partially to "recon-struct" a dialogue between Husserl and Heidegger which, we believe, illuminates the development of the thought of both. The general pattern of this interchange will be, first, a prologue in which Husserl suggests that an application of his phenomenological method to the world of the natural attitude would be a valuable enterprise, and then the following five stages:

(a) The Heidegger of *Being and Time* follows this advice and makes dis-coveries that fundamentally undermine traditional metaphysics.

(b) The full import of these results is, however, not readily apparent, even to Heidegger, and he attempts to incorporate them into a "metaphysical" system of his own. Thus, his early works are divided against themselves—in a strict sense, incoherent.

(c) Husserl sees more clearly than Heidegger the incompatibility of the latter's position with some of the basic assumptions of traditional philosophy, assumptions upon which this position itself (insofar as it is "philosophical") also depends.

(d) Husserl, however, can neither deny nor overlook the importance of Heidegger's new areas of investigation, and in his later works (*Cartesian Meditations* and *Crisis*) attempts to develop a consistent position that can accommodate them without their destructive conse-quences.

(e) Heidegger, in turn, cannot deny the force of Husserl's criticisms. But he also sees that to "accommodate" his discoveries is to falsify them, and hence he is driven to the radical rejection of metaphysics in his later work.

We shall follow this five-step sequence in the development of the questions: What kind of truths or knowledge does philosophical investigation yield? In particular, does it yield necessary truths or knowledge of essences? Is the essence/existence or necessary/contingent distinction tenable? The discussion will be subdivided into sections according to the stages of sequence a–e. Of course, the materials with which we will work aren't this neatly organized. The advantage, however, of specifying such a rigid architectonic in advance is that it allows us to bring an overall pattern into bold relief, within which the details can then take a meaningful place.

PROLOGUE: HUSSERL POINTS THE WAY

In *Ideas* Husserl delineates what he calls "the natural standpoint," which is intended to be the standpoint of the ordinary man, a man who takes the *existence* of a world of facts and values, things and practices quite for granted as he proceeds about his daily business. Husserl's strategy (a substitute for Cartesian doubt or suspension of judgment) is to "bracket" the thesis of the natural standpoint—not to doubt it but just to "make 'no use' of it" in the science of Phenomenology. This would obviate any need for a full characterization of the natural standpoint. Of such a characterization he says:

> A task such as this can and must—as scientific—be undertaken, and it is one of extraordinary importance, although so far scarcely noticed. Here it is not ours to attempt. . . . the few features pertaining to the natural standpoint which we need are of a quite general character, and have already figured in our descriptions, and been sufficiently *and fully clarified*.[1]

In *Being and Time* Heidegger undertakes this extraordinarily important and so far scarcely noticed investigation, and comes to the conclusion that far more than the most general features of the natural standpoint are relevant to philosophy. He says near the end of his first chapter:

> . . . there are still difficulties in carrying out an existential analytic, especially in *making a start*. This task includes a desideratum which philosophy

1. *Ideas* (New York, 1962), p. 95.

has long found disturbing but has continually refused to achieve: *to work out the idea of a "natural conception of the world."* [2]

The fundamental methodological importance of explicating the "average, everyday" standpoint is emphasized in a footnote to the same chapter:

> Edmund Husserl has not only enabled us to understand once more the meaning of any genuine philosophical empiricism; he has also given us the necessary tools. '*A priorism*' is the method of every scientific philosophy which understands itself. There is nothing constructivistic about it. But for this very reason *a priori* research requires that the phenomenal basis be properly prepared. The horizon which lies closest to us, and which must be made ready for the analytic of Dasein, lies in its average everydayness.[3]

Notice it is precisely the tools Husserl provided that turn out to require an analytic of everydayness.

One of Heidegger's first, and perhaps most important, discoveries (see *Being and Time*, § 15) in his study of everydayness is that we don't by and large encounter (see, talk about, deal with) "mere things," *per se,* but rather such things as matter to what we are doing or what we are concerned with. These beings he calls "equipment" or "paraphernalia" [Zeug] in a sense broad enough to include pretty much anything that's useful: tools, materials, subsidiary projects, toys, clothing, dwellings, etc. The primary point that distinguished equipment from "mere things" is its thoroughgoing interrelatedness:

> Taken strictly, there 'is' no such thing as *an* equipment. To the being of any equipment there always belongs a totality of equipment, in which it can be this equipment that it is. Equipment is essentially 'something in-order-to. . . .'[4]

An "item" of equipment isn't a separate, independent particular; it is what it is only insofar as it fits in a certain way into an "equipmental totality," or what gets called an "in-order-to structure" or a "referential context."

> Equipment—in accordance with its equipmentality—always is *in terms of* its belonging to other equipment: ink-stand, pen, ink, paper, blotting pad, table, lamp, furniture, windows, doors, room.[5]

In other words, what an item of equipment *is* is entirely dependent on how it is incorporated into the total equipmental context.

2. *Being and Time* (New York, 1962), p. 76.
3. Ibid., p. 490.
4. Ibid., p. 97; cf. p. 403f.
5. Ibid., p. 97.

SECTION A: *Being and Time*
UNDERMINES THAT DISTINCTION

If what something *is* wholly *depends* on its role in some totality, then that thing can have no *independent essence* of its own. For example, *what it is* to be a hammer (so the argument runs) is just to be related in appropriate ways to nails, carpenters, furniture, families, and so on. That is, if the interrelated equipmental context had no "slot" for hammers (e.g., "in between" carpenters' hands and nails' heads), there would be nothing that it is to be a hammer. And, conversely, if there were no hammers there would be no such "slot" for them—for, if there were no hammers, what would a nail be, etc? [6] From which it follows that hammers not only have no "essence" independent of their functional role, but they also have no "essence" independent of the *existence* of actual hammers. But to make the latter denial is just to discard the traditional distinction of essence and existence altogether.[7]

The everyday world itself, which is basically just this equipmental totality understood quite broadly, has no essence either. What could "the essence of the world" mean? It would have to mean something like: "what it would be to be the world, should the world happen to exist, but independent of whether it in fact does." But it is absurd to talk about whether the world exists or not—the world and actuality amount to the same thing; existence (in the sense of *existentia*) just is encounterability *within* the world.

> The world itself is not an entity within-the-world; and yet it is so determinative for such entities that only insofar as "there is" a world [*es Welt "gibt"*] can they be encountered and show themselves, in their Being, as entities which have been discovered.[8]

6. To ask which came first, hammers or their equipmental "slot" (since there can be neither without the other already), is like asking which came first, the chicken or the egg. Presumably some evolutionary account will be the answer in either case.

7. There is an interesting parallel between Heidegger's "material mode" attack on the notion of essence and Quine's "formal mode" attack on the notion of meaning (in "Two Dogmas"). Indeed, Quine says, "Meaning is what essence becomes when it is divorced from the object of reference and wedded to the word" (*From a Logical Point of View* [Cambridge, Mass., 1953], p. 22). His view, briefly, is that there is no sense to the notion of what an individual sentence means "in isolation from its fellows"—i.e., of a distinct meaning which a sentence has, independent of how it is incorporated into a totality, the "whole of science." From this he argues that one cannot distinguish a "linguistic component" (what it would be to be the case that P) from a "factual component" (that it is the case that P) in the truth of any sentence P. Compare this with not being able to distinguish essence (what it would be to be a hammer) from existence (that there are hammers).

8. *Being and Time*, p. 102.

But what does this argument come to? Surely, one wants to say, we can speak of possible worlds, ones which aren't actual. In one sense, of course, this is true; we can talk of *the* world possibly being different, or rearranged. Thus, I can say there could have been a hammer in the kitchen, though there isn't, or there could have been horselike animals with one horn, though there aren't. And in some contexts it's harmless enough to rephrase this as talk about "other" possible worlds than "this" one. But so far this is only a way of saying that in *the* world things might not have been as they are—which is quite different from allowing that *the* world might not have existed; *the* world different wouldn't be *a* different world.[9]

The "essence" of the world, however, as distinguished from its existence, is what it would have been to be the world even had the world not existed. But that doesn't make any sense—for how is it that we can think of something not existing? We can imagine, for example, the nonexistence of a chartreuse hammer or of a hammer in the kitchen, by imagining the total absence of any hammers of that color or in that place. But such absences are intelligible only because there actually are carpenters, nails, gray hammers in the garage, and so on. It is only in terms of this actual context that what a hammer is makes sense, and likewise, what it is for a hammer not to be there. But there could be no actual context "left behind" in terms of which the absence of the world could be understood—the world *is* the context. Nor could nonexistence of the world be understood through imagining a totality of nonexisting things. That would have to be a totality of absences; but an absence, like a gap in a fence, only make sense in terms of what isn't absent. A nonactual world as a totality of nonexisting things is no less absurd than a nonactual fence as a lineup of fence gaps.

It might, however, be supposed that the essence of the world could be specified in terms of its formal structure. Thus, if what Heidegger discovered about the everyday world is its thoroughgoing interrelatedness—i.e., the relationships he subsumes under the terms 'significance' and 'involvement'—then why not formalize these relationships? A mathematical or formal system of relationships is an abstract structure, and as such its nature can be fully specified independent of whether anything actually has that structure or not—so why not take such a system as the essence of the world? But Heidegger argues that formal or abstract relations miss the real character of, say, "hammering with" or "driving in."

---

9. A similar point is made by Kripke when he says that some modal semanticists (e.g., David Lewis) take the notion of "other possible world" too literally. He suggests the term "counter-factual situation" as perhaps less misleading. See Saul Kripke, "Naming and Necessity," in *Semantics for Natural Languages*, ed. Gilbert Harman and Donald Davidson (Dordrecht, 1972).

The context of assignments or references, which, as significance, is constitutive for worldhood, can be taken formally in the sense of a system of Relations. But one must note that in such formalizations the phenomena get leveled off so much that their real phenomenal content may be lost, especially in the case of such 'simple' relationships as those which lurk in significance. The phenomenal content of those 'Relations' and 'Relata'—the "in-order-to", the "for-the-sake-of," and the "with which" of an involvement—is such that they resist any sort of mathematical functionalization. . . .[10]

The point is that these relationships, like hammers themselves, only are what they are in terms of the actual equipmental context—including carpenters using hammers on nails—in which they occur; neither such relationships nor any "structure" of them can be "abstractly" specified.

We have seen that for Heidegger neither everyday "items" of equipment nor the everyday world itself can have an independent essence; that is, the traditional conception of essence as independent of existence breaks down. The same point is made a third time, this time regarding Dasein (human being):

> Its Being-what-it-is (*essentia*) must, so far as we can speak of it at all, be conceived in terms of its Being (*existentia*). . . . *The 'essence' of Dasein lies in its existence.*[11]

This, of course, follows from the previous point, since Being-in-the-world is constitutive for Dasein. Who Dasein *is* is determined by its involvements in the world—everyday Dasein in one way, and authentic Dasein in another. Indeed, Dasein and its world are not at root separate: "That inside which one primarily understands oneself [the world] has Dasein's kind of Being. Dasein *is* it world existingly." [12]

These three versions of the rejection of the distinction between essence and existence are part and parcel of the overthrow of a pervasive traditional ontology—what Heidegger calls the ontology of the present-at-hand [*das Vorhandene*]. Put generally, the latter is the view that what is (truly or fully) real are those things which are independent, i.e., are what they are in and of themselves. The original candidates for such *realia* were the immutable, intelligible Platonic ideas. Aristotle substituted individual substances, things that retain their (independent) identities through changes in their attributes. And the medievals more or less fused the two in the doctrine of essence, including potential and necessary properties, as opposed to existence, in which the actual and contingent (dependent) properties become determined.[13] Heidegger's observation is

10. *Being and Time*, pp. 121–22.
11. Ibid., p. 67.
12. Ibid., p. 416.
13. Further forms of the present-at-hand ontology: the independent "mere thing,"

basically that the things ("equipment") with which we ordinarily concern ourselves do not have independent or substantial essences that could
be contrasted with their instantiation in existence with accidental properties.[14]

SECTION B: *Being and Time*
IS NOT COMPLETELY FREE OF THE DISTINCTION

Being and Time is conceived as a philosophical work; it is an attempt to
discover the fundamental and necessary structures in terms of which the
meaning of Being may be clarified through "a science *of Being as such*".[15]
This goal motivates and guides even the phenomenology of everydayness,
and leads Heidegger to make in the introduction the astonishing remark
that:

> In this everydayness there are certain structures which we shall exhibit—not
> just any accidental structures, but essential ones which, in every kind of
> being that factical Dasein may possess, persist as determinative for the char-
> acter of its being." [16]

A deeper understanding of this apparent inconsistency will require
taking a look at the overall project of phenomenology as ontology.[17]
Heidegger's position is most readily approached through comparison with
that of Husserl. Husserl accounted for the possibility of a priori science
with his method of "eidetic reduction," whereby one determines the eidos
(tantamount to an essence) of a kind of thing through "free imaginative
variation." The idea is that one imagines varying a thing in multifarious
ways and checking intuitively when it would and when it would not still
count as the kind of thing in question. It is thus generally parallel to the
method of conceptual analysis, in which necessary and sufficient conditions (tantamount to nominal essences) are delineated through considering various intuitively compelling counterexamples. The eidetic sciences

---

with its defining primary qualities as opposed to dependent secondary qualities; independent, intelligible noumena, as opposed to sensible appearances (phenomena),
dependent not only on things in themselves but also on our faculties; unchanging,
intelligible, independent fundamental particles and physical laws, as opposed to
changing, sensible, dependent macroscopic objects and relationships.

14. In this regard, *Being and Time* can be seen as akin to other contemporary
challenges to the traditional modalities: cf. Quine on necessity and possibility, and
Wittgenstein on criteria and symptoms.

15. *Being and Time*, p. 272.

16. Ibid., p. 38.

17. Ibid., p. 62.

of what would count as, or what it is to be, say, a man, a psyche, a number, a physical object, etc., are called "regional ontologies."

But Husserl is after bigger game than regional ontology; he wants to understand what it is, given the eidos or essence of something, for that eidos to have an *actual* or *objective* instantiation. Toward this end he introduces his "transcendental reduction," which is a method, roughly, of transferring attention from what our thoughts are standardly about (e.g., objects and eidoses) to the very senses or meanings of those acts of thinking themselves (i.e., to the noemata of those noetic acts).[18] From this perspective he can consider the *meant* objects of thought, *not as actual* objects but only as *meant* (the *cogitata qua cogitata*). The actuality of objects and the objective world are not exactly doubted, but rather beliefs therein are scrupulously disregarded, or "bracketed," so that consideration may be restricted to what does not presuppose them: viz, the meanings, the objects as meant, and the transcendental activity or ego by which they are meant. But insofar as the meant objects, considered only as meant, are uncovered as systematically *meant to be actual*, then it appears that the essential nature of objectivity itself might be understood in terms of transcendental meaning giving.

What then remains is for this discovery to be made "scientific," in Husserl's sense of philosophy as "the all-embracing science"—that is, to be shown to be necessary and universal.

> After transcendental reduction, my true interest is directed to my pure ego, to the uncovering of this de facto [transcendental] ego. But the uncovering can become genuinely scientific, only if I go back to the apodictic principles that pertain to this ego as exemplifying the eidos ego: the essential universalities and necessities by means of which the fact is to be related to its rational grounds (those of its pure possibility) and thus made scientific (logical).[19]

Thus, the transcendental and eidetic reductions are both essential to Husserl's phenomenology—the former to uncover the objective world as a sense constituted by my de facto ego, and the latter to exhibit the possibility of this achievement in the very eidos (essence) ego, rendering it universal and necessary.[20] And, with this double-barreled method, Husserl can answer the transcendental question (which is prior to those of any regional ontology): What is it in general to be an objective instantiation of an eidos?

18. See the account of nonstandard reference in Frege, "Sense and Reference," and Dagfinn Føllesdal, "Husserl's Notion of Noema," *Journal of Philosophy* 66 (1969): 680–87.

19. *Cartesian Meditations* (The Hague, 1960), p. 72.

20. Ibid., p. 137.

Heidegger's problem is that he too wants to do transcendental philosophy.

> Being, as the basic theme of philosophy, is no class or genus of entities; yet it pertains to every entity. Its 'universality' is to be sought higher up. Being and the structure of Being lie beyond every entity and every possible character which an entity may possess. *Being is the* TRANSCENDENS *pure and simple. . . . Phenomenological truth (the disclosedness of Being) is* VERITAS TRANSCENDENTALIS.[21]

But he obviously can allow neither an eidetic nor a transcendental reduction; for precisely what is discovered in the phenomenology of everydayness is that there are neither any essences of things nor any pure meaning-giving ego distinct from the *actual* totality in which they are all involved.[22] So Heidegger has a different method, which he calls "hermeneutic," for investigating this totality, "Dasein's Being-in-the-world," as a unitary phenomenon. The hermeneutic method is one of finding *interpretations* for the totality; and, since the totality has no essence, no determinate "what it is" that could fix a horizon within which it is ultimately to be understood, hermeneutic interpretations must always be based on (be within the horizon of) such understanding as we already have.[23] That is, they must initially be based on our prephenomenological everyday understanding. The investigation and resulting interpretation can, however, themselves contribute to a more sophisticated understanding, on the basis of which, in turn, a deeper or "more primordial" investigation and interpretation are possible, and so on. Thus, we get progressively more and more primordial interpretations of the totality, and, *ipso facto*, of Dasein and Being; but we never reach an ultimate or transcendental horizon within which they are finally to be understood.[24]

The very method of hermeneutic, and the correlative abjuring of essences, seems intrinsically to rule out any *a priori*, transcendental hori-

---

21. *Being and Time*, p. 62.

22. Strictly speaking, if one rejects the notion of essence, one must correlatively reject the notion of "actuality." Likewise in speaking of "the" totality we must be careful not to think of "it" as a being.

23. Compare this attitude to Quine's: "Neurath has likened science to a boat which, if we are to rebuild it, we must rebuild plank by plank while staying afloat in it. The philosopher and the scientist are in the same boat" (*Word and Object* [Cambridge, Mass., 1960], p. 3); also see frontispiece motto).

24. "In any investigation in this field, where 'the thing itself is deeply veiled' one must take pains not to overestimate the results. For in such an inquiry, one is constantly compelled to face the possibility of disclosing an even more primordial and universal horizon, from which we may draw the answer to the question, 'What is "Being"?' " (*Being and Time*, p. 49; the quoted phrase is from Kant, *Critique of Pure Reason*, B 121).

zon within which Dasein, the world (actuality itself), or Being *must* be interpreted. How then can Heidegger say:

> The transcendental "generality" [which is "ontological and *a priori*" (same page)] of the phenomenon of care and of all fundamental *existentialia* is . . . broad enough to present a basis on which *every* interpretation of Dasein which is ontical and belongs to a world view must move. . . . [25]

The trouble is, *ontology*, as it is conceived in the early works, can hardly help but seek the special inner nature of things—i.e., try to transcend the mere factical nature of beings and characterize what it is or would be for them to be at all, whether or not they are. Ontology, in this sense, seems inevitably led to talk about essences.

> To ascribe Being-in-the-world to Dasein as the basic feature of its constitution is to make a statement about its essence—about its unique inner possibility as Dasein. Now we cannot determine anything about the essence of Dasein by asking *what sort of* Dasein exists factically, or *whether* Dasein exists factically at all. . . . Such talk concerns an *essential* condition of Dasein, one which defines Dasein *at an ontological level.* . . . [26]

In the *Being and Time* period, Heidegger still wants to know *what it is to be*, to give an account of Being as such; thus he needs what should make no sense for him: a horizon broader than Being. "Is there a way which leads from primordial *time* to the meaning of *Being?* Does *time* itself manifest itself as the horizon of Being?" [27]

SECTION C: HUSSERL POINTS OUT THE PROBLEM

Husserl, of course, has no objection to Heidegger's interest in essential structures and a transcendental perspective on actuality or Being—that, after all, is a philosopher's business. He objects, rather, to Heidegger's approach, beginning with the everydayness of factical Dasein. We can get

25. *Being and Time*, p. 244. See also *Kant and the Problem of Metaphysics*, p. 224. "The development of existential ontology, which begins by the analysis of everydayness, has as its sole objective the explication of the primordial transcendental structure of the *Dasein* in man."

26. Martin Heidegger, *The Essence of Reasons* (Evanston, Ill., 1969), p. 45.
Works of this period (the Kant book, *The Essence of Reasons*, *The Essence of Truth*) sometimes seem to exaggerate the "throwback" side of *Being and Time*, emphasized in our section b. Perhaps they represent one last try to stay "philosophical" or to satisfy Husserl. Or perhaps they are the products of unrevised earlier thinking.

27. *Being and Time*, p. 488.

an insight into Husserl's reaction to *Being and Time* from the marginalia in his own copy. Thus, adjacent to the passage that reads:

> In *which* entities is the meaning of Being to be discerned? From which entities is the disclosure of Being to take its departure? Is the starting point optional, or does some particular entity have priority when we come to work out the question of Being? Which entity shall we take for our example, and in what sense does it have priority? [28]

Husserl writes, "Can there be a privileged example in a question of universal essences? Isn't that exactly what is excluded?" [29] Heidegger is going to take everyday Dasein as his privileged starting point. But Husserl, taking "meaning of Being" to be tantamount to "essence of entities in general," can't understand why any *particular* kind of entity should be special, as though it instantiated the essence better than other instances.

A few pages later, beside the paragraph in which Heidegger says:

> We must rather choose such a way of access and such a kind of interpretation that this entity [Dasein] can show itself in itself and from itself. And this means that it is to be shown as it is *proximally and for the most part*—in its average *everydayness*.[30]

Husserl writes in the margin:

> That, in my sense, is the way to an intentional psychology of the personality, in the broadest sense, starting from personal living in the world; a founding personal type. I would have counterposed natural apprehensions of the world in natural living in the world . . . to philosophical transcendental world apprehension, and thus to a life which is not lived in the naive taken-for-granted world with a naive taking-for-granted of oneself as a man, but is rather the idea of philosophical life determined by philosophy.[31]

The argument is that if one's original direction is drawn from everyday life, in which actuality is just naively taken for granted, then a transcendental, philosophical perspective can never be reached. The best that could be attained would be an eidetic science of the everyday person.[32]

But Husserl's objections to the analytic of what he calls the life-world

28. Ibid., p. 26.
29. The marginalia are preserved in the Louvain Archives under the signature "K X Heidegger I"; our translation.
30. *Being and Time*, pp. 37–38.
31. Louvain Archives.
32. For an explicit contrast between eidetic or intentional psychology and transcendental phenomenology, see *Cartesian Meditations*, section 35 (pp. 72–73). Compare also the passage on p. 86f that says, ". . . anyone who misconstrues the sense and performance of transcendental-phenomenological reduction . . . confounds in-

[Lebenswelt] are more pointed and specific than this, for he sees more consistently than Heidegger that one is not going to find constant and universal essences in significance relations and equipmental contexts. In a short unpublished manuscript labeled "Contra Heidegger" he wrote:

> The universal practical structure of the life-world, in its universality, is not primary for the theoretical man. His practical interests vary, and therewith what is significant; and significances also vary relative to the person. Only insofar as each ego knows itself to be united with a relatively permanent community of family, estates, nation [etc.], and as a certain broader significance derives an intersubjective identity out of communal relations, are things otherwise.
>
> Theoretical interest is concerned with what is; and that, everywhere, is what is identical through variation of subjects and their practical interests, i.e., the same things, the same relations, the same changes, etc., which are there in themselves, i.e., there for "everybody". [It is concerned] with the significances themselves only insofar as they are taken in their correlation; then anybody can verify (if he takes a theoretical attitude) that this thing here, counts for subject A as such and such a piece of equipment [Zeug], for B as quite a different one, that anything can be woven into equipmental contexts of many kinds, both for the same and for different subjects.
>
> Yet whatever is cognized, it is a being that is cognized; and a being is something identical, something identifiable again and again, and ultimately, something identifiable for everybody in the subjective context of open possible communication and in its context-of-being, which, of course, because it's familiar, usually remains out of sight. All equipment and all its equipmental characteristics are beings in this primary sense. To understand their being one has to establish the whole concrete context-of-being—just as this holds also for all the other being which is hidden in the life-world, and yet "lies" in it everywhere.[33]

The point, roughly, is that to approach such variable and temporary phenomena as equipmentality and significance philosophically, one must first look to the invariant factors—the "this thing here," the subject, etc.—

---

tentional psychology and transcendental phenomenology . . . [and] falls victim to the inconsistency of a transcendental philosophy that stays within the natural realm" with what Husserl writes to Roman Ingarden in December 1927: "The new article for the Encyclopedia Britannica has cost me a great deal of effort, chiefly because I again thought through from the ground up my basic direction and took into account the fact that Heidegger, as I now must believe, has not understood this direction and thus the entire sense of the method of phenomenological reduction" (*Edmund Husserl, Briefe an Roman Ingarden* [The Hague, 1968], p. 43).

33. The passage "das ist gegen Heidegger" can be found in original manuscript form under the signature B I 32, p. 30aff; the transcription is catalogued as B I 32 II, p. 21ff. The manuscript was apparently three pages originally, of which the first is now lost. Above is our translation of the final three of the eight remaining paragraphs (except the final sentence).

and then discern progressively subtler invariant relations, structures, and so on, until the "whole concrete context" is worked out explicitly. So, interdependent and changeable equipment eventually gets understood through the constant and independent correlations among its various dependencies, changeabilties, etc. Hence, everyday significances are among the later topics in the philosopher's analysis, not at all the starting place. But notice how closely this order of proceeding is connected with the very present-at-hand ontology which Heidegger is so concerned not to take for granted.

SECTION D: HUSSERL ATTEMPTS
TO ACCOMMODATE HEIDEGGER'S DISCOVERIES

The analysis in *Being and Time* only *begins* with everydayness—it must go on from there to account for scientific and other knowledge of things more or less independent of any use we might have for them.[34] As phenomenology, Heidegger's direction apparently has the advantage over Husserl's, since "manipulating" and "coping with" things is clearly prior to scientific theory, both in individual and cultural development. So the later Husserl undertakes to show philosophically how science is founded on the life-world:

> . . . science is a human spiritual accomplishment which presupposes as its point of departure, both historically and for each new student, the intuitive surrounding world of life, pregiven as existing for all in common.[35]

But once having conceded a certain sort of priority for the life-world, Husserl proceeds philosophically (as Heidegger cannot) to develop an eidetic science of the life-world.

> What imposes itself here and must be considered before everything else is the correct comprehension of the essence of the life-world and the method of a "scientific" treatment appropriate to it. . . .[36]

This will involve, as prefigured above, the building up of the levels of what is (present-at-hand) valid within the concrete life-world.

> . . . the concrete life-world . . . must be considered in terms of the truly concrete universality whereby it embraces, both directly and in the manner

34. See especially *Being and Time*, sections 16, 24, 33, 44 and 69.
35. *The Crisis of European Sciences and Transcendental Phenomenology* (Evanston, Ill., 1970), p. 121.
36. Ibid., p. 123.

of horizons, all the built-up levels of validity acquired by men for the world of their common life. . . .[37]

This building up will begin, at the lowest level, with the passively experienced "mere thing."

> . . . anything built by activity necessarily presupposes, as the lowest level, a passivity that gives something beforehand. . . . The "ready-made" object that confronts us in life as an existent mere physical thing (when we disregard all the "spiritual" or "cultural" characteristics that make it knowable as, for example, a hammer, a table, an aesthetic creation) is given, with the originality of the "it itself," in the synthesis of a passive experience.[38]

So when Husserl seeks to accommodate philosophically Heidegger's point that things are encountered first in their everyday capacities as usabilia and only later as objective, scientifically accessible things, he proposes a special sort of "science" of the essence of the life-world: He finds that a passively given independent "thing" is presupposed by any encounter with equipment; and starting from that, all the higher level significances of the life-world (not to mention the theories of the objective sciences) can be, so to speak, added on. Heidegger's deeper discovery of the ineradicable interdependence of equipmentality is simply bypassed.

SECTION E:

HEIDEGGER GETS OVER THE TRADITIONAL DISTINCTION

In the analytic of everydayness Heidegger discovered that the equipmental world is an interrelated referential context; and, hence, that the equipment in the world cannot be regarded as a set of independent "things" which then "possess" certain independently definite properties.

> But the 'indicating' of the sign and the 'hammering' of the hammer are not properties of entities. Indeed, they are not properties at all, if the ontological structure designated by the term 'property' is that of some definite character which it is possible for Things to possess.[39]

Husserl never seems to have caught on to the deep integratedness or "holism" in our everyday world and to how that undermines the distinction between (independent) essence and (contingent) existence, and hence, the distinction between "substantial" things and dependent properties. But he did point out that, given the approach he was taking, Heidegger had no business trying to do transcendental philosophy, i.e., to find

37. Ibid., p. 133.
38. *Cartesian Meditations*, p. 78.
39. *Being and Time*, pp. 114–15.

the meaning of Being in general, and also that the everyday world in fact is not just an equipmental totality, but includes natural mere things which are neither equipment nor derivative or deficient modes thereof.

Heidegger can deny neither point; but, seeing that returning to the fold would be incompatible with his central insights, he ends up sounding less traditional and stranger than ever. Already two years after the publication of *Cartesian Meditations* bare things and works of art are quite divorced from equipment.

> We must only avoid making thing and work [of art] prematurely into sub-species of equipment.[40]

> . . . the work is not a piece of equipment that is fitted out in addition with aesthetic value that adheres to it. The work is no more anything of the kind than the bare thing is a piece of equipment that merely lacks the specific equipmental characteristics of usefulness and being made.[41]

Heidegger acknowledges that indeed, if we "keep at a distance all pre-conceptions" [42] a sort of independence must be granted the thing, a kind of defiant unwillingness to reveal or bend itself to thought.

> The unpretentious thing evades thought most stubbornly. Or can it be that this self-refusal of the mere thing, this self-contained independence, belongs precisely to the nature of the thing? [43]

And a similar self-contained stubbornness is found in equipment itself, in its requisite reliability.

> The repose of equipment resting within itself consists in its reliability. Only in this reliability do we discern what equipment in truth is.[44]

But the "independence" discovered here is not the philosopher's isolated determinateness or constancy regardless of all other things. Rather, it is something like insubordinateness, a resistance to being entirely determined by its interrelatedness in Dasein's world.

This resistant independence which is in things and in equipment, and, in another way again, in the work of art, is called "the earth." In the earlier analytic of everydayness, the determining interrelatedness of equipment was called the everyday world. In "The Origin of the Work of Art," the world is still that in which and through which things can show

40. "The Origin of the Work of Art", *Poetry, Language, Thought* (New York, 1971), p. 32.
41. Ibid., p. 38f.
42. Ibid., p. 43.
43. Ibid., pp. 31–32.
44. Ibid., p. 35.

themselves as what they are, and hence it is opposed to the earth; but it can no longer be thought as an equipmental totality, with its structure of "in-the-face-of," "in-order-to," and "for-the-sake-of." The world is rather that "all-governing expanse of [an] open relational context"[45] within which, for a people, there can be the beings there are; i.e., within which any beings (not just equipment) can have a place and be encountered. "By the opening up of a world all things gain their lingering and hastening, their remoteness and nearness, their scope and limits."[46] Thus, though there are things other than equipment and though all beings have a certain "self-contained independence," it is nevertheless only within a world that these resistant beings can show up as being what they are.

The world is the context that "lights up" beings, within which and against which they can be the beings they are; the earth is that "obscurity" of which beings are never devoid, and which leaves them always in the end inscrutable.

> "World and earth are essentially different from one another and yet never separated. . . . The world, in resting upon the earth, strives to surmount it. As self-opening it cannot endure anything closed. The earth, however, as sheltering and concealing tends always to draw the world into itself and keep it there.[47]

In the striving of the two together arise beings which are at the same time familiar (knowable, usable) and yet independent of that familiarity (unreliable, recalcitrant, surprising).

But the world or context itself is not familiar; there is no context within which "it" can be represented or "seen" as an object of any kind whatsoever. There is no "it" which "is." All that can be said is what not to say (ontological pitfalls to avoid), plus a few enigmatic sounding tautologies.

> The world is not the mere collection of the countable or uncountable, familiar and unfamiliar things that are just there. But neither is it a merely imagined framework added by our representation to the sum of such given things. The world worlds, and is more fully in being than the tangible and perceptible realm in which we believe ourselves to be at home. World is never an object that stands before us can be seen.[48]

In the later works, the world, and, hence, the Being of the beings which are lit up by it (or "show up" in it) is more clearly identified as that which is handed down to us in our tradition or culture. But since this

45. Ibid., p. 42.
46. Ibid., p. 45.
47. Ibid., p. 48f.
48. Ibid., p. 44.

handed-down world is not something we can represent to ourselves, what is left for philosophers to think about is only the "ontological difference" between that and the beings which show up in it. "The difference of Being and beings, as the differentiation of handing-down and showing up, is the outcome of the two in unconcealing keeping in concealment." [49] Indeed, we cannot think of Being *per se* at all any more, but only of this difference: "Thus we think of Being rigorously only when we think of it in its difference with beings, and of beings in their difference with Being." [50] In other words, about all that can be said of Being is that beings aren't the whole ontological story, and that the rest of the story, as a cultural achievement, is just as factical and "this-worldly" as beings.

That is, the transcendental question about the Being of beings is given up. But this does not mean that there is nothing for the thinker to do. Even without "essential necessities and universalities" to characterize the Being of beings, there are still discoveries like the importance of the differentiation of handing down and showing up, and its perennial distortion in metaphysics. Such discoveries may even "bring to light something all-pervading," though the sense of that is not so readily understandable as it might once have seemed. "Yet it remains difficult to say how this all-pervasiveness is to be thought, if it is neither something universal, valid in all cases, nor a law guaranteeing the necessity of a process. . . ." [51]

Outgrowing a tradition is not easy—progress is made by being able to look back and see how earlier steps were only part of the way out.

> In the treatise, *Being and Time*, the attempt is made, on the basis of the question concerning the truth of Being, no longer the truth of beings, to determine the essence of man in terms of his relation to Being and only out of this relation. . . . [T]he basis of the failure to understand lies in the attempt itself, which, while perhaps indeed historically developed, and not "cooked up," still comes out of the past, but which struggles to free itself therefrom, and thus necessarily and continually still falls back into the track of the tradition (Bisherigen), indeed, even calls this to aid, in order to say something entirely different.[52]

49. *Identity and Difference* (New York, 1969), p. 65 (modified translation).
50. Ibid., p. 62.
51. Ibid., p. 67f.
52. Martin Heidegger, *Nietzsche II* (Pfullingen, 1961), p. 194; our translation.

14. Richard Rorty
Overcoming the Tradition: Heidegger and Dewey

PHILOSOPHERS WHO ENVY SCIENTISTS think that philosophy should deal only with problems formulatable in neutral terms—terms satisfactory to all those who argue for competing solutions. Without common problems and without argument, it would seem, we have no professional discipline, nor even a method for disciplining our own thoughts. Without discipline, we presumably have mysticism, or poetry, or inspiration—at any rate, something that permits an escape from our intellectual responsibilities. Heidegger is frequently criticized for having avoided these responsibilities. His defenders reply that what he has avoided is not the responsibility of the thinker, but simply the tradition of "metaphysics" or "ontology." Consider the typical passage:

> "Ontology," whether transcendental or precritical, is subject to criticism not because it thinks the Being of beings and thereby subjugates Being to a concept, but because it does not think the truth of Being and so fails to realize the fact that there is a kind of thought more rigorous than the conceptual (. . . *und so verkennt dass es ein Denken gibt das strenger ist als das begriffliche*).[1]

Reprinted from *The Review of Metaphysics* 30 (December, 1976) with permission of the editor. Some of the notes are abbreviated.

1. "Brief über den 'Humanismus,'" reprinted in *Wegmarken* (Frankfurt, 1967), p. 187; "Letter on Humanism," trans. Edgar Lohner, in *Philosophy in the Twentieth Century*, vol. 3, ed. William Barrett and Henry Aiken (New York, 1962), p. 297. These are abbreviated below as *BH* and *LH*. I shall use the following abbreviations for other books by Heidegger and translations: *VA* for *Vorträge und Aufsätze* (Pfulligen, 1954); *HW* for *Holzwege* (Frankfurt, 1950); *SZ* for *Sein und Zeit*, 7th ed. (Tübingen, 1953) and *BT* for the translation of this work by MacQuarrie and Robinson, *Being and Time* (London, 1962); *US* for *Unterwegs zur Sprache* (Pfulligen, 1959) and *OWL* for its translation, *On the Way to Language* (New York, 1971),

Contemplating this distinction, one may suspect that Heidegger wants to have it both ways. On the one hand, we usually distinguish "thought" from its purportedly "irresponsible" alternatives—mysticism, art, myth-making—by identifying "thought" with argumentative rigor. But what-ever *strenger* means in this passage it is hardly what Kant or Carnap or Husserl meant by it; it has nothing to do with argument, nor with *"Phi-losophie als strenge Wissenschaft."* So presumably *strenger* means some-thing like "more difficult." From this Heideggerian angle, ontology is the easy way out; anybody can produce a new opinion on an old ontological question. Even working out whole new systems or "research programs" in ontology is not really very hard. But Heraclitus, for example, did nei-ther of these, and what he did was much harder to do. So Heidegger wants not to have to argue with his fellow philosophers, and wants also to say that he is doing something much more difficult than they try to do.

We might now be inclined to say that it would be well for Heidegger to call whatever he wants to do something other than "Thought." For surely "thinking" ought to be opposed to something else—not "emotion," perhaps, but surely to something that has more to do with the arts than the sciences, more to do with religion than with philosophy. Surely what Heidegger is doing has more to do with *that.* But Heidegger thinks that these various distinctions are themselves products of metaphysical system-building. Since all the usual divisions between disciplines, and all the usual ways of dividing man's life into stages or modes, are the products of the various writers who constitute "the tradition of Western ontology," we can hardly use these divisions to "place" the work of a man whose aim is to overcome that tradition. But one may still feel exasperated. There ought, one feels, to be *some* standard by which to judge Heidegger, some competitor running in the same race.

Tediously enough, however, Heidegger suggests that our sense of exas-peration is just one more product of the notion that philosophy is sup-posed to be a competition between arguments, a notion which we get from Plato and whose consequences, two thousand years later, were posi-tivism and nihilism. To free ourselves from the notion that there ought to be competition here would be to free ourselves from what he calls "the technical interpretation of thought." About this interpretation, he says:

---

by Peter D. Hertz and Joan Stambaugh; *N* for *Nietzsche,* 2 vols. (Pfullingen, 1961) and *EP* for *The End of Philosophy,* trans. Joan Stambaugh (New York, 1973)—a selection of passages from *N* together with a translation of "Überwindung der Metaphysik" from *VA; IM* for *Introduction to Metaphysics,* trans. Ralph Manheim (New Haven, 1959) and *EM* for *Einführung in der Metaphysik* (Tübingen, 1953); *BR* for the "Brief an Richardson" published in German and English on facing pages in W. J. Richardson, *Heidegger: Through Phenomenology to Thought* (The Hague, 1957), pp. viii–xxiii.

Its beginnings reach back to Plato and Aristotle. For them, thought is of value because it is a τέχνη, a reflective process in the service of doing and making. Reflection is already seen by them from the standpoint of πρᾶξις and ποίησις. Thus when they view thought in isolation they can think of it as not "practical." Thinking of thought as θεωρία and describing knowledge as the "theoretical attitude" is itself an episode in the "technical" interpretation of thought. It is a reactive attempt to preserve for thought some sort of autonomy over against making and doing. Ever since, "philosophy" has had to try to justify its existence to "the sciences," and it thinks it can do so by elevating itself to the rank of a "science." But this effort gives up the essence of thought. . . . Can one now call the effort to bring thought back to its own element "irrationalism"? [2]

So we cannot accuse Heidegger of irrationalism, it seems, without begging the question in favor of Plato and Aristotle. Nor can we even ask "Who then is right about thought: Plato or Heidegger?" For the question supposes there to be a topic called "Thought" on which there might be different views. But Heidegger claims no view about such a thing. He thinks that to attempt to offer views of this sort is to neglect the "essentially historical character of Being." [3] Since Thought is of Being,[4] and since Being is essentially historical, it is not as if Plato and Aristotle might have been wrong about what Thought was. It is not as if Thought had, so to speak, been waiting patiently for Heidegger to come along and put us right about it. Heidegger says that when, e.g., Plato represented Being as ἰδέα and Aristotle as ἐνέργεια, "these were not doctrines advanced by chance, but rather words of Being." [5] There is no way of getting closer to Being by getting back behind Plato and starting off on the right foot. Heidegger tells us that his own definition of Being (as "*das* transcendens *schlechthin*") in *Sein und Zeit* was not an attempt "to start over again and expose the falsity of all previous philosophy." [6] He regards the notion of "the unchanging unity of the underlying determinations of Being" as "only an illusion under whose protection metaphysics occurs as history of Being." [7] So it is not as if we might compare metaphysics-from-Plato-

2. *BH, WM*, pp. 146–47; *LH*, pp. 271–72.
3. *BH, WM*, p. 170; *LH*, p. 287 on Husserl and Sartre's failure to grasp this and on why "the Marxist view of history excels all other accounts of the past." See also *BR*, p. xiv.
4. *BH, WM*, pp. 147–48; *LH*, p. 272.
5. "*On Time and Being*," trans. Joan Stambaugh (New York, 1927), p. 9. For the original see *Zur Sache des Denkens* (Tübingen, 1969), p. 9.
6. *BH, WM*, p. 168; *LH*, p. 285. Cf. *OWL*, pp. 38ff (*US*, pp. 133ff.).
7. *EP*, p. 11 (*N*, II, p. 411). The notion that "even though the linguistic formulations of the essential constituents of Being change, the constituents . . . remain the same" which Heidegger discusses in this passage is well illustrated by, for example, P. F. Strawson, *The Bounds of Sense* (London, 1966), p. 20, in his discussion of the recurrent problem of the universal and the particular. The really fundamental "split" in contemporary philosophy, I am inclined to say, is between those (like Dewey,

to-Nietzsche on the one hand and Heidegger on the other with their common topic—Thought, or Being—and then decide which offered the better account.

To sum up, we may conclude that Heidegger has done as good a job of putting potential critics on the defensive as any philosopher in history. There is no standard by which one can measure him without begging the question against him. His remarks about the tradition, and his remarks about the limitations the tradition has imposed on the vocabulary and imagination of his contemporaries, are beautifully designed to make one feel foolish when one tries to find a bit of common ground on which to start an argument.

One may feel tempted at this point to decide that "Heidegger is not really a *philosopher* at all." This too would be foolish. Heidegger brilliantly carries to extremes a tactic used by every original philosopher. Heidegger is not the first to have invented a vocabulary whose purpose is to dissolve the problems considered by his predecessors, rather than to propose new solutions to them. Consider Hobbes and Locke on the problems of the scholastics, and Carnap and Ayer on "pseudoproblems." He is not the first to have said that the whole mode of argument used in philosophy up until his day was misguided. Consider Descartes on method, and Hegel on the need for dialectical thinking. His seemingly arrogant claim that the tradition has exhausted its potentialities [8] simply carries to its limit the sort of impatience sometimes manifested by quite mild-mannered philosophers in such remarks as "All the arguments for and against utilitarianism were canvassed well before 1900," or "All the worry about the external world is a result of confusing having a sensation with observing an object." [9] In urging new vocabularies for the statement of philosophical issues, or new paradigms of argumentation, a philosopher cannot appeal to antecedent criteria of judgment, but he may have spectacular success. The scholastics' vocabulary never recovered from the sarcasm of the seventeenth century. Half the philosophy written since Hegel attempted the sort of triumphant dialectical syntheses offered in the *Phenomenology*. Descartes and Hegel may have seemed "not real philosophers" to many of their contemporaries, but they created new problems in place of the old, kept philosophy going by the sheer brilliance of their example, and appear retrospectively as stages in a progressive development.

Heidegger, Cavell, Kuhn, Feyerabend, and Habermas) who take Hegel and history seriously, and those who see "recurring philosophical problems" being discussed by everybody from the Greeks to the authors of the latest journal articles.

8. *N*, II, p. 201.

9. When such remarks are offered wholesale (as by Wisdom, Bouwsma, and the Ryle of *Dilemmas*) they tend to be dismissed as facile and self-indulgent—as lacking the patience and the labor of the negative. But even his worst enemies would hesitate to use such terms of Heidegger; what he tries to do may be impossible or perverse, but it is not easy.

If it seems difficult to think of Heidegger coming to occupy the same position, it is because he does not, like Descartes and Hegel and Husserl and Carnap, say, "This is how philosophy has been; let philosophy henceforth be like *this*." Rather, like Nietzsche and Wittgenstein and Dewey, he asks, "Given that this is how philosophy has been, what, if anything, can philosophy now be?" Suggesting, as they did, that philosophy may have exhausted its potentialities, he asks whether the motives which led to philosophy's existence still exist and whether they should. Many philosophers—practically all those whom we think of as founding movements—saw the entire previous history of philosophy as the working out of a certain set of false assumptions, or conceptual confusions, or unconscious distortions of reality. But only a few of these have suggested that the notion of philosophy itself—a discipline distinct from science, yet not to be confused with art or religion—was one of the results of these false starts. And fewer still have suggested that we are not, even now, in a position to state alternatives to those false assumptions or confused concepts—to see reality plain. These few writers are often treated dismissively by philosophers who do claim to know where the future of philosophy lies. Heidegger's later style makes it easy to dismiss him as someone who has simply become tired of arguing, and who, taking refuge in the mystical, abandons the attempt to defend his almost respectable earlier work. But even philosophers like Dewey and Santayana, who resemble Heidegger in seeing no interesting future for a distinct discipline called "philosophy," have been dismissed as "not really philosophical" on just this ground—that they neither held out hope of the successful completion of old "research programs" nor suggested new ones. It is as if to be a philosopher one had to have a certain minimal loyalty to the profession—as if one were not permitted to dissolve an old philosophical problem without being ready to put a new one in its place.[10]

There is, however, an obvious way of distinguishing critics of the tradition like Dewey and Heidegger from the amateur, the philistine, the mystic, or the belletrist. This is by the depth and extent of their commentaries on the details of the tradition. Any freshman can dismiss "Western thought" as merely "conceptual" and have done with it. It is not so easy to explain just what being "conceptual" amounts to, and what is common to the various paradigms of "conceptual thought." Dewey and Heidegger know exactly what their predecessors were worried about, and they each offer us an account of the dialectical course of the tradition. But the self-image of a philosopher—his identification of himself as such (rather than as, perhaps, a historian or a mathematician or a poet)—depends almost entirely upon how he sees the history of philosophy.

10. This defensive reaction is especially common in discussions of Wittgenstein's later work. I consider this reaction to Wittgenstein in "Keeping Philosophy Pure" (*Yale Review* [Spring, 1976], pp. 336–56).

It depends upon which figures he imitates, and which episodes and move-ments he disregards. So a new account of the history of philosophy is a challenge that cannot be ignored. This suggests that in so far as there is any sensible question of the form "Who is right, Heidegger or the others?" it is going to be a question about historiography.[11] Not that his-toriography is less controversial than, say, epistemology or philosophy of language. Rather, the adoption of a vocabulary—one's semi-conscious de-cision about which questions one is content to dissolve or ignore and which one must set oneself to answer—is motivated almost entirely by a perception of one's relation to the history of philosophy. This may be a perception of one's place in a progressive sequence of discoveries (as in the sciences), or of the new-found needs and hopes of one's society, or simply of the relevance of certain figures in the history of philosophy to one's private needs and hopes. If we have Dewey's picture of what has happened in the intellectual history of the West, we shall have a certain quite specific account of Heidegger's role in this history; he will appear as a final decadent echo of Platonic and Christian otherworldliness. If we have Heidegger's perception, conversely, we shall have a quite specific picture of Dewey; he will appear as an exceptionally naive and provincial nihilist.

In what follows, I propose to offer sketches of Dewey as he would pre-sumably look to Heidegger and of Heidegger as he would presumably look to Dewey. This exercise will show how an extraordinary amount of agreement on the need for a "destruction of the history of Western on-tology" can be combined with an utterly different notion of what might succeed "ontology." It will, I hope, give us some ground on which to stand when trying to "place" Heidegger, by giving us a sense of how much room is left for maneuver even after one comes to see the philo-sophical tradition as having exhausted its potentialities. The frequent charges of arrogance brought against Heidegger result, in part, from the fact that he mentions few other "thinkers" of the day; he leaves one with the impression that if there are other mountain tops, they are now in-habited only by poets. Yet the vision of a culture in which philosophy was not a profession, nor art a business,[12] and in which technology was something other than "a dreary frenzy," [13] is hardly Heidegger's discov-ery. It is what Dewey offered us throughout his later life. Dewey can join Heidegger in saying that "Metaphysics—idealist, materialist, or Chris-tian—is prevented by its very *nature* from ever catching up with Europe's

11. To be sure, Heidegger warns us against taking him to offer just a new version of intellectual history—as he warns us against taking him to be doing anything that anybody else has ever done. See *EP*, p. 77 (*N*, II, pp. 483–84).
12. See *OWL*, p. 43 (*US*, p. 139).
13. See *IM*, p. 37 (*EM*, p. 28).

destiny, no matter what strained efforts metaphysics makes to unfold itself." [14] But for Dewey, Heidegger's succeeding gloss on "catching up" ("thinking in a way which reaches and gathers together what now, in a fulfilled sense of Being, is") would seem, like all his talk of Being, just one more Christian metaphysics in disguise. Dewey's *Experience and Nature*, in turn, can easily be taken as just one more variant on materialist metaphysics: a bland restatement of the triumph of nihilism.

To guard against such superficial reciprocal dismissals, let me consider some obvious points of agreement between the two men. I shall cite their parallel views on four topics: (a) the distinction, in ancient philosophy, between contemplation and action; (b) the traditional Cartesian problems that center around epistemological scepticism; (c) the distinction between philosophy and science; (d) the distinction between both and "the aesthetic."

Dewey begins a discussion of the distinction between theory and practice with a distinction between the "holy" and the "lucky." [15] He thinks of religion, and its heir philosophy, as attending to the former. Workmanship, and its heir technology, look to the latter. Because philosophy "inherited the realm with which religion had been concerned" [16] it naturally adopted "the notion, which has ruled philosophy ever since the time of the Greeks, that the office of knowledge is to uncover the antecedently real." [17] Given the further inheritance from religion of the premise that "only the completely fixed and unchanging can be real," it is natural that "the quest for certitude has determined our basic metaphysics." [18] "Metaphysics is a substitute for custom as the source and guarantor of higher moral and social values" [19] and will remain so until we recognize that "the distinctive office, problems and subject-matter of philosophy grow out of stresses and strains in the community life in which a given form of phi-

14. *BH, WM,* pp. 171–72; *LH,* p. 288. Heidegger distinguishes Europe's destiny from Russia's or America's, regions of the earth which have presumably passed beyond recall (as of 1936). See *IM,* p. 45 (*EM,* p. 34): "Europe lies in a pincers between Russia and America which are, metaphysically speaking, the same." The vulgarity of the remark should not lead one to underestimate its importance. Heidegger's intense political consciousness, which led him to make the speeches reprinted by Schneeberger in *Nachlese zu Heidegger* (Bern, 1961), needs to be recognized when trying to see what he thinks "Thought" might do, just as Dewey's must be remembered in understanding why he urged "reconstruction in philosophy."

15. See Dewey's *The Quest for Certainty* (*QC*) (New York, 1960), p. 11. Other books by Dewey whose titles I shall abbreviate are *Reconstruction in Philosophy* (*RP*) (New York, 1958); *Art as Experience* (*AE*) (New York, 1958); *Experience and Nature* (*EN*) (New York, 1958).

16. *QC,* p. 14; cf. Heidegger, *IM,* p. 106 (*EM,* p. 80): "Nietzsche was right in saying that Christianity was Platonism for the people"; see also *EP,* p. 24 (*N,* II, p. 427).

17. *QC,* p. 17.

18. *QC,* pp. 21–22.

19. *RP,* p. 17.

losophy arises" [20] and until philosophy as criticism of morals and institutions takes the place of "the whole brood and nest of dualisms which have . . . formed the 'problems' of philosophy termed 'modern.' " [21] The little dualisms of subject-object, mind-matter, experience-nature are seen by Dewey as dialectical diminutions of the great dualism between the holy and the lucky—the enduring and the day-to-day. Should we overcome all these dualisms, then philosophy might be, "instead of impossible attempts to transcend experience . . . the significant record of the efforts of men to formulate the things of experience to which they are most deeply and passionately attached." [22]

For Heidegger the confusion of Being with what endures unchangingly, can be known with certainty, and can be treated mathematically, was also the crucial first step in making philosophy what it is today. Because Greek philosophers preferred nouns to verbs,[23] and verbal substantives to infinitives [24] when they spoke of Being—because Plato left behind Heraclitus' union of πόλεμος and λόγος and coalesced φύσις with ἰδέα—we were put upon the path of ontology.

> Where struggle ceases, beings do not vanish, but the world turns away. Beings are no longer asserted (i.e., preserved as such). Now they are merely found ready-made, are data. . . . The being becomes an object, either to be beheld (view, image) or to be acted upon (product and calculation). The original world-making power, φύσις, degenerates into a prototype to be copied and imitated. Nature becomes a special field, differentiated from art and everything that can be fashioned according to plan.[25]

Here Heidegger sees the distinction between action and contemplation not as Dewey does, as reflecting the gap between the slave and the free-man,[26] but rather as arising out of an initial diremption of an original united consciousness—a diremption that is presumably to be viewed as a fatality, one of the words of Being, rather than explained causally as a product of some natural environment or social arrangement. But Dewey and Heidegger agree that this initial adoption of a spectatorial notion of knowledge and its object has determined the subsequent history of philosophy. Heidegger's claim, in *Being and Time*, that the neglect of *Zuhandensein* lies behind the Cartesian problem of the existence of the external

20. *RP*, p. v.
21. *RP*, p. xxxi.
22. *RP*, p. 25.
23. See *EP*, pp. 55–56 (*N*, II, pp. 458–59). See also Werner Marx, *Heidegger and the Tradition* (Evanston, 1971), p. 126.
24. See *IM*, p. 69 (*EM*, pp. 52–53) and compare pp. 57ff. (*EM*, pp. 43ff.).
25. *IM*, pp. 62–63 (*EM*, p. 48). I have substituted "beings" for Manheim's translation of *seienden* by "essents."
26. See *RP*, p. ix.

world [27] parallels Dewey's reiterated claim that "the brood and nest of dualisms" that appeared in the seventeenth century was due to the initial split between the enduring object of contemplation and the malleable objects of the artisan.[28] For both Dewey and Heidegger, the notion of the object as something to be viewed and represented led to subjectivism:

> When objects are isolated from the experience through which they are reached and in which they function, experience itself becomes reduced to the mere process of experiencing, and experiencing is therefore treated as if it were also complete in itself. . . . Since the seventeenth century this conception of experience as the equivalent of subjective private experience set over against nature, which consists wholly of physical objects, has wrought havoc in philosophy.[29]

Dewey's description fits in nicely with Heidegger's account of the sequence which leads from Plato through Descartes to Kant, e.g.:

> Subiectity says finally: beings are *subiectum* in the sense of the $\dot{v}\pi o\kappa\epsilon i\mu\epsilon\nu o\nu$ which has the distinction of being $\pi\rho\dot{\omega}\tau\eta$ $o\dot{v}\sigma i\alpha$ in the presencing of what is actual. In its history as metaphysics, Being is through and through subiectity. But where subiectity becomes subjectivity, the *subiectum* preeminent since Descartes, the ego, has a multiple precedence.[30]

Dewey sees the epistemological problems of modern philosophy as the adjustment of old metaphysical assumptions to new conditions. Heidegger sees them as the internal dialectical working-out of those assumptions. Heidegger comments scornfully on the notion that the modern age "discovered" that epistemology was the true foundation of philosophy [31] and on the easy retreat to the question "subjective or objective?" that characterizes thought during this period.[32] Dewey sees the quest for certainty and fixity that the ancients satisfied by nonnatural objects of knowledge as, in the modern period, transferred to show that "the conditions of the

---

27. See *BT*, sec. 15–21, especially the introduction of the notion of *Zuhandenheit* at pp. 98–99 (*SZ*, p. 69), and the claim at p. 130 (*SZ*, p. 97): "Thus Descartes' discussion of possible kinds of *access* to entities within the world is dominated by an idea of Being which has been gathered from a definite realm of these entities themselves." The latter realm is that of *Vorhandensein*. For the connection between the latter notion and Platonic and Aristotelian notions of ιδέα, ἐνέργεια, and οὐσία see Werner Marx, *Heidegger and the Tradition.*, part II, chap. 1.

28. See *QC*, p. 22, on the common assumption of idealism and realism that "the operation of inquiry excludes any element of practical activity that enters into the construction of the object known."

29. *EN*, p. 11.

30. *EP*, p. 47 (*N*, II, p. 451).

31. See the discussion of the dominance of "epistemology" in the modern era at *EP*, p. 88 (*VA*, p. 67).

32. See *What is a Thing?*, trans. W. D. Barton and Vera Deutsch (Chicago, 1967), p. 27 (*Die Frage nach dem Ding* [Tübingen, 1962], p. 20).

possibility of knowledge" are "of an ideal and rational character." [33] He thinks of the distinction between objective facts and subjective emotions, problems, and doubts as another "product of the habit of isolating man and experience from nature," [34] and remarks that modern science has joined with traditional theology in perpetuating this isolation. Dewey thereby echoes Heidegger's insistence on the underlying identity of the stance towards Being found in Aquinas's notion of an *ens a se* and modern epistemologists' notions of "objectivity." [35] Both men say things that reduce to despair the eager and sincere epistemologist, anxious to classify them as idealists or realists, subjectivists or objectivists. Consider Heidegger's exasperating remark, "Evidently truth's independence *from* man is nonetheless manifestly a relation *to* human nature." [36] Consider also Dewey's coy refusal to treat meaning and truth as relations between something "experiential" and something "in nature." [37]

When they discuss the relation between philosophy and science, both men see Cartesian, Husserlian, and positivistic attempts to "make philosophy scientific" as a disastrous abandonment of philosophy's proper function. Dewey says that "philosophy has assumed for its function a knowledge of reality. This fact makes it a rival instead of a complement of the sciences." He proceeds to endorse James's description of philosophy as "vision." [38] Heidegger's remark that philosophy's attempt to "elevate itself to the rank of a 'science' " abandons the essence of Thought has already been cited. Both see philosophy, at its best, as clearing away what impedes our delight, not as the discovery of a correct representation of reality. Both men insist on the goal of philosophy as the reattainment of innocence and the divestiture of the culture of our time.[39] Both stress the

33. *QC*, p. 41; cf. *RP*, pp. 49–51.
34. *QC*, p. 233.
35. See, e.g., *On Time and Being*, p. 7, and the discussion at *EP*, p. 22 (*N*, II, p. 424) of the relation between Christianity, truth-as-certainty, and "the modern period."
36. *Discourse on Thinking*, trans. John Anderson and Hans Freund (New York, 1966), p. 84 (*Gelassenheit* [Pfullingen, 1959], p. 66).
37. See, e.g., *EN*, pp. 321ff., and *RP*, pp. 156ff.
38. *QC*, p. 309. There is, also, another side of Dewey in which philosophy is not vision but something much more specific—a criticism of society following "the method of science" in the hope of bringing morals and institutions into line with the spirit of science and technology. See *RP*, p. xxiii. I think that Dewey was at his best when he emphasized the similarities between philosophy and poetry, rather than when he emphasized those between philosophy and engineering, but I cannot debate the matter in this paper.
39. See *EN*, pp. 37–38: "An empirical philosophy is in any case a kind of intellectual disrobing. . . . If the chapters that follow contribute to an artful innocence and simplicity they will have served their purpose." Like Heidegger he thinks, however, that "a cultivated naivete . . . can be acquired only through the discipline of severe thought." See J. Glenn Gray's essay "The Splendor of the Simple" in his *On Understanding Violence Philosophically, and Other Essays* (New York, 1970), esp. pp. 50ff.

ties between philosophy and poetry. For Dewey, when "philosophy shall have co-operated with the course of events and made clear and coherent the meaning of the daily detail, science and emotion will interpenetrate, practice and imagination will embrace. Poetry and religious feeling will be the unforced flowers of life." [40] He hopes that philosophy will join with poetry as Arnold's "criticism of life." [41] For Heidegger, "only poetry stands in the same order as philosophy"—because only in these two are beings not related to other beings, but to Being.[42]

On the other hand, both abhor the notion that poetry is supposed to offer us "values" as opposed to something else—"fact"—which we are to find in science. Both regard the fact-value distinction as springing from, and as dangerous as, the subject-object distinction. Heidegger thinks that the whole notion of "values" is an awkward attempt by the metaphysician to supply an additional *Vorhanden* in order to make good the deficiency left by thinking of Being as ἰδέα or as *Vorstellung*—an afterthought "necessary to round out the ontology of the world." [43] Heidegger thinks that the very notion of a "subject" called "aesthetics" is one more disastrous result of our distinctions between the sensuous and the supersensuous, the subject and the object, and the other distinctions that flow from Plato's original treatment of φύσις and ἰδέα.[44] Dewey would entirely agree, as he would with every attempt to keep either the "aesthetic" or the "religious" apart from the "scientific" or "empirical," and he would trace the notion of "objective value" and "purely aesthetic judgment" to the same historical roots as does Heidegger. Both of them see both poetry and philosophy

40. *RP*, pp. 212–13.
41. *EN*, p. 204.
42. See *IM*, p. 26 (*EM*, p. 20).
43. *BT*, p. 133 (*SZ*, p. 100); see also p. 132, and sec. 59. At *IM*, pp. 47–48 (*EM*, p. 36), Heidegger says that when "the spirit is degraded into intelligence, into a tool," then "the energies of the spiritual process, poetry and art, statesmanship and religion, become subject to *conscious* cultivation and planning. They are split into branches. . . . These branches become fields of free endeavor, which sets its own standards and barely manages to live up to them. These standards of production and consumption are called values. The cultural values preserve their meaning only by restricting themselves to an autonomous field; poetry for the sake of poetry, art for the sake of art, science for the sake of science." Compare Dewey's polemics in *AE* against the notion of "fine art" (chap. 1) and against Kant's isolation of the aesthetic from both experience and knowledge (pp. 252ff.), as well as his ubiquitous attempts to break down every dualism of disciplines or of faculties (art-science, reason-imagination, etc.). In moral philosophy one should compare Dewey's insistence that values are made by practice, rather than found and contemplated, with Heidegger's reply to Beufret on the relation between ontology and ethics (*WM*, pp. 183ff.). Heidegger's protest in the latter passage against the traditional ethics-logic-physics distinction should be compared with Dewey's insistence (e.g., *RP*, chap. 7) that there is no such thing as "moral philosophy" which seeks out "universal values" or "moral laws." Dewey would heartily agree with Heidegger's remark (*WM*, p. 184) that Sophocles' tragedies "hold more of ἦθος" than Aristotle's *Ethics*.
44. See *OWL*, p. 43, with pp. 14ff. (*US*, pp. 140–141, with pp. 101ff.).

as taking place where the distinction between contemplation and action does not arise, and as diminished and made pointless when this distinction is drawn.[45]

Citing all these similarities between Dewey and Heidegger may seem a *tour de force*. It is the differences that are interesting. But I think that it is important to note the similarities first. Doing so shows how both men are trying to encapsulate the whole sequence that runs from Plato and Aristotle to Nietzsche and Carnap, set it aside, and offer something new— or at least a hope of something new. Further, they are almost alone in this century in doing so. They are unique, unclassifiable, original philosophers, and both are historicist to the core. Both have been misleadingly assimilated to nonhistoricist philosophical schools. To call Dewey a pragmatist and lump him with Peirce, James, and Quine is to forget that he was swept off his feet, and into a new intellectual world, by Hegel's and Comte's visions of our past.[46] To call Heidegger a phenomenologist and lump him with Husserl, or an existentialist and lump him with (the early) Sartre, is, as Heidegger himself has pointed out, to ignore precisely the historical perspective which he prides himself on sharing with Marx, and which both derived from Hegel.[47] Both men see what Heidegger calls "the unified history of Being, beginning with the essential character of Being as ἰδέα up to the completion of the modern essence of Being as the will to power"[48] as a single, long-drawn-out event. Heidegger sees Nietzsche as where we must end if, with Plato, we take Being as presence or as representation.[49] Deweyans are inclined to see Nietzsche as an over-reaction to the realization that we shall never fulfill Plato's demand for certainty and "rationality" in morals. The realization that we shall never achieve such certainty makes us alternate between despair at there being nothing but power in the world, and intoxication at our own possession of power. No other philosophers of this century, save perhaps Wittgenstein, have so distanced themselves from the assumptions and the problems common to Plato and Nietzsche.

If Hegel is their common ground, however, their notions of what to do with Hegel are the beginnings of their differences. Dewey, like Marx,

45. See *LH*, p. 300 (*WM*, p. 191) on Thought and the theory-practice distinction, and also *IM*, p. 26 (*EM*, p. 20) on poetry. Compare Dewey, *AE*, p. 40: "The enemies of the aesthetic are neither the practical nor the intellectual. They are humdrum; slackness of loose ends; submission to convention in practice and intellectual procedure."

46. See Dewey's autobiographical "From Absolutism to Experimentalism" (1930), reprinted in *On Experience, Nature and Freedom*, ed. R. J. Bernstein (Indianapolis, 1960), pp. 3–18, esp. pp. 10–11.

47. See n. 3 above. For a good discussion of Heidegger's historicism and his relation to Hegel, see Stanley Rosen, *Nihilism* (New Haven and London, 1969), chaps. 3–4.

48. *EP*, p. 48 (*N*, II, pp. 452–53).

49. See "Plato's Doctrine of Truth" (*WM*, pp. 139ff.).

wants Hegel without the Absolute Spirit. He wants man and history to stand on their own feet, and man's history to be just that, neither Spirit's self-realization nor the fateful elephantine movements of Matter or of social classes. He does not think of "history" with a capital letter, and he is quite content, as Heidegger is not, to let his remarks on past philosophers be "one-sided and sporadic conceptual historiography." When he tells us about the consequences of the Greek separation of contemplation and action he does not think he is recollecting the words of Being—but rather, in Wittgenstein's phrase, "assembling reminders for a particular purpose." He thinks that German idealism was at bottom, and despite its achievements, a last desperate gesture in the direction of the old Platonic project of offering an ontological guarantee for the preconceptions of a leisure class.[50]

Heidegger, on the other hand, tells us that the so-called "collapse of German idealism" was not the fault of idealism but of "the age," which "was no longer strong enough to stand up to the greatness, breadth and originality of that spiritual world." [51] One of Heidegger's strongest feelings, and one that places him very far from Dewey indeed, is that ages, cultures, nations, and people are supposed to live up to the demands of philosophers, rather than the other way around. It is not Athens, Rome, Renaissance Florence, the Paris of the Revolution, and the Germany of Hitler that form the history of Being. Nor is it Sophocles, Horace, Dante, Goethe, Proust, and Nabokov. It is the sequence from Plato to Nietzsche. Not only is Thought always Thought of Being, but Thought is the *only* thing that is *of* Being in this sense (in both the subjective and objective genitive, as Heidegger says).[52] Only poetry is of the same order, but there is no indication that Heidegger thinks that poetry has a history. Less crudely put, there is no indication that Heidegger thinks that the historicity of Being can be seen in poetry, any more than it can be seen where Macauley and Acton tended to see it—in a gradually widening access to literacy, voting booths, and nourishing foodstuffs.

All this emphasis on *philosophers* would look, to Dewey, like academic parochialism. Who but a philosophy professor, after all, would think that the drama of twentieth-century Europe had some essential relation to the "*Vollendung der Metaphysik*"? Consider the following passage, in which Heidegger wants to explain why the "inherently historical asking of the question about being is actually an integral part of history on earth":

> We have said that the world is darkening. The essential episodes of this darkening are: the flight of the gods, the destruction of the earth, the standardization of man, the preeminence of the mediocre.

50. See *RP*, pp. 49–51.
51. *IM*, p. 45 (*EM*, p. 34).
52. *WM*, pp. 147–48.

What do we mean by world when we speak of a darkening of the world? World is always world of the *spirit*. The animal has no world nor any environment [Umwelt]. Darkening of the world means emasculation of the spirit, the disintegration, wasting away, repression, and misinterpretation of the spirit. . . . What makes the situation of Europe all the more catastrophic is that this enfeeblement of the spirit originated in Europe itself and—though prepared by earlier factors—was definitively determined by its own spiritual situation in the first half of the nineteenth century.[53]

That spiritual situation was, of all things, the inability of the age to live up to the "greatness, breadth and originality" of German idealism. One might think that the destruction of the earth and the standardization of man were bad enough—that the strip mines of Montana, the assembly lines of Detroit, and the Red Guards of Shanghai were enough to show the world was darkening, without bringing in the world of the spirit at all. But this would be to treat "forgetfulness of being" [54] as just a handy label for whatever it is that has been going wrong lately. Heidegger takes it much more seriously. He is not saying, like Tillich, that it is getting hard to find a good symbol of our ultimate concern. He is saying, like Kierkegaard, that symbol-hunting is sin.

This way of putting things may suggest that I am, like a good modern, neglecting the "ontological difference" between Being and beings. But in such passages as the one I just cited, Heidegger neglects it too—and it is well for him that he does. If he did not, he would no longer have anything to differentiate his talk of Being from Kierkegaard's talk of God and of Grace. Unless Heidegger connected the history of Being with that of men and nations through such phrases as "a nation's (*eines Volkes*) relation to Being," [55] and thus connected the history of philosophy with just plain history, he would be able to say only what Kierkegaard said: that when all the advances of modern civilization are utilized, all the dog tricks of the Hegelian dialectic practiced and perfected, and all the aspects of life and culture related by all the concepts one could imagine ever being evolved, we shall still be as far as ever from that which is "*strenger als das Begriffliche.*" Without the reference to the history of nations, we should obviously have only what Versényi suggests is all we get anyway: "an all too empty and formal, though often emotionally charged and mystically-religious, thinking of absolute unity." [56] With this reference, we at least seem to have an analogue of an eschatological and Augustinian sort of Christianity, rather than an analogue of Kierkegaard's private and Protestant hope that Grace may make him a New Being, able to believe the self-contradictory doctrine of the Incarnation.

53. *IM*, p. 45 (*EM*, p. 34).
54. See *IM*, p. 19, with p. 50 (*EM*, p. 15, with p. 38).
55. *IM*, p. 51 (*EM*, p. 39). See also *EP*, p. 103 (*VA*, p. 84).
56. Laszlo Versényi, *Heidegger, Being, and Truth* (New Haven and London, 1965), pp. 167–68.

I can sum up this quasi-Deweyan view of Heidegger as follows. All we are told about Being, Thought, and the ontological difference is by negation. To grasp what these are is to grasp that they have nothing to do with metaphysics. Metaphysics encompasses any conceptual thought, any causal thought, any thought of ourselves as one among a plurality of causally related beings, which is not scientific or technological thinking about a concrete issue. Metaphysics can only be explained by showing its history, by showing how people have thought to speak Being and wound up speaking of beings. So far Dewey and Heidegger can agree. Dewey thinks that the moral of the story is that metaphysics, having exhausted its potentialities, leaves us with nothing except an increased appreciation for our concrete problems—for beings. But Heidegger thinks that the historical picture sketched above offers a glimpse of something else. Yet nothing further can be said about this something else, and so the negative way to Being, through the destruction of ontology, leaves us facing beings-without-Being, with no hint about what Thought might be of. The vacant place that remains when all metaphysical thinking has been destroyed is all that we have. So whether the history of philosophy is viewed as Dewey views it (as a working out of various causal processes in an intellectual "superstructure") or as Heidegger views it (as the words of Being) does not seem to matter. For the vacant place remains for both. For Dewey, it is to be filled in with concrete attention to beings—to the strip mines, for example. For Heidegger, it is a clearing for Being. What is there to disagree about here? Once the history of philosophy is seen in the way in which Dewey and Heidegger agree on seeing it, what can be said about what remains? For Dewey, to go on talking about "Thought" is to insist that the end of metaphysics should not be the end of philosophy—without saying why it should not. For Heidegger, to say that philosophy has become obsolete is to succumb to a vulgarized version of the Nietzschean Being-as-will-to-power. It may be that any concrete phenomenona—a poem, a revolution, a person—can be viewed as just that, or as an opening for Being. Perhaps how one views it is a matter of which philosophers one has been reading lately, and of which jargon one fancies.

To take this aestheticist, relativist, quasi-Tillichian attitude is to align oneself with Dewey and against Heidegger. It is, as will by now have become obvious, the attitude and the alignment I prefer. But, before adopting it, I want to try to look at the matter through Heidegger's eyes once again. It is important, I think, to see that for Heidegger Dewey's ultimate sin is not his emphasis on the practical but precisely the adoption of the aesthetic attitude.[57] Heidegger sees the outcome of a technological age as "the world as View," and the aesthetic attitude toward philosophical sys-

57. See Versényi, pp. 72ff., on Heidegger's discussion of Nietzsche's inversion of Plato's ranking of art and mathematics.

tems that Dewey shares with Santayana as the ultimate expression of this attitude. "The basic process of modern times is the conquest of the world as picture." [58] When Dewey praises our modern manner of seeing nature as something to be used rather than contemplated he is simply falling in with modern technology's insistence on seeing "the earth's crust as a coal mine, the soil as a source of minerals." [59] This is just being realistic, and not, even on Heidegger's account, an occasion for criticism. It is when Dewey proceeds to view *philosophies*—the thought of Plato, of Thomas, of Hegel—in the same way as an engineer views ore-bearing regions of the earth that Heidegger would recoil. To treat the thought of Hegel as a *Weltanschauung* is to view him as an object of exploitation rather than a possible occasion of revelation. It is to treat philosophies as if they were means to the enhancement of human life.[60] Dewey's humanism is, for Heidegger, simply the modern consciousness incarnate, against which there is no point in protesting—except perhaps when the very possibility of Thought is denied, as it is when those philosophers who exemplify Thought are treated as mere means for the mutual adjustment of beings to beings. Heidegger's sense of the vulgarity of the age—its trivialization of everything holy—is strongest when what is trivialized is the history of metaphysics. For this history is the history of Being, and to make that history into a useful lesson for modern man is to make Being itself an instrument for our employment and an object of exploitation. To treat "the world as a view and man as a *subiectum*" [61] is simply to be in tune with the times, but to treat the great philosophers as stepping stones, or to choose among them as we choose our favorite pictures, is to make a mockery of Being itself. For Heidegger, Dewey's sketches of the history of philosophy are, at best, pathetic examples of the futility of attempting to overcome metaphysics by using the vocabulary of metaphysics (e.g., "experience" and "nature").[62] Heidegger sees even his own early attempt at overcoming—his redescription of *Dasein* in order to prepare the way for a reopening of the question of Being—as self-defeating.[63] Sometimes

58. "Die Zeit des Weltbildes" (*HW*, p. 87). A translation of this essay by Marjorie Grene appears in the Heidegger issue of *Boundary 2* (1976).

59. *VA*, p. 14.

60. "Die Zeit des Weltbildes" (*HW*, pp. 85–86).

61. *Ibid.* (*HW*, p. 85).

62. See *The Question of Being*, trans. William Kluback and Jean T. Wilde (London, 1956; original text of *Zur Seinsfrage* facing), p. 71: "What if even the language of metaphysics and metaphysics itself, whether it be of the living or of the dead God, as metaphysics, forced that barrier which forbids a crossing over of the line, that is, the overcoming of nihilism?" On the futility of Dewey's "metaphysics," see the exchange between Santayana and Dewey in *The Philosophy of John Dewey*, ed. Paul Schilpp (Evanston, Ill., 1939). I have tried to develop Santayana's point in "Dewey's Metaphysics" forthcoming in *New Studies in the Philosophy of John Dewey*, ed. S. Cahn (Universities of New England Press).

63. Some commentators on *SZ* have noted the similarities between Heidegger's non-Cartesian redescriptions of man and Ryle's. See, for example, Richard Schmitt,

he suggests that *any* overcoming of metaphysics, indeed any *mention* of the history of metaphysics, may be equally self-defeating: "A regard for metaphysics still prevails even in the intention to overcome metaphysics. Therefore, our task is to cease all overcoming, and leave metaphysics to itself." [64]

Still, Heidegger insists that in *Being and Time* he at least had the question of Being in mind when he offered us *Existentiale* in place of the "categories" of the tradition, and he still thinks that something of the sort is a necessary first step.[65] Dewey, despite the fact that he too wants to offer us a new jargon to replace the notions of "subject" and "substance" which are common to Aristotle and Descartes, will appear to Heidegger as self-deceptive and self-defeating. If one reads Dewey through Heidegger's eyes, one sees his thought as so thoroughly infected by these traditional conceptions that he has no notion of Thought as an alternative to metaphysics. Thus Dewey forgets his own Peircian subordination of truth to beauty, sees "science" as somehow replacing philosophy, or philosophy as becoming somehow "scientific." Dewey's version of the history of philosophy is designed to purify our self-image of all the remnants of the previous epochs in the history of metaphysics—all reminders of an age before technology had become supreme. He is thus a good illustration of the latest and most degenerate stage of "humanistic" philosophy, the stage which Heidegger describes as follows:

> Philosophy in the age of completed metaphysics is anthropology. Whether or not one says "philosophical" anthropology makes no difference. In the meantime philosophy has become anthropology and in this way a prey to the derivatives of metaphysics, that is, of physics in the broadest sense, which includes the physics of life and man, biology and psychology. Having become anthropology, philosophy itself perishes of metaphysics.[66]

So much for Dewey's view of Heidegger and Heidegger's view of Dewey. It would be pleasant to conclude with an impartially sympathetic synthesis. But I have no broader perspective to offer. The two men seem to me, together with Wittgenstein, the richest and most original philosophers of

Martin Heidegger on Being Human (New York, 1969), and Michael Murray, "Heidegger and Ryle: Two Versions of Phenomenology," this volume, pp. 271–90.

64. *Of Time and Being*, p. 24 (*Zur Sache des Denkens*, p. 25).

65. "Only by way of what Heidegger I has thought does one gain access to what-is-to-be-thought by Heidegger II. But the thought of Heidegger I becomes possible only if it is contained in Heidegger II." (*BR*, p. xxii).

66. *EP*, p. 99 (*VA*, pp. 78–79). Cf. *HW*, pp. 103–04 for Heidegger's dismissal of pragmatism: "Americanism is itself something European. It is an as yet uncomprehended variety of the gigantic, and the gigantic is itself still unconfined, not capable of being understood as the product of the full and complete metaphysical essence of modernity. The American interpretation of Americanism as pragmatism is still outside of metaphysics."

our time, and I have no notions about how to transcend them. The best I can do is sharpen the conflict by recurring to the questions about "the end of philosophy" with which I began and, in that context, restating Dewey's case.

I think that even if the differences in the way the two men tell the story of our tradition were somehow ironed out, there would remain this impasse: Dewey wants the tradition overcome by blurring all the distinctions it has drawn, whereas Heidegger hopes Being will overcome it for us by granting us a sense of the ontological difference. In particular, Dewey wants the distinctions between art, science, and philosophy to be rubbed out, and replaced with the vague and uncontroversial notion of intelligence trying to solve problems and provide meaning. Heidegger is equally contemptuous of the traditional distinctions, save one: he does not want *philosophy* to be lost in this shuffle, and would view Dewey's attempt to mislay it as resulting from the assumption that Thought is coextensive with ontology. One way of bringing the difference to a point is to say that Dewey thinks of philosophy, as a discipline or even as a distinct human activity, as obsolete. Heidegger, on the other hand, thinks of philosophy—of Thought as opposed to ontology—as something that might be recaptured, even though the form it might take is, in our darkened world, still invisible.

Is there anything which Dewey should oppose in such a faint, modest, and inarticulate hope? Yes, there is indeed. Heidegger's hope is just what was worst in the tradition—the quest for the holy that turns us away from the relations between beings and beings (the relations, for example, between the ghastly apparatus of modern technology and the people whose children will die of hunger unless that apparatus spreads over the rest of the planet).[67] *Tout commence en mystique et finit en politique.*[68] The politics one can imagine stemming from Heidegger's notion of technology's relation to man are more awful than the apparatus of technology itself, and for neither Dewey nor Heidegger is there a way to separate that sort of relation to politics from "philosophical truth." Heidegger's attachment to the notion of "philosophy"—the pathetic notion that even after metaphysics goes, something called "Thought" might remain—is simply the sign of Heidegger's own fatal attachment to the tradition: the last infirmity of the greatest of the German professors. It amounts to saying that even though everybody who has previously counted as a paradigm of philosophy—Plato, Thomas, Descartes, Nietzsche—turned out to be a step on a path toward chaos, we must still try to be philosophers. For "philosophy" is a name for that activity which is essential to our hu-

67. See J. Glenn Gray, "The Splendor of the Simple," pp. 65–66.
68. Charles Péguy, *Basic Verities: Prose and Poetry* (French with facing translation by A. and J. Green, New York, 1943), p. 108.

manity. No matter how much Heidegger seems to have overcome our professional urge to compete with the great dead philosophers on their own ground, no matter how much he may try to distance himself from the tradition (not to mention his fellow professors), he is still insistent that the tradition offered us "words of Being." He still thinks that the place where philosophy was is the place to be. He thinks that to cease thinking about what Plato and Kant were thinking about is to be diminished, to lose hold of what is most important, to sink into darkness. If he were true to his own dictum that we should "cease all overcoming, and leave metaphysics to itself," he would have nothing to say, nowhere to point. *The whole force of Heidegger's thought lies in his account of the history of philosophy.*

That vision demands that he place himself in a sequence that begins with the Greeks. But the only thing that links him with the tradition is his claim that the tradition, though persistently sidetracked onto beings, was really concerned with Being all the time—and, indeed, constituted the history of Being. This is like saying "*Every* previous notion of how to come unto Christ, starting with the Apostles and St. Paul and continuing on through Augustine and Luther to Tillich and Barth, has been a further step away from Him. But His Grace may still bring us to Him, if we can only overcome the tradition of theology, or even just leave it alone." Someone who said this would be trying to make an *ad hoc* distinction between "theology" and "Christianity" of the sort which Heidegger wants to make between "ontology" and "Thought."

But Heidegger wants to have it both ways, as did Kierkegaard in his day. Both need to invoke the tradition to identify what it is that has been wrongly approached, or has veiled itself. But both need to repudiate the tradition utterly in order to say what they want to say. When Kierkegaard reaches beyond Hegel and history for that which thought cannot think—the intersection of the temporal and the eternal—he has no business hinting that we should call it "Christ." Christ, after all, is what Christians think He is.[69] Being is what Nietzsche, as spokesman for the con-

---

69. As the comparison would suggest, I think that Versényi is on the right track in picking out the Kierkegaardian phrase "das ganz Andere" as a giveaway (*US*, p. 128; see Versényi, pp. 135ff. and p. 163). From a Deweyan point of view, what is wrong with Heidegger is not, as Versényi goes on to suggest, that he gives up "rational reflection," but that he insists on claiming that he is somehow in a position to do what rational reflection failed to do. In any sense in which mystic insight (or just plain insight, for that matter) does what philosophical argumentation traditionally tried to do, the common goal of both is something as vague as "lending meaning to life." What is objectionable about Heidegger is that such a vague and "humanist" goal is not enough for him. He wants Plato and Hegel and himself to be engaged in a common enterprise—speaking the words of Being—which is *not* just a fancy name for the common enterprise in which all of us, philosophers and plowmen, poets and ministers of state, are engaged.

cluding moment of the dialectic of the last two thousand years, said it was: a "vapor and a fallacy." [70] Heidegger says that *the* question" is "is 'being' a mere word and its meaning a vapor or is it the spiritual destiny of the Western world?" [71] But this suggested alternative is simply an attempt to renew our interest in Being by suggesting that our present troubles are somehow due to the Plato–Nietzsche tradition. All Heidegger can do to explain why that tradition is of more than parochial academic interest is to say that it was where the question of Being got asked. All he can do to explain why we shouldn't shrug off Being as a vapor and a fallacy is to say that our fate is somehow linked to that tradition.

To conclude: what Dewey and Heidegger both wanted was a way of seeing things that would take us as far beyond the world of historicist philosophizing that succeeded Hegel as Hegel had taken us beyond the epistemologically oriented philosophy of the eighteenth century. Dewey found what he wanted in turning away from philosophy as a distinctive activity altogether, and toward the ordinary world—the problems of men, freshly seen by discarding the distinctions that the philosophical tradition had developed. Heidegger hopes that a new path will open. But he thinks we shall only see it open if we detach ourselves from the problems of men and are still; in that silence we may perhaps hear the word of Being. Which of these attitudes one adopts depends on how devoted one is to the notion of "philosophy." Heidegger's weakness is that he cannot escape the notion that philosophers' difficulties are more than *just* philosophers' difficulties—the notion that if philosophy goes down, so will the West.

Heidegger should not be criticized for wanting something *"strenger als das begriffliche."* Few of us do not. If he is to be criticized, it is for helping keep us under the spell of Plato's notion that there is something special called "philosophy" that it is our duty to undertake. One may say of Heidegger what he himself says of Nietzsche: misled by a superficial understanding of the Platonic ideas, he tried to replace them, but instead only translated Platonism into a newer jargon.[72] By offering us "openness to Being" to replace "philosophical argument," Heidegger helps preserve all that was worst in the tradition he hoped to overcome.[73]

70. *IM*, p. 36 (*EM*, p. 27).

71. *IM*, p. 37 (*EM*, p. 28).

72. Cf. *N*, I, pp. 585–86, esp. the following: ". . . [Nietzsche's] theory fits so closely into the matrix of Plato's Theory of Ideas that it remains only a specially contrived inversion of that Theory, and thus is in *essence* identical with it." (I owe my knowledge of this passage to Versényi's discussion of it at p. 70 of *Heidegger, Being, and Truth*.) For the same point, see Bernt Magnus, *Heidegger's Metahistory of Philosophy* (The Hague, 1970), pp. 131–32.

73. I am grateful to Marjorie Grene, Walter Kaufmann, Joan Stambaugh, and Laszlo Versényi for helpful comment on a draft of this paper. I am also grateful to Frederick Olafson and Edward Lee, whose invitation to speak at a conference on Heidegger held at La Jolla in 1974 led me to write the paper in the first place.

15. Ross Mandel
Heidegger and Wittgenstein
A Second Kantian Revolution

LIKE KANT, Heidegger and Wittgenstein attempt to determine whether the relation between Knowing and Being is rendered more intelligible by seeing to what extent things conform to our language and mode of understanding. *Being and Time* and the *Philosophical Investigations* mark the crest of the second wave of Kant's Copernican Revolution. In their works Heidegger and Wittgenstein find themselves forced to reject the model of knowledge that has been most prominent throughout the history of philosophy.

Elements of this model emerge and develop in Plato, Aristotle, and the Scholastic philosophers, undergo modifications in Descartes and the Rationalists, and reappear most strongly in the early writings of Russell and Wittgenstein himself. The model states that to know a thing is somehow to possess the essence or Being of that thing. It makes the further demand that knowledge have a certain structure. It is rooted in some set of certain truths and branches into additional sets of truths by necessary connections. Often, but not necessarily, this structure is thought to reflect the ontological relations between elements in reality, with the more fundamental truths referring to the more fundamental features of reality, and dependent truths referring to dependent effects.

The best example of this model is found in Aristotle's writings. Aristotle defines knowing as having the form of the thing to be known in the mind. Form, of course, was the essence or Being of things for Aristotle, and in *De Anima* he proposes that it is the special nature of the intellectual soul, as found in man, that it can take on the form of the thing without its matter, this very operation being what he calls knowing. The structure of knowledge is found in the *Posterior Analytics*, where Aristotle states that scientific knowledge moves from premises that are true, certain, and necessary to conclusions that also possess these properties via proper syllogisms. Another example is Spinoza's *Ethics*, which moves from substance, the foundation of knowledge and the most fundamental stratum of reality, to its various modes and their properties geometrically. The logical order mirrors the ontological order. An example from modern times is the whole project of logical empiricism, especially as formulated in Carnap's *Aufbau* and *Logische Syntax*. Carnap adopts the attitude that the real is the sensible element, and taking this in addition as the foundation of knowledge, proceeds using the logical calculus of Russell to reconstruct mathematics and physics.

Heidegger and Wittgenstein turn their attention away from the products of knowing and toward the procedures of knowing. Their circle of concern encompasses such questions as how does someone come to see the world as an interaction of atomic particles? what status does an experiment have in justifying a particular theory? or how does the use of this theory transform our relations to things? Through these steps and procedures the world about us gets seen in determinate ways. The second Kantian revolution focuses on these ways in which steps and procedures determine our perspective on the world. They become the "rules of synthesis" by means of which a perspective is achieved. The foundations of knowledge become the activities of men that make knowledge possible. The logical structure of knowledge becomes those steps and procedures which make knowledge manifest. This is a shift in direction shared by many phenomenologists, ordinary language analysts, and pragmatists alike.

While Heidegger and Wittgenstein maintain similar attitudes about the foundation and structure of knowledge, they disagree on how to construe the relation of Knowing to Being. From the beginning Heidegger attempts to use this new approach to illuminate what it means for man to understand the essence of a thing. His greatest interest lies in understanding what it means for a thing to be. Wittgenstein seems to hold an attitude reminiscent of Keats's "negative capability," the capability of "being in uncertainties, mysteries, doubts, without any irritable reaching after fact and reason." [1] On the one hand, Wittgenstein says his aim is to dissolve philosophical doubts, uncertainties, and mysteries, which are merely misunderstandings of our forms of expression. On the other hand, his whole approach to language (and through language to knowledge) embodies a kind of scepticism, which just looks at the workings of language without sharing in its commitment. This is brought out by two major metaphors used in the *Investigations*.

1. John Keats in Russel Noyes, ed., *English Romantic Poetry and Prose* (New York, 1956), p. 1211.

To invent a language could mean to invent an instrument for a particular purpose on the basis of the laws of nature (or consistent with them); but it also has another sense, analogous to that in which we speak of the invention of a game.

Here, I am stating something about the word "language" by connecting it with the word "invent".[2]

The analogy of a game and the analogy of an instrument show how far Wittgenstein is from the traditional model of the relation between Knowing and Being. If language is viewed as an instrument, then knowledge becomes a tool to interact with nature, rather than to capture its essence. The game analogy implies that our expressions reflect a sense of detachment and freedom from commitments to the nature of things. "All the world's a stage, and all the men and women merely players."

Behind the *Tractatus* appears to stand the following reasoning: if logic is the essence of language and if language mirrors the essence of the world, then this logical structure must also be the essence of the world. In time Wittgenstein decided that flexible rules intimately connected with our other activities—our forms of life—were the structure and basis of language, and although he saw that these rules of usage—the grammar of expressions—determined how we experienced things, he refused to make the move from the nature of language to the nature of the world. Each form of life provides its own foundation for its own linguistic practices.

> Is it wrong for me to be guided in my actions by the propositions of physics? Am I to say I have no good ground for doing so? Isn't this precisely what I call good ground? Supposing we met people who did not regard that as a telling reason. Now how do we imagine this? Instead of a physicist they consult an oracle. (And for that we consider them primitive.) Is it wrong for me to consult an oracle and be guided by it? If we call it "wrong" aren't we using our language game as a basis to combat theirs? [3]

Wittgenstein himself did not pursue the ontological implications of his work very far. Those implications have appeared most clearly in works in the same vein as the *Investigations*, for example, Thomas Kuhn:

> One often hears that successive theories grow ever closer to, or approximate more and more closely to, the truth. Apparently generalizations like that refer not to puzzle-solutions and the concrete predictions derived from a theory but rather to its ontology, to the match, that is, between the entities with which the theory populates nature and what is "really there." . . . There is, I think, no theory-independent way to reconstruct phrases like

2. *Philosophical Investigations*, trans. G. E. M. Anscombe (New York, 1968), p. 137.
3. *On Certainty*, trans. Denis Paul and G. E. M. Anscombe (New York, 1972), p. 80.

"really there"; the notion of a match between the ontology of a theory and its "real" counterpart in nature now seems to me illusive in principle.[4]

The idea that our forms of expression refer to what is "really there" may seem illusive to Kuhn, yet these expressions possess a force which drives the user to see the world as inhabited by the entities the expressions seem to refer to. Toulmin, another writer influenced by the *Investigations*, makes the useful distinction that a scientist regards the world *as if* it were constructed out of the elements of his theory. He thinks that this does not commit the scientist to believing the world *is* constructed out of the elements of the theory.[5] This is true, in the sense that the practice of science continues oblivious to problems caused by the lack of ontological consensus. Yet, in fact, the majority of scientists do believe that the entities of their theories populate the world as it really is. This does not make the majority necessarily correct, but it shows that our expressions have an ontological force, and that philosophers are not the only ones who follow the direction of this force from language to the world, and that this is an ordinary part of using language. Wittgenstein does not simply leave ordinary language alone, but provides a new perspective, which observes the rules divorced from their ontological impetus.

Heidegger wants to preserve the perspective opened by the ontological force of our expressions and behavior. To explain just how our concepts and behavior can possess such force, it is necessary to provide a transcendental account. Such an explanation aims at demonstrating the possibility of our everyday conduct in terms of certain necessary, underlying structures. What Heidegger calls the "ontological" is in a certain sense the ordinary standpoint viewed in terms of the basic structures of Dasein. Dasein comprises the a priori structures necessary to explain how it is possible that man can apprehend the Being of things.

One fundamental element of Dasein is the understanding. The understanding constitutes things, others, and ourselves by allowing them to appear as what they are within the sphere of our awareness. This sphere of awareness Heidegger calls the world. The words "awareness" and "understanding" are not meant to be taken subjectively or psychologically. Just as Kant's threefold synthesis of the transcendental subject ordered and formed both the intuitions of things in space and time and the inner intuitions of the empirical subject, so also does the understanding of Dasein form the world, within which we find things, others, and ourselves. Dasein is this revealing, this opening up of the world. This is what Heidegger means by saying Dasein is its "disclosedness." The understanding discloses entities as a torch illuminating the night allows things to stand out from the darkness.

4. *The Structure of Scientific Revolutions* (Chicago, 1973), p. 206.
5. Stephen Toulmin, *The Philosophy of Science* (New York, 1953), pp. 163–67.

But Heidegger differs from Kant in an important respect. There is no thing-in-itself hidden from the light of understanding. Everything that in some way "is" lies within the sphere of Dasein's disclosedness. Outside this sphere there is "nothing." A discussion of the complex relations holding between Dasein and this "nothing" and their relevance for the question of the meaning of Being lies outside the scope of this paper. Let this suffice: Unlike Kant, Heidegger believes there are experiences (e.g., *Angst*) in which the ontological constitution of man as Dasein is laid bare. These experiences, in the interpretation he gives them, provide the ontical confirmation of his ontological theory. For the most part, we do not explicitly understand ourselves as Dasein, but interpret our actions, imaginings, and the like, in an everyday fashion.

The understanding determines *what* a thing is as well as *that* a thing is. To every mode of Dasein's revealing there corresponds a way in which a thing is revealed. Heidegger, for example, points out that it takes a special attitude to see things as sense data or pure sensuous intuition; seeing is always "seeing as" or "seeing that." In the pursuit of workday tasks things appear as tools, and in the pursuit of science things appear as particles or waves with special spatio-temporal properties. These different modes of understanding explain the different possibilities of experience, as if Kant had employed a different manner of synthesis for each different way a thing presents itself to us.

In addition to the difference between Heidegger and Wittgenstein in orientation, there are two major differences in points of departure. The first is that Wittgenstein's analysis focuses on language and behavior, while Heidegger develops the concept of understanding to cover all the ways we behave toward things, each other, and our own selves. Although relevant concepts are present in *Being and Time*, Heidegger does not dwell there on the theme of language. He includes discourse along with understanding and mood among the three fundamental aspects of Dasein's being. Discourse is communication, in which understanding is explicitly shared. He is unsure what status he should give to words, but the distinction between words and discourse as made in *Being and Time* appears similar to the distinction between sentences and statements. The concept of understanding, because it includes the revelation and synthesis of our behavior as well as the appearance of things, must serve as the key to Heidegger's position.

The second major difference results from the fact that most of the transcendental structures in *Being and Time* reside with the individual, while, according to Wittgenstein, the grammar of a language is necessarily a piece of public property. Each compensates, however, for his initial starting point. One of Heidegger's major interests is to interpret history as a shared understanding of a people, and Wittgenstein often points to the user's experience and behavior from the user's own point of view to explain the use of a word or procedure. The greatest differences are created by a topic like moods. Heidegger is primarily concerned with mood as an essential component of Dasein that "colors" the revealed in the revealing process. Wittgenstein is more concerned with what use must be ascribed to mood words if there are to be public criteria for correct usage. On a topic like this Heidegger and Wittgenstein seem to pass each other by, but their treatment of various issues otherwise shows similarity in attitude and concern.

One similarity is their insistence on preserving the intelligibility of ordinary life and their refusal to reduce the world as we normally experience it to something other than its own terms. Ships and sealing wax, cabbages and kings, all *are* as we ordinarily consider them. The attempt to preserve the integrity of the ways in which we ordinarily experience things applies to ourselves and others as well. There is no problem of "other minds" for either Heidegger or Wittgenstein, because we experience people as people. It takes a special effort to see a person as an automaton. When another person is in the room, we do not have to infer that he is a person, rather than a doll or a machine. Heidegger remarks that value is not something attached to some free-floating thing, but forms an integral part of a thing when we are involved with it. Wittgenstein parodies those who would analyze ordinary things into their "constitutive elements." (Is a broom in actuality a handle plus brush?) According to Heidegger, Dasein's understanding makes present the hammer as a hammer and the table as a table. This is what we see them "as" when we use them and it is this attitude toward them—just how they fit into our scheme of things—which determines what they are.

This brings up another point of agreement. Both Heidegger and Wittgenstein believe that the understanding of a particular act presupposes an understanding of a background or surroundings. In Heidegger's case the world as a whole forms a background for any particular involvement with things, while the forms of life serve the same purpose for Wittgenstein. Russell's (and in effect, the early Wittgenstein's) atomism was a reaction against Bradley's theory of relations, which implied that in order to know the truth of any one proposition you had to know the truth of all of them. Russell postulated that there must be a level of propositions whose truth could be determined by examining them alone. Both these approaches have difficulties, and Heidegger and Wittgenstein surmount them by examining the relation between instance and context. The surroundings are not assumed or unconsciously held premises. Understanding presupposes a background, but the background is of a different logical type than of the instance.

The insistence on the ordinary nature of things would only be an evasion of the question if both Heidegger and Wittgenstein did not maintain that all understanding must begin with the ordinary nature of things, and through derivative modification of this understanding arrive at those other modes of understanding. It is these derivative models which generate such difficulties for reflection, as the subject/object problem, the problem of other minds, the problem of Eddington's two tables, the mind/body problem. All take shape when we learn to see the world in another way, and then wonder how this new way is compatible with the old. Heidegger and Wittgenstein have instigated this great reversal: instead of explanations, theories, and models being used to replace the everyday sense of things, they maintain we should treat these models and explanations as emerging from the way we ordinarily experience the world and as referring back to that experience. Each asks how we use these pictures and models to illuminate our everyday sense of things.

A theory begins by seeing the familiar in other terms; the human body is seen as a machine, an object is seen as the synthesis of sense data, the meaning of a word is seen as a picture or an atmosphere. In order for salt to appear as a crystalline atomic structure, or for the earth to be seen as moving about the sun, men must change their perspective, perform certain actions, and imagine things in certain ways. It is through the establishment of a procedure and a language that the world appears in a definite manner.

Formerly the order of Knowing was distinguished from the order of Being. Those things closest to us and best known were suspected to be logically further from the bedrock of truth than those things which were harder to discover. Science had to be arranged so it began with the most fundamental truths, perhaps those most removed from our ordinary conception of things, and expanded to those truths which were logically dependent and most likely resembled the ordinary facts. When the everyday nature of things is accepted in its own right, a new kind of description of logical relations is necessary. A logic of procedure replaces a logic of product. The former is a description of the method of knowing, how one moves from the everyday perspective of the world and back again, and how one justifies those moves in practice. The rules for these procedures become of paramount importance. From this follows Wittgenstein's description of the philosophical grammar of language use and Heidegger's exposition of the modes of understanding and its determinations.

A description of these procedures is not a description of discovery. Poincaré's stepping on a bus and discovering a mathematical theorem will not be a part of this new logic. The description will concern itself more with the order of instruction, what steps are necessary to move an ignorant man from the everyday perspective to the perspective of the theory, and what steps are necessary within the perspective of a theory to explain a given problem.

What consequences does this new approach to the foundation and structure of knowledge hold for the relation between Knowing and Being? To answer this question, a comparison with Kant's original project is in order. Much has been made of the Kantian nature of the *Tractatus*, yet the Kantian nature of the *Philosophical Investigations* is not often pointed out. An analogy between the *Investigations* and the *Critique of Pure Reason* can be carried out if it is noticed how much the linguistic community behaves like a transcendental subject for itself. The forms of life and the rules of grammar play the same role in Wittgenstein's description of experience as the forms of intuition and the concepts of understanding. The linguistic practices of a community become conditions through which we see the world. In so far as seeing is "seeing as" and "seeing that," the way we live, the role of objects in our lives, determines how we perceive them. "Grammar tells us what kind of object anything is." [6] Only in a language can a description be given, and, as Wittgenstein points out, there must be rules for description and agreement in judgments. All these are determined by the community which shares a language.

Just as Kant traced the necessary and the a priori back to the forms of intuition and the pure concepts of understanding as rules for the synthesis of experience, Wittgenstein grounds necessity in the rules of linguistic practice. A statement that appears as if it had to be true draws its necessity from the connections in the grammar of the language. This can best be seen in *The Remarks on the Foundations of Mathematics*, where he hammers out the theme that mathematics is a form of expression invented prior to experience which serves as a standard to be used in experience. The mathematician "invents" essence, and the necessity found in mathematics shows us its role in our forms of life as a standard which must be agreed upon before measurement (calculation as a standard meter).

Kant attempted in the Transcendental Dialectic to demonstrate how the misapplication of concepts entangles the intellect in illusion. Analogously, Wittgenstein believes that philosophical problems arise when expressions stray outside their normal employment into areas of discourse where they take on extraordinary senses. The remedy for this kind of bewitchment is a clear understanding of the rules of use for an expression, which delimit the boundaries of that expression. The new form of philosophy that Wittgenstein proposes is the path to that understanding.

Wittgenstein may be said to supply the transcendentally ideal perspective of our language forms, as compared to the empirically real attitude that we have when we are using them. From this point of view language is projected onto the world, not discovered in it. He suspends the ontological force that seizes those using an expression.

6. *Investigations*, p. 116.

This attitude will not save us from tangling our language forms, unless Wittgenstein means to suggest that since language is only an invention, no concern should be shown when it goes astray. The ontological force, the drive that makes men populate the world with entities seemingly postulated by their form of speech, leads men into these tangles. Moreover, their behavior cannot be understood unless this force is taken into account.

Wittgenstein does not raise these questions explicitly, but a good idea of the effect can be gauged by examining a work like Toulmin's *Philosophy of Science*. As noted before, Toulmin believes that many of the ontological problems caused by science could be solved by distinguishing between regarding the world *as if* it is populated by the entities of a theory and giving to these entities the full-blooded status of reality. Turning to the topic of the existence of microscopic entities, Toulmin points out that within science itself there are certain criteria that separate those things thought to be explanatory fictions and those things which are in some way thought to exist. He goes on to caution us about judging the usefulness of a given theory on the basis of its having its elements confirmed as existing.[7] Although this is an accurate picture of the role of existential judgments in science, it cannot explain the intention of these judgments. What possible distinction could be made between a confirmed theory and an explanatory fiction, if both are going to be used only *as if* the world were as they described?

A cursory look at the procedures and interpretations used in confirmation experiments reveals that the criteria for their existence resemble the criteria used for ordinary things. Cloud chambers and Geiger counters, though bound to a theoretic context, reveal evidence that brings our view of the theoretical entity closer to our view of the table or chair. As soon as the intention of existential judgments in science is accepted, science and common sense seem to be at odds. This returns us to those metaphysical issues such as the mind/body problem and Eddington's two-tables problem.

Kant found it necessary to introduce transcendental structures to explain the possibility of synthetic a priori judgments. Wittgenstein believes that explanation comes to an end by indicating the established procedure and leaving it alone. He identifies the foundation of knowledge with the power to set rules for language, but does not explain how it is possible that such power can lie in the hands of a community of speakers. For example, although the role that mathematics plays may dictate universal agreement to its propositions, the mere description of the status of mathematics in our language cannot explain the property of unequivocal consensus. In democratic societies, everyone agrees that there should be one

7. *Science*, pp. 134–39.

set of laws and one government, but this agreement neither determines or explains who should govern or which laws should be enacted. The fact that one never needs to reach a compromise in mathematics should make suspect the idea that the universal agreement found in mathematics can be explained by pointing to its status alone. An apotheosis of language occurs in the *Investigations* by virtue of its role as that which explains everything but which cannot be explained by anything. Wittgenstein refuses to explain languages or provide justifications. Why must all theories of language be suspect?

Heidegger supplies us with the explanation that Wittgenstein refuses to give. His ontological analysis of Dasein provides us with a transcendental explanation that is also self-explanatory. In his analysis of dread, Heidegger tries to show how the understanding of Dasein can grasp its own situation, so that it acknowledges that it is responsible for the revealing of the world and the things within the world, and the very manner in which those things are. This interpretation may not be correct. In fact, Heidegger's own thought moves in a direction that forces him to rescind his previous interpretation. The important point is that an attempt is made to give a coherent account of the relation of men to things, an account that explains knowledge and understanding in a way that can be used to explain how the conception of the theory itself is possible. It is not clear in Kant's case, for instance, why transcendental knowledge, knowledge which justifies the synthetic a priori, is itself justified, and not a transgression of the bounds of human understanding.

Heidegger calls for an "existential conception of science." [8] The existential conception of science would clarify how by modifying our understanding things are revealed in new ways. For Heidegger, our changes of perspective, our carrying out of experiments, our working out formulas actually bring about the scientific worldview. The responsibility of the understanding is to reveal the Being of things, and until the understanding reveals that a thing is and what a thing is, in no way can that thing be said to be. This responsibility forms the basis for regarding human action and behavior as the foundation and structure of knowledge.

Heidegger calls "what a thing is revealed as" the Being of a thing. In this way he hopes to preserve the ontological force of our everyday understanding and our scientific understanding. Our workday understanding discloses the hammer as a hammer, not as a mere lump of iron attached to a piece of wood, while our scientific understanding discloses salt as a crystalline atomic structure. Moreover, the relation between the different kinds of Being are made intelligible by pointing to the changeover in

8. *Being and Time*, trans. John Macquarrie and Edward Robinson (New York, 1962), marginal pagination, p. 357.

understanding. These transformations show the relations between the salt on the table for the evening meal and the salt in the laboratory.

But does Heidegger's ontological explanation preserve ordinary understanding or overwhelm it? The ontological perspective so alters the ontical perspective that the latter cannot be understood as formerly.

> To say that before Newton his laws were neither true nor false cannot signify that before him there were no such entities as have been uncovered and pointed out by these laws. Through Newton the laws became true; and with them, entities became accessible in themselves to Dasein. Once entities have been uncovered, they show themselves precisely as entities which beforehand already were. Such uncovering is the kind of being which belongs to "truth." [9]

This problem might also be raised by Toulmin's analysis of the role of theory: Does an electron exist when no one is theorizing about it? Heidegger's explanation does indeed explain how we understand the electron, yet goes beyond that understanding. To exist at all times and to be revealed as existing at all times do not mean the same thing, although no test could distinguish between them. The fact that the understanding of Dasein has the responsibility of revealing entities changes the meaning of their Being.

Although Heidegger's analysis of Dasein alters our ordinary understanding of things (just as Wittgenstein's description of language changed the way we normally think about language), this would not be a strike against it, if it proved to be more consistent and contained more explanatory power than our existing ways of thinking about things. After all, philosophy has played some role in determining our ways of expression in the past; why should it not in the future?

Yet there are structural defects in Heidegger's program that make adoption of it hard to accept. Many of the defects arise from the fact that Dasein is identified with the self of each of us and the understanding which reveals ourselves and things within the world. This wedding of something like Kant's conception of the empirical self and the transcendental self is unable to explain error. If to be is to be revealed by the understanding, then it makes no sense to say that we understand something to be other than it is. As long as someone misunderstands something, it "is" how he misunderstands it. On the other hand, in Kant there is no guarantee that the empirical self will comprehend the synthesis of experience performed by the transcendental self. The transcendental self can be synthesizing according to rules while the empirical self errs.

Another defect lies in the fact that the transcendental structures are

9. Ibid., p. 227.

largely centered about the individual. Each one identifies himself with his own understanding, and each understanding is responsible for revealing a world. Heidegger says that each world is revealed as a world shared with others, but there persists a sense of numerically distinct worlds with no visible means of coordination.

These problems probably account in part for the celebrated Turn of Heidegger, in which he moves from the analysis of Dasein toward an understanding of how men and things belong together in a unitary world. The questions about Being, time, and man arise again as he tries to articulate the transcendental source of this "belonging together."

The destination of Wittgenstein's thought seems riddled with as many uncertainties and mysteries as the problems he sought to leave behind. Heidegger's Turn may lead in the more profitable direction for the second Kantian revolution, for here Heidegger seems to have developed an approach that can incorporate many insights into how the behavior of man plays a role in establishing the Being of a thing without degenerating into solipsism or other pitfalls to which philosophical theories seem vulnerable. Those insights of Heidegger and Wittgenstein into the procedures of men and their role in the knowing process seem to be our only clues in facing the uncertainties, mysteries, and doubts of philosophy.

16. Michael Murray
Heidegger and Ryle: Two Versions of Phenomenology

In an effort to throw light on some issues of recent philosophical history, I propose to examine a cluster of matters common to Ryle's *The Concept of Mind* (1949) and to Heidegger's *Sein und Zeit* (1927). A very pertinent element for such a discussion is Ryle's feature-length review of *Sein und Zeit*, published in 1929; [1] attention also should be drawn, however, to three additional writings: his paper "Phenomenology" (1932),[2] a review (1946) of *The Foundation of Phenomenology*,[3] and most recently a paper delivered at the Royaumont Conference in 1962, "Phénoménologie contre *The Concept of Mind*." [4] From them one learns something about the development of Ryle's thought, its relation to phenomenology in general and Heidegger in particular.

An alternative title for this discussion might have run: "Heidegger or *The Concept of Mind*." Its ambivalence provides a direction. Read in an inclusive or appositional way "or" has the sense of "Heidegger Revisited,"

Reprinted from *The Review of Metaphysics* 27 (September, 1973) with permission of the editor. The present version includes revision and incorporates comments kindly provided by Gilbert Ryle in correspondence.

1. *Mind* 38 (April, 1929) : 355–70); reprinted in Gilbert Ryle, *Collected Papers* (New York, 1971), vol. 1, pp. 197–214, and the present volume, pp. 53–64. Hereafter cited as Rev/SZ, page references are to this volume. *The Concept of Mind* (London, 1949) is cited as *CM*. *Sein und Zeit* is cited from the 7th ed. as *SZ;* trans. J. Mac-Quarrie & E. Robinson (New York, 1962), with marginal pagination.
2. *Proceedings of the Aristotelian Society,* Supp. vol. 11 (July, 1932) : 68–83. *Collected Papers,* vol. 1, pp. 167–78. Hereafter cited as "P."
3. An exposition of Husserl by Marvin Farber. *Philosophy* 21 (1946) : 263–69; *Collected Papers,* vol. 1, pp. 215–24. Hereafter cited as Rev/FP.
4. *La philosophie analytique,* ed. Leslie Beck, Coll. Cahiers de Royaumont, Philosophie IV (Paris, 1962), pp. 62–104; *Collected Papers,* vol. 1, 179–96. Hereafter cited as *P-CM*.

while interpreted exclusively it confronts us with the necessity to choose
between two incompatible versions. No one would seriously dispute that
there are significant differences in technique, motive, and goal between
Heidegger's *Sein und Zeit* and Ryle's *Concept of Mind*, and in their philosophizing generally. Ryle's technique is that of the linguistic portrayal or
sentence-frame analysis; his goal is not a science or a clarification of the
meaning of Being, but rather a "theory of mind" or philosophical psychology. His method lies within what may be termed a behaviorist perspective (*CM*, pp. 327–28) and, implicitly, he adopts the verification
principle of meaning. The source of the behavioral indicators of "mind"
as well as its measure (i.e., the criterion for true judgments), unlike the
source and measure of Skinnerian behaviorism, is provided for by ordinary, cultivated English. In Heidegger's work the appeal to the evidence
of ordinary language, the language of everyday being in the world, is also
frequent. He often cites linguistic usage for guidance in his analyses, as
for example the passages on the hammer (*SZ* pp. 73, 154, 360–61), on
social inauthenticity (pp. 127–28, 174, 178, 252–58), on temporal expressions (pp. 330, 349, 406–09, 416), and on the grammar of listening and
hearing (pp. 163–64, 173–74, 271). At this stage he is not nearly as self-
conscious of this method as is Ryle in a later period, although it is conso-
nant with Heidegger's emergent stress on the importance of language. For
Heidegger, of course, these analyses of ordinary language are not ends in
themselves, because this realm is meant to exhibit certain a priori structures of human existence, which he calls the "existentials" in contradistinction to the "categories" applicable to things. Furthermore, his interest in
these existential clarifications is governed by his contention that they
afford a necessary basis for and prelude to ontology, for which reason he
designates this endeavor "fundamental-ontology." The analysis of being
human, consequently, can never, according to Heidegger, be autonomous
and self-sufficient, because man's very constitution is meshed (a fact
which subjectivism misses) with that of others, things, and instruments,
with works of art, thought, and politics, and above all with Being. His
analysis also differs in an important way from Ryle's in his view that our
understanding of the world is ensnared in the conflicting claims of
authentic and inauthentic possibilities for life. As a result, from the outset,
ordinary language, the theme to which he later returns in his essays on
Hölderlin, represents a threat as well as a rich fund of expression. Lastly,
there is nothing in Ryle resembling Heidegger's detailed examination of
gossip, hearsay, and curiosity, boredom, fear, and dread, time, freedom,
and death.

The notion of a striking contrast and incompatibility between Heidegger and Ryle tends to be taken for granted, and with some good reason as
I have indicated. But a second interpretation, which does not cancel out

these differences, is possible; and precisely because of the obviousness of the first, it would be more interesting and worthwhile to press the seemingly implausible view that there exists a substantial affinity between their works. At the close and at some intervenient points, I shall return to the connection between the plausible and the implausible interpretations.

According to the implausible interpretation, the various parallels discernible between the two mentioned works show the unmistakable impact of *Sein und Zeit* and its type of phenomenology on Ryle. The same subjects, same forms of argument, same families of concepts and sometimes even examples found in *Sein und Zeit* (which Ryle had read very closely) reappear in *The Concept of Mind*. First among them comes a renewed critique of Cartesian philosophy, a program very conspicuous in *Sein und Zeit*, and defined in detail specifically in part I, division iii, § 19–21 on the nature of "world." Heidegger entitles section 18b: "A Contrast between our Analysis of Worldhood and Descartes's Interpretation of World." There he presents an incisive analysis of Descartes's concepts which he fills out more in later writings. Weighed historically Heidegger's analysis is all the more striking since it appears against the background of the avowed Cartesianism of Husserl, his close friend and teacher. Ryle devoted considerable attention to pre-Heidegger phenomenology and was well aware of this fact as he noted at the time of the review (Rev/SZ, p. 56), although he did not fully appreciate it until much later. Husserl's phenomenology, he then says, "burgeoned into a full Cartesian metaphysics" (Rev/FP, p. 267). Ryle's own anti-Cartesian design is an underlying theme of *The Concept of Mind* and is introduced in the first chapter: "Descartes' Myth." Despite this, however, just who gets criticized in the critique of Descartes (CM, p. 8) and even the full content of "the official doctrine" remain in a kind of twilight land: "It would not be true to say that [it] derives solely from Descartes' theories . . ." (CM, p. 23; cf. p. 11). In Ryle's version the relation between the legend and history remains less clear than it should, but the general features emerge nonetheless: the mind occupies the place of a ghost inside a machine as the soul is inside of the body. And as a result, theoretical discourse is ruled by a dualism of psychic and mechanistic talk, of inner and outer, internal and external, segregated and estranged from one another; and lastly, this inner self is a transparent consciousness capable of absolute certainty of itself and of complete doubt about the external world, physical and custommade. Ryle's purpose is to dismantle this doctrine as a mismarriage of conceptual frameworks and to substitute a more effective account of mind in its place (CM, chap. 1, et passim). I shall sketch comparatively the consequences of the Cartesian dualism which both attack—such as the intellectualist model of consciousness, the problem of other minds, and language as assertion—but let me indicate first the orientation of Heidegger's criticism. In the Cartesian view, since knowing "is not some external characteristic [bodily property], it must be 'inside'" (SZ, p. 60), whereas human being-in is conceived as "the Being-present-at-hand of some corporeal Thing (such as a human body) 'in' an entity present-at-hand" (SZ, p. 54; cf. pp. 107–08). Heidegger stresses more than Ryle the underlying ontological suppositions of Descartes and Galilean science: "The idea of Being as permanent presence-at-hand . . . keeps [Descartes] from bringing Dasein's ways of behaving into view in a way which is ontologically appropriate" (SZ, p. 98). Instructively, Heidegger never uses the word "consciousness" except within quotation marks, in order to make plain its theory-ladeness. The thesis of the published part of Sein und Zeit is a declaration of conceptual independence from the Cartesian and Galilean deformation of the meaning of human existence. Thus "man's 'substance' is not spirit as a synthesis of soul and body; it is rather existence" (SZ, p. 117; see also pp. 62, 119, 205, and passages cited below).

In his review of Heidegger, Ryle criticizes Heidegger's theory of "being a self in the world" and asserts that scientific knowledge has been smuggled in beneath the primitive situation thus described, "which knowledge necessitates universals and categories" (Rev/SZ, p. 59). An important point concerning the "language" of Sein und Zeit is raised, one still worth discussion, and as we know, Heidegger himself has acknowledged that this language was not yet wholly emancipated from the language of metaphysics. But Heidegger's reservation goes in the direction opposite Ryle's desire here to argue for the priority of the categories of objects and things over those of persons and events. His claim is not that in Sein und Zeit Heidegger's language is insufficiently freed from the grammar of "mere entities" and thus interferes with its purpose, but rather the more traditional one that, since the logical grammar of science is fundamental, attempts to escape it are misdirected. Such suggests that at this stage in his thinking Ryle himself is too Cartesian to grasp the meaning of the Cartesian critique, a suggestion borne out by another passage: "For instance the general characterization of our conscious being as a 'being-in-the-world' surely implies that underlying our other reactions and attitudes there is knowledge. We 'have' or are 'in-the-world' only if we know that at least one 'something' exists" (Rev/SZ, p. 63). Ryle fails to recognize that in his very assertion of the necessary priority of knowledge of an object, some sense of the world has been presupposed. At the same time he tacitly promotes the myth of a world-less "subject" which is the counterpart of the epistemological "object," prior to the world, revealing in another way Ryle's commitment to both the subject and the object poles of the Cartesian outlook.

World cannot be based on advance "knowledge" of some res, because we never encounter anything except within a context or against a background. The theoretician may ignore or pass over in silence this context but this does not eliminate it. There can be knowledge of the requisite sort only within a world horizon, one which the "knower" inhabits and lives through. Heidegger's argument is not intended to throw out the concept of knowledge, but rather to distinguish between what we might call knowledge *within* the world and knowledge *of* the world, or in his terms, between the original founding mode of transcendental being-in (constituted by the existential of understanding) and the regional or special areas of things that provide the reflective subject matter of particular sciences (SZ, p. 59). Related to this question is the *way* that Ryle construes Heidegger as redirecting our attention to the *sum* and the *ego* of the *cogito* and his persistent mistranslation of Dasein (human being; lit. "there-being") as "I" (Rev/SZ, pp. 58, 59, 60, 62). On this last point Heidegger was quite emphatic and in another way gave voice to his break with Descartes: "It is of course misleading to exemplify the aim of our analytic historically in this way. One of our first tasks will be to prove that if we posit an 'I' or subject as that which is proximally given, we shall completely miss the phenomenal content of Dasein" (SZ, p. 46; cf. p. 116).

A profound shift has taken place from the Ryle of the Heidegger review to the later-Ryle of *The Concept of Mind*, a shift indicated by his own words: "The assumptions against which I exhibit most heat are assumptions of which I myself have been a victim. Primarily I am trying to get some disorders out of my own system" (CM, p. 9). Now he maintains that "during the three centuries of the epoch of natural science the logical categories in terms of which the concepts of mental powers and operations have been coordinated have been wrongly selected" (CM, p. 8; cf. pp. 18–23). More than two decades earlier, Heidegger undertook to demonstrate how traditional ontology had invariably subjected human being to objective categorial structures (*Vorhandensein*), above all "Nature" as conceived by the natural sciences, and traced this penchant even further back to its roots in Greek thought (SZ, pp. 24–26, 45, 48, 63, 70, 98, 106, 361, 428–29, 437). In his review of *Sein und Zeit* Ryle took explicit note of the fact that Heidegger was trying to penetrate beneath "the technical terms which science and philosophy in the course of a long development have established" (Rev/SZ, p. 57). To "categories" as traditionally conceived, Heidegger opposed the "existentials" or structures of human existence, and substituting the former for the latter would constitute, in Ryle's own terms, "a category mistake" (CM, p. 16). Ryle's move is a strictly analogous one in the sense that he is attempting to articulate a set of concepts appropriate to an account of mind together with a critique of the inappropriateness of the influential categories of the modern natural sciences.

In this new search Ryle underscores, in a manner reminiscent of his interpretation of Heidegger (Rev/SZ, p. 56), that his positive goal is not some new speculative construction. In *The Concept of Mind* he wants to get at "the knowledge we already possess" (*CM*, p. 7). (Elsewhere Ryle states the same thing with regard to Husserl, though he doubts that Husserl was true to his own belief.) Compare this with his quite apt explication of Heidegger: "He [Heidegger] is simply telling us explicitly what we must have known 'in our bones' all the time . . . he is telling us something which we, when told, recognize that we knew implicitly from the start" (Rev/SZ, p. 61). Explicating this osteological sense of things entails the rejection of the traditional accounts of "other minds" and the related, so-called problem of the "external world." To be human is to be in a world actively engaged with others, a given existential structure that Heidegger calls Dasein's being-with (*Mitsein*) (SZ, pp. 116–30); our relation to others is not that of merely "looking at" an object situated in space (e.g., a body) but is specifically that type of care directed to other human beings called solicitude (SZ, p. 121). In the face of the apparent inaccessibility of the other, a theoretical consequence of the Cartesian philosophy and for him a problem most recently revived again by Husserl, Heidegger writes:

> Theoretically concocted 'explanations' of the Being-present-at-hand of Others urge themselves upon us all too easily; but over against such explanations we must hold fast to the phenomenal facts of the matter . . . namely, that Others are encountered *environmentally*. . . . [SZ, p. 119]

Ryle takes up the same argument against English philosophy, which in this respect shares a more or less common bent with Continental thought, as well as against features of his own previously held position. Summarizing the problem in its most skeptical form, Ryle explains:

> Contemporary philosophers have exercised themselves with the problem of our knowledge of other minds. Enmeshed in the dogma of the ghost in the machine, they have found it impossible to discover any logically satisfactory evidence warranting one person in believing that there exist minds other than his own. [*CM*, p. 60; cf. pp. 13, 15]

The way out of the Robinson Crusoe conclusion (*CM*, p. 13) is simply a superior description of the phenomena to that given by either objectivist mechanism or subjectivist mentalism. "I discover," argues Ryle, "that there are other minds in understanding what other people say and do. In making sense of what you say, in appreciating your jokes . . . I am not inferring to the workings of mind, I am following them" (*CM*, pp. 60–61). While in these formulations there is basic agreement between Heidegger and Ryle, Heidegger does not provide the precedent for Ryle's extreme and, I think, rightly criticized statement that knowledge of others is at virtual "parity" with self-knowledge and that they differ only in degree (*CM*, pp. 155, 179).[5] Explaining away rather than explaining our being with others, this solution nearly eliminates the difference between myself and yourself, the disappearance of which is the definition of the social anonymity of the inauthentic One (*das Man*).

According to Ryle there is something mistaken and confused in the entire employment of the inner-outer, mind-matter pairs, which is the assumption behind the problem of the external world (*CM*, p. 22 passim). To the metaproblem of this problem Heidegger dedicated the section of *Sein und Zeit* titled "Reality as a Problem of Being, and Whether the 'External World' Can Be Proved" (sect. 43a). Exposing this extensively debated problematic is an important part of Heidegger's critical analysis.

> When Dasein directs itself towards something and grasps it, it does not somehow first get out of an inner sphere in which it has been proximally encapsulated, but its primary kind of Being is such that it is always 'outside' alongside entities which it encounters and which belong to a world already discovered. Nor is any inner sphere abandoned when Dasein dwells alongside the entity to be known, and determines its character. . . . And furthermore, the perceiving of what is known is not a process of returning with one's booty to the 'cabinet' of consciousness after one has gone out and grasped it. . . . [*SZ*, p. 62]

For Heidegger is in exact agreement with Ryle (or vice versa) that the very question posed by the traditional, modern model of consciousness is a misprision. "The question of whether there is a world at all and whether its Being can be proved makes no sense if it is raised by *Dasein* as Being-in-the-world; and who else would raise it?" (*SZ*, p. 202). "The 'scandal of philosophy,'" Heidegger observes in his critique of Kant and Descartes, "is not that this proof has yet to be given, but that *such proofs are expected and attempted again and again*" (*SZ*, p. 205).

The later Ryle follows Heidegger in attacking the theoretical prejudice of Western philosophy which treats theorizing as the paradigm of mental act and the theoretician's "object" as the solely "real thing." Ryle wants to maintain that, "On the contrary, theorizing is one practice among others . . ." (*CM*, p. 26; cf. pp. 26–28, 137), and he offers the same explanation as Heidegger of a motive behind the conventional view: theorists have been preoccupied with the task of investigating theoretical cogni-

5. "The sorts of things that I can find out about myself are the same sorts of things that I can find out about other people. . . . " (*CM*, p. 155).

tion. "Preoccupation with 'theories' has led to ignoring the question what it is for someone to know how to perform tasks" (*CM*, p. 28). Heidegger attributes this distortion to the focus on *intuitus* and "seeing" in most conceptions of knowledge (*SZ*, p. 358). Yet he also emphasizes that theoretical behavior *is* a form of behavior, a way of being in the world, with a *praxis* of its own, determined by a special mood of its own (*SZ*, pp. 69, 138, 358). This intuitive-sight model is the model of a "just looking" according to a *method* (*SZ*, p. 69), oriented toward objective uniformities ('present-at-hand'), which requires the mood of "a tranquil tarrying alongside" (p. 138).

Such a model of knowledge is radically incomplete because it is incapable of self-understanding even its own specialized activities (not to mention others) and research skills—reading off measurements in experiments, making up "preparations" for microscopic observation, doing calculations and writing out theories (*SZ*, p. 358). Indeed, there is a *rough* but quite clear epistemological correspondence between what Ryle calls knowing-that and knowing-how (*CM*, chap. 2, esp. pp. 27–35, 40–42, 59–60) and Heidegger's fundamental distinction between the kind of understanding involved with mere entities and essences (*Vorhandensein*) and the understanding of instruments and signs ready-at-hand (*Zuhandensein*) (*SZ*, pp. 55, 61, 69, 71, 74, 83–84, 87, 183). Understanding a hammer is knowing how to use it in contexts of utility and significance. Heidegger portrays knowing-how in general terms thus: "As a disclosure, understanding always pertains to the whole basic structure of being-in-the-world . . . that which is ready-to-hand is discovered in its service*ability*, its us*ability*, and its detriment*ality*" (*SZ*, p. 144). Theoretical knowledge, in contrast, is always of a thematic sort, a knowledge that something appears such and such, that such and such is the case. Of this kind of knowing Heidegger says: "Looking at something in this way [in the way they look, their *eidos*] is a definite way of taking up a direction toward something—of setting our sights toward what is just there as an entity (present-at-hand)" (*SZ*, p. 61). Ryle aims "to prove that knowledge-how cannot be defined in terms of knowledge-that, and further, that knowledge-how is a concept logically prior to the concept of knowledge-that." [6] Though Heidegger would cast it in the vocabulary of the 'primordial' and the 'derivative,' this is a perfect statement of a major intent of *Sein und Zeit*.

Know-how, Ryle tells us, is going by unformulated rules and, although know-how is learned, learning-how is accomplished by practice, not by just knowing the rules of chess or language (*CM*, pp. 41–42) or of being informed of this or that truth (*CM*, p. 27). One can know the grammar of a language without knowing-how to speak it, or know-how to speak it

6. "Knowing How and Knowing That," *Proceedings of the Aristotelian Society* 46 (1946); reprinted in *Collected Papers*, vol. 2, pp. 212–25; see p. 215.

without expressly knowing or even having learned the grammar (*CM*, p. 42). The kind of beings other than men which knowing-how engages is precisely the type Heidegger terms "equipment," whose nature it is to be ready-at-hand for use. In Ryle's two cases, the equipment is, in the one, the chess pieces and board, and in the other, the linguistic signs whether written or phonetic or both. The sense of things accessible in the mode of knowing-that includes a range of theoretic and thematic awareness but is typified by a proposition like "The hammer has the property of heaviness" (see analysis below) or by concerns like that of Descartes who asserts that the truth of nonmental reality is extensive magnitude, or *res extensa*. What characterizes in common the "hammer" or all of physical reality in this mode of knowing is its mere present-at-handness.

Now in fact there are some uses of Ryle's "knowing-that" which are quite different from the corresponding notion in Heidegger, and there are dialectical objections possible to both their views on this which cannot be taken up here. When Ryle declares that the intellectualist legend assimilates knowing-how to knowing-that (*CM*, pp. 29, 31, 40f), he echoes Heidegger's repeated complaint that philosophers have too long overlooked the most everyday and immediate contexts of human life, equating the whole of experience with the theoretician's mode of it.

One particular application of the theoretician's bias is featured in both their accounts of the nature of language. Heidegger in *Sein und Zeit* (pp. 153–60) and only much later, Ryle, in *The Concept of Mind* (pp. 185, 311), attack the all too exclusive dominance assumed by the assertoric proposition. To quote from Heidegger:

> Prior to all analysis, logic has already understood 'logically' what it takes as a theme under the heading of the "categorical statement"—for instance, 'The hammer is heavy.' The unexplained presupposition is that the 'meaning' of this sentence is to be taken as: "This Thing—a hammer—has the property of heaviness." In concernful circumspection there are no such assertions 'at first.' But such circumspection has of course its specific ways of interpreting, and then, as compared with the 'theoretical judgment' just mentioned, may take some such form as 'The hammer is too heavy,' or rather just 'Too heavy!', 'Hand me the other hammer!' Interpretation is carried out basically not in a theoretical statement but in action . . . —laying aside the unsuitable tool, or exchanging it, "without wasting words." [*SZ*, p. 157; cf. pp. 360–61]

Ryle observes that "theorists like to define intellectual operations as operations with propositions" but neglect or camouflage the fact that this is language in the didactic mode of lesson-giving, lesson-taking, and lesson-using activities (*CM*, p. 311). To understand theoretical propositions as presupposing an instructional situation enriches our awareness and supplements the account that Heidegger wants to give.

In discussing Heidegger in his review essay, Ryle correctly noted

Heidegger's stress on the importance of examining man in his "average everydayness," essential yet constantly neglected since it is the closest to us; and Ryle was struck by Heidegger's use of ordinary language instead of a technical metaphysical language. What he does use, Ryle describes as "the many barrelled compounds of everyday nursery words and phrases" (Rev/SZ, p. 57) and uses them, as earlier pointed out, to get beneath "the technical terms which science and philosophy . . . have established." Ryle's point here is worth repeating especially because this side of Heidegger has been almost totally submerged in the legend of his metaphysical jargon. At the same time we must not lose sight of the fact that Ryle's pretext for these remarks is that he felt the pathway through ordinary language to be a threat to his own conception of philosophy. Of this pathway, on which he himself later embarks, he then wrote: "The hypothesis seems to be a perilous one, for it is at least arguable that it is here, and not in the language of the village and the nursery that mankind has made a partial escape from metaphor" (Rev/SZ, p. 58). Of course, in *Sein und Zeit* the everyday idioms, usage, and metaphors are in the service of phenomenological inquiry; they are valuable only if they serve to disclose the phenomena and if not, new ones must be and are forged. And to be sure many of the concepts by which Heidegger describes Dasein (facticity, existence, temporality, transcendental horizon) plainly are not found in the vocabulary of the village or nursery, even German ones.

In a recent discussion with Urmson, Ryle declared that in his "Systematically Misleading Expressions" (1931–32)—written about the same time as his Husserl paper (P)—he was under the direct influence of the doctrine of the ideal language (= logical form) and that he now (1962) rejected it as a bad method.[7] It is not difficult to see and perhaps Ryle would agree that the same "bad method" held sway in 1929 when he felt the appeal of the tractarian mode (see n. 15) and continued at work in "Categories" (1938–39).[8] The question can be raised how completely Ryle in his later writings breaks away from the "theoretical" conception of language, that is, of language *as* logic (CM, pp. 8, 126, 150, 155–56, 171, 194, 198). At one juncture, for instance, Ryle describes his entire book as "a discussion of the *logical behavior* of some of the cardinal terms" (CM, p. 126, italics added), and since for him the problems and mistakes are logical, so must be the solutions. Elsewhere he rejects the claim of Husserl that phenomenology can function as First Philosophy (*erste Philosophie*), because that would assign it priority *even* over logic (P, p. 77); the same misgiving runs throughout "Phénoménologie contre *The Concept of Mind*."

7. "Histoire de l'analyse," *La philosophie analytique*, pp. 11–39.
8. *Logic and Language*, 2nd series, ed. A. Flew (Oxford, 1955), pp. 286–88, 291.

Nevertheless, there are several significant parallels between the later Ryle and the Heidegger conceptions of language vis à vis a Cartesian orientation. Both are alert to the clear-distinct bias in the image of theorizing as sight (*CM*, p. 303; *SZ*, pp. 171f.). As we have noted, Ryle, like Heidegger, points out the heavy influence of this train of thought upon interpretations of language. The logician's "either categorical *or* hypothetical is highly misleading" (*CM*, p. 140), and true-false propositions do not all connect up attributes to objects (*CM*, p. 120). According to Heidegger, assertion itself is a derivative variety of interpreting (*SZ*, pp. 153–60)—a mode of interpreting because it represents a particular stance toward what is asserted and expresses itself in a select grammatical emphasis and vocabulary; and derivative rather than original because asserting presupposes as a condition of its possibility an already given and open context of signs, instruments, and speech. Interpretation is the way in which the understanding of the world becomes concrete and actual, and interpretedness should be regarded not as a special local feature but as deployed throughout the lived world. While assertion is a species of interpretation, not all interpreting is assertive.

Against the traditional insensitivity, encouraged by the supreme importance granted the assertion in theoretical discourse, Ryle calls attention to the sheer variety of talk:

> What is said is said either conversationally, or coaxingly or reassuringly, or peremptorily, or entertainingly, or reproachfully, and so forth. Talking in a bargaining way is different from talking in a confessional way, and both are different from talking anecdotally . . . Even what we write is meant to be read in a special tone of voice, and what we say to ourselves in our heads is not "said" in a monotone. [*CM*, p. 310]

The above passage on language is strikingly similar to one of Heidegger's published in 1927 and studied by Ryle in 1929:

> Being-with-one-another is discursive as assenting or refusing, as demanding or warning, as pronouncing, consulting, or interceding, as 'making assertions,' and as talking in the way of 'giving' a talk. Talking is always talking about something . . . Even a command is about something. And so is intercession . . . What is talked about in talk is always 'talked to' in a definite regard and within certain limits . . . As being-in-the-world man is already 'outside' when he understands . . . Being-in and its disposition are made known in discourse and indicated in language by intonation, modulation, the tempo of talking, "the way of speaking." [*SZ*, p. 162]

Ryle uses "disposition" in what Heidegger would call both an existential sense as applied to persons, and a categorial sense pertinent to things. His discussion is complex and many of its subtleties are dependent upon special properties of English. Heidegger makes no effort to inventory the wealth of terms and sentences which Ryle does, but is chiefly interested in root characteristics of man, the existential a priori which underlies the manifold and variable forms of expression. (The question of the relation thus is whether the linguistic distinctions and nuances become *intelligible*, supposing Heidegger's existentials to be necessary.) While there is no elaborate resemblance between Ryle and Heidegger here, two specific points of contact deserve mention, "dispositions" and "feelings."

Ryle employs "disposition" as a property concept of certain things, such as the brittleness of glass or the solubility of sugar, which denotes a liability and propensity toward a particular state, such as being broken or dissolved. Ryle's analysis of the dispositional property of "hardness" adheres rather closely to an account that Heidegger offers in his critique of Descartes (*SZ*, pp. 91, 97, 209). Ryle concludes that to express it properly we should "have to produce an infinite series of different hypothetical propositions" (*CM*, p. 44), whereas Heidegger claims that "hardness" is the experienced resistance of some entity to human effort and as such implicates a context of significant action. The "discovery of what is resistant to one's endeavor is possible ontologically because of the disclosedness of the world" (*SZ*, p. 211).

These accounts have something in common, although Ryle's strikes me as the more odd, and the reason for its peculiarity appears to be the inadequately developed sense of world in his theory of mind. For Ryle speaks not about what is the case but what *would* be required for its meaning to be made out, where Heidegger speaks of what must already be the case for such an experience—for instance, the oak tree resisting the axe of the lumberman—to take place. In Heidegger's terms the role of the infinitude of propositions is occupied by the temporal transcendence of Dasein. What Ryle does not really explain is the unity of the properties or its contextual supposition which Heidegger's account encompasses, e.g., the experience of the resistant oak. Ryle's analysis could be extended to stipulate that the individual expressions of a language always presuppose a background of other expressions. These other expressions form the local context of an expression's meaningfulness and utilizability. Such a range of reference corresponds to Heidegger's notion of a 'region" (*SZ*, p. 103), an empirical circumstance as is the region of the workshop for the carpenter's utterance, "Too heavy!" Of course this analysis can and must be extended further, because the local range of utterance itself draws from and delves into the totality of expressions, or language as a whole. If we reflect upon the background of any possible expression, expressibility as such, we are close to Heidegger's existential, transcendental concept of world.

If we turn to "disposition," as a mental property in the Ryle sense, we can recognize certain comparisons. Ryle's use of "disposition" as a category of mind to signify its capacities, tendencies, and propensities is expressed in dispositional nouns like "habit" or dispositional adjectives like "greedy" and dispositional verbs like "know," "believe," and "aspire" (*CM*, p. 118). This concept group is akin to a family of existential concepts introduced by Heidegger who says that Dasein *is* its potentiality-for-being (*Seinkönnen*), since its essence is its self-understanding (*Verstehen*), and basic state-of-mind (*Befindlichkeit*), while its being is structured by care for things, self, and others, and is founded in an "ec-static" temporality. Dasein stands out and stretches itself into future, past, and present. With these positive notions Heidegger seeks to overthrow the atomistic theory of "inner states" and modern subjectivism and also the traditional equation of the actual with the present (or Now).

Heidegger and Ryle both give "disposition" a distinctively temporal meaning and also contrast it with discrete episodes or occurrences (*CM*, p. 118). Disposition traits are essential to an interpretation of man and as early as the Heidegger review, Ryle expressly recognized such a theoretical direction in Heidegger, even so far as noting down the concept of a "disposition" (Rev/SZ, pp. 56, 58). Ryle's statement that know-how is a "disposition" (*CM*, p. 46)—say the skill of the chess player in Ryle's example or the knack of the craftsman in Heidegger's—conforms to the way Heidegger describes Dasein's involvement in the signifying structures of the ready-to-hand (*Zuhandenes*) with its in-order-to (*um . . . zu . . .*) and that-for-the-sake-of-which (*umwillen*). As Ryle translates it rather well, Dasein in the world is "a 'being-*about*' (*besorgen*)" (Rev/SZ, p. 58), and the *praxis* of man's being-about is not a "blind" behaving but has its own kind of circumspection (*Umsicht*), which is close to the intent of Ryle's view that "understanding is a part of knowing-*how*" (*CM*, p. 54) and to his characterization of practice as intelligent or skilled performance (*CM*, pp. 33, 45, 60).

Ryle's treatment of mental disposition is burdened with a difficulty that Heidegger's is not, similar to his problem with thing-dispositions previously considered, namely the inability to explain the unity and identity of mind. This is a consequence of his view that the nature of mind can only be truthfully articulated by "an infinite series of propositions" and his rough equation of the mind with "the topic of sets of testable hypothetical and semi-hypothetical propositions" (*CM*, p. 46). In this regard Ryle has only overthrown Descartes to become, perhaps not surprisingly, the heir of Hume.

In *Sein und Zeit* Heidegger calls for a more thorough-going phenomenology of the "affects," which he describes as having made little serious progress since Aristotle's *Rhetoric* (SZ, p. 138). Ryle's fascinating and intricate studies on this subject can be construed as at least consistent with and at best as a response to this asserted need. Heidegger avoids the concept of "emotion" because it has gained the popular sense of being the anticorrelate of "cognition" and he rejects the accepted view of both (*SZ*, pp. 138–39). Ryle is alive to this issue too (*CM*, pp. 104, 258), and in the foreword to his chapter on emotions, he says that the word designates at least three or four different things: "inclinations," "moods," "agitations," and "feelings" (*CM*, p. 83). Appreciating the importance Heidegger assigns in principle to this topic, Ryle wrote: "Feelings . . . are at least as directly constitutive of my world as ideas or concepts . . ." (Rev/*FP*, p. 269). Heidegger had worked especially with the notion of "state-of-mind" or "disposition" (*Befindlichkeit*) and "mood" (*Stimmung*) as the concrete attunement (*Bestimmtheit*) of the individual life.

We cannot rehearse the details of Ryle's discussion or review any of Heidegger's significant later thoughts on the problem, but consider for instance Ryle's concept of "mood" (*CM*, pp. 98–104), which plays an important role for him and bears an obvious resemblance to Heidegger's concept of *Stimmung*. "In saying that he is in a certain mood," explains Ryle, "we are saying something fairly general . . . that he is in the frame of mind to say, to do and feel a wide variety of loosely affiliated things." And, he goes on, "Moods monopolize. To say that he is in one mood, is, with reservations for complex moods, to say that he is not in any other" (*CM*, p. 99). Heidegger makes "disposition" and "mood" primary and necessary constituents of existence in the world, and as Ryle himself had properly noted, essential to Dasein's "being-itself" are "moods, tenses, and inflections" (Rev/*SZ*, p. 59). Both agree that moods and feelings must be distinguished, and both agree that these states are not "subjective" in the popular sense of a merely "inner" self.

The objection must be met that the clue to the direction, if not the thrust of Ryle's thought might naturally be expected to have derived from the thought of Wittgenstein. Chronologically speaking, we know that when he wrote his feature review of *Sein und Zeit* in 1929, Ryle was unfamiliar with the later Wittgenstein. This is hardly strange if one recalls that Wittgenstein had not returned to Cambridge until early the same year. Wittgenstein states in the 1945 preface to the *Philosophical Investigations* (part 1 : 1945; part 2 : 1947–49) that the work goes back to 1929. Apart from the fact that Wittgenstein distrusted promulgation of his teachings, the turn of his thinking required a transitional period which has been variably described. Rhees argues convincingly in his introduction to *The Blue and Brown Books* (1933–36) that the latter are rather more in the shadow of the *Tractatus* than in the light of the *Investigations*.[9] Wittgen-

9. (New York and London, 1958; 2nd ed., 1960), pp. viii, x, xiv, xvi.

stein himself seems to be of the same opinion when he labels the revisionary effort of the *Brown Book* "worthless." [10]

If Wittgenstein can be said to have taught some of the notions discussed prior to *The Concept of Mind* (just which ones cannot be set forth here), the following facts must be kept in mind: that the second part of the *Investigations* was written contemporaneously with *The Concept of Mind;* that the former work was unavailable in its full published form until *after* the latter; that *still earlier* these notions had been systematically explored by Heidegger; and that Ryle was fully acquainted with Heidegger's work, having called attention to these notions in his review.[11] In addition certain general features of *The Concept of Mind* distinguish it conspicuously from the episodic structure of the *Investigations. The Concept of Mind* is a book organized around a central concept and problem, and laid out in a fairly systematic manner with conventional forewords, chapters, and subdivisions. Formally speaking the resemblance is closer to Heidegger's book or to others than to Wittgenstein's.

Ryle later abandons most of the reasons for which he took Heidegger to task in the review, and his new approach involves analyses and concepts comparable in significant regards to ones in *Sein und Zeit.* Even then Ryle declared explicitly that the contemporary "danger" to phenomenology "is not necessitated by the idea of Phenomenology, which I regard as good" (Rev/SZ, p. 55). On that occasion his concluding judgment on Heidegger was enormously honorific and open:

> He shows himself to be a thinker of real importance by the immense subtlety and searchingness of his examination of consciousness, by the boldness and originality of his methods and conclusion, and by unflagging energy with which he tries to think beyond the stock categories of orthodox philosophy and psychology. [Rev/SZ, p. 64]

Evaluated from the angle of Ryle's philosophical aims, the extractible similarities between the two works are rather great. Yet a few years before publishing *The Concept of Mind,* Ryle announced that he had washed his hands of phenomenology and thus contradicted both his word and deed: "In short, Phenomenology was, from its birth, a bore" (Rev/FP, p. 268). It is still hard to see how his original estimation can have been so completely amiss.[12] On the other hand, one *might* be tempted to con-

---

10. Ibid. Applied to the present text (1960 edition) at about p. 154. See note p. viii.

11. When Merleau-Ponty asked Ryle whether he adhered to Wittgenstein's program, he replied, "I certainly hope not!" adding that for him Wittgenstein had opened up ways but provided no solutions to problems (P-CM, p. 98).

12. On this point Ryle writes, "My . . . 'as from its birth, a bore' referred to Husserl's 1913 and post-1913 Phenomenology. And it is, was, will be a bore! Heideg-

strue Ryle's cryptic remark, made barely three years before *The Concept of Mind*, as a kind of advanced notice for his book: "For it is a part of culture to believe that all culture comes from Paris, so Martin Heidegger's graft upon his former master's [Husserl's] stock is not unlikely before long to be adorning Anglo-Saxon gardens" (Rev/*FP*, p. 268).

A still further possibility would be that Ryle does not care about the question at all because he does not consider it to be of itself a philosophical question. This possibility implies a thesis about the nature of the relation of philosophical work to history and raises a question that cannot be left unanswered. Among Anglo-American philosophers a belief prevails that the history of philosophy, not to mention history, *is* separate from philosophy proper, that the history of philosophy is rather more the business of historians than of philosophers. The task of philosophers is to analyze or dispell problems and dilemmas. The separatist position, to give it a name, does not make the philosophical demand that one philosopher's estimation of another be a truthful reflection, but imagines itself to be honoring truth in some higher nonhistorical sense. That this position could be regarded as detrimental to philosophical discourse or as a mere form of *divertissement* seems not to occur. A recent case in point is Ryle's cavalier retort to an altogether justified criticism of his account of Husserl, that he did not care whether or not it was a "caricature" (*P-CM*, p. 87). Such an attitude indeed more typifies Ryle today than at the time of his *Sein und Zeit* study where he does appear genuinely concerned for an accurate representation of phenomenology. What can a title such as "Phénoménologie contre *The Concept of Mind*"—or what has been rightly suggested as more appropriate: "*The Concept of Mind* contre Phénoménologie"—*mean* when its author concedes that his description of the opponent is a caricature? Does that not make the *contre*, the opposition or strife itself a caricature?

When a thinker or his advocate attributes revolutionary significance to a work,[13] the separatist view runs into an unresolvable impasse. In such a context "revolution" is necessarily an historical concept; a nonhistorical conception of revolution would imply less the idea of decisive shift or advance than that of mere turning about in circles—its original astronomical meaning. One of those who endorsed the separatist theory of revolution was Wittgenstein when he held that it made no difference to him what others had said (note its family resemblance to his other contention

---

ger (which for other reasons I could not face re-reading) is quite explicitly *not* covered by this phrase of mine. By 1946 it was clear to me (tho' not in 1929) that Heidegger's stuff was not Phenomenology, or not what Husserl meant by 'Ph[enomenology]' " (31/10/73).

13. See *The Revolution in Philosophy*, introduction by Gilbert Ryle (London, 1957).

that, whatever it was, it was only mystification), and that he had "found, on all essential points, the final solution." [14] Such a standpoint, already hallowed in Descartes's *Discours de la méthode*, continues only slightly impaired in the *Investigations*. Analytical philosophy prides itself on its talent for dissolving and banishing traditional philosophical problems (therapy); and yet often it has not bothered in any careful way to ascertain what *were* and *are* the essential philosophical problems (diagnosis).[15] Quite obviously, good therapy must presuppose thoughtful and perceptive diagnosis. If one is *spoken to*, and the texts of the tradition do speak, one must listen before one can understand and reply. Any other approach is irresponsible or, to continue the medical analogy, quackery. Both the diagnostic and the therapeutic sides are required if *philosophical* work is to be responsible and whole. Precisely because philosophy is concerned with the issue, it is concerned with history, and indeed history in a sense that interests few historians, namely as the life of philosophical truth. Without this concern it becomes impossible to speak meaningfully of advance, revolution, or of setback.

Now we are in a position to underscore the second, exclusive "or" (the reasons for which have been summarized) and to ask whether Ryle's appropriation of Heidegger does not, in fact and in principle, miss a dimension of genuine revolutionary significance. This can best be understood by considering a key theme in Ryle's criticism that runs through all four papers on phenomenology, namely his repudiation of phenomenology as "first philosophy" (in Husserl's phrase borrowed from Descartes and Aristotle) or as "strict science" (*strenge Wissenschaft*) and Heidegger's related though different interpretation of it as "fundamental ontology."

In the review of *Sein und Zeit* Ryle feels that the dangerous move by Husserl occurs when phenomenology "is given primacy over all other sciences, and is itself presuppositionless . . ." (p. 55) ". . . a vital ambiguity [is] present in that expanded theory of Phenomenology which makes it the logical 'prius' of not only psychology but logic, metaphysics, and the mathematical and natural sciences" (p. 62). Next, in the essay "Phenomenology," Ryle maintains that phenomenology is a part of philosophy and is a priori, but that it is neither science nor rigorous science nor "science of sciences" (p. 69). This follows from the view of phenomenology as "science of the manifestations of consciousness," one equivalent to epistemology (p. 70). In his review of *The Foundation of*

14. *Tractatus Logico-Philosophicus*, trans. D. F. Pears and B. F. McGuinnes (London, 1961), p. 3.
15. Examples ready at hand: Carnap (*ergo* Ayer, Quine, and Pitcher) on Heidegger; Russell and Popper on Hegel; Bowsma on Descartes. For a good critical survey of analytical philosophy in relation to philosophical history, see Richard Bernstein, *Praxis and Action* (Philadelphia, 1971), pp. 230–304, 316–20.

Phenomenology, a presentation of Husserl by Marvin Farber, Ryle describes Husserl's best work as that part of the *Logische Untersuchungen* devoted to the reconstruction of epistemology and philosophy of mind. Heidegger, he adds, modifies the representational theory of perception but retains the "intentionality dogma" (p. 268).[16] Lastly, in "Phénoménologie contre *The Concept of Mind*" Ryle says that his book may be described as a sustained attempt at phenomenology, not as a contribution to any science whatever, but rather philosophical psychology (pp. 75, 82; cf. *CM*, p. 319). Conceptual research is not a science of sciences; it differs according to type but not hierarchically. Ryle assigns the philosophy of mind no privileged position and, speaking on behalf of British philosophers, states: "we doubtless incline to say that it is logic which controls and deserves to control the other researches" (p. 68).

In the above line of criticism two things should be observed that are at the heart of the *difference* between Heidegger and Ryle. These are, first of all, the correctness of Ryle's inference and the falseness or question-begging character of his premise. If we accept the reduction of phenomenology to psychology, it follows—as both Husserl and Heidegger would agree—that phenomenology can only provide a regional ontology rather than a foundation for ontology. This is what Ryle does by reading *Sein und Zeit* as a design for a philosophical psychology, albeit a revolutionary one as he argues. The premise of the argument, however, is one that Husserl and Heidegger would both strongly reject. If *Sein und Zeit* is looked upon as another regional ontology (i.e., the region of "mind"), then what is most important for Heidegger is ignored.

Despite the numerous particular parallels in their attacks on Cartesianism and in their positive concepts, Ryle in his critique and in his own work remains on the plane of traditional ontology rather than fundamental ontology. The aim of fundamental ontology is to lay bare the indispensable relation of man to things in their Being. The existentials are so-called not because they describe the nature of man which might later be correlated with a general metaphysics, as Ryle seems to think (Rev/*SZ*, pp. 61, 64); rather they show up Dasein's relation to beings, to others, to its own self as pregnant with a sense of Being and as the questioner of the meaning of Being. Man's understanding of Being affects the what and how of his nature. Heidegger's subsequent working out of the question of the meaning of Being assumes many paths, including a reevaluation of the results of his own earlier work, yet he continues to pursue the same question. (Contemporary linguistic physicians are prone to confuse performing a

16. Despite the fact that the word appears but once in *Sein und Zeit*, in a footnote on Husserl (p. 363), accompanied by the statement that "intentionality" must be thought through on another, more fundamental basis, viz., temporality. The argument is pursued in *Vom Wesen des Grundes* (1929), *The Essence of Reasons*, trans. T. Mallick (Evanston, 1969), pp. 28–29, 110–15.

task wrongly with performing the wrong task.) Heidegger would agree with Ryle that philosophy is not a superscience, but that is because the question of Being is more fundamental than any science or logic.

Ultimately one cannot do full justice to the concrete and close analysis of phenomena—to which Ryle has made signal contributions—in independence of fundamental questions. This fact can be brought home by comparing again Heidegger and Ryle's respective treatments of moods. Heidegger describes and distinguishes the specially revelatory moods of fear, which is object-oriented towards some fearsome thing within the world (SZ, pp. 140–43) and dread (*Angst*) which has no inner-worldly object (SZ, pp. 182–91). Dread is dread in the face of being-in-the-world as such, not of a particular threatening item within it and, in this sense, is dread of "nothing." For this very reason the experience of dread casts light across existence as a whole and so discloses the world in its worldliness.

For Ryle there can be no connection of the dread experience with the world, because he does not recognize the phenomenological sense of world as a lived transcendental horizon. Everyday speech busies itself constantly with know-how and things ready-to-hand (SZ, p. 186), hence with items within the world, and this *is* the primary field of Ryle's attention. "For, roughly, the mind is," Ryle writes, ". . . the topic of sets of testable hypothetical and semi-hypothetical propositions" (CM, p. 46). The mind or the world thus defined lacks unity and self-identity like the bundle of Humean impressions which is its ancestor. One might well argue that Ryle lacks the world in the mentioned sense just because he makes no room for the experience of dread. A better guide is Wittgenstein who, some months after the Ryle review, expressed sharp appreciation for Heidegger's notion of dread as that which reveals the limits of existence and points to Being.[17] We can now speak more precisely of two versions of phenomenology to signify the sense in which each thinker is a phenomenologist and each expresses views about the nature of phenomenology. The differences between Heidegger and Ryle include radical ones, and Ryle scarcely concurs in the philosophical program of Heidegger, still less that of Husserl, but acknowledgment of Ryle's substantial debt to Heidegger is overdue.

NOTE

In his pithily condensed "Autobiographical," Ryle takes due note of the fact that among the first courses he taught was one dealing with Brentano

17. *Ludwig Wittgenstein und der Wiener Kreis, Gespräche aufgezeichnet von Friedrich Waismann*, Schriften 3 (Frankfurt am Main, 1967), pp. 68–69. For the full

and Husserl and that his first published things were the reviews of In-garden and Heidegger. While respectfully, but emphatically, denying that his colleague John Austin had any philosophical influence on him, of his possible youthful indebtedness to Husserl he says "there is not much truth" in this opinion. About the philosophical proximities to Heidegger (or for that matter the distances), he confines himself to the remark: "I was amused to find [Husserl's Phenomenology], together with Heideg-ger's Existentialism, becoming the *dernier cri* in France after the Second World War." [18] More recently, in a letter that greeted the preceding dis-cussion "with interest and general approval," Ryle indicated his own view about the influence of Heidegger:

> I don't suppose in 1928–29 I exchanged a word with anyone about Heidegger. Logical Positivism did capture my colleagues and in good measure me. . . . Of course I have no idea how much *Sein und Zeit* affected me. My anti-psychologism, which expanded into anti-Cartesian dualism later on, was alive and kicking as early as in my first reading of Frege, Husserl, Meinong, and Brentano, when Austrian intentionality-theory partly paralleled Cambridge anti-idealism. But I may well have found in *Sein und Zeit* (not the Meaning/Nonsense theory that I wanted), but anti-dualistic *cum* pro-behavioristic thoughts which were later congenial to me.
>
> I did work hard over my *Sein und Zeit* review; but don't *think* it got as deep under my skin as did some of the other things. But it is not *now* for me to say! I'm pretty sure that I never lent (or refused to lend!) my *Sein und Zeit* to any colleague or pupil. But this could all have been "cover up" for an indebtedness that I wanted to keep dark.[19]

---

translation and my commentary, see "On Heidegger on Being and Dread," this volume, pp. 80–83.

18. *Ryle: A Collection of Critical Essays*, ed. by Oscar P. Wood and George Pitcher (Garden City, New York, 1970), pp. 1–15; cf. p. 9.

19. To the author, dated 31/10/73, Oxford.

Politics and Philosophy of History

17. Hannah Arendt
Martin Heidegger at Eighty

Martin Heidegger's eightieth birthday was also the fiftieth anniversary of his public life, which he began not as an author—though he had already published a book on Duns Scotus—but as a university teacher. In barely three or four years since that first solid and interesting but still rather conventional study, he had become so different from its author that his students hardly knew about it. If it is true, as Plato once remarked, that "the beginning is also a god; so long as he dwells among men, he saves all things" (*Laws* 775), then the beginning in Heidegger's case is neither the date of his birth (September 26, 1889, at Messkirch) nor the publication of his first book, but the first lecture courses and seminars which he held as a mere *Privatdozent* (instructor) and assistant to Husserl at the University of Freiburg in 1919. For Heidegger's "fame" predates by about eight years the publication of *Sein und Zeit* in 1927; indeed it is open to question whether the unusual success of this book—not just the immediate impact it had inside and outside the academic world but also its extraordinarily lasting influence, with which few of the century's publications can compare—would have been possible if it had not been preceded by the teacher's reputation among the students, in whose opinion, at any rate, the book's success merely confirmed what they had known for many years.

There was something strange about this early fame, stranger perhaps than the fame of Kafka in the early twenties or of Braque and Picasso in the preceding decade, who were also unknown to what is commonly understood as the public and nevertheless exerted an extraordinary influence. For in Heidegger's case there was nothing tangible on which his fame could have been based, nothing written, save for notes taken at his

Reprinted from *The New York Review of Books* (October, 1971). Translated by Albert Hofstadter. © 1971 by Hannah Arendt. Reprinted by permission of Harcourt Brace Jovanovich, Inc.

lectures, which circulated among students everywhere. These lectures
dealt with texts that were generally familiar; they contained no doctrine
that could have been learned, reproduced, and handed on. There was
hardly more than a name, but the name traveled all over Germany like
the rumor of the hidden king.

This was something completely different from a "circle" centered
around and directed by a "master" (say, the Stefan George circle), which,
while well known to the public, still remained apart from it by an aura
of secrecy, the *arcana imperii* to which presumably only the circle's members are privy. Here there was neither a secret nor membership; those
who heard the rumor were acquainted with one another, to be sure, since
they were all students, and there were occasional friendships among them.
Later some cliques formed here and there; but there never was a circle
and there was nothing esoteric about his following.

To whom did the rumor spread, and what did it say? In the German
universities at the time, after the First World War, there was no rebellion
but widespread discontent with the academic enterprise of teaching and
learning in those faculties that were more than professional schools, a dis-
quiet that prevailed among students for whom study meant more than
preparing for making a living. Philosophy was no breadwinner's study,
but rather the study of resolute starvelings who were, for that very reason, all the harder to please. They were in no way disposed toward a
wisdom of life or of the world, and for anyone concerned with the solution of all riddles there was available a rich selection of world views and
their partisans: it wasn't necessary to study philosophy in order to choose
among them.

But what they wanted they didn't know. The university commonly offered them either the schools—the neo-Kantians, the neo-Hegelians, the
neo-Platonists, etc.—or the old academic discipline, in which philosophy,
neatly divided into its special fields—epistemology, aesthetics, ethics, logic,
and the like—was not so much communicated as drowned in an ocean of
boredom. There were, even before Heidegger's appearance, a few rebels
against this comfortable and, in its way, quite solid enterprise. Chronologically, there was Husserl and his cry "To the things themselves"; and
that meant, "Away from theories, away from books" toward the establishment of philosophy as a rigorous science which would take its place
alongside other academic disciplines.

This was still a naïve and unrebellious cry, but it was something to
which first Scheler and somewhat later Heidegger could appeal. In addition, there was Karl Jaspers in Heidelberg, consciously rebellious and
coming from a tradition other than the philosophical. He, as is known,
was for a long time on friendly terms with Heidegger, precisely because
the rebellious element in Heidegger's enterprise appealed to him as some-

thing original and fundamentally philosophical in the midst of the academic talk *about* philosophy.

What these few had in common was—to put it in Heidegger's words—that they could distinguish "between an object of scholarship and a matter of thought" (*Aus der Erfahrung des Denkens*, 1947)[1] and that they were pretty indifferent to the object of scholarship. At that time the rumor of Heidegger's teaching reached those who knew more or less explicitly about the breakdown of tradition and the "dark times" (Brecht) which had set in, who therefore held erudition in matters of philosophy to be idle play and who, therefore, were prepared to comply with the academic discipline only because they were concerned with the "matter of thought" or, as Heidegger would say today, "thinking's matter" (*Zur Sache des Denkens*, 1969).

The rumor that attracted them to Freiburg and to the *Privatdozent* who taught there, as somewhat later they were attracted to the young professor at Marburg, had it that there was someone who was actually attaining "the things" that Husserl had proclaimed, someone who knew that these things were not academic matters but the concerns of thinking men —concerns not just of yesterday and today, but from time immemorial— and who, precisely because he knew that the thread of tradition was broken, was discovering the past anew.

It was technically decisive that, for instance, Plato was not talked *about* and his theory of Ideas expounded; rather for an entire semester a single dialogue was pursued and subjected to question step by step, until the time-honored doctrine had disappeared to make room for a set of problems of immediate and urgent relevance. Today this sounds quite familiar, because nowadays so many proceed in this way; but no one did so before Heidegger.

The rumor about Heidegger put it quite simply: Thinking has come to life again; the cultural treasures of the past, believed to be dead, are being made to speak, in the course of which it turns out that they propose things altogether different from the familiar, worn-out trivialities they had been presumed to say. There exists a teacher; one can perhaps learn to think.

The hidden king reigned therefore in the realm of thinking, which, although it is completely of this world, is so concealed in it that one can never be quite sure whether it exists at all; and still its inhabitants must be more numerous than is commonly believed. For how, otherwise, could the unprecedented, often underground, influence of Heidegger's thinking

---

1. See "The Thinker as Poet" in *Poetry, Language, Thought*, trans. A. Hofstadter (New York, 1975).

and thoughtful reading be explained, extending as it does beyond the circle
of students and disciples and beyond what is commonly understood by
philosophy?

For it is not Heidegger's philosophy, whose existence we can rightfully
question (as Jean Beaufret has done), but Heidegger's thinking that has
shared so decisively in determining the spiritual physiognomy of this century. This thinking has a digging quality peculiar to itself, which, should
we wish to put it in linguistic form, lies in the transitive use of the verb
"to think." Heidegger never thinks "about" something; he thinks something. In this entirely uncontemplative activity, he penetrates to the
depths, but not to discover, let alone bring to light, some ultimate, secure
foundations which one could say had been undiscovered earlier in this
manner. Rather, he persistently remains there, underground, in order to
lay down pathways and fix "trail marks" (a collection of texts from the
years 1929 to 1962 had this title, *Wegmarken*).

This thinking may set tasks for itself; it may deal with "problems"; it
naturally, indeed always, has something specific with which it is particularly occupied or, more precisely, by which it is specifically aroused; but
one cannot say that it has a goal. It is unceasingly active, and even the
laying down of paths itself is conducive to opening up a new dimension
of thought, rather than to reaching a goal sighted beforehand and guided
thereto.

The pathways may safely be called *Holzwege*, wood-paths (after the
title of a collection of essays from the years 1935 to 1946), which, just
because they lead nowhere outside the wood and "abruptly leave off in
the untrodden," are incomparably more agreeable to him who loves the
wood and feels at home in it than the carefully laid out problem-streets on
which scurry the investigations of philosophical specialists and historians
of ideas. The metaphor of "wood-paths" hits upon something essential—
not, as one may at first think, that someone has gotten onto a dead-end
trail, but rather that someone, like the woodcutter whose occupation lies
in the woods, treads paths that he has himself beaten; and clearing the
path belongs no less to his line of work than felling trees.

On this deep plane, dug up and cleared, as it were, by his own thinking,
Heidegger has laid down a vast network of thought-paths; and the single
immediate result, which has been understandably noticed, and sometimes
imitated, is that he has caused the edifice of traditional metaphysics—in
which, for a long time, no one had felt quite at ease in any case—to collapse, just as underground tunnels and subversive burrowings cause the
collapse of structures whose foundations are not deeply enough secured.

This is a historical matter, perhaps even one of the first order, but it
need not trouble those of us who stand outside all the guilds, including
the historical. That Kant could with justice, from a specific perspective,

be called the "all-crushing one" has little to do with who Kant was—as distinguished from his historical role.

As to Heidegger's share in the collapse of metaphysics, which was imminent anyway, what we owe him, and only him, is that this collapse took place in a manner worthy of what had preceded it: that metaphysics was *thought* through to its end, and was not simply, as it were, overrun by what followed after it. "The end of philosophy," as Heidegger says in *Zur Sache des Denkens;* but it was an end that is a credit to philosophy and holds her in honor, prepared for by one who was most profoundly bound to her and her tradition. For a lifetime he based his seminars and lectures on the philosophers' texts, and only in his old age did he venture to give a seminar on a text of his own. *Zur Sache des Denkens* contains the "protocol for a seminar on the lecture '*Zeit und Sein*,' " which forms the first part of the book.

I have said that people followed the rumor about Heidegger in order to learn thinking. What was experienced was that thinking as pure activity—and this means impelled neither by the thirst for knowledge nor by the drive for cognition—can become a passion which not so much rules and oppresses all other capacities and gifts, as it orders them and prevails through them. We are so accustomed to the old opposition of reason versus passion, spirit versus life, that the idea of a *passionate* thinking, in which thinking and aliveness become one, takes us somewhat aback. Heidegger himself once expressed this unification—on the strength of a proven anecdote—in a single sentence, when at the beginning of a course on Aristotle he said, in place of the usual biographical introduction, "Aristotle was born, worked, and died."

That something like Heidegger's passionate thinking exists is indeed, as we can recognize afterward, a condition of the possibility of there being any philosophy at all. But it is more than questionable, especially in our century, whether we would ever have discovered this without the existence of Heidegger's thinking. This passionate thinking, which rises out of the simple fact of being-born-in-the-world and now "thinks recallingly and responsively the meaning that reigns in everything that is" (*Gelassenheit*, 1959, p. 15),[2] can no more have a final goal—cognition or knowledge—than can life itself. The end of life is death, but man does not live for death's sake, but because he is a living being; and he does not think for the sake of any result whatever, but because he is a "thinking, that is, a musing being" (ibid.).

A consequence of this is that thinking acts in a peculiarly destructive or critical way toward its own results. To be sure, since the philosophical

2. *Discourse on Thinking*, trans. J. M. Anderson and E. H. Freund (Harper & Row, 1966), p. 46.

schools of antiquity, philosophers have exhibited an annoying inclination toward system building, and we often have trouble disassembling the constructions they have built when trying to uncover what they really thought. This inclination does not stem from thinking itself, but from quite other needs, themselves thoroughly legitimate. If one wished to measure thinking, in its immediate, passionate liveliness, by its results, then one would fare as with Penelope's veil—what was spun during the day would inexorably undo itself again at night, so that the next day it could be begun anew. Each of Heidegger's writings, despite occasional references to what was already published, reads as though he were starting from the beginning and only from time to time taking over the language already coined by him—a language, however, in which the concepts are merely "trail marks," by which a new course of thought orients itself.

Heidegger refers to this peculiarity of thinking when he emphasizes that "the *critical* question, what the matter of thought is, belongs necessarily and constantly to thinking"; when, on the occasion of a reference to Nietzsche, he speaks of "thinking's recklessness, beginning ever anew"; when he says that thinking "has the character of a retrogression." And he practices the retrogression when he subjects *Being and Time* to an "immanent criticism," or establishes that his own earlier interpretation of Platonic truth "is not tenable," or speaks generally of the thinker's "backward glance" at his own work, "which always becomes a *retractatio*," not actually a recanting, but rather a fresh rethinking of what was already thought (in *Zur Sache des Denkens*, pp. 61, 30, 78).

Every thinker, if only he grows old enough, must strive to unravel what have actually emerged as the results of his thought, and he does this simply by rethinking them. (He will say with Jaspers, "And now, when you just wanted really to start, you must die.") The thinking "I" is ageless, and it is the curse and the blessing of thinkers, so far as they exist only in thinking, that they become old without aging. Also, the passion of thinking, like the other passions, seizes the person—seizes those qualities of the individual of which the sum, when ordered by the will, amounts to what we commonly call "character"—takes possession of him and, as it were, annihilates his "character," which cannot hold its own against this onslaught. The thinking "I," which "stands within" the raging storm, as Heidegger says, and for which time literally stands still, is not just ageless; it is also, although always specifically other, without qualities. The thinking "I" is everything but the self of consciousness.

Moreover, thinking, as Hegel, in a letter to Zillmann in 1807, remarked about philosophy, is "something solitary," and this not only because I am alone in what Plato speaks of as the "soundless dialogue with myself" (*Sophist* 263e), but because in this dialogue there always reverberates something "unutterable" which cannot be brought fully to sound through

language and articulated in speech, and which, therefore, is not com-
municable, not to others and not to the thinker himself. It is presumably
this "unsayable," of which Plato speaks in the Seventh Letter, that makes
thinking such a lonely business and yet forms the ever varied fertile soil
from which it rises up and constantly renews itself. One could well imagine that—though this is hardly the case with Heidegger—the passion of
thinking might suddenly beset the most gregarious man and, in consequence of the solitude it requires, ruin him.

The first and, so far as I know, the only one who has ever spoken of
thinking as a *pathos*, as something to be borne by enduring it, was Plato,
who, in the *Theaetetus* (155d), calls wonder the beginning of philosophy;
he certainly does not mean by this the mere surprise or astonishment that
arises in us when we encounter something strange. For the wonder that
is the beginning of thinking—as surprise and astonishment may well be
the beginning of the sciences—applies to the everyday, the matter-of-
course, what we are thoroughly acquainted and familiar with; this is also
the reason why it cannot be quieted by any knowledge whatever. Heidegger speaks once, wholly in Plato's sense, of the "faculty of wondering
at the simple," but, differently from Plato, he adds, *"and of taking up and
accepting this wondering as one's abode"* (*Vorträge und Aufsätze*, 1954,
Part III, p. 259).
   This addition seems to me decisive for reflecting on who Martin Heidegger is. For many—so we hope—are acquainted with thinking and the
solitude bound up with it; but clearly, they do not have their residence
there. When wonder at the simple overtakes them and, yielding to the
wonder, they engage in thinking, they know they have been torn out of
their habitual place in the continuum of occupations in which human affairs take place, and will return to it again in a little while. The abode of
which Heidegger speaks lies therefore, in a metaphorical sense, outside the
habitations of men; and although "the winds of thought," which Socrates
(according to Xenophon) was perhaps the first to mention, can be strong
indeed, still these storms are even a degree more metaphorical than the
metaphor of "storms of the age."
   Compared with other places in the world, the habitations of human affairs, the residence of the thinker is a "place of stillness" (*Zur Sache des
Denkens*, p. 75). Originally it is wonder itself which begets and spreads
the stillness; and it is because of this stillness that being shielded against
all sounds, even the sound of one's own voice, becomes an indispensable
condition for thinking to evolve out of wonder. Enclosed in this stillness
there happens a peculiar metamorphosis which affects everything falling
within the dimension of thinking in Heidegger's sense. In its essential seclusion from the world, thinking always has to do only with things absent,

with matters, facts, or events which are withdrawn from direct perception. If you stand face to face with a man, you perceive him, to be sure, in his bodily presence, but you are not *thinking* of him. And if you think about him while he is present, you are secretly withdrawing from the direct encounter. In order to come close, in thinking, to a thing or to a human being, it or he must lie for direct perception in the distance. Thinking, says Heidegger, is "coming-into-nearness to the distant" (*Gelassenheit*, p. 45 [*Discourse on Thinking*, p. 68]).

One can easily bring this point home by a familiar experience. We go on journeys in order to see things in faraway places; in the course of this it often happens that the things we have seen come close to us only in retrospect or recollection, when we no longer are in the power of the immediate impression—it is as if they disclose their meaning only when they are no longer present. This inversion of relationship—that thinking removes what is close by, withdrawing from the near and drawing the distant into nearness—is decisive if we wish to find an answer to the question of where we are when we think. Recollection, which in thinking becomes remembrance, has played so prominent a role as a mental faculty in the history of thinking about thinking, because it guarantees us that nearness and remoteness, as they are given in the sense perception, are actually susceptible of such an inversion.

Heidegger has expressed himself only occasionally, by suggestion, and for the most part negatively, about the "abode" where he feels at home, the residence of thinking—as when he says that thinking's questioning is not "part of everyday life . . . it gratifies no urgent or prevailing need. The questioning itself is 'out of order.' " (*An Introduction to Metaphysics*, Anchor Books, 1961, pp. 10–11). But this nearness-remoteness relation and its inversion in thinking pervades Heidegger's whole work, like a key to which everything is attuned. Presence and absence, concealing and revealing, nearness and remoteness—their interlinkage and the connections prevailing among them—have next to nothing to do with the truism that there could not be presence unless absence were experienced, nearness without remoteness, discovery without concealment.

Seen from the perspective of thinking's abode, "withdrawal of Being" or "oblivion of Being" reigns in the ordinary world which surrounds the thinker's residence, the "familiar realms . . . of everyday life," i.e., the loss of that with which thinking—by which nature clings to the absent— is concerned. Annulment of this "withdrawal," on the other side, is always paid for by a withdrawal from the world of human affairs, and this remoteness is never more manifest than when thinking ponders exactly these affairs, training them into its own sequestered stillness. Thus, Aristotle, with the great example of Plato still vividly in view, has already strongly advised philosophers against dreaming of the philosopher-king who would rule *ta ton anthropon pragmata*, the realm of human affairs.

"The faculty of wondering," at least occasionally, "at the simple" is presumably inherent in all humans, and the thinkers well known to us from the past and in the present should then be distinguished by having developed out of this wonder the capacity to think and to unfold the trains of thought that were in each case suitable to them. However, the faculty of "taking up this wondering as one's permanent abode" is a different matter. This is extraordinarily rare, and we find it documented with some degree of certainty only in Plato, who expressed himself more than once and most drastically in the *Theaetetus* (173d to 176) on the dangers of such a residence.

There too, he tells, apparently for the first time, the story of Thales and the Thracian peasant girl, who, watching the "wise man" glance upward in order to observe the stars only to fall into the well, laughed that someone who wants to know the sky should be so ignorant of what lies at his feet. Thales, if we are to trust Aristotle, was very much offended—the more so as his fellow citizens used to scoff at his poverty—and he proved by a large speculation in oil presses that it was an easy matter for "wise men" to get rich if they were to set their hearts on it (*Politics*, 1259a ff.). And since books, as everyone knows, are not written by peasant girls, the laughing Thracian child had still to submit to Hegel's saying about her that she had no sense at all for higher things.

Plato, who, in the *Republic*, wanted not only to put an end to poetry but also to forbid laughter, at least to the class of guardians, feared the laughter of his fellow citizens more than the hostility of those holding opinions opposed to the philosopher's claim to absolute truth. Perhaps it was Plato himself who knew how likely it is that the thinker's residence, seen from the outside, will look like the Aristophanic Cloud-cuckoo-land. At any rate, he was aware of the philosopher's predicament: if he wants to carry his thoughts to market, he is likely to become the public laughingstock; and this, among other things, may have induced him, at an advanced age, to set out for Sicily three times in order to set the tyrant of Syracuse right by teaching him mathematics as the indispensable introduction to philosophy and hence to the art of ruling as a philosopher king.

He didn't notice that this fantastic undertaking, if seen from the peasant girl's perspective, looks considerably more comical than Thales's mishap. And to a certain extent he was right in not noticing; for, so far as I know, no student of philosophy has ever dared to laugh, and no writer who has described this episode has ever smiled. Men have obviously not yet discovered what laughter is good for—perhaps because their thinkers, who have always been ill-disposed toward laughter, have let them down in this respect, even though a few of them have racked their brains over the question of what makes us laugh.

Now we all know that Heidegger, too, once succumbed to the temptation to change his "residence" and to get involved in the world of human affairs. As to the world, he was served somewhat worse than Plato, because the tyrant and his victims were not located beyond the sea, but in his own country.[3] As to Heidegger himself, I believe that the matter stands

3. This episode, which today—now that the embitterment has cooled and, above all, the innumerable canards have been somehow set right—is usually called an "error," has many aspects, among others that of the Weimar Republic, which didn't at all display itself to those who lived in it in the rosy light in which, viewed against the horror of what followed, it is nowadays often seen.

Moreover, the content of Heidegger's "error" differed considerably from the current "errors" of the period. Who in the midst of Nazi Germany could possibly have thought that "the inner truth . . . of this movement" consisted in "the encounter between global technology and modern man" (*Introduction to Metaphysics*, p. 166)— something about which the vast Nazi literature is entirely silent—except, of course, somebody who had read instead of Hitler's *Mein Kampf* the writings of the Italian futurists who indeed had some connections with fascism, as distinct from national socialism.

There is no doubt that these writings make more interesting reading, but the point of the matter is that Heidegger, like so many other German intellectuals, Nazis and anti-Nazis, of his generation never read *Mein Kampf*. This misunderstanding of what it was all about is inconsiderable when compared with the much more decisive "error" that consisted in not only ignoring the most relevant "literature" but in escaping from the reality of the Gestapo cellars and the torture-hells of the early concentration camps into ostensibly more significant regions.

Robert Gilbert, the German folk poet (somehow in the tradition of Heine) and popular song writer, described even then in four lines of an unforgettable verse what actually happened in the spring of 1933:

> *Keiner braucht mehr anzupochen*
> *Mit der Axt durch jede Tür—*
> *Die Nation ist aufgebrochen*
> *Wie ein Pestgeschwür.*

> No one needs to give a knock,
> With an ax through every door—
> Burst open, the nation spews its matter
> Like an abscessed sore.

This escape from reality turned out to be more characteristic and more lasting than all the *Gleichschaltungen* of those early years. (Heidegger himself corrected his own "error" more quickly and more radically than many of those who later sat in judgment over him—he took considerably greater risks than were usual in German literary and university life during that period.) We are still surrounded by intellectuals and so-called scholars, not only in Germany, who, instead of speaking of Hitler, Auschwitz, genocide, and "extermination" as a policy of permanent depopulation, prefer, according to their inspiration and taste, to refer to Plato, Luther, Hegel, Nietzsche, or to Heidegger, Jünger, or Stefan George, in order to dress up the horrible gutter-born phenomenon with the language of the humanities and the history of ideas.

One can indeed say that escape from reality has in the meantime blossomed into a profession, and this in the literature of both the Hitler and the Stalin period. In the latter we still find the notion that Stalin's crimes were necessary for the industrialization of Russia—even though this "industrialization" quite obviously was a gigantic failure—and in the former we still read grotesquely highfalutin and sophisticated

differently. He was still young enough to learn from the shock of the collision, which after ten short hectic months thirty-seven years ago drove him back to his residence, and to settle in his thinking what he had experienced.

What emerged from this was his discovery of the will as "the will to will" and hence as the "will to power." In modern times and above all in the modern age, much has been written about the will, but despite Kant, despite even Nietzsche, not very much has been found out about its nature. However that may be, no one before Heidegger saw how much this nature stands opposed to thinking and affects it destructively. To thinking there belongs *"Gelassenheit"*—serenity, composure, release, a state of relaxation, in brief, a disposition that "lets be." Seen from the standpoint of the will the thinkers must say, only apparently in paradox, "I will nonwilling"; for only "by way of this," only when we "wean ourselves from will," can we "release ourselves into the sought-for nature of the thinking that is not a willing" (*Gelassenheit*, p. 32f. [*Discourse on Thinking*, pp. 59–60]).

We who wish to honor the thinkers, even if our own residence lies in the midst of the world, can hardly help finding it striking and perhaps exasperating that Plato and Heidegger, when they entered into human affairs, turned to tyrants and Führers. This should be imputed not just to the circumstances of the times and even less to preformed character, but rather to what the French call a *déformation professionelle*. For the attraction to the tyrannical can be demonstrated theoretically in many of the great thinkers (Kant is the great exception). And if this tendency is not demonstrable in what they did, that is only because very few of them were prepared to go beyond "the faculty of wondering at the simple" and to "accept this wondering as their abode."

With these few it does not finally matter where the storms of their century may have driven them. For the wind that blows through Heidegger's thinking—like that which still sweeps toward us after thousands of years from the work of Plato—does not spring from the century he happens to live in. It comes from the primeval, and what it leaves behind is something perfect, something which, like everything perfect (in Rilke's words), falls back to where it came from.

---

theories with whose spirituality the gutter never had anything to do. We move there in a ghostly realm of motions and "ideas" which has slid so far from every documented and experienced reality that every thought, even those of the great thinkers, loses its solidity, a realm in which ideas, like cloud formations, easily and effortlessly pass and blend into one another.

18. Karsten Harries

Heidegger as a Political Thinker

> Wenn die Seele dir auch über die eigne Zeit
> Sich die sehnende schwingt, trauernd verweilest du
> Dann am kalten Gestade
> Bei den Deinen und kennst sie nie.
> —Hölderlin, *An die Deutschen*

Asked whether, in the light of recent attempts to use philosophy to change our goals and to help transform society, he saw a social mission for his philosophy, Heidegger gave a negative reply: "If one wants to answer this question, one has to ask first: what is society? and consider that society today is only the absolutization of modern *subjectivity* and that from this perspective a philosophy which has overcome the stand-point of subjectivity is not even permitted to participate in the discussion." [1] What rules out such participation is the fact that Heidegger's thinking, as he himself interprets it for us, has pushed beyond his own time in such a way that given all that the age considers important it must seem beside the point. The work of the later Heidegger is an extended untimely meditation. This untimeliness helps to explain the apolitical character of this work.

Heidegger has not always understood his thinking in this way. The actions and words of 1933 and 1934, especially the *Rektoratsrede*, his inaugural address as rector of the University of Freiburg, speak of a quite

Reprinted from *The Review of Metaphysics* 24 (June, 1976), with permission of the editor.
The epigraph can be translated, "Though your soul swerves beyond your own time / Winged by its yearning, mournful you linger here / On the cold shore then / Among your own and know them not."

1. Richard Wisser, ed., *Martin Heidegger im Gespräch* (Freiburg und München: Karl Alber, 1970), p. 68.

different conviction.[2] They force us to raise the question: what, if any, relationship is there between the apolitical stance of both *Being and Time* and the later works, and Heidegger's political engagement in 1933?

But is this even a philosophical question? Does it not rest on a confusion of biography and philosophy? The achievement of the philosopher, it has been suggested, should not be confused with the man's sins.[3] This suggestion makes sense only if one is willing to admit the inauthenticity of Heidegger's work.[4] Authenticity, as Heidegger himself understands it, rules out such a separation of the political stance of the author and his philosophy.[5] Those who argue that the ideal which finds expression in the *Rektoratsrede* stands in no relationship to his philosophy make that philosophy as rootless as most thinking in this "age of need."

But was Heidegger's warm reception of National Socialism not as a matter of fact a brief aberration which had little connection with his preceding work and was soon followed by disenchantment and opposition? The latter cannot be denied: Heidegger's tenure as rector lasted only ten months; his unwillingness to cooperate with the Nazis left him no choice but to resign.[6] But the former must be questioned. The connections which link the *Rektoratsrede* to *Being and Time* cannot be overlooked; at the same time the address leaves no doubt concerning Heidegger's sympathies with National Socialism, in spite of the fact that it was found subversive by some Nazis. Thus it is not too surprising that in 1953, when the *Introduction to Metaphysics* was finally published, Heidegger left what he had said in 1935 about "the inner truth and greatness" of the movement stand-

2. Martin Heidegger, *Die Selbstbehauptung der deutschen Universität* (Breslau: Korn, 1933), abbreviated *SU*. See also Guido Schneeberger, *Nachlese zu Heidegger. Dokumente zu seinem Leben und Denken* (Bern, 1962). Schneeberger's bias makes it necessary to use this collection with care. For a more balanced view, see François Fédier, "Trois attaques contre Heidegger," *Critique*, Vol. XXII, No. 234, 1966, and Jean-Michel Palmier, *Les écrits politiques de Heidegger* (Paris: l'Herne, 1968).

3. Ludwig Marcuse, for example, wants to dissociate Heidegger's "fall into sin" from "the extraordinary book *Being and Time*. . . . *Being and Time*, the shameful Freiburg productions of the thirties, and the opaque orphic platitudes of the Hölderlin and Trakl essays may not be mixed together. No one can 'defend' his propaganda for Hitler (in the guise of philosophy). No madman can destroy his epochal *Being and Time*." Letter in *Der Spiegel*, Vol. XX, No. 11, 1966. See also Eric Weil, "Le cas Heidegger," *Les temps modernes*, Vol. II, No. 22, July 1947.

4. See Theodor W. Adorno's rather superficial *Jargon der Eigentlichkeit. Zur deutschen Ideologie*, 5th ed. (Frankfurt am Main: Suhrkamp, 1970), which discusses Heidegger's use of language as an example of idle talk. The charge is supported with greater care by Robert Minder in "Heidegger und Hebel oder die Sprache von Messkirch," "*Hölderlin unter den Deutschen*" und andere Aufsätze zur deutschen *Literatur* (Frankfurt am Main: Suhrkamp, 1968), pp. 86–153.

5. This follows from Heidegger's association of authenticity and entirety. As opposed to the inauthentic person, who has scattered himself into different roles and activities, the life of the authentic person is essentially one.

6. See the already cited works by Fédier and Palmier. Also Otto Pöggeler, *Philosophie und Politik bei Heidegger* (Freiburg und München: Karl Alber, 1972).

ing without comment,[7] although in other places he did not hesitate to edit and interpret the earlier lectures. Heidegger thus reminds us himself that his turn towards National Socialism was genuine and cannot be erased from the development of his thought. The nature of this term must be understood if we are to understand that development.

In this paper I will try to show that the *Rektoratsrede* has an important place in the evolution of Heidegger's thought. While its roots are in *Being and Time*, it also announces new themes which are developed in *An Introduction to Metaphysics* (1935) and *The Origin of the Work of Art* (1935/36). The political philosophy to which these themes lead lets us understand what Heidegger saw and hoped to see in Hitler. One is reminded of the place Nietzsche assigned to Wagner. Like Nietzsche, Heidegger was soon forced to recognize how disastrously misplaced his enthusiasm had been and how unfounded his hope for a new beginning which would rescue Germany from disintegration and madness. This recognition forced a rethinking of his own philosophy and of its relationship to the age. National Socialism is now understood in somewhat Spenglerian terms as a characteristic expression of a late age from which Being has withdrawn itself.[8] Heidegger ties this withdrawal to the triumph of subjectivity in modern technology. Given this association it is not surprising that *Die Zeit des Weltbildes* (1938), the essay in which Heidegger offers a first analysis of the technological world, concludes with the lines from Hölderlin's *An Die Deutschen* which I placed at the beginning of this essay.[9] Sadly the thinker, whose reflections have led him beyond his age, recognizes how untimely he has become. Heidegger's opposition to the Nazis is inseparable from a self-interpretation which places him at a distance from the modern world.

It is unfortunate that Heidegger's changing political views, fragmentary as they are, have received so little attention, for it is here that the questionable character of his thought becomes most readily apparent—questionable in the sense of both demanding and deserving challenge.[10] Werner

7. *Einführung in die Metaphysik* (Tübingen: Klostermann, 1953), p. 152; *Introduction to Metaphysics*, trans. R. Manheim (New Haven: Yale University Press, 1959), p. 199. Cf. Jürgen Habermas, "Zur Veröffentlichung von Vorlesungen aus dem Jahre 1935," *Philosophisch-politische Profile* (Frankfurt am Main: Suhrkamp, 1971), pp. 67–75.

8. In "Hölderlin und das Wesen der Dichtung," first presented as a lecture in 1936, Heidegger makes Hölderlin's characterization of his age as *die dürftige Zeit* his own. *Erläuterungen zu Hölderlins Dichtung*, 2nd. ed. (Frankfurt am Main: Klostermann, 1951); trans. D. Scott, "Hölderlin and the Essence of Poetry," *Existence and Being*, ed. W. Brock (Chicago: Regnery, 1949), p. 289.

9. *Holzwege* (Frankfurt am Main: Klostermann, 1951), p. 89; "The Age of the Worldview," trans. Marjorie Grene, *Boundary 2*, Vol. IV, no. 2 (1976), pp. 341–55.

10. I know of only three books which must be mentioned. Alexander Schwan's *Politische Philosophie im Denken Heideggers* (Köln und Opladen: Westdeutscher Verlag, 1965) remains the best study of Heidegger's political thought. Basing his

Marx has warned of the danger posed by Heidegger's thought.[11] The more seriously we take Heidegger, the more weight we must give to this warning; the more we feel ourselves drawn to the path which he has cleared, the more carefully we must consider where he is leading us and by what authority.

The attempt to show connections between the *Rektoratsrede* and *Being and Time* can succeed only if we keep in mind their very different goals. The *Rektoratsrede* is shaped by Heidegger's political engagement; it is addressed to the teachers and students of the university and calls them to a specific place. *Being and Time* on the other hand has no clear political implications; it does not call us in a definite direction. And this, it would appear, is as it should be: as a work in fundamental ontology it must remain formal and abstract; as a transcendental inquiry it can only describe possibilities of human existence without prescribing where man is to go.

But can *Being and Time* be considered a pure example of fundamental ontology? Do terms like "authenticity" and "inauthenticity" function in a purely descriptive manner? Rather, does Heidegger not choose them to call us, if not to a particular life, at least to a way of living? *Being and Time* can be read as an edifying discourse disguised as fundamental ontology. Heidegger may insist that "inauthenticity" and "idle talk" are not being used in a derogatory sense (*SZ* 43, 167),[12] but he himself acknowledges that finally we cannot divorce ontological inquiry from the concrete stance adopted by the inquirer. "Is there not, however, a definite ontical way of taking authentic existence, a factical ideal of Dasein, underlying our ontological Interpretation of Dasein's existence? That is so in-

---

analysis especially on "The Origin of the Work of Art," Schwan shows convincingly that Heidegger understands the *polis* as a work of truth. Schwan does not, however, make clear the connection between resolve and such work; the relationship of Heidegger's work analysis to *Being and Time* remains unclear. Jean-Michel Palmier develops Heidegger's suggestion in *Einführung in die Metaphysik* that "the inner truth and greatness" of National Socialism should be sought in the encounter between global technology and modern man in *Les écrits politiques de Heidegger*. Special emphasis is placed on the impact of Ernst Jünger's *Der Arbeiter* on Heidegger's thought. In *Philosophie und Politik bei Heidegger* Otto Pöggeler criticizes Schwan for having placed too much emphasis on "The Origin of the Work of Art" and for having romanticized Heidegger's conception of truth. According to Pöggeler, any attempt to develop a political philosophy along Heideggerian lines must begin with the global rule of a technologically determined world civilization. Heidegger's thinking seeks to keep open the possibility which would allow man to escape total subjection to that rule.

11. *Heidegger und die Tradition* (Stuttgart: Kohlhammer, 1961), pp. 246–47.; trans. T. Kisiel & M. Greene, *Heidegger and the Tradition* (Evanston: Northwestern University Press, 1971), pp. 247–48.

12. Page references in the text are to *Sein und Zeit*, 7th ed. (Tübingen: Niemeyer, 1953), abbreviated *SZ*; trans. J. Macquarrie and E. Robinson, *Being and Time* (New York: Harper and Row, 1962).

deed. But not only is this Fact one which must not be denied and which we are forced to grant; it must also be conceived in its *positive necessity*, in terms of the objects which we have taken as the theme of our investigation" (*SZ* 310). Heidegger's ontological analysis thus shows the purity of fundamental ontology to be an illusion. His choice of terms communicates the ideal underlying his ontological investigations: *Being and Time* calls its readers to authenticity, to that honest acceptance of man's own being which Heidegger terms "resolve." The theme of resolve returns, but in a different key, in the *Rektoratsrede*. A careful analysis of that term can thus help to make clearer what links the two works.

In *Being and Time* resolve is understood as the authentic response to the call of conscience, while conscience is said to call man to acknowledge his guilt (*SZ* 289–97). Man is guilty in being his own foundation, but in such a way that he is in the hands of nothingness, cast into the world, vulnerable and mortal. This use of the word "guilt" shares with the ordinary understanding an emphasis on authorship and negativity. We call someone guilty when he is the author of something which should not have been done, or not the author of something which should have been done. Heidegger calls man guilty because as a free being he is author of his actions and bears responsibility for what he is, yet is cast into the world, subjected to it and to death. Using a more traditional language we can say that man is guilty because he has eaten of the Tree of Knowledge, but not of the Tree of Life. If man is to seize himself as he is, he has to acknowledge that his freedom is tied to impotence, that his project of pride, of becoming his own foundation, must fail. If man is to exist authentically he must accept his guilt.

Authenticity does not simply refer to a possible mode of human existence, but that possibility has a claim on man. We are called to authenticity. Heidegger interprets this call as the call of conscience. Here "conscience" may not be taken in the sense in which we use the word when we speak of having a bad conscience because of something we did or failed to do. In the call of conscience man's own guilty being calls him out of the absorption in the accepted and expected back to himself and to an acknowledgment of the groundlessness of his being.

Conscience demands to be heard. Resolve is the authentic response to that demand. Resolved man seizes himself in his entirety, that means in his freedom, but also and especially in his subjection to what is, in his impotence, his vulnerability, and his mortality. Resolve is inseparable from an openness to the uncertainty of human existence. The resolute individual has surrendered all claims to something like a ground on which he can base his life and which can offer final security.

Like "guilt" and "conscience," "resolve" is left empty and abstract. Heidegger's call to resolve calls man to a form of life, not to a particular life. But man cannot exist as pure form. To affirm what Heidegger terms guilt, man must also accept his facticity and the necessity of choosing himself concretely, in the world and with others. Resolve becomes genuine only when expressed in particular resolute action. The formal character of *Being and Time* makes it thus like a vessel which demands to be filled. This demand does not come to fundamental ontology from without, but is generated by the ontological analysis itself. Only in particular decisions does man genuinely seize himself and thus become authentic. The ontological analysis of authenticity and resolve remains incomplete until it has been shown how such decisions are possible.

But how does *Being and Time* allow for the realization of resolve in concrete decision? Resolve is inseparable from an acknowledgment of guilt, from the recognition that man cannot secure his being and decisions by relating them to a higher authority in which he could be said to have his measure. Only inauthentic existence receives such a measure by subordinating itself to an established way of life; the authentic individual knows about the groundlessness of all such measures. Authentic measures appear only with resolve; they are not antecedently given to guide resolve.[13]

Is this claim any more intelligible than Sartre's closely related attempt to make freedom the foundation of value?[14] A freedom which knows no criteria is indistinguishable from spontaneity. Freedom requires, if perhaps not a moral sense, at least an intuition that some things matter and that not all things matter equally. Furthermore, that they matter cannot be something that I have freely chosen, for if this were so we could ask why this particular choice was made. To say that things matter is to say that man is called to his place or perhaps to different and even incompatible places. Where there are no criteria to evaluate what is to be done and decision is blind, it is impossible to distinguish responsible action from arbitrariness. When pushed so far that it frees itself from all measure and authority, freedom subverts itself; it must remain tied to criteria or to an authority on which a decision can be based. But how are we to reconcile this with Heidegger's analysis of resolve?

Due to its formal character, *Being and Time* invites a resolve to be resolved, a readiness to commit oneself without prior assurance that there is a cause worthy of our commitment. To insist on such assurance would be a mark of inauthenticity. But what is to distinguish the readiness to be

13. See *Holzwege*, pp. 43–44; trans. Albert Hofstadter, "The Origin of the Work of Art," *Poetry, Language, Truth* (New York: Harper and Row, 1971), p. 55. "Every decision, however, bases itself on something not mastered, something concealed, confusing; else it would never be a decision."

14. Jean-Paul Sartre, *Being and Nothingness*, trans. Hazel E. Barnes (New York: Philosophical Library, 1956), pp. 625–28.

resolved from a readiness to be seized? Resolved to be resolved, man is in a vulnerable position. He opens himself to attack and seizure, even if such seizure is what the individual has chosen for himself. Heidegger suggests this in those later works where *Entschlossenheit* (resolve) is said to be *Ent-schlossenheit:* [15] the hyphen is to suggest that the resolved individual has unlocked and opened himself, ready to listen and to respond to what is. The shift in emphasis is hardly surprising. Already in *Being and Time* resolve is said to free man for his world (*SZ* 297). From Heidegger's understanding of authenticity as complete self-possession and of man as essentially in the world and with others it follows that resolve is only inadequately understood when it is interpreted as the authentic response to the silent call of conscience. This would transform the authentic individual into a homeless stranger, who, like Kierkegaard's knight of faith, has suspended his ties to the world. Authenticity would become an inner quality which remains hidden from others. But to become authentic man must affirm himself in his entirety. We find Heidegger thus insisting that resolve does not imply a leave-taking from the world and does not yield a free-floating self, but "pushes" the self back into the world and the community (*SZ* 298). Such involvement does not yet furnish the authority which is needed to make sense of decision. In the absence of criteria which transcend the particular situation it is difficult to see why the authentic individual would decide on one course of action rather than on another. Without a higher measure man becomes an empty vessel into which the world pours its contents.[16]

Heidegger recognizes the need for an authority which will allow man to escape from arbitrariness and thus make authentic action possible. In *Being and Time* he seeks such authority in the past which has helped con-

---

15. *Einführung in die Metaphysik*, p. 16, *Holzwege*, pp. 55 and 321. See also *Gelassenheit* (Pfullingen: Neske, 1959), p. 61.

16. Passages like the following—"But on what basis does Dasein disclose itself in resoluteness? On what is it to resolve? *Only* the resolution itself can give the answer." (*SZ* 298)—have invited a decisionistic interpretation of *Being and Time*. Karl Löwith may have been the first to suggest a connection between Carl Schmitt's political decisionism and Heidegger's thought in "Les implications politiques de la philosophie de l'existence chez Heidegger," *Les temps modernes*, Vol. II, No. 14, Nov. 1946, p. 348. See also Eric Weil, "Le cas Heidegger," p. 136; Jürgen Habermas, "Die grosse Wirkung," *Philosophisch-politische Profile*, pp. 81–82; and Christian Graf von Krockow, *Die Die Entscheidung. Eine Untersuchung über Ernst Jünger, Carl Schmitt, Martin Heidegger* (Stuttgart: Enke, 1958). Beat Sitter ("Zur Möglichkeit dezisionistischer Auslegung von Heideggers ersten Schriften," *Zeitschrift für philosophische Forschung*, Vol. XXIV, No. 4, 1970) admits on one hand that Heidegger's early writings are open to a decisionistic interpretation (519) and that such an interpretation is invited by the emptiness of Heidegger's ontological categories (523), but rightly insists that for Heidegger the ground of decision cannot be sought in an intuition which cannot be questioned and justified; decisionism is a "phenomenon of inauthenticity" (532).

stitute the present and illuminates the future. Authentic action is repetition, where repetition should be thought of not as a mechanical reenactment of what has been, but as a response which does not forsake the present for the past (SZ 386). "The sole authority which a free existing can have" is said to be the "repeatable possibilities of existence" (SZ 391). The inherited past, however, even if looked at as a repeatable possibility, is not as such authoritative. The past event becomes one which should be repeated only when it is recognized to be worthy of repetition. Heidegger does not speak of recognition, but of the individual choosing his hero (SZ 385). This choice endows a past existence with something like an archetypal significance. Heidegger gives no examples and does not elaborate. Is he thinking of the believer's choice of Christ? In what sense and how is the hero chosen? Is the choice, like the choice of what Sartre terms the fundamental project, the ground of further justification and as such groundless? [17] Is it a decision to believe in the archetypal significance of a precursor? But can such belief be willed? There must be something about the present individual and his situation which allows him to recognize in the precursor's stance the measure of his own. If the present is mute without the voice of the inherited past, it is nevertheless only the present which can lead authority to this voice. We fall back into arbitrariness unless choice is tied to recognition. How is this to be thought? *Being and Time* gives no answer. But as long as this question remains unanswered, the ontological analysis of authenticity remains incomplete.

What are the political implications of Heidegger's analysis of authenticity and resolve? Richard Schmitt is not the only one to suggest that Heidegger's emphasis on self-possession surely "would incline him toward an anarchism like that of Henry David Thoreau, who proclaims, 'That government is best which governs least.' " [18] In support of this suggestion one can point to a remark made by Count Yorck von Wartenburg, and quoted with apparent approval in *Being and Time:* "To dissolve elemental public opinion, and, as far as possible, to make possible the moulding of individuality in seeing and looking, would be a pedagogical task for the state. Then, instead of a so-called public conscience—instead of this radical externalization—individual conscience—that is to say consciences—would again become powerful" (SZ 403). Schmitt cites one of Heidegger's own statements, adding the comment that

> Where all authority is suspect and feared as a temptation for the individual to give over his responsibility for choosing genuine self-possession, one is not

17. Sartre, *Being and Nothingness*, pp. 563–64.
18. Richard Schmitt, *Martin Heidegger on Being Human* (New York: Random House, 1969), p. 250.

surprised to read that "Resoluteness constitutes the *fidelity* of existence to its own self. As resoluteness which is ready for *dread*, fidelity is at the same time respect for the only authority that existing freely can have." [*SZ* 391] [19]

Unfortunately Schmitt does not quote the second sentence in its entirety and as a result misinterprets what is being asserted: according to Heidegger resolve must root itself in the inherited past.[20] This past, given the fact that man exists essentially with others, is not only the individual's own, but determines the destiny of a people. (*SZ* 384) "Dasein's fateful destiny in and with its 'generation' goes to make up the full authentic historizing of Dasein" (*SZ* 385).

Heidegger's understanding of destiny rules out all attempts to draw anarchistic consequences from *Being and Time*.[21] Once we recognize that authenticity demands the subordination of the individual to a common destiny, it becomes impossible to see the *Rektoratsrede* as diametrically opposed to *Being and Time*. Consider the following passage from the address which Schmitt finds particularly difficult to reconcile with what is said in *Being and Time*:

> The highly touted "academic freedom" is being banished from the German university: being merely negative, this freedom was spurious. It meant indifference, arbitrariness of goals and inclinations, actions without restraint. [*SU* 15] [22]

Heidegger precedes this sentence with the Kantian sounding "To give the law to oneself is highest freedom." Freedom is understood as autonomy; autonomy requires obedience to a law which the individual draws from his own essence and thus gives himself. But in what sense does Heidegger's understanding of the essence of man enable us to give content to

19. Ibid.; the translation is Schmitt's own.
20. "Als *angst*bereite Entschlossenheit ist die Treue zugleich mögliche Ehrfurcht vor der einzigen Autorität, die ein freies Existieren haben kann, vor den wiederholbaren Möglichkeiten der Existenz" (*SZ* 391)
21. That *Being and Time* has anarchist implications is also asserted by Graeme Nicholson in "Camus and Heidegger: Anarchists," *University of Toronto Quarterly*, Vol. XLI, autumn 1971, and "The Commune in *Being and Time*," *Dialogue*, Vol. X, No. 4, 1971. Nicholson argues that Heidegger's understanding of authenticity implies rupture and crisis which find their political expression in a revolt and the choice of "an unfinished commune, one without institutions." This interpretation, suggestive and provocative as it is, is supported by a very selective reading of Heidegger. Nicholson recognizes that Heidegger's understanding of history and destiny does not fit his interpretation, but he does not take this to be a serious objection, arguing instead that this part of *Being and Time* is incompatible with Heidegger's existential theory. The reader is left to wonder whether that theory, especially Heidegger's conception of authenticity, has not been truncated.
22. The translation is by Schmitt. All other translations from the *Rektoratsrede* are my own.

such a law? Kant could appeal to the authority of pure reason. But if Heidegger's analysis is accepted, that authority is no longer available. To give some content to the notion of autonomy Heidegger draws on history: to understand what his own essence commands, the individual has to understand also the origin of that essence and the destiny which ties him to others, to his people (*Volk*) (*SZ* 384; *SU* 15).

This much we can get from *Being and Time*. New and all too timely is the emphasis which the *Rektoratsrede* places on leadership. Heidegger strikes this theme with the very first sentence: the assumption of the rectorate is the acceptance of the duty to provide the university with spiritual leadership (*SU* 5). And since the university should not only be the school which trains "the leaders and guardians of the fate of the German people" (*SU* 7, 18), but itself a place of "spiritual legislation" (*SU* 21), this leadership cannot be confined to the academic sphere, but should have an impact on the entire nation. The disintegration of the old order, the collapse of an already ruined culture, which threatens to sweep everything into confusion and madness (*SU* 22), gives particular urgency to this task. Heidegger's description of the students of 1933 underscores this urgency: Germany's students are "on the march," but this march still lacks direction. This makes it into a search for those leaders, who through "word and work" would reveal to these students their vocation (*SU* 14).

It is remarkable that with all this talk of leadership no mention is made of Hitler. The tensions between the reality of Hitler's leadership and what Heidegger has to say are indeed striking. Heidegger's understanding of leadership rests on his analysis of resolve. Resolve implies autonomy, while autonomy demands that the individual understand his own essence and what it commands; this, in turn, cannot be separated from an understanding of the destiny of the community of which he is a member. And yet this destiny, and thus the place of the individual, are not simply given to us by history, but must be wrested from it. History must be interpreted. Heidegger's leadership thus takes the form of interpretation.

As the title of the *Rektoratsrede, Die Selbstbehauptung der deutschen Universität*, suggests, Heidegger's concern in that address is directed not so much towards the individual as towards the threatened autonomy of the German university. The university, he insists—or does this insistence conceal a plea?—will continue "to set its own task and to determine the way and manner of its realization" (*SU* 6).[23] But it can do so only if the

23. Heidegger's insistence on the autonomy of the university challenged those who wanted to make it into a tool of the movement and reduce it to a vocational school, while his emphasis on the spiritual opposed Rosenberg's subordination of spirit to race and biology. This is not to suggest that Heidegger's commitment to the Nazis was less than genuine. He appears to have been convinced at the time that in spite of the threat posed by party functionaries and ideologues, the engagement of people like

members of the university community, instead of permitting its disintegration into independent faculties and departments, know about and commit themselves to its essence. Such a commitment is said to be inseparable
from a commitment to science (*SU* 7). But what is science? The heart of
Heidegger's address is given over to his answer to this question, which
leads him back to the beginning of science in Greek philosophy, a beginning which, Heidegger asserts, "does not lie *behind us* as something which
has long since happened, but stands *before* us" (*SU* 11) and continues to
preside over the destiny, not only of the university, or of science, but of
the German people.

Heidegger's determination of the essence of science recalls the analysis
of *Being and Time*, although science is now given far greater importance.
In *Being and Time* physics is considered as the classical example not only
of science, but of ontological analysis in general (*SZ* 362). What makes
mathematical science paradigmatic is the way in which its approach to
entities is governed "by the prior projection of their state of Being" (*SZ*
262). Such projection presupposes that man has already distanced himself
from and opposed himself to all that is. All science rests on objectification and thus on a distancing from more engaged ways of existing in the
world.

In keeping with this analysis, the *Rektoratsrede* seeks the origin of science in Greek philosophy because here, for the first time, Western man
opposes himself to all that is and questions and seeks to grasp it in its
being (*SU* 8). The distancing essential to science should not lead us to
understand science as mere detached contemplation. Instead it must be
understood as a product of human labor. The Greeks are said to have
recognized this and to have understood *theoría* as "the highest mode of
enérgeia," of man's "being-at-work" (*SU* 10). Science, instead of letting
what is be, strives to subject it to man's projective vision and thus to over-
power it. According to Heidegger, the Greeks knew that such attempts
could never succeed. The finally unsurmountable resistance of what is
being investigated must be recognized if investigation is to be more than
idle speculation; this resistance renders all genuine knowledge questionable. Heidegger speaks of the "creative impotence of knowledge" and suggests that it is only the failure of even the most resolute attempt to over-

himself could help to shape the Nazi movement in such a way that it would become
a force which could rescue Germany from crisis and confusion. Such engagement
could be effective only if the gap between the language of philosophy and that of
politics could be closed. Heidegger thus was willing to fuse his own philosophical
terminology with Nazi jargon, a fusion which had to contaminate his style. An
embarrassing example of this are those three pages of the *Rektoratsrede* where
Heidegger discusses *die drei Bindungen, Arbeitsdienst, Wehrdienst,* and *Wissens-
dienst.* Palmier is right to point back to the three orders of Plato's *Republic* (*Les
éscrits politiques,* p. 163), but, no matter what the antecedents, in the context of the
time this had to be understood as propaganda for Hitler.

power what is which reveals the unfathomable determinacy of what confronts us and gives to knowledge its truth (*SU* 9).

But what, if any, political significance does this determination of science have? To see that significance it is important to keep in mind that science, as Heidegger understands it in the *Rektoratsrede*, establishes an order which encompasses all entities, including man himself. This, if Heidegger is right, is what science meant to the Greeks: a power encompassing human existence in its entirety (*SU* 10). And when Heidegger recalls his audience to the Greek beginning of science, he calls for a thinking which, no longer content with the splintering of science into sciences, will help to establish or reestablish the "spiritual world" of the German people, and thus help to overcome the disintegrating tendencies of the age.

According to the analysis of *Being and Time*, resolve demands that man know his place in the world (*SZ* 298). In the *Rektoratsrede* Heidegger suggests that this world is established and reestablished by human work. Authenticity depends on such establishment. Thus it demands of those who lack the strength to create their own work the subordination to the work of a creative leader which assigns them their place and joins them in a community. Such subordination may not be an unquestioning acceptance of the assigned place. Implicit in the demand for authenticity is the demand that no one follow a leader without challenging his leadership. "Every following carries resistance with it. This essential tension between leading and following may not be obscured, let alone eliminated" (*SU* 21).

We can make sense of the conflict between leaders and followers only if the leader's work is not an arbitrary establishment, but remains responsive to a reality whose claims cannot be denied and to which the followers have independent access. Heidegger's insistence on the importance of questioning is tied to a demand that man open himself to this reality, to the powers which preside over our existence and he mentions "nature, history, language; people, custom, state; poetry, thought, faith; disease, madness, death; law, economy technology" (*SU* 13). Questioning leads to recognition of *das Unumgängliche*, of what cannot be gotten around. Only out of such openness can the spiritual world of a people arise.

> For "spirit" is neither empty cleverness, nor the uncommitted play of the intellect, nor the limitless drift of conceptual distinction, and it is especially not world reason; spirit is primordially attuned, knowing resolve towards the essence of being. And the *spiritual world* of a people is not a superstructure erected by culture, no more than it is an armory stuffed with useful bits of knowledge and values, but it is the power which most deeply preserves the forces stemming from earth and blood as the power which most deeply moves and profoundly shakes our being. [*SU* 13]

Resolve is still understood as man's affirmation of himself in his entirety, but Heidegger now insists that such affirmation is possible only when man

opens himself to forces which transcend him. Embarrassingly close to the
Blut und Boden vocabulary of the Nazis, Heidegger speaks of the *erd- und
bluthaften Kräfte eines Volkes;* [24] the works which follow speak more
simply of the earth. This introduction of a transcendent reality which
moves and claims man allows Heidegger to give an answer to the question: what makes the leader's work more than arbitrary establishment and
lets others recognize its authority? Such recognition is possible because
such work is not free invention, but an interpretation of the meaning of
the earth. This meaning must be brought to light, must be articulated if
man is to know his place. And this articulation must allow the individual
to recollect his own vocation if authenticity is to be preserved.

An Introduction to Metaphysics, The Origin of the Work of Art, and
Hölderlin and the Essence of Poetry develop the conception of the creative leader whose work lets others discover their own essence and place.
Heidegger's reflections now center on the artist, especially on the poet,
but thinkers and statesmen are included among those creators who "cast
their work against overwhelming nature and in it capture the world which
is thus opened up" (*EM* 47, 146; *HW* 50).[25] Not only that: the work of
the statesman is given a privileged place in that it "grounds and preserves"
the work of other creators (*EM* 146). Heidegger never developed the
suggestion that the *polis* or the state should be understood on the model
of the work of art, but, as has been shown convincingly by Alexander
Schwan, any attempt to understand Heidegger's political thinking in the
thirties has to begin with his analysis of the work of the artist and the poet.

The nature of such work is discussed most fully in *The Origin of the
Work of Art*. In this essay Heidegger is speaking first of all of the visual
arts, but, as he himself points out, "*All art*, as the letting happen of the
advent of the truth of what is, is, as such, *essentially poetry*. The nature
of art, on which both the art work and the artist depend, is the setting-
itself-into-work of truth" (*HW* 59). Poetry is understood as "illuminating
projection" which "nominates beings *to* their being *from out of* their
being" (*HW* 60–61).

Inseparable from such projection is the establishment of a world. By
world Heidegger does not mean the totality of facts. We come closer to
what he has in mind when we think of a space of intelligibility. Consider

24. The Nazis were, however, not the only ones to use this vocabulary at that
time. For a fuller discussion of the phrase see François Fédier, "A propos de Heidegger," *Critique*, Vol. XXIV, No. 242, July 1967, p. 681.
25. Page references in the text are to the already cited editions of *Einführung in
die Metaphysik* (*EM*) and *Holzwege* (*HW*). Translations from "The Origin of the
Work of Art" in the latter volume by Albert Hofstadter in Martin Heidegger,
Poetry, Language, Thought (New York: Harper and Row, 1971), pp. 17–87. The
other translations are my own.

the thesis of *Being and Time* that entities are considered first of all as to hand. To understand such entities—Heidegger uses the example of a hammer—is to understand what they are good for. Such understanding places them in a wider context, e.g., the context provided by some activity. With respect to this activity I can ask again: what is it good for? And such questioning can continue until we come to a final horizon which cannot be surpassed: to the world. To truly know what something is, is to know its place in the world. "The world is not the mere collection of the countable or uncountable, familiar and unfamiliar things that are just there. But neither is it a merely imagined framework added by our representation to the sum of such given things. . . . World is the ever-nonobjective to which we are subject as long as the paths of birth and death, blessing and curse keep us transported into Being. Wherever those decisions of our history that relate to our very being are made, are taken up and abandoned by us, go unrecognized and are rediscovered by new inquiry, there the world worlds" (*HW* 33). To know one's place in the world is to know what matters; to know what matters is to know what is to be done. "He who truly knows what is, knows what he wills in the midst of what is" (*HW* 55). To create a world is thus to establish a place for man to dwell.[26] Heidegger calls this dwelling place man's *ethos*.[27] Resolve and knowledge of this *ethos* belong together. Only that person can be resolved and know what is to be done who has been assigned his place in the subordination to some work.

Heidegger includes the statesman among the genuine creators. The statesman's work establishes the *polis*, the place in which poet, artist, and thinker, as well as those who lack the strength to be creators, find their places. "To this place of history belong the gods, the temples, the priests, the festivals, the games, the poets, the thinkers, the ruler, the council of elders, the assembly of the people, the army, and the ships" (*EM* 117). The modern state is seen in the image of the Greek *polis*. In the *Rektoratsrede* Heidegger thus speaks of a people knowing itself in the state. Only the commitment to a state lets a people discover its own essence and destiny and thus itself as one people.[28] Heidegger insists that like all genuine creators, political leaders must be violent and willing to use power. This willingness lets them stand out in history and at the same time lets

---

26. "Bauen Wohnen Denken," *Vorträge und Aufsätze* (Pfullingen: Neske, 1954), pp. 145–204; "Building, Dwelling, Thinking," *Poetry, Language, Thought*, trans. A. Hofstadter, pp. 145–61.

27. *Über den Humanismus* (Frankfurt am Main: Klostermann, 1949), p. 39; trans. E. Lohner, "Letter on Humanism," *Philosophy in the Twentieth Century*, ed. W. Barret and H. Aiken (New York: Harper and Row, 1962), p. 296.

28. Pöggeler is right to insist that we can no longer speak of a people (*Volk*) as German idealism had done, looking back to the Greek polis (*Philosophie und Politik*, p. 29).

them become *apolis:* "without city and place, lonely, uncanny, without expedients in the midst of all that is, without law and limit, without structure and order, because *as* creators, they themselves must lay the foundation for all this" (*EM* 117). Similarly the *Rektoratsrede* demands of the leader "the strength to be able to walk alone" (*SU* 14).

The connection between these ideas and Heidegger's turn toward National Socialism cannot be denied. Heidegger's understanding of the state as the work of a violent creator leads quite readily to such assertions as "The Führer himself and he alone *is* the German reality of today and for the future, and its law." [29] As the creator of measure and law, the creative statesman cannot be subjected to them: his work cannot meaningfully be challenged, for the criteria which would have to be presupposed by such challenge are themselves only established through his work.[30]

Heidegger soon recognized what a terrible mistake he had made, and, as Hannah Arendt points out, "he was still young enough to learn from the shock of the collision which after ten short hectic months . . . drove him back to his residence, and to settle in his thinking what he had experienced." [31] This timely retreat from the world of action into thoughtful contemplation poses more questions than the initial engagement. Does Heidegger's understanding of the creative statesman allow us to distinguish the genuine leader from his false counterpart? Did the reality of Nazi Germany collide with the philosopher's thoughts? And why did Heidegger's recognition of his own error not lead him into more active opposition, but to retreat from the political sphere altogether? Should we

---

29. "Deutsche Studenten," *Freiburger Studentenzeitung*, Nov. 3, 1933, reprinted in Schneeberger, p. 136.

30. One may want to challenge these implications of Heidegger's work on Heideggerian grounds by arguing that there is nothing which prevents each individual from being himself the author of the work from which he derives his measure. This would deny the distinction between leader and led and challenge the priority of the political. It would, however, be difficult to reconcile such an interpretation with Heidegger's understanding of community. A Heideggerian defense of democracy has been attempted by Karl-Heinz Volkmann-Schluck in his *Politische Philosophie. Thukydides, Kant, Tocqueville* (Frankfurt am Main: Klostermann, 1974). Volkmann-Schluck points to Heidegger's understanding of *Gelassenheit*, which he takes to imply a willingness to let the other, be it a person or a nation, freely unfold its essence (p. 232). European history fulfills itself in democracy; the "will to equality," which determines the shape of our political-social world, is said to have its origin in the Greek determination of the essence of man and in the character of reflection which governs modern thought (p. 142). Beat Sitter similarly interprets the history of the West as a movement towards freedom. ("Zur Möglichkeit dezisionistischer Auslegung," p. 524) But if Heidegger's analysis permits us to understand democracy as a characteristic expression of our age, the movement towards equality and freedom is tied by him to the ever deepening loss of Being and thus rendered questionable. See pp. 322–26 of this article.

31. Hannah Arendt, "Heidegger at Eighty," *New York Review of Books*, Vol. XVII, No. 6, Oct. 1971, p. 54, reprinted in this volume, pp. 293–303.

see this retreat as a perhaps regrettable, but only too understandable, expression of human weakness, or are philosophical thought and concrete decision once again more intimately connected?

Let us consider the first of these questions: how, given Heidegger's understanding of the state as a violent setting-itself-into-work of truth, can we distinguish the genuine leader from his false counterpart? The decision becomes particularly difficult to make when we keep in mind those passages where Heidegger ties truth and untruth so closely together that all attempts to distinguish one from the other seem to be ruled out from the very beginning. If truth is in its essence untruth (*HW* 43) must not every setting-into-work of truth be at the same time an establishment of error? Werner Marx thus suggests that Heidegger is mistaken when he makes not only mystery, but error, deception, and evil equal partners in the truth relationship. If we insist on that partnership, National Socialism, precisely in so far as it represented a genuine setting-itself-into-work of truth, had to fall into violence and error.[32]

When "truth" and "error" are so closely linked the terms threaten to become meaningless; their identification would reduce Heidegger's philosophy to absurdity. Heidegger cannot be claiming their identity. But how then is the partnership of truth and error to be understood? Already in *Being and Time* we read that "the proposition that 'Dasein is in the truth' states equiprimordially that 'Dasein is in untruth' " (*SZ* 222). To say that Dasein is in the truth is to understand it as the place where the hidden emerges into the light, the place where beings reveal themselves. Only because there is such a place can truths in the usual sense be discovered; the truth of assertions presupposes the truth of Dasein. Heidegger likens Dasein to a forest clearing: human being is the place where Being opens itself and unconcealment happens. To say that man is equally in truth and untruth is to maintain that "the clearing in which beings stand is in itself at the same time concealment" (*HW* 42).

The thesis is less paradoxical than some of Heidegger's formulations make it appear. As a being who must share his world with others, man's understanding is inevitably "dominated by the way things are publicly interpreted" (*SZ* 222). Most of the time we find ourselves assigned a place which we have neither created nor appropriated, but have inherited without questioning this inheritance. Bound to others, man has already subjected himself to ways of living, speaking, and understanding which are not his own. We understand as one understands and thus cover up what is to be understood even as we understand it. "Being towards entities has not been extinguished, but it has been uprooted. Entities have not been completely hidden; they are precisely the sort of thing that has

---

32. Marx, *Heidegger und die Tradition*, p. 247; and Schwan, *Politische Philosophie*, pp. 39, 76–77.

been uncovered, but at the same time they have been disguised" (*SZ* 222). First of all and most of the time man exists inauthentically. And because inauthenticity is inseparable from man's being with others, man can be said to exist in untruth.

Does Heidegger's insistence on the partnership of truth and untruth mean that the two are identified or equally significant? Quite the contrary: the call to authenticity is also a call to truth. Heidegger demands that Dasein "explicitly appropriate what has already been uncovered, defend it *against* semblance and disguise, and assure itself of its uncoveredness again and again. The uncovering of anything new is never done on the basis of having something completely hidden, but takes its departure rather from uncoveredness in the mode of semblance" (*SZ* 222). To demand authenticity of man is to demand of him also that he make what others have established his own. This precludes any unquestioning following of some leader. The leader must respect the autonomy of his followers if their following is to be authentic. And those who would follow a leader must first recognize that the place they are assigned by his work is indeed their own. This twofold demand had to collide with the reality of Hitler's leadership.

But the question remains: how are we to distinguish truth from semblance, the genuine leader from his false counterpart?

To know is to uncover what is as it is. Heidegger speaks in this connection of robbery (*SZ* 222). Searching for truth, man seeks to appropriate what is not his. But such attempts can never lead to total appropriation. Finally our aggression must meet with refusal: something unmastered and hidden will always remain. Were our appropriation to become total the otherness of what we are trying to understand would disappear. Thought would have absorbed reality, but such absorption would prevent us from making any sense of truth at all. Genuine knowledge is inseparable from the recognition of what must remain concealed. And yet, this is not to say that all our attempts at understanding are equally inadequate. What remains concealed provides the measure which gives direction to our search for truth. All making overt, all establishment of Being in human work, must remain open to what has remained hidden. Heidegger thus insists that we have understood only one side of genuine work when we have understood it as the establishment of a world. In the *Rektoratsrede* he demands that "the spiritual world of a people" preserve "the forces stemming from earth and blood"; somewhat transformed this demand reappears in *The Origin of the Work of Art* as the claim that establishing a world, the work must also preserve the earth.[33]

33. Although hardly developed, the conception of the earth is at least hinted at in *Being and Time*. Dermot Moran called my attention to the function of the earth in

What does Heidegger mean by "earth"? How does "earth" relate to "world"? Perhaps consideration of an analogous, but more traditional formulation can help us to understand this relationship. It has often been suggested, by, among others, Heidegger himself in his *Habilitations-schrift*,[34] that to know what something is is to know its place in a logical or linguistic space. This place is never so fully determined that it could not be occupied by some other, very similar thing. The measures which we bring to reality, for instance when we call something a fir tree, have their measure in, but cannot capture what is before us in its concrete particularity, but only in certain respects which make it comparable to other objects. This limitation is not a failure of language, but its very point. In language revelation and concealment must go together. Their conjunction discloses the rift which separates language and reality: just as the material presence of the object, its givenness, prevents thought from fully penetrating and subjecting it, so that the victory thought seeks must finally elude it, and some opacity, something not mastered, will always remain, so by forcing what is to be known into our moulds we place our human measures before reality which thus presents itself to us as other than it is. While the language-space transcends given matter in that it has room not only for what happens to be the case, but for infinitely many other possible facts, given matter transcends that space and does not totally disclose itself in it. We can thus distinguish between a *formal* and a *material transcendence*, between the transcendence of language and the transcendence of things. The former furnishes a space which allows objects to appear, but it does not account for the fact that they do appear. The being of entities can be understood as the interplay of formal and material transcendence. In this play revelation and concealment, truth and untruth, are inseparably joined.

Heidegger does not speak of formal and material transcendence, but of world and earth. Not that these pairs of terms say the same thing: the spectatorial stance of traditional philosophy, from which the distinction between formal and material transcendence is thought, has reduced reality revealed in practice to objectivity present to a subject. The transformation of the world which assigns us our place into a transcendental space, of the Dionysian earth which claims and moves us into the mute presence of things, has its foundation in that reduction.

Heidegger seeks the essence of work in the establishment of a struggle between earth and world; establishing this struggle the work establishes

---

the *Cura* fable (*SZ* 197–98) and to *SZ* 381, where Heidegger speaks of "die Umweltnatur als 'geschichtlicher Boden.'" This anticipates *HW* 62, where Heidegger suggests, "ein geschichtliches Volk" has "seine Erde."

34. *Die Kategorien- und Bedeutungslehre des Duns Scotus* (Tübingen: Mohr, 1916), p. 96.

Being. Heidegger speaks of a struggle rather than of a resting together because earth and world, while they belong together, are inescapably in tension. In so far as the establishment of a world is a making overt and public, it tends to conceal the dimension of the hidden. As the established world comes to be taken for granted such concealment leads to a forgetting of the earth. The inherited and accepted world tends to obscure the tension between the place it assigns to us and the many ways in which the earth more immediately claims and moves us. Preserving the earth, genuine work shatters the security offered by the established and accepted. By opening man to what transcends his world it renders that world questionable and at the same time places it on the only ground which it can have. The word "ground" should not be misunderstood. If by ground we understand a securely established foundation, the hidden earth cannot be considered a ground. It is not *Grund*, but *Abgrund*, abyss.

Heidegger understands genuine work as a creative interpretation of the past which articulates "only the withheld vocation of the historical being of man himself" (*HW* 63). Such interpretation is inseparable from a questioning appropriation or repetition of that original interpretation of Being which still governs the shape of our world. When Heidegger asks: what is Being? he seeks to recover the Greek beginning of our historical existence, to recall us to that beginning, not to have us simply repeat it, but to transform it into a new beginning. For to understand that first beginning is also to open oneself to what transcends that beginning, to the earth, to "the original realm of the powers of being" (*EM* 29), which is both prior and posterior to our world. All genuine work not only reestablishes the world, but recalls us to the earth and thus to the precariousness of what has been established. Authenticity demands openness to the earth. Only such openness allows the individual to recollect in the leader's work his own vocation. Such recollection is always a decision. "Every decision, however, bases itself on something not mastered, something concealed, confusing; else it would never be a decision" (*HW* 44). This, however, is not to say that the decision is arbitrary, only that it is precarious, that the possibility of error cannot in principle be avoided, and that because of this the decision must continuously be questioned and renewed or perhaps revoked.

Heidegger's thinking, with its emphasis on the precariousness of human existence and its insistence on challenge and questioning, had to collide with an ideology which claimed to offer an adequate and total world interpretation. Any such claim must cover up what Heidegger terms the earth; thus it precludes the possibility of authentic following. But while this helps us to understand Heidegger's retreat from National Socialism, the question remains: why does this retreat take the form of a retreat from all political activity?

Heidegger's subsequent interpretation of National Socialism gives the answer: instead of finding leadership capable of rescuing the West from that Spenglerian decline which is conjured up in the *Rektoratsrede* before its final call to resolve, Heidegger discovered that the Nazis were very much part of this age of need, an age which, according to Heidegger, receives its shape from technology. Heidegger's retreat from politics is inseparable from his characterization of the essence of technology.[35]

What is technology? Heidegger interprets it as the culmination of the history of metaphysics. That history, as Heidegger asserts again and again, begins with the Greeks. Here, for the first time, man opposes himself to all that is and attempts to grasp it in its being. Establishing the essence of what is, such determination tends to cover up what must remain hidden. The covering up and forgetting of what Heidegger terms the earth is part of the essence of metaphysics.

Already in the *Rektoratsrede* Heidegger sketches the three stages of metaphysics so familiar from his later works (*SU* 10–11). With the Greeks the attempt to seize and thus to secure Being leads to an interpretation of Being not simply as presence, but as constant presence, for how can we seize the ephemeral? Elusively fleeting sensible appearance is thought of as dependent on a permanent higher reality. A decisive second step is taken when this higher reality is understood as God and every other entity as *ens creatum*. God's creative intellect knows no hiddenness; the thought of God, in Whom everything is secured, has to cover up the earth. Metaphysics enters its third and final stage with Descartes: only what can be known clearly and distinctly can be said to be, and what can be known in this manner can be manipulated. Cartesian metaphysics triumphs over the earth in technology. This triumph and the complete forgetting of the earth belong toegther. But how, then, is it possible to be authentic in a technological age? If authenticity demands openness to the earth it also demands that we take a step beyond the technological world which is our inheritance.

It is in this context that the parenthetical remark in *An Introduction to Metaphysics*, suggesting that "the inner truth and greatness" of National Socialism be sought in the encounter between global technology and modern man, should be understood (*EM* 152). Alexander Schwan maintains that Heidegger sees this greatness in the appropriateness of National Socialism to an age from which Being has withdrawn itself: National Socialism provides in a preeminent way what the essence of the age demands.[36] This is indeed how Heidegger later came to interpret National Socialism, but the claim is difficult to reconcile with the lectures of 1935:

---

35. See especially "Die Frage nach der Technik," *Vorträge und Aufsätze*, pp. 13–44.
36. Schwan, p. 136.

not Hitler's Germany, but Russia and America are said there to have realized most completely the technological essence of the modern world; they
are "metaphysically seen, the same: the same dreary rage of an unchained
technology and the bottomless organization of ordinary man" (*EM* 28).
Technology is seen here as a danger; the destruction of the essence of
man which its total triumph implies should not simply be accepted as inevitable. Instead technology should be understood, appropriated, and surpassed. Heidegger's understanding of history and destiny suggests how
difficult such a surpassing must be. For our destiny has been shaped by
technology; the authentic response to technology can therefore not be a
simple refusal. Such a refusal would cause us to lose touch with our inheritance, thus with ourselves. It must rather take the form of an appropriation which, in recovering the origin of technology in the origin of
metaphysics, repeats and surpasses that beginning and thus preserves the
forgotten earth.

What Heidegger hoped for from National Socialism was such preservation. Heidegger soon came to see that his hope had been vain and misguided, that the Nazis' *Blut und Boden* had little in common with Hölderlin's *Erde*. This recognition forced Heidegger to reinterpret the nature
of their leadership. Hitler's Germany now comes to be seen as Russia and
America were described in *An Introduction to Metaphysics*.

Central to this reinterpretation is Heidegger's thesis of the totalizing
tendency of that interpretation of Being which shapes the modern world.[37]
To the extent that for modern man what is can be understood, organized,
and controlled, he can no longer give place to the earth. And if genuine
work must preserve the earth, then the modern world will no longer
know genuine work, be it the work of the artist, of the thinker, or of the
statesman. Nor will it know truth in Heidegger's sense, for truth and
genuine work belong together. The present world is thus interpreted as
the *Irrnis*, the "realm of error," which by its very essence must cover up
the earth in which it yet has its roots.[38] This covering up is inseparable
from that will to security in which metaphysics has its origin, a will which
is just the other side of man's inability to accept what in *Being and Time*
is called man's guilt. This will to security finds its first clear philosophical
expression in Plato, who sees man's temporal existence as lacking, man as
an erotic being, striving to overcome that lack. Plato also saw that such
striving could not gain its goal in time. Only the turn to a realm of being
beyond time could give man satisfaction. Later man turned to God and
thus gained a sense of final security, but, as Nietzsche points out, modern

37. Besides the already mentioned essays, see especially Heidegger's *Nietzsche*, 2
vols. (Pfullingen: Neske, 1961). Also Hans-Georg Gadamer, "Über die Planung der
Zukunft," *Kleine Schriften I* (Tübingen: Mohr, 1967), pp. 161–78.
38. *Vorträge und Aufsätze*, pp. 92ff. Abbreviated *VA*.

man is unable to give content to such a turn. For him there is no escape from time. To make temporality constitutive of human existence is also to place a lack at the center of man's being. This is to say that man's search for security cannot come to an end. Hobbes offers a good description of modern man, as Heidegger understands him, when he writes:

> I put for a general inclination of all mankind, a perpetual and restless desire of power after power, that ceaseth only in death. And the cause of this, is not always that a man hopes for a more intensive delight, than he has already attained to; or that he cannot be content with a moderate power: but because he cannot assure the power and means to live well, which he hath present, without the acquisition of more.[39]

Man never has enough power; security is always inadequate. Heidegger understands technology as the organization of this lack. "Everywhere, where there is too little of what is—and increasingly there is too little of everything for the will to will which is ever raising itself—technology must leap into the breach and create *Ersatz* and use up raw materials. But in truth *Ersatz* and the mass production of *Ersatz* things is not a passing stopgap, but the only possible form in which the will, the 'complete' securing of the organization of organizing maintains 'itself' and thus can be the 'subject' of everything" (*VA* 95–96). For a humanity which has lost touch with the earth, everything must become *Ersatz*. Instead of entrusting himself to what is, man encounters what is only as material for his plans and calculations. The progressive organization of everything can come to no end.

Heidegger does not understand technology as an instrument at man's disposal; this would require that man has the ability to consider what is and himself apart from technology. Just this Heidegger questions. Technology, he suggests, determines the shape of our world. As modern man puts himself in God's place and seeks to secure his existence, he subjects himself to an endless process of planning and calculation.

According to Heidegger the modern leader is just a functionary of that process. "The born leaders are those who, on the basis of their attunement, allow themselves to be employed by this process as its steering organs" (*VA* 96). This process does not stop before man. Rather it reduces man to "raw material" and subjects him to the same planning that has already transformed nature into a source of raw materials. Before this process an old-fashioned morality, which finds this transformation incompatible with human dignity, is powerless. Somewhat mockingly Heidegger speaks of the moral indignation of those "who do not yet know what is" (*VA* 93). The progressive organization of everything knows no limits.

39. *Leviathan*, Part I, chap. 11.

Thus the attempt to subject human sexuality and reproduction to planning should be expected. "One should not, out of an antiquated prudery, seek refuge in differences which no longer exist" (*VA* 95). Terms like *Schrifttumsführung* and *Schwängerungsführung* suggest that Heidegger is thinking of the Nazis, but the tendency towards totalitarianism and one-dimensionality is part of a process which cannot be understood as a peculiarly German, or for that matter, a peculiarly Russian or American development, but which has a global significance.[40] "Because reality consists in the homogeneity of what can be subjected to planning and calculation, man must enter into this uniformity in order to be up to reality. Today a man without uniform already makes the impression of being unreal, of no longer belonging" (*VA* 97).

Unwilling to don the uniform, no longer counting himself among the leaders, Heidegger has become a questioner and listener. *Entschlossenheit* has given way to *Gelassenheit*. The latter suggests not so much resolve, as a willingness to let things be, not in the sense of accepting them, but in the sense of not trying to interfere. Heidegger characterizes this attitude as a "simultaneous yes and no" to the technological world.[41] The "no" is born of the recognition that the triumph of technology as he describes it must destroy the essence of man. To save that essence we must keep ourselves open to that other dimension for which the technological world leaves no room and which is yet its origin. Heidegger's work seeks to preserve such openness in the present age. But he can give little content to this other dimension. Lacking the strength to oppose to this world another, better world, the philosopher acquiesces in the technological world, permits it to enter his life, and at the same time keeps his distance. He lives in this world, but as an outsider, whose thinking prevents him from really belonging to it. Seeing no possibility for world-establishing work and genuine community in this age, Heidegger has forsaken political activity. He has become *apolis* in the sense in which all true creators are said by him to be *apolis*. But unlike them Heidegger lacks the strength to fashion a work which would lead us in new directions. Left is the strength to listen to the now all but silent call of the earth. "Invisible and outside the wasteland of the devastated earth dwell the shepherds" (*VA* 97).

Heidegger's inner emigration raises as many questions as his brief and misguided but genuine political engagement. That engagement was born of a

---

40. For the impact of Ernst Jünger's *Der Arbeiter* (1932) on Heidegger's interpretation of technology, see Palmier. Also Heidegger, *Zur Seinsfrage* (Frankfurt am Main: Klostermann, 1956); trans. W. Kluback and J. Wilde, *The Question of Being* (New York: Twayne, 1959).

41. *Gelassenheit* (Pfullingen, 1959), p. 25; trans. J. Anderson and E. Freund (New York: Harper and Row, 1966), *Discourse on Thinking*, p. 54.

widely shared sense of crisis and of the conviction that, given the state of the society in which he lived, the philosopher could not remain aloof, but had to engage himself and play a leading part in its transformation. Heidegger's subsequent recognition that, instead of leading, he permitted himself to be used, issued in a despairing denial of a social mission to his thought. The present world is now judged to be such that authenticity is possible only to the outsider. To guard Being and the threatened essence of man, the "shepherd of Being" must take leave from that world. But where can he go? If the technological world is indeed *the* world for us, there is no place he can go. He must remain where he is. To the world his dwelling outside remains invisible.

But does Heidegger's conception of authenticity not demand a more complete self-affirmation than such an inner emigration allows? An affirmative answer was presupposed by Heidegger's extension of his analysis of the work of art to the state. That extension, with its emphasis on the earth, rests on a critique of the claim that modern science and technology can give us *the* key to what is. To the extent that technology becomes a power which dominates society, the individual will lose his own essence to what he has created. Heidegger's return to the Greek origin of science was to free us from such dominion and thus prepare for a more humane future.

Unfortunately this project became intertwined with a rejection of the modern conception of the state, with its separation of the ethical and the political, of the private and the public, separations which are difficult to reconcile with the kind of unity and self-integration demanded by Heidegger's conception of authenticity. Recalling Nietzsche's hope for a creative resurrection of Greek tragedy, Heidegger calls for a state which would be a "repetition"—in his sense of the word—of the Greek *polis,* a state which would assign man his *ethos,* his place as member of a genuine community. It is this romantic conception of the state with its fusion or confusion of the political and the social which we must question. The attempt to restructure the modern state in the image of the *polis* will tend towards totalitarianism.

To question this conception of the state we must also question the conception of authenticity which lends it support and the implicit idealization of unity at the expense of plurality. The antipluralistic side of Heidegger's thought reappears in the later claim that the tendency towards totalitarianism is inseparable from our world, shaped as it is by technology. Technology tends towards total dominion. But is Heidegger's monolithic world understanding correct? Again we meet with an emphasis on unity which does violence to the many facets of our being in the world. Heidegger sees the history of the West as the working out of just one theme: our destiny is governed by the history of metaphysics, which conceals a finally futile search for security. Unless he learns to take a step beyond that history, man will lose his essence. Only this linear view of history leads Heidegger to his despairing analysis of the present age as so deeply fallen that all attempts to criticize and reform are already caught up in that fall.

But does the history of metaphysics, as Heidegger understands it, offer us *the* theme of our world? I would not question that Heidegger points to one, perhaps even the most important theme. Still, our world is too varied to be understood in this simple manner. We must recognize other, perhaps older themes, and we can appeal to these themes to put technology in its proper place. Indeed, this is what Heidegger himself does when he invites us to think beyond our world to the *Geviert*, the fourfold gathering of earth and sky, divinities and mortals.[42] That we can follow this invitation presupposes that Heidegger's one-dimensional interpretation of the modern world is only a caricature of our world. Once this is recognized, the misguided optimism of the *Rektoratsrede* is likely to seem less questionable than Heidegger's more recent denial of a social mission to his philosophy.

42. See especially "Das Ding," *Vorträge und Aufsätze*, pp. 163–81; trans. A. Hofstadter, "The Thing," *Poetry, Language, Thought*, pp. 165–86.

19. David Couzens Hoy
History, Historicity, and Historiography in Being and Time

PHILOSOPHY COURSES ON *Being and Time* rarely cover the sections on history, and published discussions of Heidegger's analytic of Dasein often fail to consider how these sections add to the description of human existence. Yet Heidegger's concept of historicity is a crucial part of the structure of Dasein, and his theory of historiographical methodology is an essential propaedeutic for the later destruction of the history of ontology. If Heidegger does indeed eventually occupy a major place in the history of philosophy, this will be due both to his profound concern with the historical nature of human existence and to his rethinking of the history of thought. He is a philosopher's philosopher who denies that philosophy can begin with a presuppositionless starting point and work toward an unhistorical, eternal truth, and who accordingly follows his own dictum that philosophy must learn how "to conceive the possibilities prepared by its 'precursors'" (*SZ* 19).[1]

The failure to take the sections on history seriously can lead to several important consequences. First, the popular fascination with Heidegger's description of being-toward-death may cloud Heidegger's insistence that Dasein is not an isolated, private ego but most primordially a social, communal, and historical being. Secondly, the difficult distinction between the ontic and the ontological may be misunderstood unless it is put to a test where something concrete hangs on the distinction. The relation of Heidegger's notion of historicity to the procedures of historiography represents such a test, and it creates difficulties for the early Heidegger's

1. All translations from the German texts of Heidegger are my own responsibility. References to *Being and Time* are cited according to the pagination in *Sein und Zeit* (*SZ*), the tenth edition (Tübingen, 1963). The terms *Geschichtlichkeit* and *Historie* have been translated as "historicity" and "historiography" rather than as "historicality" and "historiology" as in the Macquarrie and Robinson translation.

foundationalist theory of science. These difficulties raise the historical question of how Heidegger himself became motivated to generate the ontological philosophy of history in *Being and Time*.

A third general problem concerns the philosophical project of *Being and Time* itself, for the fundamental ontology that makes a basic premise of the principle of historical and temporal change must reflect upon its own status if it is not to succumb to a paradoxical historicism. Heidegger himself in his later writings has misgivings about the ontological or metaphysical character of *Being and Time*, and doing philosophy for him becomes more and more indistinguishable from redoing the history of philosophy. Possibly, however, the methodology described in *Being and Time* for the subsequent destruction of the history of metaphysics should itself have been abandoned for the same reason that the project of overcoming metaphysics was to be relinquished. In the later essay "Time and Being" Heidegger remarks that the attempt to destroy metaphysics from within still involves a positive regard for metaphysics. To accomplish his antimetaphysical task, he now intends "to cease all overcoming, and leave metaphysics to itself." [2] Nevertheless, there are many other later writings for which the discussion of historical methodology in *Being and Time* prepares the way, however problematically.

This third problem area raises questions about the whole of Heidegger's thought. In order to deal in sufficient detail with § 72 through § 76 of *Being and Time*, questions about later writings will not be explicitly considered here.[3] The ontological analysis of history in *Being and Time* invites an independent consideration of the problem of giving an adequate hermeneutical theory of the methodology of the historical disciplines. In order to understand and evaluate the theory Heidegger presents in *Being and Time*, the historical background of his own thinking on the philosophy of history should be known. Then his reasons for moving beyond an analytic or ontic philosophy of historiography to an ontological philosophy of historicity in *Being and Time* will be more apparent, and we will have the proper basis for a critical examination of his views on the methodology of the historical sciences.

THE PROBLEM OF HISTORY IN THE EARLY WRITINGS

In contrast to previous phenomenology with its Cartesian assumptions of the possibility of attaining unhistorical, presuppositionless certainty, *Being*

2. Martin Heidegger, *On Time and Being*, trans. Joan Stambaugh (New York, 1972), p. 24.
3. See David Couzens Hoy, "The Owl and the Poet: Heidegger's Critique of Hegel" in *Boundary 2* 4 (Winter, 1976): pp. 393–410; also, Michael Murray, *Modern Philosophy of History: Its Origin and Destination* (The Hague, 1970).

and Time allows for historical change in man's nature and existence. In fact, one of its basic tenets is that Dasein *is* historical. The assertion that man is an essentially historical being, however, is itself historical. Philosophy should recognize that it too is an activity conditioned by its tradition. Heidegger approves the remark of Count Paul Yorck von Wartenburg that philosophy should be "historized" (*SZ* 402).

The assertion that thought is necessarily relative to a historical origin is itself a thought, however, and as with any formulation even vaguely suggestive of historicism, a familiar paradox arises. The ontological statement that "Dasein is historical" emerges at a moment in history, but is it true for all moments of history, or is it relative to its own historical context? Is truth itself historical, and if so, what would it mean to say that "truth is historical" is true? "Truth" is a word bearing unhistorical, absolutist overtones in the philosophical tradition. Part of Heidegger's project is to suggest other ways to speak meaningfully about truth. He specifically develops a notion of truth for an ontology emphasizing the historical character of human existence. The question is, if Heidegger asserts that "the questioning into Being" of his own philosophical enterprise is itself characterized by historicity (*SZ* 20), does that commit him to historical relativism, and if so, is this a vicious relativism?

In the introduction to *Being and Time* (see § 6), Heidegger maintains that his own view is radically opposed to historical relativism. The philosophical rethinking of the tradition involves becoming aware of how the tradition shapes the conceptualization of existence, and this awareness should preclude an ahistorical blindness to basic assumptions. We are not to continue thinking in the traditional manner, for that would be to think in a certain way simply because others have always thought that way. Such a thinking would not know *why* it takes a particular direction, and hence, where it is going. A rethinking of the tradition, if it is genuinely thoughtful, involves a criticism, deconstruction, or "destruction" of traditional ways of thinking and of the traditional history of philosophy. The possibility of such a criticism or destruction, however, is itself made possible by the tradition. The "new" standpoint following the destruction is itself not an arbitrary, free-floating position, but is rooted in the possibilities of the thought of its predecessors. Heidegger affirms, then, that "this demonstration of the origins of basic ontological concepts through an investigative exhibition of their 'birth certificates' has nothing to do with a vicious relativizing of ontological standpoints" (*SZ* 22). He believes that the rethinking of the tradition confronts the evident failures of traditional thinking with the possibility of another interpretation of the tradition—a possibility inherent in the tradition all along, but only now becoming clear. The destruction is not of the tradition or the past per se, but of a present way of thinking that has become merely traditional, losing sight of the genuine goals and real historical potency of the tradition.

Although Heidegger is sometimes accused of relativism and historicism, he is clearly aware of the paradoxes involved in these positions. From his earliest writings where he defends logicism against psychologism to his latest writings where he identifies historicism not with his own thought, but with the technological thinking of the decadent, modern world view,[4] he maintains that his thought is not susceptible to such paradox. Seen from the perspective of Husserl's transcendental phenomenology, Heidegger's hermeneutic phenomenology may appear to be on the brink of historicism. But Heidegger's attacks on historicism are as corrosive as Husserl's in *Philosophy as Rigorous Science*. Of course, Heidegger's disclaimers should not veil the fact that his theory of history in *Being and Time* owes much to Dilthey, and Husserl's attack on historicism is sometimes interpreted as a criticism of Dilthey (despite the perhaps merely polite insistence by Husserl that he does not have Dilthey himself in mind.)

The rejection of relativism and historicism in *Being and Time* depends upon the success of Heidegger's fundamental ontology. Earlier writings also show, however, that Heidegger is concerned with refuting these positions, although he comes to realize that his refutations are inadequate and eventually rejects some of his neo-Kantian arguments in favor of the ontological turn he takes in *Being and Time*. In a 1914 review of C. Sentroul's *Kant und Aristoteles*, for instance, Heidegger argues for rather traditional criteria of philological objectivity.[5] He scolds the author for failing to relate Kant and Aristotle to their own historical contexts. One is of course reminded of similar criticisms of Heidegger's own historical scholarship, and his perhaps justified complaint that his philosophical rethinking of past philosophers has not been understood.

A more surprising defense of historiographical objectivism that contrasts with *Being and Time* to some extent occurs in his *Habilitationsvortrag*, "Der Zeitbegriff in der Geschichtswissenschaft," published in 1916.[6] In direct opposition to his polemic in *Being and Time* against historiographical "facts," he follows Droysen in affirming that the first task of historiography is to ascertain the objective factuality (*Tatsächlichkeit*) of the historical reality to be explained by the historian (ZG 185). Hence, contrary to a relativism maintaining that facts depend on and derive from

4. In the essay "Overcoming Metaphysics," which may be a veiled reply to Carnap, Heidegger writes: "The consequence of lack of destiny is the unhistorical. Its characteristic is the dominance of historiography. Historiography's being at a loss is historicism." See Martin Heidegger, *The End of Philosophy*, trans. Joan Stambaugh (New York, 1973), pp. 92–93. For a similar claim, see SZ 396.

5. See *Literarische Rundschau für das katholische Deutschland* 40 (Freiburg, 1914): pp. 330–31, p. 330.

6. Martin Heidegger, "Der Zeitbegriff in der Geschichtswissenschaft," *Zeitschrift für Philosophie und philosophische Kritik* 161 (Leipzig, 1916): pp. 173–188; hereafter cited as (ZG).

a particular theory or interpretation, Heidegger believes at this period that facts come first and that the scientific task of examining the sources for factuality is the proper beginning for historical understanding. In accepting that the second task of historiography is to depict the relations of connection (*Zusammenhang*) between the "*priorly determined facts*" (ZG 186), Heidegger clearly denies the relativist assertions that determining facts and finding relations are not distinct operations and that what count as "facts" depends upon a prior interpretive and evaluative understanding of the relations.

In *Being and Time* Heidegger rejects this view about the priority of facts, but there is no radical break with the previous text. He is opposed to relativism because he does not believe the historical past is essentially unknowable. In the earlier essay he explicitly denies that the past is an incomprehensible otherness (ZG 184). His argument that both the present and the past are manifestations of common possibilities of human life is inconclusive, however, and he will come to realize that this notion of "life" is problematic. Although he is opposed to relativism, he is also opposed to positivism, and the final conclusion of the essay is that the value-laden character of historiography makes it irreducible to other kinds of science. History is qualitative and not quantitative like the natural sciences, and he accepts the neo-Kantian distinction between the *Naturwissenschaften* and the *Geisteswissenschaften*.

Certain difficulties with the "Zeitbegriff" essay, however, lead Heidegger to give up some of his neo-Kantian views and to search for a new approach to the problem of historical relativism. For example, further philosophical questions need to be answered about this common human life underlying the qualitative differences between historical ages. The thrust of Heidegger's analysis in the "Zeitbegriff" essay is to ground reflective thought and abstract science in actual life and concrete existence rather than in atemporal, metaphysical constructs. If "life" is conceived as historical and changing, however, it is unclear how this concept can provide the common denominator linking different ages and allowing one age to compare itself with another. If, for Heidegger (following Rickert), historical understanding essentially involves an evaluation (*Wertbeziehung*) grounded in an interest and presupposing a viewpoint, what prevents the possibility that the values of one age will have only the vaguest family resemblance to those of an earlier one? Furthermore, what prevents the occurrence of such an extensive conflict of values that an earlier period remains incomprehensible? If each view is only a perspective, and there is no aperspectival overview as long as there is historical change, where is the guarantee of the certainty or truth of any historical insights? Or are such insights merely creative fictions or temporarily useful hypotheses?

The "Zeitbegriff" essay involves another kind of difficulty that leads

Heidegger to look for a new approach to the problem of history. Heidegger's ontological turn is partly motivated by his dissatisfaction with the essay's method of taking historical science as a given and examining the way historians proceed. In this early essay Heidegger cites historians on the subject of historiographical methodology, but the way historians think they proceed is not necessarily the way they do proceed. In *Being and Time* Heidegger refuses to start an analysis of history with a discussion either of what historians think they do, or of what they actually do. Rather, he proposes an ontological questioning of history, thus superseding the neo-Kantian assumption that history is only one special area among others for philosophical analysis. This ontological turn raises the more fundamental question whether philosophy itself is historically conditioned.

Heidegger's move toward the latter question is clearly influenced by Dilthey, although Heidegger thinks Dilthey's notions of life and empathy are inadequate. Perhaps because of these inadequacies, Heidegger finds it more convenient to speak through Dilthey's acquaintance, Count Yorck, in spelling out the reasons for going beyond his own earlier standpoint. The critique of Ranke by Count Yorck that Heidegger cites in *Being and Time* is particularly revealing both of his dissatisfaction with the analytic, neo-Kantian method and of his reasons for moving from an ontic to an ontological questioning. Ranke is an "ocularist" (*ein grosses Okular*—SZ 400), writes Yorck, meaning that Ranke is concerned merely with the immediately visible, the more dramatic surface appearances of history, such as the political. Ranke's attempt to do history as objectively as possible— simply giving the "facts" in a pure description and letting the "story" tell itself—is empty and formalistic, argues Yorck, for it forgets that the main purpose of historical thinking is to go beneath the sources to what is hidden.

Of course, the objectivist can reply that this so-called search for the hidden is simply a free ticket entitling one to speculate and romanticize. Yorck's point, however, shows that he sees historical thinking as fulfilling a somewhat different task. To use Nietzsche's language, history fulfills a service to life. Indeed, like Nietzsche, Yorck attacks the antiquarians who merely dig up history for history's sake—thus aestheticizing history and cutting it off from life—when the real purpose of historical thinking is to provide a *critique* (SZ 401).

If Heidegger's philosophy of history is to escape the danger of relativism, such a critique must be possible. The historian must be able to criticize conflicting historiographical accounts, and the philosopher must be able to criticize conflicting views of the meaning of history. Heidegger owes his awareness of the necessity of criticism more to Nietzsche than to the potentially relativistic world view philosophy of Dilthey, and he develops his account of criticism through an explication of Nietzsche's essay "The Use and Abuse of History for Life."

But what is the *object* of historical critique? A critique of the past might be enlightening, but it could not change anything. It would be of merely superficial interest and, in Nietzschean terms, of no real use. Thus, antiquarianism—the mere presenting of the past for the past's sake—remains uncritical. Critique is essentially critique of the present. Criticism must have a basis, however, and history is precisely that which makes comparison and contrast possible by bringing out similarities and differences not only between the present and the past, but also between the actual past and a merely imagined one. Hence, even though history arises out of the present situation and is essentially critical, the antiquarian attempt to give an unbiased picture of the past is a legitimate and necessary moment in the historiographical process. Criticism of the present on the basis of what is past has little force, however, unless there are possibilities inherent in the past that, although overlooked and distorted by a confused and blind present, are still possibilities for the future. The history that reveals these possibilities is called monumental history.

To Nietzsche's three moments of historical thinking—the antiquarian, monumental, and critical—Heidegger adds his own interpretation in distinguishing authentic from inauthentic historical thinking. Each of these moments becomes inauthentic when carried out separately and without concern for the other moments. Authentic historiography, according to Heidegger, must entail a painful detachment from the public confusion of "today": "As authentic, the monumental-antiquarian historiography [*Historie*] is necessarily a critique of the 'present' [*Gegenwart*]. Authentic historicity [*Geschichtlichkeit*] is the foundation for the possible unity of the three kinds of historiography" (*SZ* 397).

Drawing on Dilthey, Yorck, and Nietzsche, Heidegger in *Being and Time* thus moves to a different level of concern with history from that found in his reading of Droysen and such neo-Kantians as Rickert and Windelband. In fact, Heidegger aims at a level of analysis "deeper" than that achieved by the tradition of *Lebensphilosophie*, where "life" is left as an ambiguous remainder (see *SZ* 46ff.). But shifting to another level is not satisfactory unless that level is also philosophically explained and justified. In terms of historical reality as such, Heidegger agrees with Yorck that philosophy is itself historical (*geschichtlich*) and that asking about the way historians do history will not answer philosophical questions about the very conditions for the possibility of historical thinking (see *SZ* 402). Yorck is trying both to establish the essential connection between history and life and to distinguish this more fundamental sense of history from the ontical, factual orientation of the "ocularists." Yet as long as "life" remains unclarified and ontologically "indifferent" (*SZ*

209), there will not be sufficient criteria to decide between the two levels. For the historical to be demonstrated as more fundamental than the ontical, Heidegger thinks it is necessary to go beyond Yorck's distinction and show how the two are grounded in an overall unity—one that can only be shown by fundamental ontology. This principle of unity is for Heidegger the question into the meaning of Being that is the concern of *Being and Time* as a whole.

Although one can thus trace the history of Heidegger's dissatisfaction with previous philosophy of history and understand his motivation for developing an ontological philosophy of history in *Being and Time*, there is no reason to take this ontological turn uncritically. The question must also be raised whether it really makes sense to "ground" historical science in historical existence, as Heidegger—following Dilthey and Yorck—attempts to do. Heidegger distinguishes between history as science (*Historie*) and history as what actually happens (*Geschichte*). In *Being and Time* he introduces a new notion, that of human historicity (*Geschichtlichkeit*). This idea that human existence is a temporal happening (*Geschehen*) that is aware of itself as happening and changing, as stretching along between birth and death, has the status of a condition for the possibility of both *Geschichte* and *Historie*. Is this ontological grounding of history in historicity necessary, and will it actually have important consequences for historiography? This question can only be approached after first considering why Heidegger in *Being and Time* thinks that the move from *Historie* and *Geschichte* to *Geschichtlichkeit* and the etymologically connected *Geschehen* is really a transition to more fundamental, ontological levels and not simply a change of problem or a shift to semantically related but actually distinct senses of the terms.

THE TURN TO HISTORICITY

One way to understand Heidegger's discussion of history in relation to the rest of *Being and Time* is to ask why historical reflection would arise, given Heidegger's description of human existence prior to § 72. Why would Dasein need to think historically? A forward-looking, futural being already immersed in the world might not need to engage in the reflective abstraction involved in studying history, especially the history of far distant pasts or foreign cultures with little relation to the present. Heidegger's account is designed, however, to avoid the gap between immediacy and reflection. Dasein becomes aware of how it *is* its past (and the past of its generation, i.e., its tradition) insofar as the past is an essential part of the *constitution* of Dasein's understanding of its futural possibility. Dasein may relate to this constitution by trying to overcome the way the tradition conditions or limits its possibilities. For this purpose even the distant past or the past of other traditions provides useful contrasts. Of course, in order for the past to contrast with the present its *difference* must be recognized. Thus, as far as possible the past must be recreated on its own terms.

The theoretical intentions of *Being and Time* condition the way history becomes a problem and must be recognized as influencing the way history is "phenomenologically" analyzed. The results of the analysis in *Being and Time* do not necessarily conflict with the overall results of the "Zeitbegriff" essay, but there is a difference in orientation. The "Zeitbegriff" essay begins with reflection on the past and argues that the otherness of the past forces the present into reflective consciousness (*ZG* 184). Historiography can thus lead to an awareness of essential differences between past and present, and this contrast can bring about greater self-understanding. *Being and Time*, on the other hand, starts with the problem of self-understanding and must account for, among other things, the possibility of and interest in abstract reflection on objectively different and distant times. The latter account is said to be more fundamental than the former. This claim to be more fundamental, however, is not necessarily borne out by the subject matter, history, but instead appears to follow only from the methodological requirements of another problematic, in this case, Heidegger's analytic of Dasein.

The neo-Kantian project of constructing a logic of historiographical concepts—the project behind the "Zeitbegriff" essay—will not, Heidegger asserts,[7] answer ontological questions about "how history can possibly become an *object* for historiography" (*SZ* 375). Historiography or historical *reflection* is not the most important aspect of history to be explained. Otherwise one could criticize Heidegger for arbitrarily choosing historiography as the human science to be explained when other sciences such as sociology or psychology are possibly even more problematic in the contemporary situation. Of course, Heidegger does think the cultural, historical sciences are in fact in a state of crisis (see *SZ* 9–13). He also thinks, however, that theology, biology, physics, and mathematics likewise face a crisis. History apparently takes priority because of its closer relation to the analytic of Dasein rather than because of its status qua science, even though this too is important.

What motivates Heidegger in *Being and Time* to turn to history? At least two reasons for an ontological analysis of history can be immediately inferred from Heidegger's text itself. First, given the state of the analytic of Dasein prior to § 72, Heidegger must account for the way man remains self-identical through time, the way man can authentically project a uni-

7. See *SZ* 375 and 393 for explicit criticisms of Rickert.

fied future and past for himself in view of the ultimate limit that death imposes. Since Heidegger holds that not everybody has a self—a unique and individual existence—and that most people remain lost and dispersed in everydayness and in *das Man*, he must explain the "connectedness of life" and the self-constancy of Dasein. The analysis eventually shows that the question about the "connectedness of life" is itself based on a false understanding of the nature of human existence, an understanding starting from man's inauthenticity, that is, from the way man is dispersed and fragmented. Such an understanding is naturally unable to explain either formal self-identity or material self-constancy since the self is what the individual has yet to create for himself (*SZ* 390). Most people choose not to create themselves but to let themselves be formed by what "others" expect of them. Even this latter alternative is a choice, however, and it shows at least a capacity to create a self over time and to have a history. This capacity is the movement of Dasein as it stretches itself out through time,[8] and is called Dasein's happening or *Geschehen*—a term etymologically related not only to *Geschichtlichkeit* but also to *Geschick* (destiny). For Heidegger the ontological principle of historicity is a fundamental feature of this human existence which is so essentially a *Geschehen*, and it is also constitutive of the possibility of man's authentic self-understanding.

The second reason for the ontological analysis of history is that Heidegger, as already noted, intends to prepare the way for the "clarification of the task of a historiographical destruction of the history of philosophy" (*SZ* 392). Accordingly, he attempts to "ground" the ontic science of historiography in this ontological structure. This foundationalist "grounding" will be discussed in the third section of this paper, following a closer examination of the principle of historicity.

The concept of historicity is easily misunderstood. It is a rather rich notion, taking a great deal of its meaning from other parts of Heidegger's fundamental ontology. There are other reasons besides the two already mentioned for giving an ontological analysis of history, and if these are overlooked, the concept will be misinterpreted. For instance, the notion of historicity might seem to leave out much of what is normally under-

8. This stretching along is grammatically reflexive (it is an "*erstreckten Sicherstreckens*"—*SZ* 375). Thus more is implied than that man is simply *conscious* of his being stretched along, of his undergoing change in time, for otherwise this point could have been made simply with the passive voice. *Geschichtlichkeit* is not to be reduced to a psychological phenomenon, but is already philosophical in that its necessity is determined by the task of constructing a nondualistic ontology more than by a desire to be "faithful to experience." This explains Heidegger's assertion in his critique of Yorck that history must not merely be distinguished from the ontical (with its dichotomy between a subject that experiences or undergoes an objective succession of quantitative moments), but must also be grounded in the question of Being, i.e., in a new "ontology" that avoids the metaphysical reduction of man to subject and of Being to the range of possible objects.

stood by the term "history." Talking about how an individual has a history or a unified life is not the same as talking about how a people or a nation has a history. Thus, Nathan Rotenstreich attacks Heidegger for "reducing" history to temporality and to Dasein's *personal* anticipation of death.[9] The emphasis on personal death is translated by Rotenstreich into the concept of "doom." Since historicity is a mode of Dasein's temporality, and since, according to Rotenstreich's interpretation, temporality is essentially bound up with individual existence and consciousness of personal doom, Rotenstreich concludes that grounding history in historicity is basically a grounding of the impersonal in the personal. He thinks Heidegger makes the personal primary and the impersonal secondary, and he disputes this ordering. Since for Rotenstreich history normally involves the impersonal, world-historical, public domain (e.g., institutions such as the state and the law), Heidegger's discussion of historicity has nothing to do with and can have no consequences for history.

But this interpretation of Dasein as a personal, private subject, an inner consciousness over against a world, incorrectly reads psychological meanings into Heidegger's ontological, philosophical analysis. Such readings confuse the ontic and the ontological: structures that constitute conditions for the possibility of empirical, psychological states are themselves taken to be such states. Thus, while it is true that for Heidegger being-toward-death *individuates* Dasein, it does not necessarily *subjectivize* Dasein. While anxiety and the anticipation of death force one to question one's existence and selfhood, the "self" is not some internal, subjective being radically distinct from external, objective projects and situations. Heidegger deliberately avoids the psychological vocabulary of a philosophy of consciousness based on a subject-object dichotomy.

Although according to Heidegger's account I am on my own in facing my death, my authentic appropriation of myself is thus not merely a matter of subjective inwardness. The authentic self is not the existentialist hero who is alone and isolated, and Heidegger insists that to be alone is only a derivative, deficient mode of our more primordial being-with-others (*SZ* 120). The confrontation with death does not subjectivize Dasein and relativize all values to a subjective volition, leaving man radically alone and disengaged from the world. Dasein is defined as being necessarily in-the-world, and this necessity holds as well for *authentic* Dasein, despite the awareness of death, precisely because of the irrecusable structures of temporality and historicity—ontological structures that are not merely ontic, psychological states. The awareness of death does not lead one out of the actual world to other possible worlds where one would be a dif-

9. Nathan Rotenstreich, "The Ontological Status of History," *American Philosophical Quarterly* 9 (January, 1972): pp. 49–58.

ferent person by engaging in other possible life projects. It leads rather
to a recognition of the compelling situation of the actual historical world
and to an urgent commitment to what is most unique and individual about
one's own way of being-there. The freedom man attains through authentic
being-toward-death is still conditioned by historicity: man is not free not
to have a history. He is also not free to have another historical past than
the one he actually has.

Of course, one could recognize the purpose of the analysis of historicity and still reject the results. Calvin O. Schrag, for instance, believes
that Heidegger fails to accomplish the transition that brings Dasein back
from the radical alienation of its anticipation of death to a truly social
and historical community.[10] Again, however, an overly psychological
reading that breaks up the ontological connections between being-toward-
death and historicity misconstrues the result. Being-toward-death is not
the reflection of a subject on some objective state that will eventually
occur. Rather, it is an ontological principle explaining how Dasein is the
kind of being that can find and understand itself in a definite situation.
Historicity accounts for the possibility not only of formal self-possession
(i.e., that Dasein can be "my own"), but also of the inclusion of concrete
meanings in my appropriation of myself. In other words, historicity explains *how* the "my own" includes a past and a future, and how this past
and future are essentially interconnected with the past and future of other
human beings. In brief, the confrontation with the possibility of death
takes on the mode of a concern for one's fate, that is, for one's death in
view of a definite worldly situation. Death makes possibilities implicit in
this situation explicit, and in terms of this explicitness Dasein first has the
possibility of dying not blindly, but fatefully, with an understanding of
its commitment to the situation. Since Dasein's situation fundamentally
involves other people, this co-presence in a situation means that Dasein's
fate will be irrecusably tied to the destiny of a people or nation and to
an independent historical reality.

Destiny (*Geschick*) and fate (*Schicksal*) are technical terms for Heidegger. Contrary to Rotenstreich's interpretation, there are no indications
that destiny is not a true, authentic aspect of historicity. In fact, Heidegger
explicitly points to the authenticity of destiny in defining the concept:
"The full, authentic happening (*Geschehen*) of Dasein is constituted by
Dasein's fateful destiny in and with its 'generation'" (*SZ* 384–85). Fate
represents the way Dasein becomes definite and actual through its relation
to events in the world. It is the crucial point when Dasein understands itself as being free to choose, yet not free to choose, distinct possibilities

10. Calvin O. Schrag, "Heidegger on Repetition and Historical Understanding,"
Philosophy East and West 2 (July, 1970): pp. 287–295, p. 291.

presented by the situation (*SZ* 384). Destiny, on the other hand, concerns more than the fate of the *individual;* it involves the essential connection of the individual to the *community* or a *people:* "Since, however, fateful Dasein, as being-in-the-world, exists essentially with others, its happening (*Geschehen*) is a co-happening (*Mitgeschehen*) and is determined as destiny" (*SZ* 384). Dasein's original *Mitsein,* its essentially social nature, manifests itself through this *Mitgeschehen.*

As the property of a community, destiny is nevertheless not impersonal. Dasein is not to be confused with a private subject that arbitrarily decides the meaning of its historical place. The concept of destiny also implies that freedom is finite and that the fate of the individual is conditioned by the destiny in which he stands. "Destiny is not composed of individual fates any more than being with others can be understood as finding a number of subjects together. Fates are already *guided in advance* by being with others in the same world and by being resolved for definite possibilities" (*SZ* 384—emphases added). Of course, it is also true that destiny would not be possible unless fate were also possible, and Heidegger goes on to say, "The anticipatory handing oneself down in the thereness of the instant of insight that lies in resoluteness we call fate. In it is also grounded destiny, which we understand as Dasein's happening in being together with others" (*SZ* 386). Both fate and destiny are "grounded" in the structure of Dasein, and specifically in Dasein's resoluteness. Being "grounded" does not mean that something else occurs *before* destiny or fate in some genetic, causal relation—as fate before destiny, destiny before fate, or resoluteness before both—but rather that each is necessary for the others to be possible.

The structure of historicity is an essential condition for Dasein's ability both to understand itself and to appropriate itself and take responsibility for its situation. Dasein is not an isolated ego, a subject ontologically distinct from its possibilities. Dasein, says Heidegger, makes itself historical "in its freedom for death by *handing itself down* to itself in a possibility that it has inherited, yet has chosen" (*SZ* 384). Dasein does not spontaneously create its possibilities. The past *conditions* the range of possibilities. Yet it is up to Dasein to recognize its possibilities as such and to incorporate them in its existence.

The personal-impersonal distinction thus misses the point and can easily be overcome. History, or the inherited historical community and tradition, is in fact an extremely personal matter. The person for Heidegger is essentially social and historical. Of course, the individual is free to combat this tradition as well as to lose himself in the politics of the day. Thus, the general modern skepticism about the possibility of having historical goals does not constitute a counterexample to Heidegger's analysis. For Heidegger this skepticism is characteristic of a false sense of the "world-

historical" which takes historical happening to be a function of changes
of ready-to-hand and present-to-hand entities "within the factically existent world." For him historical happening is a function, rather, of the
world as such—"the world in its essential, existent unity with Dasein"
(*SZ* 389). In other words, the false view that thinks history is impersonal
is itself based on an incorrect model of historical understanding, a model
that makes history an object over against a subject observing a multiplicity
of things and events before him. If man is wrongly construed as a subject
ontologically separate from objective history, then the attempt to explain
man's role in history is already doomed to failure. The search for the
meaning of world history already signifies that such meaning has been lost.

The immersion in the skeptical indifference toward authentic history in
the everyday mode of existence is itself a way of choosing to relate to
one's inheritance. More needs to be said, however, about the meaning of
"choosing one's inheritance." That an inheritance can be "chosen" does
not imply the absolute freedom of a subject to constitute the meaning of
his objective situation. Choosing an inheritance is like choosing a fate. The
ordinary notion of fate implies, of course, that fate is predetermined and
not freely chosen. Heidegger's sense of the term "fate" is not entirely unrelated to this ordinary notion, for fate is tied to the facticity of the historical situation the individual has inherited. The difference is that a naive
interpretation of historical determinism must be left behind. The "situation" includes more than unavoidable physical forces. The way men understand themselves is also an important factor in their situation. Therefore, a change in the understanding of the situation is a change in the
situation itself. If men think that the historical situation is hopeless or
meaningless, then that understanding will condition their actions, probably
by leading to an inability to act because of an inability to *believe* in the
possibility of positive action. Coupled with the nihilistic loss of belief in
history-producing action is a loss of even the possibility of having a genuine fate. Having a fate demands the possibility of believing that the historical situation is constituted in a particular and definite way requiring a
concrete course of action. To choose a fate means both to believe that
the historical situation is constituted in a particular way and to be resolved to live by the consequences of that belief.

Heidegger is thus concerned not only with the epistemological problems
of historical relativism but also with the historical nihilism of the modern
era, where man's fate is to be "fateless." The problems about epistemological relativism are connected with the problems about historical values
and actions. Relativism undercuts the ability to *believe* that an understanding of the historical situation is *true*, and is therefore implicitly nihilistic. Historicity is precisely the ontological principle intended to keep the
ontological project of *Being and Time* from lapsing into a subjectivistic

relativism and into nihilism. For one thing, because fate and destiny are intertwined, and because the individual's vision of his fate is a vision into a situation including the destiny of a community, Heidegger's account cannot be cited in support of subjectivism. Since one's fate has social implications, its meaning is not indifferent to the community, but is at once radically personal and communal. Furthermore, nihilistic indifference is also precluded in that the historical understanding involved in the choice of an inheritance includes an essential moment of *criticism*, and criticism implies that all historical understanding is not equally valid. In fact, it can be argued that both evaluative nihilism and epistemological skepticism are most effectively combatted by the essential role of criticism in the structure of historicity. There is a serious flaw in Heidegger's account, however, if he fails to support his insistence on the necessity of criticism with an account of how criticism is logically possible and with an account of the criteria for judging and evaluating different historical interpretations.

First of all, in what way does historical understanding involve criticism? For Heidegger, as noted, historical understanding does not merely involve what Nietzsche called *antiquarian* historiography—the knowledge of history merely for the sake of knowledge. Heidegger speaks of "choosing a hero" (*SZ* 385), indicating his concern not simply with academic knowledge of the past but with what Nietzsche called *monumental* history. Choosing a hero, Heidegger argues, is conditioned by the possibility of "retrieving" meanings from the past, of "repeating" these "past" meanings. A distinction must be drawn here between the past as *Vergangenheit* —a state of affairs whereby some *thing* once present-to-hand (*vorhanden*) is gone for good—and the past as *Gewesenheit*—a state where the "has been" still conditions the "is." This distinction corresponds to the grammatical distinction between the past perfect and the imperfect tenses. Dasein *is* as a being that *has been*. Man is a being with a past in the sense of *Gewesenheit*, and this past is an essential aspect of what he is and *will be*. The structure of historical thinking, then, does not merely involve the relation of past to past, or past to present, but also indicates an essential relation to the future. A concern with the way man *is* involves both a concern with the way he *has been* and the way he *will be*. To think about history is to think the essential unity of past, present, and future in man's being.

This unity, however, implicitly includes an essential negativity. The repetition or retrieve (*Wiederholung*) of past possibility (where "possibility" is to be taken in Heidegger's technical sense of immanent structure rather than in the sense of a potency that does or does not become actual) entails a rejoinder (*Erwiderung*) and a countermand (*Widerruf*) to other possibilities (*SZ* 386). The repetition is a rejoinder insofar as appropriating one meaning implies the existence of other possible meanings. Further-more, the repetition constitutes a countermand since the appropriation of one possibility implies the rejection of others.[11] Heidegger's account is not a defense of either tradition for tradition's sake or progress for prog-ress's sake. History is tied to the present as well as to the past and future, and it is tied to the present in an essentially critical way. Historical under-standing involves an awareness, however dim, of the possibility of modes of existence and ways of thinking different from those readily apparent in the present.

According to Heidegger, historicity, or the understanding that involves this movement of repetition, rejoinder, and countermand, need not in-volve an explicit reflection. This fundamental way of relating to historical action and events (*Geschichte*) could take place, he says, "without the need of any historiography" (*SZ* 386). Even primitive tribal behavior would manifest historicity. To establish this connection one might be able to link historicity to mythical-religious beliefs. Ancestor worship, for instance, is at least *prima facie* connected to a confrontation with death, and it also serves the need of maintaining the tribal traditions and pre-serving the unity of the tribe. Whether the categories of Heidegger's on-tology need be extended to primitive peoples is an open question, but at least on the surface pointing to "prehistorical" tribes would not be a tell-ing counterexample against his claim that historicity is a fundamental fea-ture of existence. Even cultures that have been historically important because of the high achievements of their civilization need not be ages particularly inclined to historical reflection: "Unhistoriographical eras," says Heidegger, "are not as such also always unhistorical" (*SZ* 396). Fur-thermore, for Heidegger as for Nietzsche, an era of advanced historio-graphical achievements need not manifest great historical achievements.

The ontological analysis, then, produces a category characteristic of human existence in general and is not applicable only to a specific culture or historical tradition, such as that of Western Europe. Furthermore, an important feature of Heidegger's ontological analysis of historicity is that nothing follows from the analysis about what the *content* of history must

---

11. Macquarrie and Robinson's explanatory footnote in their translation of *Being and Time*, p. 438, is somewhat misleading. They say that the point of the counter-mand (*Widerruf*) is a disavowal as a "rebuke to the past." To say, however, that the *past* is rebuked can mislead one into thinking that the past can be denied, or that responsibility for the present can be shifted to the past. (To take an abstract example: rebuking one's predecessors for starting a war that one nevertheless continues with very similar principles and policies to those which caused the war in the first place.) This interpretation overlooks the fact that to rebuke the *past* is not to change any-thing. Heidegger's point is more that the *Widerruf* is a rebuke to the present and to certain forces in the present that claim to be the fulfillment of the past.

be. Hegel's concept of history, in contrast, is far more prescriptive.[12] Heidegger's ontology does not prescribe how particular ontic manifestations—in this case, historical events—are to be interpreted, for the ontological categories are also conditions for merely imaginable but likely counterfactual occurrences. Ontological concepts are more formal than material: they describe only the form of existence and not the particular content of individual experiences and events. Heidegger often insists that the apparent lack of specific ontic manifestations of structures such as anxiety or historicity is not evidence against them. Ontological explanation is different from ontical (or scientific) explanation.

This difference presents a problem, however, for it is difficult to see how the ontological foundation affects the ontical activity of historical research. Unlike Hegel's view, Heidegger's position in *Being and Time* does not enjoin that history be seen one way rather than another. Historicity is a formal notion, more like a Kantian category, and Heidegger claims that existence is essentially characterized by the structure of historicity. Any historical thinking, and any piece of historiography, therefore, manifests this structure.

Yet criticism is supposed to be an essential aspect of historicity. The claim that history should involve an explicitly critical self-awareness says very little unless it is also known what constitutes good grounds for criticism. Criticism must be based on specific standards and criteria. The question is, on what grounds can such criteria be derived from "merely" ontological conditions? The ontological account claims only that criticism must be present to some degree. Suppose, however, that two critical but antithetical historical accounts appear. A theory of the science should say more about how these histories can adjudicate their differences. The simple fact that they contain critical elements does not decide between them, and in fact their critical force must be suspended until it is known which of the two accounts is true. For criticism to have force, there must be reason to believe that the critical account is true and not false or arbitrary. For the ontological account to have ontical force or applicability, further criteria for determining the validity or even the value of historical ac-

---

12. Hegel emphasizes the connection more than the separation of the historical and the historiographical—the events of history and the writing of history—on the grounds that the notion of "history" involves preconceptions determining both the individuation of "historical" events and the writing about these events. History, Hegel maintains, is itself the story of the development of the idea of freedom, and as such, the minimal material conditions for "having a history" could be set forth. Thus, his view is that without notions like the law and the state there is no sense in writing a "history." See part 4 of Hegel's introduction to the *Lectures on the Philosophy of World History* in the new English translation by H. B. Nisbet (Cambridge, 1975), pp. 135ff.

counts must be specified. Of course, Heidegger's account does not necessarily fall back into relativism if such specifications are not given. But unless more can be said, relativism is not satisfactorily dismissed.

THE IMPLICATIONS FOR HISTORIOGRAPHY

Heidegger's turn away from the neo-Kantian approach to philosophy of science toward a more "fundamental," ontological questioning is based on a belief that sciences face a crisis and that philosophy is capable of "leaping ahead" of the sciences to show them the way out of their difficulties by setting research on a new foundation (SZ 9–10). Of course, such a belief is not unique to Heidegger. Husserl's notion of philosophy as rigorous science is an important antecedent. This belief, however, generates what may be a decisive failure for "fundamental ontology," for it is precisely at the point where ontology is to be reconnected with the ontic sciences that Heidegger is least convincing. In his account of the connection between historicity and historiography, Heidegger explicates more clearly than anywhere else in *Being and Time* how ontological philosophy helps an ontic science out of its state of crisis. This account, therefore, has implications for sciences other than historiography. It becomes paradigmatic for the whole ontological enterprise of "laying the foundations" for the sciences. But can an ontological construct have the ontic force Heidegger imputes to it? If the account fails, this does not, of course, prove that the project is not feasible. But history, because of its intimate connection with philosophy, is perhaps the area where the project is most likely to succeed, if it is capable of succeeding at all. Examining Heidegger's theory of historical science in § 76 provides a crucial test of his foundationalist theory of science.

For Heidegger science is a thematizing (SZ 393). On the basis of a prescientific interest a specific region is delimited, and entities within this region are investigated according to a method and a conceptual framework. What is it that historical science thematizes? For Heidegger the object of history is Dasein that has been (*dagewesenes Dasein*). This delimitation of the region of history does not impose much of a boundary on the science, however, and merely provides a condition for the possibility of our openness and access to the past. This openness does not restrict what can be said about the past, and might imply an arbitrariness in historical explanations, or even worse, a complete relativism whereby anything at all can be said. Heidegger can be defended here, however, because of the limitations imposed by his restriction that the thematizing be "accomplishable" (*vollziehbar*—SZ 393). Since the object of history for Heidegger is Dasein that has been, and since Dasein always exists in a world, *all* the factual (*vorhanden* and *zuhanden*) remains of Dasein and of that world must be included in the account and explained. So Heidegger's concept of historical science includes the ordinary criteria of completeness (the collection of all the relevant data) and coherence (the consistent account of all this data). So far there is nothing that conflicts with traditional demands for the most rigorous scholarship.

The next step is more problematic. Simply having the factual material, Heidegger goes on to say, does not explain why the material appears historical. Rather, the material must be understood as pertaining to and belonging to a world, and to factical Dasein existent in that world. The acquisition and sifting of the material is not the *start* of the return to the past, but rather *presupposes* a prior possibility of "*historical being toward* Dasein that has been there" (*SZ* 394).

To see what Heidegger means here one can begin with what he does not mean. First, he is not suggesting a theory of empathy, for empathy implies treating men as subjects ontologically separated and linked only by vague intuitions (see *SZ* 124). Secondly, he is not suggesting that history is concerned with the *uniqueness* of past events. For Heidegger, the historian should retrieve the existential possibilities of the past age for his own age. Thirdly, he is also denying that history reduces to deterministic laws (see *SZ* 395). Although history must account for the data, Heidegger's basic point is that history's theme should *not* be merely the factual.[13] The facts, he says, are themselves only the *result* of a resolute choosing of existence, and the historian's task is most essentially not the reconstruction of facts, but of possibilities, that is, of the existential choices underlying the historical fate of individuals and the destiny of peoples.

This reconstruction is more properly a repetition or retrieve because it is not merely a question of reconstructing or rebuilding, for instance, a collapsed ruin. The ruin itself is only a sign for a mode of existence that must be retrieved or repeated by the historian. The mode of existence is not a thing but a possibility in and through a series of factual manifesta-

13. This point depends on a central distinction in Heidegger's terminology. Once that distinction is granted, the point becomes almost trivially true. Heidegger distinguishes *Tatsächlichkeit*, or factuality (the noun form being *Tatsache*) and *Faktizität*, or facticity (the noun form being *Faktum*). "Factuality" can apply to inanimate (*vorhanden* and *zuhanden*) things, whereas facticity applies only to human beings (see *SZ* 7, 56, 135, 145, 394). An important difference between the mode of existence of things and the mode of existence of humans is that while what is factually the case with things can usually be directly perceived, what is factically the case in the existence of persons is *never* directly perceived but only inferred (*SZ* 135). Given the terminology, then, the historian's recreation of the state of affairs in the past must go beyond directly observable factual objects in order to infer what the factical existence of the people was like. But this terminological distinction does not resolve the important question as to whether it can be *ascertained* that an account of what was factically the case is a true account, and in what sense of "true."

tions. Understanding a possibility is different from knowing a fact. But even to recognize what the fact signifies, the historian must understand and interpret the total context conditioning the individuation of that fact. On Heidegger's view, the context itself is not a fact but a possibility that surrounds or runs through the facts. There will always be a demand for a substantiation of the interpretation by the facts, but it should be clear that the same facts can fit into different contexts and that the context itself represents a choice by the historian. This choice is as much a response (*Erwiderung*) to the historian's own situation as to the past situation. History has an essential relation to the present (and to the anticipated future). Since it represents an act of detachment from the present, it is at least implicitly a questioning of the "today." When history recognizes its own critical potential, in Heidegger's eyes it becomes authentic (*SZ* 397).

Heidegger, of course, fully realizes the paradox in claiming that historians should and must deal with possibilities rather than with facts. Sciences generally deal with facts, but Heidegger continues his earlier project in pointing to an essential difference between the human sciences and the natural sciences. Even a weaker sense of "science," however, should still include criteria for rational discourse in order to make discursive arbitration possible. In shifting from the necessary to the possible, has Heidegger eliminated such criteria for history?

Although much of what Heidegger says about historical science is true, at least to a certain extent he appears to say too much. For example, he holds that historiography cannot be believed to have "universal validity" (*SZ* 395). If Heidegger is merely suggesting that no historical account will be true forever, there is no special difficulty. But if he is claiming that an account could not possibly be acknowledged as valid at a particular time by competent historians, then his view is dangerously paradoxical. He implies himself in another book that a certain account is true for a given age (see *Einführung in die Metaphysik*, p. 134; English trans., p. 147f.). In *Being and Time*, moreover, he clearly intends the analysis of historiographical methodology to lead to a destruction of the history of philosophy (*SZ* 392). What is the status of Heidegger's own inversion of the history of philosophy? When Heidegger's rethinking of the tradition leads to the primordial origins for categories and concepts—origins since forgotten by the tradition itself (see *SZ* 21–22)—is his account of these origins "true"?

At least in *Being and Time* Heidegger appears to claim that his own historical account is valid, for he sees this destruction of the history of philosophy as itself a "criticism aimed at 'today' and the dominant way of handling the history of ontology" (*SZ* 22–23). His project of destruction is itself a kind of historiography—and an authentic one, since it is so essentially critical of what is "false" in philosophy today. But then, it must also be reverently antiquarian and faithful in its scholarship.

At least two senses of truth, however, are involved here. These two senses correspond to a distinction Heidegger himself draws between truth as the uncoveredness (*Entdecktheit*) of entities (when a particular thing is seen as *that* thing) and the disclosedness (*Erschlossenheit*) of the *whole* that makes possible the uncovering of particular entities (*SZ* 220). The former is ontical; the latter, ontological. When Heidegger emphasizes that historical science should be concerned with the possible, and when he says that such historiographical truth should be explained from "the authentic disclosedness ('truth') of historical existence" (*SZ* 397), he is therefore saying that historiography is grounded in ontological truth.

This claim may seem to pay history a compliment, for it unites history with philosophy and art in being "true" in the more profound sense of opening up new ways of seeing, a new world. But is this unity desirable? In his *Habilitationsschrift* Heidegger himself points to a difference between history and philosophy. He sees the history of philosophy belonging more essentially to philosophy than to historical research (see *Die Kategorien- und Bedeutungslehre des Duns Scotus*, p. 5). His description of "authentic" historiography and its ontological kind of "truth" is more likely to be applicable to the history of philosophy, at least in his own sense of a rethinking of philosophy and its history, rather than to historiography per se. Of course, even the history of philosophy may not involve the ontological kind of truth that allows for the reinterpretations resulting from Heidegger's deconstruction of the history of traditional ontology. Yet arguments for this point are different from those showing that the concept of truth presupposed by historiography is not the ontological truth of authentic disclosure. The latter point needs to be shown here.

Heidegger claims that the task of historical science is the "*disclosure of historical beings*" (*SZ* 393). This disclosure is a repetition involving the understanding of past Dasein in its past, but repeatable, possibility. "What is meant by the 'birth' of historiography out of authentic historicity is that the primary thematizing of the historiographical object is a projection of past Dasein's own existential possibility" (*SZ* 394). This possibility is not limited to the "private" life of an individual but includes larger historical forces.

Heidegger's basic point may simply be that the historian is trying to understand human beings and not machines. Human beings are not things, and so the criteria for understanding them are not the same as for knowing about things such as machines. Knowledge about a thing is true or false in a different sense from the way in which understanding a person is true or false. But although this may hold for living people, historical people are different in that we know their deeds. We do not have to worry about future actions which may gainsay our knowledge about the actions that have already taken place. What notion of truth is presupposed, therefore, by a historiographical account of historical human beings?

For one thing, the account must be confirmable or disconfirmable. Heidegger himself claims that past philosophers have not been truly understood. He does not seem to be saying that many interpretations are possible and that his is as plausible as any other. His accounts are supposed to be more compelling than that. In fact, he explicitly denies that grounding history in historicity makes history subjectivistic. He affirms the objectivity of historical science, although he redefines the term "objectivity":

> The historiographical disclosure of the "past" that is based in fateful repetition is so far from "subjective" that it alone guarantees the "objectivity" of historical science. For the objectivity of a science is primarily regulated by whether it can *bring* uncovered *before* understanding that thematic being in its primordial Being. [SZ 395]

Heidegger does have a point against Ranke and the historicists, for "the way it really was" ("wie es eigentlich gewesen ist") involves more than simply the facts. This is a rather facile point. It does not follow from this that the facts can be interpreted any way at all. Furthermore, if Heidegger intends to preserve the objectivity of history, even in his own sense of the term, he must give clearer methodological reasons why one description of the possible is more compelling than another, especially if the second description conflicts with the first.

For Heidegger truth as disclosure involves what he calls untruth, but it does not involve the false. Judgments are capable of truth or falsity (in the sense of *entdecken* and *verdecken*). Disclosure, however, is the opening up of a whole context of meaning, and is not capable of being false, but only of failing to disclose. This failure to disclose Heidegger calls untruth. Furthermore, the truth of disclosure, since it pertains to Dasein, is always accompanied by untruth, for disclosure is finite—disclosing one reigon entails not disclosing another.

Historiography would inevitably be in untruth, since there is always more to be said about the past. For historical accounts to be convincing, however, they must be capable of arbitration. It must make a difference whether they are true, for otherwise they are only speculative. Historical accounts consist of statements and assertions that purport to tell what is and is not the case about actual occurrences in the world. Of course, for Heidegger assertions are derivative and depend for their truth on the more profound "truth" of their disclosive context. Yet history is not poetry, and statements by historians, even about existential possibility, are statements intended to be true about the past situation, and also intended to be confirmable or disconfirmable. Truth as disclosure, ontological truth, therefore, is not something to which history *qua science* can attest or not. Moreover, it is not possible to discriminate between conflicting historical accounts on the basis of such truth. Methodologically, such a concept is not presupposed by the science as such. Nor does science supply evidence for Heidegger's ontological theory.

For a historical account to serve as criticism, it must be held true. Of course, for the criticism to be effective, the account may not be true, but if an account is recognized as false, it loses its critical force. Even the most vehement advocate of "relevance" in historiography must admit that sound factuality is better than an emotionally appealing but factually empty account. Even those who insist that historiography is influenced by political differences should recognize that discourse and dialogue are possible only as long as accounts are backed by the possibility of confirmation or disconfirmation and frameworks are justified or justifiable by discursive reasoning.

Another feature of truth as disclosedness that has less applicability to historiography than one might think is the appeal to authenticity. Heidegger writes, ". . . Dasein discloses itself to itself in and as its own possibility of being [*Seinkönnen*]. This authentic disclosedness shows the phenomenon of primordial truth in the mode of authenticity" (*SZ* 221). When he says that historiographical truth is to be explicated in terms of authentic disclosedness (*SZ* 397), he means that there is an essential moment of reflection, of self-understanding involved in doing history. But how is it involved? While it may be true that the historian as a person can reflect on what history means to him and his existence, this is a different matter from the truth of the historical account itself. In fact, Heidegger's own example of an "authentic" historian would indicate that the *content* of the research is not the most relevant factor in determining authenticity. To distinguish between historians who are pursuing historical research authentically and those who are not, he says:

> The historian who "throws" himself from the start into the *Weltanschauung* of an era has not yet proved thereby that he understands his object in an authentically historical way and not just "aesthetically." And on the other hand, the existence of an historian who "only" edits sources may be characterized by an authentic historicity. [*SZ* 396]

More relevant for determining whether historiography is authentic is the degree to which the historian combines monumental and antiquarian interests with critical interests. If the results of the fact-grubbing source editor's labors show that a particular past situation has been misunderstood and that the dominant assumptions about this situation must be changed, his work is indeed valuable. But if his work only corroborates the dominant assumptions (perhaps contrary to his original hopes), should it be judged less valuable and less authentic? Both cases manifest resoluteness and an experience of the possibility of critical history. Whatever the answer, there is good reason to distinguish the question of the truth of the historical account from the meaning it has for the historian himself. Certainly the attempt to adjudicate between conflicting historical accounts by an investigation of their authenticity is less likely to yield convincing results than a reexamination of the historians' sources and methods.

Can the self-reflection involved in the "authentic disclosedness" take place within the boundaries of historical science as such? Can history *qua* *history* reflect on its own foundations and reveal to itself its own status in the present? One may think it can, perhaps by giving a history of itself. But in a later essay Heidegger asks a similar question about history and, for good reasons, answers negatively. This negative answer can also illuminate the essential disconnection between historical science and its ontological foundation in existential truth.

In the essay "Wissenschaft und Besinnung," Heidegger argues that sciences are incapable of discovering their own essence, of taking into account "scientifically" their own boundaries and conceptual frameworks. There might appear to be one exception:

> Historiography has *qua* science like every science a history. Therefore historical science [*Geschichtswissenschaft*] *can* take account of itself in terms of its themes and methods. Certainly. Through such accounting historiography grasps the history of the science that it is. But by doing so, historiography can never grasp its own essence as historiography, that is, as science. If one wants to say something theoretical about mathematics, then one must abandon mathematical objects and manners of presentation. What mathematics itself is can never be calculated mathematically.[14]

The truth of theoretical statements about the nature of history will be essentially different from the truth of historical statements themselves. If theoretical statements about mathematics leave the validity of mathematical calculations unchanged, why should it be assumed that ontological statements about historical science as such will change the validity of assertions in that science? A discussion of the "ontological genesis" of historiography is *only* a discussion of genesis, and does not alter the validity of historical accounts. Such a discussion also shows the radical difference between the kind of truth involved in historiography and the self-generating, self-confirming kind of truth involved in the genetic account of a foundationalist ontology. Of course, the ontological enterprise may have its own validity and its own function. Even if that were granted,

14. Martin Heidegger, *Vorträge und Aufsätze* (Pfullingen, 1967), part 1, p. 57.

however, Heidegger's analysis of historiography provides no evidence for thinking that the ontological enterprise should or could leap ahead and guide the science out of crisis in any concrete way. The "crisis" appears to be "only" a philosophical one.

Bibliographical Guide

A COMPLETE BIBLIOGRAPHY of Heidegger's published German works, together with the English translations, would be enormous. Klostermann is in the process of publishing a complete critical edition of all of Heidegger's writings. The first grouping, of previously published works, runs to sixteen volumes; a second, covering the lectures from Marburg and Freiburg, about forty volumes; and two other sections will include the unpublished treatises and notes and sketches. The guide below includes virtually all of the major published works that have or are soon to appear in English translations, followed by their German sources.

HEIDEGGER'S WORKS

The abbreviations given in the first two sections below are used in the third, which is a chronological bibliography listing works in the order of their composition.

Collections in English Translation

BW Basic Writings. Edited by David Krell. New York: Harper and Row, 1977. Contains Introduction to *Being and Time*, translated by Joan Stambaugh; "What is Metaphysics?" translated by David Krell; "On the Essence of Truth," translated by J. Glenn Gray; "The Origin of the Work of Art," translated by Albert Hofstadter; "Modern Science, Metaphysics, and Mathematics," translated by W. D. Barton and Vera Deutsche; "The Question Concerning Technology," translated by William Lovitt; "Building Dwelling Thinking," translated by Albert Hofstadter; "What Calls for Thinking?" translated by Fred D.

Wieck and J. Glenn Gray; "The End of Philosophy and the Task of Thinking," translated by Joan Stambaugh.

EGT Early Greek Thinking. Translated by David Krell and Frank Capuzzi. New York: Harper & Row, 1975. Contains "The Anaximander Fragment," "Logos (Heraclitus, Fragment B50)," "Moira (Parmenides VIII, 34–41)," "Aletheia (Heraclitus, Fragment B16)."

EP The End of Philosophy. Translated by Joan Stambaugh. New York: Harper & Row, 1973. Contains "Metaphysics as History of Being," "Sketches for a History of Being as Metaphysics," "Recollection in Metaphysics," "Overcoming Metaphysics."

EB Existence and Being. Edited and with an introduction by Werner Broch. Chicago: Henry Regnery-Gateway, 1967. Contains "Remembrance of the Poet," "Hölderlin and the Essence of Poetry," trans. David Scott; "On the Essence of Truth," and "What is Metaphysics?" trans. R. F. C. Hull and Allan Crick.

NWPA Nietzsche I: Will to Power as Art. Translated and edited by David Krell. New York: Harper & Row, forthcoming. Contains "Will to Power as Art."

NER Nietzsche II: The Eternal Recurrence of the Same. Translated and edited by David Krell. New York: Harper & Row, forthcoming. Contains "The Eternal Recurrence of the Same," "Who Is Nietzsche's Zarathustra?"

NWPK Nietzsche III: Will to Power as Knowledge and as Metaphysics. Translated and edited by David Krell. New York: Harper & Row, forthcoming. Contains "The Will to Power as Knowledge," "The Eternal Recurrence of the Same and the Will to Power," "Nietzsche's Metaphysics."

NN Nietzsche IV: Nihilism. Edited by David Krell and translated by Frank Capuzzi. New York: Harper & Row, 1978. Contains "European Nihilism, "Nihilism and the History of Being."

OWL On the Way to Language. Translated by Peter Hertz, except "Words," translated by Joan Stambaugh. New York: Harper & Row, 1971.

PT The Piety of Thinking. Translated, with notes and commentary, by James G. Hart and John Maraldo. Bloomington: Indiana University Press, 1976. Contains "Phenomenology and Theology," "The Problem of a Non-Objectifying Thinking and Speaking in Today's Theology," "Review of Ernst Cassirer's *Mythical Thinking,*" "Principles of Thinking."

PLT Poetry, Language, Thought. Translated and edited by Albert Hofstadter. New York: Harper & Row, 1971. Contains "The Thinker as Poet," "The Origin of the Work of Art," "What Are Poets For?" "Building Dwelling Thinking," "The Thing," "Language," " '. . . Poetically Man Dwells . . .' "

QT *The Question Concerning Technology and Other Essays*. Translated and with an Introduction by William Lovitt. New York: Harper & Row, 1977. Contains "The Question Concerning Technology," "The Turning," "The Word of Nietzsche: 'God is Dead,' " "The Age of the World Picture," "Science and Reflection."

German Collections

H *Holzwege*. Frankfurt am Main: Klostermann, 1950.
N *Nietzsche I, II*. Pfullingen: Neske, 1961.
US *Unterwegs zur Sprache*. Pfullingen: Neske, 1959.
VA *Vorträge und Aufsätze*. Pfullingen: Neske, 1954.
WM *Wegmarken*. Frankfurt am Main: Klostermann, 1967.

Chronological Bibliography

In each entry the English title and publication data are given first, followed by the German title and publication date.

1912

"The Problem of Reality in Modern Philosophy." Translated by Philip J. Bossert. *Journal of the British Society for Phenomenology* 4 (1973) : 64–71. "Das Realitätsproblem in der modernen Philosophie." *Philosophisches Jahrbuch* 25 : 353–63.

1927

Being and Time. Translated by John Macquarrie and Edward Robinson. New York: Harper & Row, 1962. A new translation by Joan Stambaugh that will replace this is forthcoming. The Introduction appears in *BW*. *Sein und Zeit*, 7th ed. Tübingen: Niemeyer, 1953. Parts go back to lecture courses from 1919–24.
"What Are Poets For?" *PLT*. "Wozu Dichter?" H.

1929

On the Essence of Reasons. Translated by Terrence Mallick. With German text. Evanston: Northwestern University Press, 1969. *Vom Wesen des Grundes*.

Kant and the Problem of Metaphysics. Translated by James S. Churchill. Bloomington: Indiana University Press, 1969. *Kant und das Problem der Metaphysik.* With a new foreword. Frankfurt am Main: Klostermann, 1951. Based on lectures from 1925–26.

What Is Metaphysics? EB, BW. Was ist Metaphysik? 9th ed. Frankfurt am Main: Klostermann, 1965.

1930

"On the Essence of Truth." *EB, BW. Vom Wesen der Wahrheit.* Frankfurt am Main: Klostermann, 1943, *W.*

1935–36

What is a Thing? Translated by W. D. Barton and Vera Deutsche. Chicago: Henry Regnery-Gateway, 1968. *Die Frage nach dem Ding. Zu Kants Lehre von dem transzendentalen Grundsätzen.* Tübingen: Niemeyer, 1962.

An Introduction to Metaphysics. Translated by Ralph Manheim. New Haven: Yale University Press, 1974. *Einführung in die Metaphysik* Tubingen: Niemeyer, 1953.

1936

"Hölderlin and the Essence of Poetry." *EB.* "Hölderlin und das Wesen der Dichtung." *Erläuterungen zu Hölderlins Dichtung.* 2nd ed. Frankfurt am Main: Klostermann, 1951.

"The Origin of the Work of Art." *PLT, BW.* "Der Ursprung des Kunstwerkes." *H.*

"The Will to Power as Art." (1936–37) *NWPA.* "Der Wille zur Macht als Kunst." *N* I.

1937

"The Eternal Recurrence of the Same." *NER.* "Die ewige Wiederkehr des Gleichen." *N* I.

1938

"The Age of the World View." Translated by Marjorie Grene. *Boundary 2* 4 (1976) : 341–55. Or "The Age of the World Picture." *QT.* "Die Zeit des Weltbildes." *H.*

1939

"On the Being and Conception of *Physis* in Aristotle's *Physics* B 1." Translated by Thomas Sheehan. *Man and World* 4 (1977): 219–70. "Vom Wesen und Begriff der *physis*, Aristoteles Physik B 1." *WM.* "The Will to Power as Knowledge." *NWP.* "Der Wille zur Macht als Erkenntnis." *N* I.

1940

"European Nihilism." *NN* "Nietzsche's Metaphysics." *NWPK.* "Europäische Nihilismus" and "Nietzsches Metaphysik." *N* II.

1941

"Metaphysics as History of Being," "Sketches for a History of Being," "Sketches for a History of Being as Metaphysics" and "Recollection in Metaphysics." *EP.* "Die Metaphysik als Geschichte des Seins," "Entwürfe zur Geschichte des Seins als Metaphysik," "Die Erinnerung an die Metaphysik." *N* II.

1942

"Plato's Doctrine of Truth." Translated by John Barlow. *Philosophy in the Twentieth Century*, vol. 3. Edited by William Barrett and Henry D. Aiken. New York: Harper & Row, 1962. *Platons Lehre von der Wahrheit.* Bern: Franck, 1947, and *WM.*

1943

"Postscript" to "What Is Metaphysics?" *EB, WM.*
"Aletheia (Heraclitus, Fragment B 16)." *EGT.* "Aletheia (Heraklit, Fragment B 16)." *VA.*
"The Word of Nietzsche 'God is Dead.' " *QT.* "Nietzsches Wort 'Gott ist tot.' " *H.*

Hegel's Concept of Experience. Translated by Kenley Dove. New York: Harper & Row, 1970. "Hegels Begriff der Erfahrung." *H*.

1944

"Logos (Heraclitus, Fragment B50)." *EGT*. "Logos (Heraklit, Fragment 50). *VA*.

1946

"Overcoming Metaphysics" (1936–46). *EP*. "Überwindung der Metaphysik." *VA*.

1947

"Letter on 'Humanism.' " Translated by Edgar Lohner. *Philosophy in the Twentieth Century*, vol. 3. edited by William Barrett and Henry D. Aiken. New York: Random House, 1962, and *BW; Über den 'Humanismus'*. Frankfurt am Main: Klostermann, 1949, and *WM*.

1949

"The Pathway." Translated by Thomas O'Meara. *Listening* 2 (1967) : 88–91. *Der Feldweg*. Frankfurt am Main: Klostermann, 1953.
"The Turning." *QT*. "Die Kehre." *Die Technik und die Kehre*. Pfullingen: Neske, 1962.
"The Way Back into the Ground of Metaphysics" ("Introduction" to *"What is Metaphysics?"*). Translated by Walter Kaufmann. *Existentialism from Dostoevsky to Sartre*. New York: Meridian, 1956. "Der Rückgang in den Grund der Metaphysik." *Was ist Metaphysik?* 9th ed. Frankfurt am Main: Klostermann, 1965.

1950

"The Thing." *PLT*. "Das Ding." *VA*.
"Language." *PLT*. "Die Sprache." *US*.

1951

Elucidations of Hölderlin's Poetry. Translated by Keith Hoeller. University, Ala.: University of Alabama Press, 1978. *Erläuterungen zur Hölderlins Dichtung.* Frankfurt am Main: Klostermann, 1951.

1952

"Building Dwelling Thinking." *PLT, BW.* "Bauen Wohnen Denken." *VA.*
What is Called Thinking? Translated by Fred D. Wieck and J. Glenn Gray. *Was heisst Denken?* Pfullingen: Neske, 1954. See also *BW.*

1953

"The Question Concerning Technology." Enlarged from 1949 Address in "The Framework." *QT.* "Die Frage nach der Technik." *VA.*
"Who is Nietzsche's Zarathustra?" Translated by Bernard Magnus. *Review of Metaphysics* 20 (1967): 411–31, and *NER.* "Wer ist Nietzsches Zarathustra?" *VA.*
"Language in the Poem." Translated by Peter Hertz. *On the Way to Language.* New York: Harper & Row, 1971. "Die Sprache im Gedichte." *Unterwegs zur Sprache.* Pfullingen: Neske, 1959.
"A Dialogue on Language." *OWL.* "Aus einem Gespräch von der Sprache." *US.*
"Science and Reflection." *QT.* "Wissenschaft und Besinnung." *VA.*

1954

"The Thinker as Poet." *PLT. Aus der Erfahrung des Denkens.* Pfullingen: Neske, 1954.
" '. . . Poetically Man Dwells . . .' " *PLT.* " '. . . dichterish wohnet der Mensch . . .' " *VA.*

1955

The Question of Being. Translated by William Kluback and Jean T. Wilde. With German text. Boston: Twayne, 1958. *Zur Seinsfrage.* Frankfurt am Main: Klostermann, 1956.
Discourse on Thinking. Translated by John Anderson and E. Hans Freund.

New York: Harper & Row, 1966. *Gelassenheit*. Pfullingen: Neske, 1959.
What is Philosophy? Translated by William Kluback and Jean T. Wilde.
With German text. Boston: Twayne, 1958. *Was ist das—die Philosophie?*
Pfullingen: Naske, 1956.

1957

Identity and Difference. Translated and with an introduction by Joan
Stambaugh. New York: Harper & Row, 1969. *Identität und Differenz*.
Pfullingen: Neske, 1957.
"The Essence of Language" (1957–58). *OWL*. "Das Wesen der Sprache."
US.

1958

"Words." *OWL*. "Das Wort." *US.*

1959

"The Way to Language." *OWL*. "Der Weg zur Sprache." *US.*

1962

"Kant's Thesis about Being." Translated by Ted Klein and William E.
Pohl. *Southwestern Journal of Philosophy* 4 (1973) : 7–33; *Kants These
über das Sein*. Frankfurt am Main: Klostermann, 1962.
On Time and Being. Translated Joan Stambaugh. New York: Harper &
Row, 1972. *Zur Sache des Denkens*. Tübingen: Niemeyer, 1969.
"Letter to Fr. Richardson." With German text. Preface to *Heidegger:
Through Phenomenology to Thought*. The Hague: Martinus Nijhoff,
1963.

1963

"My Way to Phenomenology." Translated by Joan Stambaugh. *On Time
and Being*. New York: Harper & Row, 1972. "Mein Weg in die
Phänomenologie." *Zur Sache des Denkens*. Niemeyer: Tübingen, 1969.

1964

"The End of Philosophy and the Task of Thinking." Translated by Joan Stambaugh. *On Time and Being.* New York: Harper & Row, 1972. "Das Ende der Philosophie und die Aufgabe des Denkens." *Zur Sache des Denkens.* Niemeyer: Tübingen, 1969.

SECONDARY LITERATURE

The most comprehensive bibliography of secondary writings is Hans-Martin Sass, *Heidegger-Bibliographie* (Meisenheim: Verlag Anton Hain, 1968) and the supplement, *Materialien zu einer Heidegger-Bibliographie* (Meisenheim: Verlag Anton Hain, 1975), an international compilation covering the years 1929–1972. A useful work for following up related discussions or topics in Heidegger is Hildegaard Feick, *Index zu Heideggers "Sein und Zeit,"* 2nd. rev. ed. (Tübingen: Max Niemeyer Verlag, 1968), which is, in fact, a general index to most of the published writings in the German editions.

Books

Demske, James M. *Man, Being, Death.* Lexington: University Press of Kentucky, 1970.

Erikson, Stephen. *Language and Being: An Analytic Phenomenology.* New Haven: Yale University Press, 1970.

Marx, Werner. *Heidegger and the Tradition.* Translated by Theodore Kisiel and Murray Greene. Evanston: Northwestern University Press, 1971.

Mehta, J. L. *The Philosophy of Martin Heidegger.* New York: Harper & Row, 1971.

Murray, Michael. *Modern Critical Theory: A Phenomenological Introduction.* The Hague: Martinus Nijhoff, 1975.

Richardson, William. *Heidegger: From Phenomenology to Thought.* The Hague: Martinus Nijhoff, 1963.

Rosen, Stanley. *Nihilism: A Philosophical Essay.* New Haven: Yale University Press, 1969.

Seidel, Georg. *Martin Heidegger and the Presocratics.* Lincoln: University of Nebraska Press, 1964.

Sherover, Charles. *Heidegger, Kant, and Time.* Introduction by William Barrett. Bloomington: Indiana University Press, 1971.

Schmitt, Richard. *Martin Heidegger on Being Human.* New York: Random House, 1969.
Versényi, Lazlo. *Heidegger, Being, and Truth.* New Haven: Yale University Press, 1965.

Collections of Essays

Frings, Manfred S., ed. *Heidegger and the Quest for Truth.* Chicago: Quadrangle Books, 1968.
Kockelmans, Joseph, ed. and trans. *On Heidegger on Language.* Evanston: Northwestern University Press, 1972.
Sallis, John, ed. *Heidegger and the Path of Thinking.* Pittsburgh: Duquesne University Press, 1970.
Ballard, Edward G., and Charles E. Scott. *Martin Heidegger in Europe and America.* The Hague: Martinus Nijhoff, 1973.

Articles of Special Interest

Aler, Jan. "Heidegger's Conception of Language in *Being and Time.*" In *On Heidegger on Language*, edited by Joseph Kockelmans, pp. 33–62.
Alderman, Harold. "The Work of Art and Other Things," In *Martin Heidegger in Europe and America*, edited by Edward Ballard and Charles Scott, pp. 157–169.
———. "Heidegger's Conception of Metaphysics," *Journal of the British Society for Phenomenology* 2 (1971) : 12–22.
Ballard, Edward G. "Heidegger's View and Evaluation of Nature and Natural Science. In *Heidegger and the Path of Thinking*, edited by John Sallis, pp. 37–64.
Goff, Robert Allen. "Wittgenstein's Tools and Heidegger's Implements." *Man and World* 1 (1968) : 447–62.
Harries, Karsten. "Wittgenstein and Heidegger: The Relation of the Philosophy to Language." *Journal of Value Inquiry* 2 (1968) : 281–91.
Kockelmans, Joseph. "Ontological Difference, Hermeneutics, and Language." In *On Heidegger and Language*, edited by Joseph Kockelmans, pp. 195–234.
Marshall, Donald G. "The Ontology of the Literary Sign: Notes toward a Heideggerian Revision of Semiology." *Boundary* 2 4 (1976) : 611–24.
Pöggeler, Otto. "Heidegger's Topology of Being." In *On Heidegger and Language*, edited by Joseph Kockelmans, pp. 107–33.
———. " 'Historicity' in Heidegger's Late Work," *Southwestern Journal of Philosophy* 4 (1973) : 53–73.

———. "Heidegger Today," In *Martin Heidegger in Europe and America*, edited by Edward G. Ballard and Charles E. Scott, pp. 1–36.

Sherover, Charles M. "Kant's Transcendental Object and Heidegger's *Nichts*." *Journal of the History of Philosophy* (1969) : 413–22.

Biography and Autobiography

Heidegger, Martin. "Letter to Father Richardson." With German text, Preface to William Richardson, *Heidegger: Through Phenomenology to Thought* (The Hague: Martinus Nijhoff: 1963).

———. "My Way to Phenomenology." trans. Joan Stambaugh, *On Time and Being* (New York: Harper & Row, 1972), pp. 74–82.

———. "Only a God Can Save Us," *Der Spiegel* Interview with Heidegger on September 23, 1966, published May 30, 1976, trans. Maria P. Alter and John D. Caputo, *Philosophy Today* (Winter, 1976), pp. 267–84.

Biemel, Walter. *Heidegger*. Translated by J. L. Mehta. New York: Harcourt Brace Jovanovich, 1976.

List of Contributors

Harold Alderman, Department of Philosophy, California State College at Sonoma.

Hannah Arendt (deceased).

Albert Borgmann, Department of Philosophy, University of Montana.

Rudolf Carnap (deceased).

Ronald Bruzina, Department of Philosophy, University of Kentucky.

Hubert Dreyfus, Department of Philosophy, University of California, Berkeley.

Hans-Georg Gadamer, Department of Philosophy, University of Heidelberg.

Karsten Harries, Department of Philosophy, Yale University.

David Hoy, Department of Philosophy, Barnard College.

John Haugeland, Department of Philosophy, University of Pittsburgh.

Ross Mandel, Cambridge University.

Michael Murray, Department of Philosophy, Vassar College.

Otto Pöggeler, Department of Philosophy, The Ruhr University at Bochum.

Paul Ricoeur, Divinity School, University of Chicago, and Department of Philosophy, University of Paris at Nanterre.

Richard Rorty, Department of Philosophy, Princeton University.

Stanley Rosen, Humanities Institute, The Pennsylvania State University.

Gilbert Ryle (deceased).

George Vick, Department of Philosophy, California State University at Los Angeles.

Ludwig Wittgenstein (deceased).

Index